2nd CLASS SEASON
VALID FOR 4 DEC 1961
UNTIL 22 DEC 1961
BETWEEN PETTS WOOD
AND VICTORIA
VIA West Dulwich
Also available on L.T. Railways BETWEEN VICTORIA
SLOANE SQUARE
2529
KATHMANDU
HV8421 174
HV8421 175
G. Ticket
Tren accelerat
Comb. cu suplim. de tren
Cluj Napoca 20
CJ
pînă la stația
Val. 1—250 km
Cl. II Lei 1800
2752
24 SEP
CASINO TO BRISBANE
Azienda Tranvie Municipali
TORINO
BIGLIETTO di CORSA SEMPLICE
Tariffa Speciale
Da presentare a richiesta degli Agenti dell'Azienda.
Serie 27
85473
NO. 3810
2014年01月30日 08:53开
14车 14D号
一等座
上海虹桥 D105次 宜春
ShangHaiHongQiao YiChun
¥296.50元 折
限乘当日当次车
3101041989****3633 检票口14A
3067-1091-4101-1200-7906-3
和谐号
GOOD ONLY SAT. 8:00 P.M.
MULTI-TRIP WEEKLY SUBURBAN
MURARRIE
DARRA
BRESCIA
I0820981
Also available on L.T. Railways
VICTORIA and SOUTH KENSINGTON
GLOUCESTER ROAD
Standard Class

BETWEEN LEIGH-ON-SEA
AND FARRINGDON
VIA Whitechapel and Aldersgate
Also available to and from FENCHURCH STREET
Signature of holder
FOR CONDITIONS ENQUIRE AT TICKET
This Ticket is NOT TRANSFERABLE and must be given up on expiry
Nº
BRITISH RAILWAYS BOARD (S)
2nd CLASS SEASON TICKET
04 JUN
BETWEEN SYDENHAM
Also available on L.T. Railways
Economy Return
CHILD'S TICKET
LEDGER CHARGE
BRISBANE
TO
CAIRNS
III-06
LIRE
SERVIZI URBANI
STEFFER
BRESCIA
ROMA
metrebus
A Roma paghi la sosta anche con il telefonino!
atac.roma.it/sosta
Economy Ordinary Return
LAIDLEY
TO
GATTON
15 km
2818
Economy Return
LEDGER CHARGE
BRISBANE
TO
Maryborough
120
TUMSAR RD
北京
Z1次
Beijing
2010年11月14日21:14开
¥411.00元
当日当次车有效
10001200921112 G091714
HALF FARE
CASINO
TO
BRISBANE
See By-Laws
TRAVEL
Valabil
CL. II Lei 15800
6023
VICTORIA
WEST DULWICH
2nd CLASS WEEKLY SEASON TICKET
BRITISH TRANSPORT COMMISSION
HMANDU
RATP
METRO
AUTOBUS
RÉDUIT
PICCADILLY CIRCUS
5p
ATM MILANO
LINEE ORDINARIE URBANE
VALE 70 MINUTI
MILANO Pulita è bella.
0.497.707
735
FREE TICKET
by ROAD MOTOR
IPSWICH
TO
TOOWOOMBA
Not Transferable
ECONOMY
HALF FARE
TOOWOOMBA
50
LIRE
002
serie 8316
9966
175 km
I.E.T.T.
ECONOMY SINGLE
CHILD'S TICKET
LEDGER CHARGE
ROCKHAMPTON
TO
BRISBANE
Not Transferable
2058
D. Ticket
Tren accelerat
Cluj Napoca 20
pîng la staţia
CJ
RATP
2

THE RISE OF THE RAILROAD

RCTS
32424
SPL
112

DK
Smithsonian
THE RISE OF THE
RAILROAD
PULLMAN
32424

CONTENTS

Rush hour This image from 1924 shows crowds gathering at the platform gates at London Waterloo station, a key terminus for commuting within and out of London.

Forging ahead Railroads around the world, like this one at Landwasser in Switzerland, used pioneering engineering techniques to overcome natural obstacles, such as mountains, rivers, and deserts.

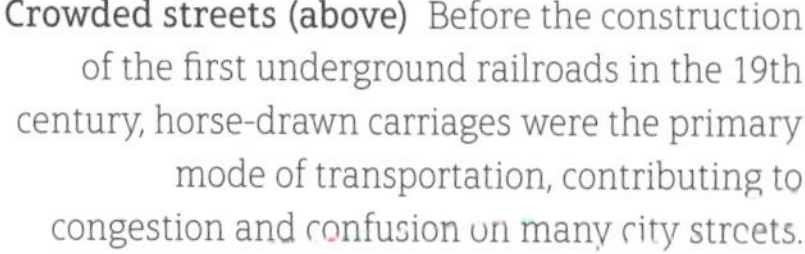

Crowded streets (above) Before the construction of the first underground railroads in the 19th century, horse-drawn carriages were the primary mode of transportation, contributing to congestion and confusion on many city streets.

Railroad time (above right) Meticulous maintenance of railroad clocks was essential to ensure timely signaling and maintaining train schedules.

Commuter railroads (right) With railroads reducing travel times, people could come into cities for work from surrounding areas.

INTRODUCTION

Of all the great inventions of the Industrial Revolution, the railroads arguably had the most impact. In a world before rail, travel over any distance was a major undertaking. Regions of even small countries, such as France or England, could be up to seven days' journey from the capital, while large countries like the United States, China, or Russia could take months to cross. Until the early 19th century, most people lived their whole lives within the confines of the town or rural area in which they were born, and no one had ever gone faster than a horse could gallop. Travel was simply too difficult and too expensive for the vast majority of people, which in turn limited the spread of ideas and technology.

Lack of mobility was a major barrier to economic and social development. In the absence of rapid transportation, people could starve within only a few hundred miles of plentiful food supplies. The slow transit of goods by horse and cart, or along rivers and canals, meant that perishables had to be consumed very rapidly. Sending a letter across the country took days, and newspapers were a misnomer, since they were effectively full of old information. It took months for people to learn the fate of loved ones at war, and news of major events, from even just a short distance away, filtered through slowly.

Limitations on travel also translated into social restriction—people had little choice of spouse, since opportunities to meet potential marriage partners from even neighboring towns were rare. Concepts of time, too, were different before the railroads. Daily life was regulated by the sun, and towns just a few miles east or west of each other could operate on different schedules.

Then the railroads arrived and changed everything. One of their first major impacts was to force countries to standardize their measurements of time, both nationally and internationally, since railroad timetables would otherwise be too confusing. Greenwich Mean Time, the standard by which the world sets its clocks, was created partly as a result of the railroads, and continental US was divided into four time zones for the same reason. The Trans-Siberian, the longest railroad in the world, still operates according to Moscow time, even though the line crosses seven other time zones on its way to Vladivostok. Punctuality and time-keeping thus became vital, not just with regard to the railroads, but in all spheres of life. The railroads created the structured day, which, prior to their arrival, had been 10 hours long, rather than today's norm of eight. In other words, they created the "nine-to-five" routine.

Creature comforts (below left)
Sleeper cars on railroads were part of the many improvements of onboard services, which helped encourage travel for long-distance journeys.

Waging war (below center)
The railroads played a key role in many conflicts, as they could be used to transport troops and matériel to the front.

Moving faster (below right)
Over their 200-year history, railroads have constantly innovated with the result that modern high-speed trains can be used in 25 countries across the world.

The railroads overthrew all established concepts of distance and time, and social upheaval followed. The last vestiges of feudalism were swept away, since people were no longer tied to the land—indeed, they could now work far from home. People worked standard hours and expected to do so for a wage. Thus, the growth of capitalism went hand in hand with the expansion of the iron road. As people no longer had to find employment near their homes, towns and cities could become far larger than would previously have been possible. Suburban sprawl, often thought of as a product of the automobile age, is, in fact, the result of the development of commuter lines.

Access to long-distance travel, in relative comfort at fairly low cost, changed people's horizons and opened up their imaginations. What had previously been impossible became routine—such as going to the seaside or visiting an exhibition. On a social level, the scope for potential marriage partners suddenly broadened, being no longer confined to the immediate vicinity.

The exchange of ideas took off as national conferences could now be convened, and the inventions of the Industrial Revolution spread—first across Britain then across the world. Professional sport became feasible as clubs and their supporters could travel long distances to play other teams, and league size was limited only by how far a team could travel in a day.

Warfare, too, was revolutionized by the railroads. Armies had traditionally sustained themselves by foraging and pillaging—an unreliable practice that made it impossible to keep troops in the same place for long, since supplies, especially for the animals, inevitably ran out. These logistical restrictions meant that battles took place over days rather than weeks or months. With the rise of railroads, armies no longer needed to be constantly on the move, since they could be supplied with food and munitions from the nearest railhead. They were also invaluable in transporting troops quickly to quell domestic riots or launch wars against neighbors.

Nation states became more cohesive as country-wide railroad systems developed. The railroads, often state-owned, were the glue that bound a country together, linking disparate regions and enabling governments to expand their influence in remote, previously lawless areas. The railroads also stimulated large movements of people: Siberia and the American West were both populated after major lines were built. Settlements everywhere congregated around the tracks; indeed, in the US, several towns that were bypassed by the iron road simply moved to be closer to it. Stations became hubs, attracting development and commerce.

As the railroads expanded, they brought change in their wake. Railroad companies were often the largest organizations in their respective countries and, due to their size, required new types of business management and even accounting methods. The very engines of capitalism—bank loans, stock markets, information on investment—suddenly became possible. Railroad companies needed banks to fund their expansion and, in turn, banks found railroad companies to be their best clients, since they were the biggest and most ambitious. It was no coincidence that banks and railroad companies were the driving force of mid- and late-19th century capitalism.

Moreover, since the railroad companies employed many workers, it was inevitable that, as the trade union movement was born and developed, the railroads became the industry in which they flourished. Indeed, they were the site of many of the fiercest disputes between capital and labor.

The story of the railroads is not just one of trains and technology, and this richer history, set in a wider social context, is the one this book aims to tell. Despite a strong challenge from the automobile, the railroads remain a brilliant technological feat and a great way to travel—but they are, in fact, much more than that, as every page will show.

Railroad art The railroads have long captured people's imaginations, inspiring works of art and literature. This vibrant woodblock print of a train at Takanawa, Japan, was made just before the country's first line opened in 1872.

鉄道之全圖
山甚
山甚板

LIVERPOOL
LIVERPOOL
TIMES
MANCHESTER
RAILWAY COMPANY
LIVERPOOL
MANCHESTER
RAILWAY COMPANY
LIVERPOOL
TREASURER
MANCHESTER
RAILWAY COMPANY
LIVERPOOL
DESPATCH
RAILWAY COMPANY

NORTH STAR
L P M
R Y

JUPITER

Early train travel Right from the start, rail passengers were divided into different classes with varying levels of comfort, as these coaches that ran on the Liverpool and Manchester Railway in 1834 demonstrate.

The first tracks

Today's railroads are a combination of inventions that were made over millennia, starting with the wheel around 3500 BCE and culminating in the steam engine in the late 17th century. By the early 1800s, steam engines—which began as huge, cumbersome machines—were small enough to be put on wheels, and so the self-propelling "steam locomotive" was born. The next stage was simply to hitch the locomotive to a train—consisting either of wagons carrying freight or of coaches bearing passengers.

There were many who argued that train travel would never be popular, or that horses should provide the power, but once the world's first major railroad, the Liverpool and Manchester line, opened in England in 1830, there was no stopping the spread of the iron road. The United States quickly followed, and the invention spread throughout Europe—tentatively at first, but then quite rapidly. Lines were opened to enormous fanfare, and people flocked to the new stations—many to begin routines of traveling to work by rail, many just to enjoy the new technology.

There were some initial setbacks, however. Every aspect of the railroads, from tracklaying and signaling to training staff and building stations, had to be learned from scratch. This was the birth of a completely new industry and complications were inevitable. There were accidents and fires, and investors fell prey to fraudsters and confidence tricksters. Indeed, locomotives were prone to blowing up or breaking down, and a prominent British politician, William Huskisson, was killed at the opening of the first railroad when he failed to respond quickly enough to warnings of an incoming train while standing on the tracks. Nevertheless, all these difficulties were overcome, and within a couple of decades trains were traveling at twice the speed of a galloping horse and covering huge distances. The railroad age had begun.

FROM WAGONWAYS TO RAILROADS

The railroad was the culmination of decades of experimentation with tracks, wagons, and engines. As wooden tracks gave way to metal rails, transportation became faster and more efficient, laying the foundation for modern railroad systems.

The world's first railroad, the Liverpool and Manchester, opened in England in 1830, as a result of the Industrial Revolution. But the railroad was also an ancient technology. The wheel had been invented more than 5,500 years earlier and had soon been given a track. By the time of the Ancient Greeks (1200–323 BCE), the wheels of carts and coaches were running in specially dug-out channels that prevented them from sliding off the road in wet weather, and similar tracks have been found in the ruins of Pompeii and Sicily. Myth has it that Greek king Oedipus unknowingly slew his father when the two crossed paths on one such road and argued over who had the right of way.

Early tracks and trains

The earliest image of wooden tracks being used for transportation dates back to 1350 and can be seen in a church in Freiburg im Breisgau, Germany. Within a couple of centuries, numerous wagonways (or paths made of such tracks) had been built in Germany and Britain to haul heavily loaded wagons out of mines.

The late 18th-century Willington Waggonway is the world's oldest complete section of wooden railroad yet discovered

Wooden wagon Pictured here is a replica of the type of wagon used to carry coal and other minerals on the early wagonways in the 17th and 18th centuries.

The first of these appeared in Saxony, which had become a major tin and silver mining region by the 14th century. Activity in the Saxon mines peaked in the 16th century, thanks to the development of the *Leitnagel Hund*—a four-wheeled mining truck that was far more efficient than its predecessors. It had an iron bar that projected from its underside into a groove between a pair of wooden tracks, to keep it from veering off course. Operating the truck demanded great skill, and there were inevitably accidents, but it soon revolutionized the German mining industry, making it possible to transport much larger quantities of ore to the surface for smelting. At first, this system was entirely dependent on human labor, but soon horses replaced people, enabling even heavier loads to be moved.

The next development was the introduction of rails for the trucks to travel on. The earliest of these, found in Germany and known as *Karrenbahnen*, were made of wood, and by the early 18th century, in the coal region of the Ruhr, they had a lip—an L-shaped flange that kept the wagons on the tracks. On some wagonways, the flange was fitted to the wheels of the trucks rather than the tracks, an arrangement that later became standard on the railroads.

By the time the flange had been introduced, Britain had also developed a system of wagonways. It was based on the German system but soon became more extensive than its precursor. Britain was the cradle of the Industrial Revolution, and its wagonways connected an ever-expanding network of mines to an increasing number of factories, and to waterways that enabled coal and minerals to be shipped even

Wylam Colliery Established in England in the middle of the 18th century, this large coal mine greatly benefited from the use of steam engines, which enabled it to be far more profitable.

farther afield. This transportation system had a huge economic impact on Britain, and both the industrial and domestic consumption of coal increased tenfold between 1700 and the early 1800s. The network that emerged in the northeast of England in the 17th century was so busy with traffic that it became known as the Newcastle Roads. By 1660, there were nine wagonways on Tyneside alone, and several others in the Midlands to the south. In 1726, a group of coal mine owners called the Grand Allies went a step further by linking their collieries to a shared wagonway. They even created a "main line," the Tanfield Wagonway, much of which had two tracks, permitting a continuous flow of inbound and outbound vehicles. The route linked several pits with the Tyne River, crossing the Causey Arch—a bridge with a 105 ft (32 m) span over a rocky ravine—en route. Costing £12,000 (around £2 million or $2.6 million in 2025 money), the arch was built by stonemason Ralph Wood and still stands today. At the time it was the longest single-span bridge in Britain. It accommodated two tracks—the "main way" to take coal to the river, and the "bye way" for returning empty wagons. At its peak, more than 900 horse-drawn wagons crossed the arch each day. There were several such wagonways in Britain and the rest of Europe, but cooperative ventures were rare—many pit owners deliberately built wagonways that prevented rivals from reaching the waterways.

Iron railroads

It was not until the late 18th century that iron rails were first used near Hanover, Germany. Soon afterward, iron rails were laid to move trucks around the ironworks at the key industrial site of Coalbrookdale in the Midlands, England. The initial idea was to cover existing wooden rails with an iron cap so that they would last longer

The Causey Arch Shown here in a watercolor by Joseph Atkinson, the Causey Arch, built 1725–1726, is thought to be the oldest surviving single-arch railroad bridge in the world. The line has long since closed, but the bridge still serves as a footpath.

(they had previously been replaced every year), but advances in smelting technology soon made it possible to construct the entire rails from iron. It was around this time that the words "railroad" and "railway" were adopted for the wagonways of the Midlands, which now carried lime, ore, and pig iron as well as coal. Throughout this period, railroad wagons also became larger and were able to carry loads of more than 2½ tons (2.3 metric tons), and the gauge of the tracks (the distance between them) was largely standardized at 5 ft (1.5 m). This width best suited the horses that hauled the wagons (any wider and they were too heavy to pull), and it was close to the gauge that eventually prevailed across much of the world—4 ft 8½ in (1,435 mm), or today's "standard" gauge.

These iron railroads flourished for about 40 years. At their peak, thousands of miles of iron tracks stretched across Britain, as opposed to the mere hundreds of miles of wooden equivalents that preceded them, and they reached far beyond the coalfields, linking mines and quarries with ports, rivers, and canals. Their main purpose was to transport minerals to the nearest waterway, but a few carried passengers on a casual basis—usually workers hopping on for a ride to or from a mine or a quarry. Some lines, such as the Swansea and Mumbles line in South Wales, provided carriages for people, but the main business was freight.

La Roulette This illustration shows the *Roulette*—a wagonway installed in 1691 by Louis XIV of France. It had a nearly 787 ft (240 m) wooden track on which his guests could ride in a gilded carriage.

Powering the railroads

A few canny mine owners devised more sophisticated railroad systems, involving cables and the use of gravity. Ralph Allen, the owner of a quarry above Bath Spa, designed a wagonway on which the loaded wagons descending the hill into the city pulled the unloaded ones back up the incline behind them. Such "gravity railroads" became common in the 18th century. The simplest ones used gravity to roll the wagons downhill and horses to pull the empty ones back up. An entirely frivolous example was the *Roulette*, built for Louis XIV of France in the gardens of the Palace of Versailles, near Marly in France. The Sun King liked to entertain his guests by giving them a ride on the *Roulette*. Although technically a gravity railroad, this was really more like a roller coaster built into a hill. The carved, gilded carriage thundered down a wooden track into a valley and then shot up the other side. The passengers boarded from a small, classical building that could lay claim to being the world's first railroad station, then

TOP SPEEDS THEN AND NOW

Nicolas-Joseph Cugnot's locomotive, 18th century

2½ mph

(4 km/h)

Train à Grande Vitesse (TGV), 21st century

357 mph

(574 km/h)

Early steam power The development of steam power often involved cooperation between inventors, including Robert Boyle and Denis Papin, pictured here discussing their experiments.

three bewigged valets pushed the coach to the top of the incline, from where gravity took over, giving the aristocrats a novel thrill.

For all their variety, the early railroads still required horses or humans to pull them along. What they needed was an engine to drive them, and just such a device was being developed. This was the steam engine, which began life as a stationary machine that generated power to drive water pumps, but was soon adapted to provide rotary power to drive wheels. It was a small leap to connect the engine to the wheels it was driving, thus creating a self-propelling, steam-powered vehicle.

The idea of steam power goes back to Classical times—Archimedes recognized it, and Heron of Alexandria experimented with it—but it was only in the late 17th century that Frenchman Denis Papin harnessed it with his "steam digester," a crude pressure cooker that he adapted to make an "atmospheric engine"—essentially a cylinder containing a piston that could oscillate under the pressure of steam expanding and condensing. Applying the principles that Papin had documented, Englishman Thomas Newcomen, an ironmaster from Devon working in the early 18th century, developed the idea of producing steam engines to pump water from mines, and made 60 of them. After Newcomen died and the patents ran out, engineers copied his ideas and similar engines were built in many countries,

The first locomotive Devised by Nicolas-Joseph Cugnot in 1769, this three-wheeled "steam trolley" is thought to have been the first self-propelled vehicle and ran at 3 mph (4.8 km/h) with the aim of hauling artillery.

including the US, the German states, and the Austrian Empire, where one was used to power the fountains for Karl Philipp, prince zu Schwarzenberg's palace in Vienna. However, it was Scottish engineer James Watt who first made steam power commercially viable, by making a series of technical improvements to Newcomen's designs so that they could be adapted to carry out a wide variety of tasks. He formed a partnership with English manufacturer Matthew Boulton, and soon their engines were powering looms, mills, and ships across the world.

Trailblazing steam power

Nicolas-Joseph Cugnot, an artillery lieutenant from eastern France, made the first attempt to put a steam engine on wheels around 1769, when he designed what he hoped would be a motorized cannon platform. On a test run in Paris, his engine propelled itself slowly forward, but then it veered off course and crashed into a wall, prompting the city authorities to ban it as a public danger. There were various other attempts, in Britain and the US, to build steam-powered road vehicles, but they were so heavy they destroyed the roads—a problem that was solved by Cornishman Richard Trevithick, who first put the engine on rails. Trevithick had a setback in 1801, when his "road carriage" caught fire, but three years later, he produced a locomotive that traveled at 5 mph (8 km/h) at Penydarren, an ironworks in Wales. Later still, he demonstrated his invention on a circular track near the present site of Euston station, London, playfully calling it *Catch Me Who Can*. Like Louis XIV's *Roulette*, however, it was more of a funfair ride than a serious commercial enterprise, and Trevithick went off to develop stationary steam engines for the gold and silver mines of Peru.

By the time Trevithick left England, all the technology needed for a modern railroad was in place. Like railroad tracks, the steam locomotive was slow to develop—indeed, it seemed for a while that horses would power the railroads. It took time for new methods to replace the old, and for many years, the railroads were a patchwork of iron and wooden tracks, with steam locomotives being trialed while horse-drawn lines were being built. What the railroads needed was a genius to bring these disparate elements together. That genius was civil engineer George Stephenson—a great synthesizer of ideas, who was soon dubbed the "father of railroads."

> **"Denis Papin... is the name which stands next recorded in the progressive invention of the steam engine."**
>
> DIONYSIUS LARDNER, *THE STEAM ENGINE EXPLAINED AND ILLUSTRATED*, 1840

Steam digester Invented in 1679 by French physicist Denis Papin, this device used steam to extract fat from bones under high pressure.

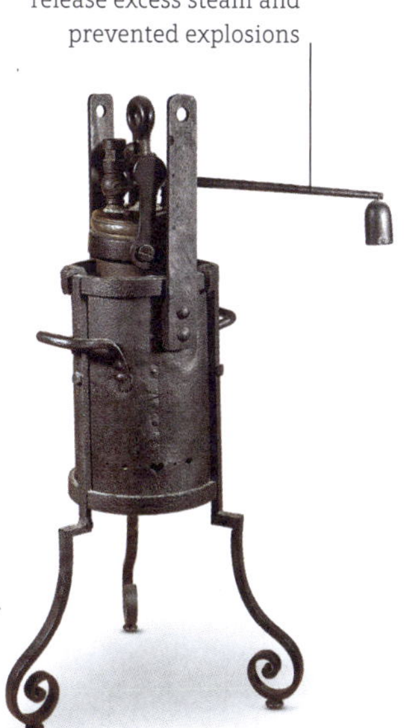

Safety valve helped release excess steam and prevented explosions

THE FATHER OF THE RAILROADS

Of the hundreds of inventors who contributed to the creation of the railroads, one stands out, not because he was the most innovative, but because he was the best at exploiting the ideas of others and turning them into workable concepts.

Born in Wylam, near Newcastle-upon-Tyne, England, George Stephenson was a barely literate, self-educated man who did not suffer fools gladly, but who deserves the title of "the father of the railroads." He played an important role in the development of two important lines: the Stockton and Darlington, completed in 1825, which was really the last and most sophisticated of the wagonways (see pp.16–21); and the Liverpool and Manchester, whose opening five years later heralded the real start of the railroad age. He continued to play a vital role in the spread of the railroads, both in Britain and abroad, until his death in 1848.

Starting strong

Stephenson started out young, working as a pit boy from an early age. While his mechanical aptitude held him in good stead, he decided to complete his education at night school. Before long, he found work as an engine wright and was put in charge of all the stationary engines at Killingworth, a large coal mine in North Tyneside situated in the now-ceremonial

George Stephenson A self-taught engineer, Stephenson pioneered a steam locomotive that ran on rails and built the world's first fully fledged steam railroad, the Liverpool and Manchester line, which opened in 1830.

county of Northumberland. He understood that the key to making better use of steam technology was to enable the engines to run on rails and haul loads directly, rather than using the cable system whereby stationary engines reeled in cables attached to wagons (see p.71), and he persuaded the colliery owners to give him the means to build a "traveling machine"—his name for the locomotive. The result was unveiled in 1814—a steam engine somewhat oddly named after Gebhard Leberecht von Blücher, a Prussian general who led his army to several victories against Napoleon, the common enemy of Britain and Prussia at the time. Incorporating features from Trevithick's engines (see pp.20–21), *Blücher* was built in the colliery workshop and proved to be more powerful than any of its predecessors, as it could haul 30 tons (27 metric tons) of coal up an incline at 4 mph (6.5 km/h).

The success of *Blücher* spurred Stephenson to build another 16 locomotives over the next 10 years, most of which were commissioned by local collieries. One went to the Kilmarnock and Troon Railway in 1817, but was withdrawn because it damaged the line's cast-iron rails. The same fate befell a second engine that

Power wheel The large wheel, shown in this c.1910 image, is the same power wheel that Stephenson used to operate a lathe—a metal shaping machine—at the Killingworth Colliery.

Planned route The Stockton and Darlington Railway was the first to carry both passengers and freight hauled by a steam engine. This 1821 map shows the intended route of the line.

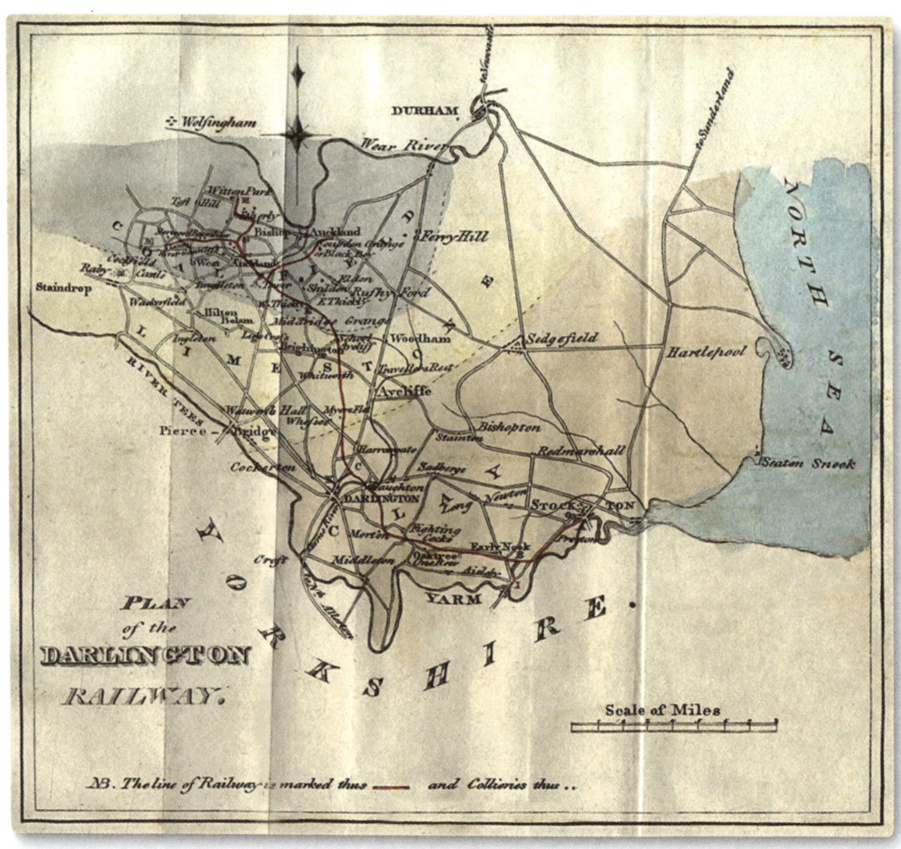

was sent to the railroad at Scott's Pit at Llansamlet, near Swansea, in 1819. These failures demonstrated the great difficulty in developing engines that were light enough not to break the primitive tracks but powerful enough to haul a reasonable load. Showing his versatility as an engineer, Stephenson initially solved this problem by using steam pressure to create a "steam spring" to cushion the weight of the load. He then simply increased the number of wheels to distribute the weight.

Connecting towns

Stephenson's engines, however, continued to suffer difficulties, and he did not have the resources to solve them. In the early 1820s, he became quite despondent at their failings, but developments in the coal town of Darlington lifted his spirits. A group of prosperous Quaker colliery owners, led by Edward Pease and his son Joseph, wanted to create a railroad that would connect Darlington to Stockton at the mouth of the Tees River, where coastal shipping from London docked. They wanted to reduce the price of coal by making it cheaper to transport and to counter a rival plan being mooted to build a canal. Stephenson was the obvious choice to prepare such a route and build the Stockton and Darlington Railway and was summoned to the Peases' home to discuss their plan. He was duly appointed surveyor and engineer on the project, and since he had formed a company in 1823 with his son, Robert, to build locomotives at a works in Newcastle, he could use his own engines on the railroad. Nevertheless, when Stephenson surveyed the area to be crossed, he encountered considerable opposition from local landowners and had to map out a route that would avoid their fox-hunting grounds.

The scheme was far more ambitious than any of the former wagonways. Tracks had to be laid along a route of nearly 26 miles (42 km), and there were major physical obstacles, too, notably the Myers Flat swamp and the Skerne River at Darlington. Stephenson eventually created a firm base in the swamp by filling it with many tons of hand-hewn rock and called on a local architect to help him design a stone bridge to cross the river. Despite its length and logistical difficulties, the line took only three years to construct, but even as it opened, debate raged over what form of traction to use. Stephenson and his son produced the steam engine *Locomotion No. 1*, which, on the opening day of September 27, 1825, pulled a train of around 34 wagons carrying about 600 passengers and a variety of goods through the countryside. However, this was not enough to convince the Peases. The truth was that Stephenson's locomotives were unreliable—they often ran out of steam and frequently needed repairs—so most of those early trains were hauled by horses; at one point, the Peases even considered making the whole line horse-driven. Eventually, however, a much better locomotive designed by an engineer at Stephenson's works, Timothy Hackworth, saved the day, and it was the horses who were withdrawn.

The completed Stockton and Darlington Railway was recognized as a major technical advance over its predecessors, but given the initial use of horses, it was still effectively a superior type of wagonway. It was also flawed. There were few passing loops—which allow trains traveling in opposite

First day The opening of the Stockton and Darlington Railway, depicted in this 20th-century illustration, captured the imagination of the public.

Stephenson's railroad gauge of 4 ft 8½ in (1,435 mm) became the world standard

directions to pass each other—so arguments and even fights between drivers were common. The owners also made the mistake of allowing anyone who was prepared to pay a fee to use their vehicles on the line, which meant that all kinds of conveyances, rickety and unstable, were used, resulting in frequent breakdowns. Nevertheless, the railroad attracted a lot of traffic, and although it took time to become profitable, it established an important precedent—Stephenson had decided on a gauge, which became standard across much of the world's railroad network.

From Liverpool to Manchester

The intense traffic on the Stockton and Darlington line encouraged entrepreneurs across Britain to promote local railroad plans. Many of these were never built, but the most important was Stephenson's next big project—the Liverpool and Manchester line, which was conceived on a much larger scale than the Stockton and Darlington and would become the world's first modern railroad. A group of wealthy industrialists in the northwest of England, annoyed at paying local canal owners' extortionate rates to transport their goods, sought to link the two towns with a railroad. The 31-mile (50 km) line was much more ambitious than the Stockton and Darlington, and although originally conceived as a freight railroad, it would also carry passengers, as it connected two very important towns that had a combined population of roughly 410,000. To ensure reliability, the trains would be run directly by the company, which set the pattern for nearly all future railroad lines. Stephenson was invited by the directors to determine the route. Again, there was a major area of swampy peat bog, Chat Moss, to overcome, as well as a series of streams and rivers that needed fording, requiring no fewer than 64 bridges, including a nine-arch viaduct over the Sankey River. Nothing on this scale had ever been attempted before. Stephenson was again both surveyor and engineer and personally studied the terrain. Local landowners strongly opposed the line, and there was a false start when the initial Parliamentary Bill (which needed to be passed for the line to be built) was thrown out at the behest of the rival canal owners—partly a result of an embarrassing performance in front of the members of parliament by Stephenson, who proved to be tongue-tied in the intimidating atmosphere of Parliament. For a time, Stephenson was replaced as surveyor and engineer, but he was soon reinstated, and work began in 1827. Stephenson personally oversaw construction all along the line, often riding long distances on horseback to check on progress. His solution to the Chat Moss problem was to float the railroad embankment on a bed of brushwood and heather. He also excavated a 2-mile (3.2 km) cutting through Olive Mount at the entrance to Liverpool and built the Sankey Viaduct with sandstone blasted out of the cutting.

The Rainhill Trials

The form of traction to be used remained an issue throughout the line's construction. The directors of the railroad favored locomotives but were unsure whether the existing engines were up to the task, so they launched a competition, the Rainhill Trials, to decide who should design the engines for the railroad. Five entrants took

Sankey Viaduct The viaduct over the Sankey River was one of the trickiest engineering challenges that George Stephenson faced in constructing the Liverpool and Manchester Railway.

part in the trials, which were held on a completed section of track starting on October 6, 1829. The trials continued over nine days and in front of more than 10,000 spectators. The technical requirements were strict, particularly regarding weight, which was fixed at a maximum of 6 tons (5.4 metric tons), and the engines had to complete 10 return trips, or 20 total, 1.5-mile (2.4-km) trips at an average speed exceeding 10 mph (16 km/h).

One of the entrants, *Cycloped*, turned out to be a prank (the engine was, in fact, a horse on a treadmill), so *Rocket*, the entry of George Stephenson's son, Robert, faced only three rivals: John Braithwaite and John Ericsson's *Novelty*, Timothy Hackworth's *Sans Pareil*, and Timothy Burstall's *Perseverance*. In the event, the trial was easily won. *Perseverance* never managed more than 6 mph (10 km/h), and the other two failed to finish the course. Meanwhile, *Rocket* thundered up and down the track, ensuring that the Stephensons won the £500 prize to help develop their engines.

Since the line carried freight in both directions—the raw materials from the port at Liverpool, and the manufactured goods in the other direction—as well as passengers, it was double-tracked from

Rainhill trials A set of trials were held in 1829 at Rainhill to assess the best locomotive to power the Liverpool and Manchester Railway. The trials were won by Robert Stephenson's *Rocket*, shown here racing ahead under the bridge.

Railroad fatality The grand opening of the Liverpool and Manchester Railway in September 1830 was marred by the death of a local member of parliament, William Huskisson, who was hit by a train as he attempted to get out of the way.

> **"George Stephenson told me as a young man that railways will supersede almost all other methods of conveyance."**
>
> JOHN DIXON, QUOTED IN *LIFE OF GEORGE STEPHENSON*, 1875

the outset, which greatly increased capacity. The opening day on September 15, 1830, was an epoch-making event, attracting people from around the world, several of whom would return home to inspire the building of railroads in their own country. The celebrations, however, were marred by tragedy—an accident that resulted in the death of William Huskisson, a prominent politician. Huskisson crossed the tracks to greet the Prime Minister and 1st Duke of Wellington, Arthur Wellesley, at his train carriage, when the ceremonial trains stopped at Parkside, halfway down the line. Panic set in when another train, *Rocket*, approached. Huskisson failed to climb onto the Duke's carriage in time and fell under the oncoming train. His leg was shattered and, although Stephenson took him to Eccles, near Manchester, for help on the *Rocket*—reaching an amazing speed of 35 mph (56 km/h) en route—Huskisson died that evening.

An enduring impact

While the completion of the Liverpool and Manchester marked the peak of George's career, the Stephenson name lived on. George went on to build numerous railroads and his son, Robert, who concentrated mainly on improving the locomotives produced by his eponymous company, constructed a far longer railroad, the 112-mile (180-km) London and Birmingham line, which is now part of the West Coast Main Line. Robert Stephenson & Co Ltd. thrived and eventually produced more than 3,000 engines before being absorbed by a larger company in 1937. George Stephenson also advised early American rail promoters (see pp.34–35) and assisted in the construction of lines in Belgium (see p.44) and Spain. The Stephensons certainly left an enduring mark on the railroads. When the line celebrated its 150th anniversary in 1980, Peter Parker, the then-chairman of British Rail observed: "The world is a branch line of the Liverpool and Manchester."

Improving engines (right) This poster demonstrates the rapid progress in locomotive technology. It shows how the very basic engine devised by Stephenson had, by the end of the century, turned into sleek, modern locomotives.

Fueling the engine The steam engine required two people, a driver and a fireman, to keep it running. Here, a fireman (left) is shoveling coal into the firebox.

POWERING THE ENGINE

Steam-powered devices appeared in the writings of Heron of Alexandria as early as the 1st century CE. However, it was not until the late 17th century that steam power was put to practical use in the form of stationary engines, the principles behind which were refined simultaneously by Oliver Evans in the US and Richard Trevithick in England. Trevithick developed the idea of using high-pressure steam, which allowed the engine to be small enough to be mounted on wheels. This meant that steam could be used for propulsion. His *Puffing Devil*—the world's first steam locomotive—made its maiden journey on Christmas Eve 1801.

How steam is created

In his 1829 *Rocket*, George Stephenson pioneered the fire-tube boiler. Earlier engines used a single fire tube to heat the water in the boiler, but Stephenson used 25 copper fire tubes to greatly increase the heat transfer between the firebox and the boiler, meaning that steam could be created more efficiently. Later engines used superheater elements in place of the fire tubes.

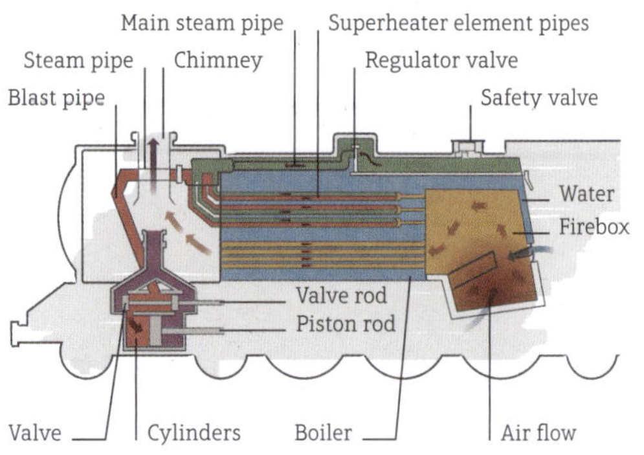

KEY

- Steam exhaust
- Saturated steam
- Superheated steam
- Hot gases

Forward motion In a typical steam engine, coal is burned to heat water and create steam that is passed at high pressure to the cylinders to turn the gear.

Steam propulsion

Steam from the boiler is superheated to over 212°F (100°C) and transferred to the cylinders at high pressure, pushing the pistons that turn the driving wheels via a series of pivots and rods, converting linear motion to rotation.

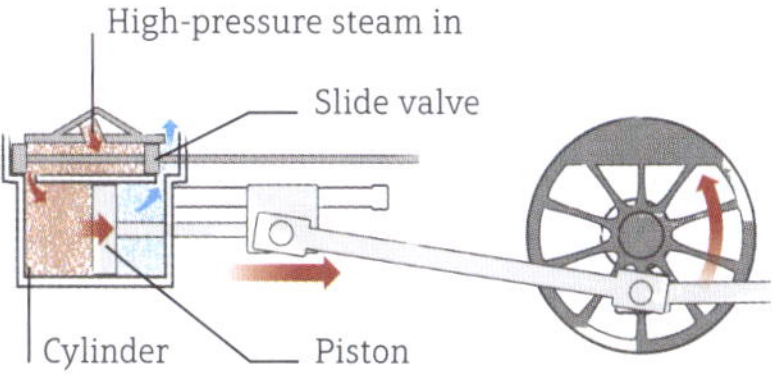

Phase 1: Outward stroke
High-pressure steam is fed via a slide valve into the cylinder, where it expands and pushes the piston to rotate the wheels by a half-turn.

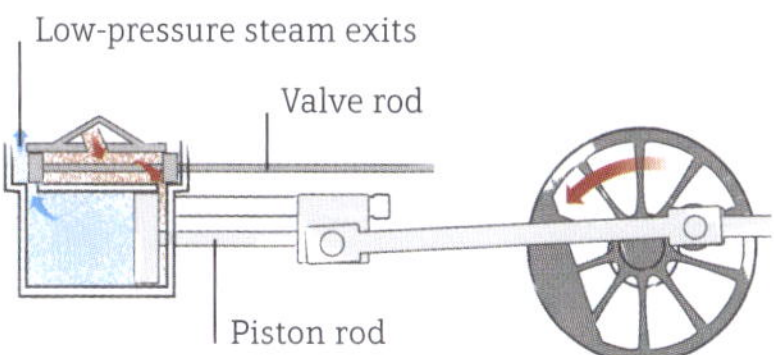

Phase 2: Exhaust
A series of rods that connect the wheel to the slide valve open the valve to allow the steam, which has now lost pressure, to escape.

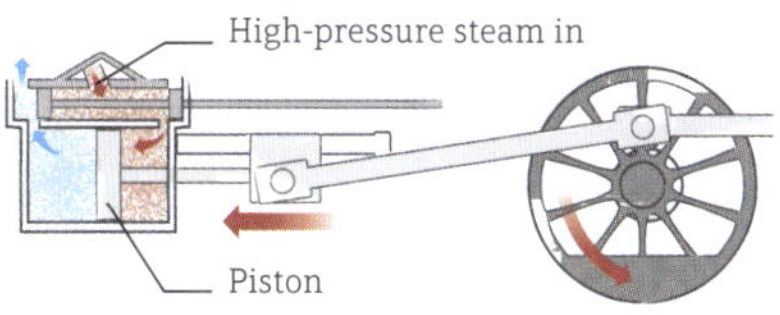

Phase 3: Return stroke
The movement of the valve allows the steam to enter the back of the cylinder, and the return phase of the stroke begins.

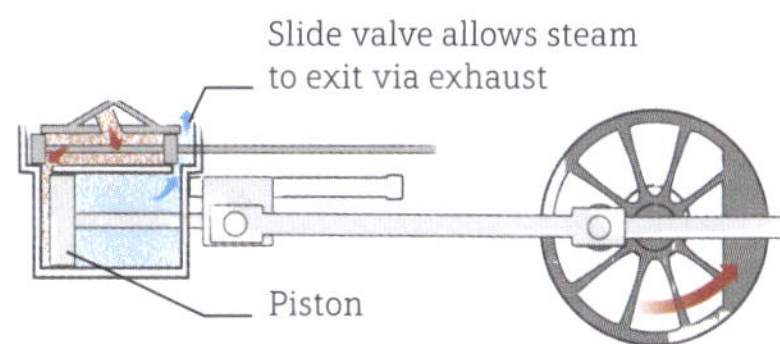

Phase 4: Exhaust
Once the wheels make another half turn, the spent steam escapes the cylinder, fresh steam enters it, and the cycle begins again.

THE FIRST AMERICAN RAILROADS

The United States entered the railroad age later than Britain, but before long, it developed one of the largest railroad networks in the world.

In 1828, the 90-year-old Charles Carroll stepped up to make the inaugural speech at the breaking ground ceremony for the new Baltimore and Ohio Railroad. Carroll had witnessed the birth of the US firsthand—he was the only surviving signatory of the American Declaration of Independence. Half a century later, as he commemorated the launch of this ambitious project that aimed to reach into the heartland of the continent, his words proved to be remarkably prescient: "I consider this among the most important acts of my life, second only to my signing the Declaration of Independence, if even it be second to that."

The US, which had only recently freed itself from the shackles of colonialism, was far behind Great Britain, its former colonial master, in terms of

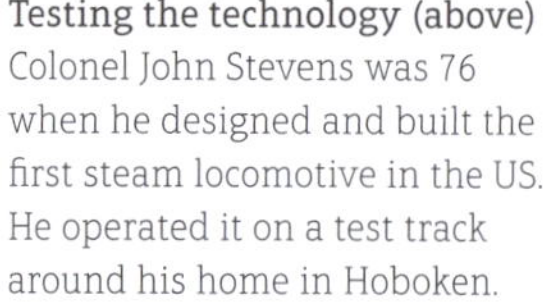

Testing the technology (above) Colonel John Stevens was 76 when he designed and built the first steam locomotive in the US. He operated it on a test track around his home in Hoboken.

Pioneering lines The early railroads in the US mostly linked inland towns such as St. Louis (shown here) with ports on the eastern coast.

technological development. Its earliest railroads—it soon adopted the name "railroads"—were dependent on British imports, as were its riverboats, factories, and mining operations, all of which ran on British steam engines. To catch up, American industrialists kept a close eye on British railroad developments, and often traveled across the Atlantic to pick up the latest information. The size of the US, and the ambition of its people, made it fertile ground for the iron road, and it was perhaps inevitable that the new nation would soon boast more miles of track than the rest of the world put together. In fact, the US would end up, at the peak of the railroad boom in 1916, with more than 250,000 miles (400,000 km) of line, by far the biggest rail network the world has ever seen.

Early days

Until the advent of the railroads, transportation in the US had been difficult and slow. There were a few canals, but these iced up in winter. The roads were very poor, owned by turnpike trusts that were unable to maintain them properly as the tolls that were collected were insufficient. Steamboats were the best form of transportation, but they gave access to only certain parts of the country. The first American railroad pioneer was Colonel John Stevens, a successful steamboat designer and operator who was obviously rather

The first chartered railroad in the US was the Granite Railway of Massachusetts, which opened in 1826

taken with the railroads since he wrote a pamphlet entitled *Documents Tending to prove the Superior Advantages of Rail-ways and Steam-Carriages over Canal Navigation*. As early as 1815, he obtained the first railroad charter for permission to construct a line linking the Delaware River near Trenton with the Raritan River in New Jersey, though in the event it was never built—no investors came forward to finance the scheme, which was far ahead of its time. Undeterred, in 1825 Stevens designed and built a steam locomotive, which ran on a circular track on a narrow-gauge line at his estate.

Stevens and his two sons were involved in a number of other early projects, notably the Philadelphia and Columbia line, which was built to link the port of Philadelphia with Columbia on the Susquehanna River to give merchants in Philadelphia access to Harrisburg and Western Pennsylvania. They also founded the Camden and Amboy Railroad, which ran from Camden, across the Delaware River from Philadelphia, to South Amboy, on the New Jersey shore opposite New York. Initially, all these lines were horse-drawn, but inevitably, given the distances involved, locomotive traction was considered—and for that, British technology was needed. John Stevens's son Robert traveled to Britain and brought back a locomotive, *John Bull*, built in the Robert Stephenson Works. It arrived in parts and was assembled by Isaac Dripps,

John Bull Built in Britain and imported to the US in 1831, this locomotive is seen here at the 1893 Columbia World Exposition with a cowcatcher—Isaac Dripps's invention to push cattle away from the tracks.

North American Railroads in 1860 The early American railroads were concentrated in the northeast of the US, developing as a result of, and driving, industrialization.

an engineer who fitted pilot wheels at the front to help guide the locomotive around the sharper bends on the American railroad, and who was also credited with inventing the "cowcatcher"—in reality, a cow killer that pushed away cattle or deer that had roamed onto the line, invariably fatally.

Railroad development

Building lines in the US in the early 19th century was by no means easy. First, the promoters had to obtain a charter from the state government, then they had to persuade investors, who were often local people, to support the scheme, and finally they had to find sufficient workers to build the line as there was often a shortage of labor. There was one key advantage compared with other countries. Once a charter was obtained, the state gave the railroad company "eminent domain"—the right to take over any land required for the line's construction. Sometimes, though, the law was difficult to apply in practice. When the Erie Railroad was being constructed across upstate New York, it was planned to cross land belonging to the Seneca people. The local people demanded $10,000 (in modern terms, around $340,000, or £260,000) for the right of way. The railroad works manager blustered that the land was no good for anything else apart from growing corn or potatoes. The local chief responded: "Pretty good for railroad," and got the money.

Most of the early railroad development was stimulated by competition between the great cities of the eastern US, such as Baltimore, Philadelphia, New York, and Boston. Each wanted to obtain cheap access to the Midwest, where towns were growing rapidly, creating an important market for produce. Baltimore proved to be the most adventurous in promoting a railroad stretching deep into the hinterland. The Baltimore and Ohio was the most significant of these early schemes,

In 1829, the *Stourbridge Lion*, imported from the UK, became the first steam locomotive to operate in the US

being the first attempt to build a rail link between an Atlantic port and the Ohio River, and so reaching the Midwest.

Steam replaces horse

As with so many of these early lines, the promoters of the Baltimore and Ohio were unsure about whether to use horses or steam locomotives to haul the trains. Given that they wanted the line to reach the town of Wheeling, nearly 400 miles (650 km) from Baltimore, it is extraordinary that they even considered using equine power, but they arranged a competition between the hay eater and the coal burner. A locomotive builder, Peter Cooper, had built a little engine, nicknamed *Tom Thumb*, for the line, and it proceeded to impress the promoters with a test run on the initial 13 miles (21 km) of track that had been completed, reaching an exhilarating 18 mph (29 km/h). On the run back toward Baltimore, Cooper foolishly agreed to race his locomotive against a powerful gray horse. The animal soon took the lead, thanks to its faster acceleration, but was then overtaken by the steady little engine when Cooper opened the safety valve to provide extra power. However, he overreached himself: after the locomotive had gained a significant lead, the belt that drove its pulley snapped, and the engine

Small wonder In 1830, inventor and businessman Peter Cooper's pioneering engine *Tom Thumb* became the first successful American steam locomotive. This image shows a reenactment of its historic journey on the Baltimore & Ohio Railroad.

eased to a halt. The equine victory proved pyrrhic, however, as Cooper had done enough to persuade the promoters that steam haulage, rather than horsepower, was the only way to make the line viable. Although work started in 1828, and trains started operating on part of the line two years later, it was not until 1853 that the tracks reached Wheeling on the Ohio River owing to legal, financial, and technical difficulties.

A new "friend"

Farther south, there was a far longer pioneering line, which was completed much more quickly and used American technology. The Charleston and Hamburg was an attempt to revive Charleston's foreign exports, which had gone into decline, and its local merchants hoped to secure the trade of the rich cotton-growing area in the region. They chose steam power from the outset, and the first engine, the *Best Friend of Charleston*, built at the West Point Foundry in New York, pulled its first train in December 1830. Unfortunately, a couple of months later, the pioneering locomotive suffered an untimely demise when an inexperienced fireman, annoyed at the sound made by the escape of steam from its safety valve, blocked it. The pressure of the accumulated steam caused the boiler to explode, killing the fireman and scalding the driver. Despite this mishap, the line was complete by 1833, and at 136 miles (219 km), it was, for a time, the longest in the world.

> **"The introduction of so powerful an agent as steam to a carriage on wheels will make a great change in the situation of man."**
>
> THOMAS JEFFERSON, 1802

A distinct identity

American railroads differed from their European counterparts in several respects. The key contrast was one of scale, not just in the extent of their reach, as they gradually extended farther and farther west, but also in the size of the trains and locomotives themselves. Their characteristically huge, bulbous chimneys—needed to contain the sparks that might otherwise set fire to the countryside—were far taller than their European equivalents, for the American lines had few bridges or tunnels. Consequently, even today American trains are almost 3 ft (1 m) taller than those in Europe, enabling them to carry much greater loads. Overall, US railroads were bigger in every sense than those across the Atlantic. They covered greater distances, and were longer and heavier

The background depicts the charter granted to the railroad in 1827

Honoring the past Marking the 125th anniversary of the opening of the Baltimore & Ohio Railroad, this stamp features a horse-drawn car, *Tom Thumb*, and a 1952 diesel locomotive.

Carriage comfort From the start, American railroads had open-plan carriages with a through corridor, such as the one shown here from c.1905, unlike their European counterparts, which had individual compartments.

because they used stronger and larger locomotives, all of which gave them a distinctive style (see pp.40–41). The efforts to cut the costs of the new lines were successful, and US railroads were far cheaper to build than their European equivalents, but as a result, they were also less reliable and slower. Some aspects of the railroads were, however, better from the start. Locomotives, for example, were fitted with cabs for the crew, a "luxury" that was necessitated by the rigors of the US climate, but which did not become universal elsewhere until much later. Right from the start, too, passengers traveled in carriages that were open plan, rather than in individual compartments, such as those in Europe. These were necessary because traveling longer distances meant that travelers required ready access to conveniences, a facility that was not available on most European trains until well into the second half of the 19th century.

Rapid progress

These early lines were successful and mostly profitable, which attracted a wave of investment into this burgeoning industry. By 1837, at least 200 railroads were being promoted. Many of these were unrealistic or put forward by crooks intent on cheating potential investors, but many schemes were completed, and by the end of the decade about 2,750 miles (4,425 km) of railroad were in operation—a remarkable rate of progress. The spur for most of these lines was freight, particularly

The South Carolina Canal and Railroad Company ran the first American steam-powered passenger train in 1830

coal and minerals, but increasing numbers of passengers also flocked to the trains. Soon, these inaugural short lines were followed by long trunk railroads such as the Erie and the Pennsylvania lines, linking the Eastern Seaboard with the Midwest. It was only in the second half of the 19th century that the transcontinentals brought the railroads to the West.

Building a nation around iron roads

Before long, every town wanted to be connected to the railroad network as it was considered vital for their prosperity. Prominent local citizens would band together and form a company to obtain a charter, often investing their own money. A mere 20 years later, at the outbreak of the Civil War (see pp.60–65) in 1861, there were nearly 30,000 miles (48,280 km) of railroad in the US. The railroads, in fact, grew symbiotically with the US economy, transforming the nation from a predominantly agricultural country into the industrial powerhouse of the world, all within a few decades. It is impossible to know whether the tracks spread so quickly because of the rapid growth in wealth, or whether it was the other way around, but there is no doubt that the US thrived because of the growing railroad system and that the railroads welded this vast nation together (see also pp.114–121).

Locomotive works In 1848, Schenectady Locomotive Works opened in New York. It was responsible for the manufacture of several early locomotives, including Central Pacific Railroad's *Jupiter*, which was present at the 1869 ceremony to mark the completion of the transcontinental railroad.

THE EARLY YEARS OF AMERICAN STEAM

Starting with the Baltimore and Ohio Railroad in 1827, the growth of the American railroad network enabled the Industrial Revolution to take hold in the northeastern US and opened up the west coast to exploration and colonization. US locomotive engineers produced some innovative designs, including geared locomotives and the first rack railroad (see pp.104–105).

John Bull **(1831)**
Built by Stephenson & Co., *John Bull* was exported to the US, where it worked from 1831 to 1866. American engineer Isaac Dripps added a two-wheel bogie (see p.58), to which he attached the first cowcatcher, as well as a headlight, spark-arresting chimney, and covered tender and cab.

Baltimore and Ohio Grasshopper No.2: *Atlantic* (1832)
Named because its long connecting rods and vertical cylinders gave it an insect-like appearance when moving, the Grasshopper *Atlantic* was the first US-designed locomotive to see commercial service on American soil.

Baltimore and Ohio Grasshopper No.8: *John Hancock* (1836)
The *John Hancock* was an improved model of the Grasshopper class, featuring a covered cab and dual-powered axles. It was used continuously on the Baltimore and Ohio Railroad from 1836 until 1892.

Baltimore and Ohio No.57: *Memnon* (1848)
One of the oldest surviving freight locomotives in the US, the *Memnon* was designed to transport coal. Its hauling power was aided by eight driving wheels, the central pair of which are "blind" (lacking flanges) to enable the locomotive to better negotiate curves in the line.

Baltimore and Ohio No.147: *Thatcher Perkins* (1863)
Named after its designer, the company's Master of Machinery, *Thatcher Perkins* was rushed into service to meet the demands of the American Civil War. Its six driving wheels and four leading wheels were designed to cope with the steep tracks in the Allegheny Mountains.

Cumberland Valley Railroad No.13: *Pioneer* (1851)
The *Pioneer* was a lightweight locomotive with only one pair of driving wheels. It was used to haul up to three passenger carriages and is pictured here in the livery of its retirement in 1901.

Shay No.1: *Leetonia* (1906)
The *Leetonia*, one of engineer Ephraim Shay's geared locomotives, used toothed driveshafts driven by three vertical cylinders to power all 12 of its wheels, making it ideal for hauling timber at low speeds on steep grades and tight curves.

Moore-Keppel and company Climax No.4 (1913)
Similar to the Shays, the Climax-class geared engines were used by lumber companies. A cylinder on either side of the boiler powered eight wheels via a centrally mounted transmission.

Reading company No.1251 (1918)
Built using parts from older locomotives, No.1251 was a shunting engine with six driving wheels. Its "saddle tank" design meant that no tender was required—water was carried in a tank on top of the boiler.

EUROPE TAKES TO THE RAILS

As Britain was pioneering the railroads, the cafés of Paris were abuzz with news of the recent developments—but not everyone was as enthusiastic.

Just as railroad opponents in Britain had warned that it might be impossible to breathe when traveling at more than 30 mph (50 km/h), or that cows would stop producing milk because of the noise of the railroad, in France and the rest of Europe, too, there were eminent doubters of this new technology. Indeed, the French habit of philosophizing over major issues meant that Parisian intellectuals discussed the pros and cons of the new railroads in great detail—the writer Edmond de Goncourt warned that when traveling on the railroad, "one was so jolted about that it was quite impossible to collect one's thoughts."

However, despite the naysayers, the major European countries—particularly France, Belgium, and the German

Locomotive inspection
Railroad workers took great pride in their engines, which were subject to regular inspections. This 1855 picture shows the locomotive *La Petite* being inspected in Sotteville-lès-Rouen, France.

Confederation—were now scrambling to construct their own lines. The economic advantages of doing so were obvious, but there were political reasons too—railroads were both vital assets in war and, paradoxically, they could also help bind nations together.

The French initiative

At first, Europe was dependent on Britain both for technology and drivers, but many countries soon developed their own technology, notably France, whose early efforts were close behind Britain's. In 1823, during a brief revival of the French monarchy, Louis XVIII signed an Act that permitted the construction of France's first railroad. The 13-mile (21 km) track ran between St.-Étienne and Andrézieux in the Massif Central and was built to carry coal from the mines to the Loire for shipment to the rest of the country. The line opened in 1828 and, although horse-drawn, it was an instant success. As a result, extensions were added, and by 1832 the line, which now used locomotives and carried passengers as well as freight, stretched to the major city of Lyon. The elaborate French coaches were an improvement on the rather more austere British trains and were divided into compartments, an arrangement that soon became standard across Europe.

France's equivalent of George Stephenson (see pp.22–29) was Marc Seguin, a scientist and inventor who had in fact advised Stephenson on how to improve the boilers of his locomotives. He produced two locomotives for the extended St.-Étienne–Lyon railroad, each featuring a multitube boiler (see pp.30–31) and a mechanical fan to deliver oxygen to the fire. Later, in another case of Anglo-French cooperation, Robert Stephenson built

Donkey power Before steam engines became widely used, railroads tried animal power, such as these French carriages being hauled by a donkey.

By 1840, there were 350 miles (560 km) of track in France, and 2,000 miles (3,200 km) of track in Britain

locomotives designed by Seguin. However, the lengthy debate over the advantages and disadvantages of railroad construction slowed the pace of development in France.

The cause of the railroad promoters was not helped when the world's first major rail disaster occurred between Versailles and Paris, in May 1842. The train, returning from Versailles, was so heavily laden with vacationers who had been watching the celebrations for the king's fête that it required two locomotives to haul it. The leading engine suffered a broken axle—a relatively commonplace event in the early days of railroads—and then derailed, along with three carriages, which quickly burst into flames. The death toll was at least 50 and may have been as many as 200; people couldn't escape because they were locked in their compartments and many bodies were consumed by the inferno. As a result, the French authorities stopped locking passengers into their carriages, although the practice continued elsewhere, contributing to the high death toll of the 1889 Armagh disaster, the worst in Irish history (see p.132).

Railroad disaster This 19th-century painting depicts the 1842 Versailles rail disaster. The derailment of the locomotive resulted in a massive fire in the train's wooden carriages.

Burgeoning railroad in Belgium

Many other countries around Europe joined the Railway Age in the 1830s, and the state was usually much more directly involved than in Britain, where the government had remained aloof. Nowhere was this more true than in Belgium, a new country carved out of the Netherlands in 1830 and anxious to demonstrate its independence. The railroads were an ideal way of doing so, since building a railroad system was thought to stimulate a sense of national identity. Consequently, the country's first king, Leopold I, approved the design of a whole network, and in 1834 construction started on the first line. This crossed the entire country from Antwerp in the north to Mons in the west, and into Prussia via Aachen in the east—a total of 154 miles (248 km), a very ambitious scheme at that time. Together with an Ostend–Liege line forming an east–west axis, Belgium quickly created a fully planned national railroad system—the first of its kind in the world. Inevitably, George Stephenson was involved, his company providing the first three locomotives and he himself traveling incognito in 1835 on the first train carrying the royal party. When the train broke down, Stephenson went to the engine to help fix the problem, and was knighted by the king for his pains. The support of the government gave Belgium a lead in railroad development, and by 1843 most of the heart of Belgium's railroad network—which forms a "cross" shape centered on Brussels—had been built, giving the heavily industrialized country the densest network in the world.

Germany's rail network

Germany's first railroad also opened in 1835, doing so in Bavaria, where King Ludwig approved a steam-hauled line that ran the 3.7 miles (6 km) between Nuremberg and Fürth. Unlike most of the inaugural lines, this was built mainly for passengers, as it relieved traffic on the busiest highway in Bavaria between the two towns. The congestion was the result of peculiar local circumstances. For centuries, the Nuremberg authorities had forbidden laborers and foreigners to live in the town, so they had to commute from Fürth, which had become a dormitory

town, presaging a use for the railroad that remains commonplace today. Saxony, another important German state, followed Bavaria's lead, building Germany's first major railroad, linking Leipzig with Dresden. Saxony was the industrial heartland of Germany, similar in character to the northwest of England, where the pioneering Liverpool and Manchester line had been built (see pp.26–29). More than 200 factories had sprung up in the region, and local industrialists, realizing that a railroad was essential to carry the minerals and ore needed by the factories, quickly raised the money to build the 65-mile (105 km) line, which was built remarkably swiftly thanks to the use of British technology and personnel.

The railroads were particularly important for Germany as a means of unifying the country. As early as 1817, economist and visionary thinker Friedrich List had understood the importance of the railroads for Germany. He argued that a nation could prosper only through trade and industry, and that a fast, efficient rail network could carry food and industrial products throughout the country. His theory was borne out. Customs duties between states were soon scrapped as impractical, and within a generation of the first rail line being completed, Germany's railroad system had helped it become a powerful unified state.

Like the Nuremberg–Fürth line, the first line in the Netherlands, another relatively early starter, was also built

Centennial celebration This image shows a 1938 replica of the locomotive *Adler*. It was built to mark the 100th anniversary of the opening of the initial section of the Berlin–Potsdam railroad, the first line in Prussia.

9,400

The number of locomotives in Germany by 1880

The railroads come to Italy This 1839 painting by Salvatore Fergola depicts the inaugural train leaving Portici station in Naples, Italy. The line was Italy's first railroad, and today forms part of the Naples–Salerno line.

for passengers rather than freight. The Holland Iron Railway between Amsterdam and Haarlem opened in 1839 and reached Rotterdam eight years later. It was extremely successful, killing off the competing coach and barge traffic that had previously dominated the route between the country's two main cities. The Netherlands, though, did not have the centrally planned scheme of its Belgian neighbor and so never developed such an intensive network.

The Belgian, German, and Dutch railroads were all steam-hauled, but the idea that railroads could be operated successfully by horses lingered. In Austria, remarkably, the early network was entirely horse-drawn and grew to an extensive size. It included the world's longest horse-drawn railroad—a 80-mile (129 km) line linking Linz in Upper Austria with Budweis in Bohemia (home of the world-renowned beer, now in Czechia). The horse-drawn system was later extended further to the saltworks at the Upper Austrian health resort of Gmunden, and by 1836, it had reached an impressive 122 miles (197 km). Only then did the Austrians replace horses with steam engines.

Horse-drawn railroad While most early railroads were steam powered, the Budweis–Linz line in Austria initially used horses. This 19th-century image shows the first carriage used on this horse-drawn railroad.

Italian and Russian railroads

The railroads of both Italy and Russia began as royal initiatives, albeit for the private purposes of connecting royal palaces. In Italy, the King of the Two Sicilies, Ferdinand II, fancied connecting his main palace in Naples to his other residence on the Bay of Naples at Portici with a 4½-mile (7.2 km) railroad line, which was completed in October 1839. The idea had been recommended to him by a Frenchman, Armand Bayard de la Vingtrie, who was eager to make money from railroad schemes. The first section of the line was built quickly and proved to be immensely popular, carrying up to 1,000 people per day. Oddly, the king himself eschewed traveling on the inaugural journey, perhaps because he was aware of the risks of early train travel.

In Russia, Czar Nicholas I built the first railroad line between his main residence in St. Petersburg and

Railroad memorabilia The opening of railroads was often accompanied by memorabilia such as this medal, which commemorates the 1839 inauguration of the first rail line in the Netherlands.

Inaugural ceremony This 19th-century painting depicts the arrival of the first train from St. Petersburg into Tsarskoye Selo on October 30, 1837.

Tsarskoe Selo, the enormous royal residence favored by Catherine the Great. He was advised by Austrian engineer, Franz Anton von Gerstner, who was eager to bring Russia into the railroad fold and had sought to build a far more ambitious line between St. Petersburg and Moscow. Initially, however, only the Tsarskoe Selo line was commissioned, and opened in 1837 with the first train, carrying eight full coaches, taking a mere 28 minutes to reach Tsarskoe Selo—an impressive average speed of almost 30 mph (50 km/h).

Expanding to Pavlovsk

The following year, the line was extended by 16 miles (26 km) to Pavlovsk, a small vacation resort complete with buffets, concerts, and a ballroom to entertain the St. Petersburg crowds on their day trips. To attract the crowds, the railroad subsidized the public entertainment at Pavlovsk, which is described in Dostoevsky's *The Idiot* as "one of the fashionable summer resorts near St. Petersburg." At first, the line was hauled by horses and various locomotives imported from Britain and Belgium, but before long, the animals, exhausted from pulling the heavy trains, were put out to grass and steam locomotives were introduced. The line was a great success, with people flocking to the railroad both out of curiosity and the desire to sample the attractions. More than 725,000 people traveled on the line in its first year, an average of 2,000 per day. The 400-mile (640-km) long St. Petersburg–Moscow line was completed in 1851, becoming one of the longest and most impressive trunk routes in the world at the time.

Most countries in Europe adopted the 4 ft 8½ in (1,435 mm) gauge devised by Stephenson (see p.25), and this proved vitally important in ensuring that a continental network was created, with trains passing through borders relatively easily—although customs and technical factors relating to signaling and driver training usually meant delays at the frontier. Russia and Spain were exceptions—both used a 5 ft (1½ m) gauge for fear of invasion from hostile neighbors, reckoning correctly in the case of Russia that making trains change gauge would prove a useful defensive barrier.

Travel regulations

Traveling on these early lines was not always made easy, either by the regimes of the day or the railroad companies. Governments were suspicious of their citizens' desire to travel, and the companies were diligent in collecting fares. On the Leipzig–Dresden line, for example, there were no advance ticket

> **"Railway! A magical aura already surrounds the word; it is a synonym for civilization, progress and fraternity."**
>
> PIERRE LAROUSSE, 1867

sales and access to the station was allowed only a quarter of an hour before the train left—a practice that persists in remote parts of Europe even today. Passengers were required to purchase a return ticket and children under 12 were banned. In Russia, there was also an extraordinary amount of bureaucracy involved in taking a train. Passengers had to obtain an internal passport before traveling, and then go to their local police station to obtain permission for the journey. Even today, Russians have to show their internal passport before buying a ticket for a long-distance journey. Nevertheless, despite the bureaucracy and the technical problems incurred on many pioneering lines, all these early railroads proved popular and successful, spurring the rapid spread of rail travel throughout Europe and to many other parts of the world.

Pavlovsk station Many early railroad stations were grand affairs designed to show off the wonders of the railroads. This 19th-century illustration depicts the impressive station at Pavlovsk in St. Petersburg.

WESTERN EUROPEAN RAILROADS

After the opening of the pioneering Liverpool & Manchester Railway in 1830, the concept of railroad technology was picked up quickly across Europe. The early railroads were so successful that the creation of networks in all the most developed European countries was rapid and inevitable. The lines spread in the ensuing decades until Europe was crisscrossed with a vast web of railroads. While most of these used standard gauge, allowing for easy cross-border travel, Spain and Portugal in the southwest and Russia in the far east chose different gauges, partly for military reasons. This map shows the network of early 21st-century European railroads.

Reluctant joiners The first line in France used horse power and opened in 1828 near St.-Étienne. This line was extended to Lyon in 1832, with locomotives replacing horses. However, a reluctance to embrace this concept persisted as a result of bureaucracy and strong opposition from those who felt this invention would ruin the beauty of the country. A disastrous fire on a train near Versailles in 1842 also hampered progress, but eventually a huge network was built with state support in the second half of the century.

The Dublin and Kingstown Railway (D&KR), which was the first dedicated commuter railroad in the world when it opened in 1834, is now a part of the Dublin Area Rapid Transit (DART) line

Spain's high-speed railroad network is the longest in Europe and second longest in the world, with nearly 2,500 miles (4,000 km) of tracks

KEY

— Main line

○ City/Town

State support The progress of railroads was quickest in countries where the state, often working with private contractors, supported the idea. Thanks to strong encouragement by the King, Belgium was well on its way to having a network of lines by the end of the 1830s. The image above shows the first train en route from Brussels to Mechelen in 1835. On the other hand, in neighboring Holland (the Netherlands), the first short line did not open until 1839, because of lack of state interest and objections from canal companies, who viewed the railroads as a threat to their monopoly of transportation networks.

According to the latest data, the Czech Republic has the greatest density of railroads in relation to its land mass in the world

In 2024, the total rail network in Türkiye was 8,650 miles (13,919 km), including 1,400 miles (2,251 km) of high-speed lines

Railroad opposition Campaigners against the early railroads used posters such as this 1846 one, entitled "Hyde Park as it will be," to portray a dystopian world that would be brought about by the advent of the railroads. Here, it depicts the desecration of the environment at London's Hyde Park.

RAILROAD MANIA

The success of the first railroads stimulated enormous interest from potential investors and promoters of new lines across the world, creating periods of railroad mania.

Starting in the early 19th century, periods of railroad mania occurred in nearly every country that developed a network. Unfortunately, not all those who tried to climb the railroad bandwagon were honest. Some had the sole intention of trying to make people part with their money.

Early adopters

The first mania happened before a single line was completed. In the early 1800s, during the run-up to the opening of the Stockton and Darlington Railway (see pp.24–25), British entrepreneurs put forward ideas for other lines despite it being an unproven technology. However, a downturn in the economy following a poor harvest in 1825 and a spate of banking failures soon soured the optimism, and almost all of these programs were quietly forgotten. The success of the Liverpool and Manchester line (see pp.26–29) prompted another spate of railroad promotion in the mid-1830s, but it was the huge surge in applications for new lines from 1844 onward that led to the use of the term "railroad mania." The phenomenon recalled previous promotional fevers such as the canal mania of 1791–1795, and foreshadowed more recent frenzies such as the dot-com boom of the 1990s.

In Britain, by the mid-1840s, railroad construction was established as a legitimate and profitable business, and the healthy economic conditions were ripe for a major boom. The usual method for raising capital was to organize local public meetings at which investors would buy "scrip"—vouchers that could later be exchanged for future shares—for a small deposit in the proposed company. Having raised part of the capital, the promoters would then go to Parliament for approval of their proposal. There had been something of an economic slump in the

In 1825–1835, prospectuses for around 54 railroad lines were published in Britain

Bristol railroad station
Early stations, such as this one in Bristol that opened in 1840, did not have a platform or any other facilities for passengers.

early 1840s, but as the economy recovered, there was an upsurge in railroad promotion. Railroads were seen as a method of making a quick buck, and from 1844 to 1847, British parliamentary approval was obtained for more than 8,000 miles (12,800 km) of line—nearly five times the amount that had already been laid, and a large proportion of Britain's current rail network of 9,846 miles (15,846 km). At the time, building a railroad was a relatively simple task, provided the terrain was favorable—no more difficult than opening a local shop or erecting a row of houses. Once permission was obtained, it was a matter of creating a narrow permanent way, laying the track, and putting in the odd raised wooden platform at stations. There was none of the complexity of today's technically sophisticated railroads.

The mania took hold with astonishing rapidity. In 1843, only 100 miles (160 km) of new line were approved by the British Parliament, but over the next three years the figures were respectively around 800 miles (1,200 km), nearly 3,000 miles (4,800 km), and 4,500 miles (7,200 km), as 272 acts were granted. The scale of this boom can be judged by the fact that it represented a theoretical amount of £700 million worth of capital investment—10 times Britain's annual exports at the time. However, the boom collapsed faster than it grew. The economy slumped in 1847, and as a result, only 17 miles (27 km) of new line were approved by 1849, but two-thirds of the mileage approved thus far was eventually completed within a few years. Some of the failed projects were revived in the smaller booms of 1852–1853 and the 1860s.

Although most of the projects, even the failed ones, were genuine attempts at building a railroad, some of them were blatantly fraudulent, while others were based on the belief that the expansion would last forever. This was how the biggest fraudster of the period, George Hudson, created a massive empire, which inevitably collapsed when the bubble burst. He built several railroads, including the core of the Midland Railway, which was one of the most extensive lines in Britain. He had some other good ideas, too, such as establishing a ticket-clearing house through which railroad companies were reimbursed for running trains on each other's tracks. As he grew in confidence, however, he used

"This big swollen gambler... deserved a coalshaft from his brother mortals."

THOMAS CARLYLE, PHILOSOPHER AND WRITER, ON GEORGE HUDSON

Caught in a web (right)
In the 1840s, so many railroad programs were being put forward that people began perceiving them as a threat to their traditional way of life, as depicted in this illustration from 1846.

the money he raised for new programs to pay dividends on previous projects—what is now called a Ponzi scheme. His accounting practices had, in fact, been so dubious that on his demise it was impossible to find out where all the money had gone. He had become rich, as one wag put it, "by keeping everything but his accounts." His career, so glittering that he was elected Lord Mayor of York and later a Member of Parliament for Sunderland, came to an abrupt end in 1865 when his dishonesty was exposed, after which he vanished and died in obscurity.

Spreading across Europe

Switzerland underwent a period of railroad mania in the 1850s, helped by Alfred Escher, a powerful Swiss businessman and politician, and a keen advocate for the railroads. He had observed the growth of railroads in other countries and feared that Switzerland was missing out on the economic prosperity offered by a rail network and would become "the sad face of Europe's backwater." In 1852, he helped push through a law allowing private companies to build and run railroads. This launched a frenzy of construction by competing firms—joined by Escher himself, who founded Swiss Northeastern Railway and enjoyed great success. Over the following decades, the Swiss rail network extended across the country, including the ambitious Gotthard Railway in the 1870s (see pp.102–103).

In France, a law passed in 1865 to encourage railroad construction in remote areas led to a period of rapid railroad expansion. At the time, France's railroads were controlled by six large companies, and the idea was to encourage new entrants on to the network to ensure better coverage of rural areas where the six were reluctant to go. The law allowed local authorities to

Gotthard Railway
This pioneering railroad, which opened in 1882 after 10 years of construction, was the first to cross the southern alps, linking Switzerland with Italy.

sponsor these lines, and speculators piled in, seeing the possibility of making money out of the grants being offered, despite the fact that most of these lines would never be viable. Within 10 years, nearly 3,000 miles (4,800 km) of remote lines had been built, many narrow gauge to reduce costs. However, few made a profit and they soon had to be rescued by the state, forming the core of what later became the French nationalized railroad system, SNCF.

By 1917, the extent of railroad tracks in the US peaked at 254,000 miles (408,773 km)

In Italy, the government stimulated a period of rapid expansion. Creating a national rail network was seen as essential after the unification of Italy in 1861, and the state sponsored the expansion through a concession system. However, most of the companies that built the lines had insufficient capital and fell into financial difficulties when the lines, which were poorly constructed, failed to attract sufficient passengers. The state took over and eventually nationalized the railroads.

Railroad fever in the US

Perhaps unsurprisingly, it was the US that suffered the biggest bout of "railroad fever," as they called it. There

Interurban station The Superior Street interurban station in Toledo, Ohio, shown in this postcard was one of the many short-lived initiatives that sprang up in the US in the early 20th century.

were, in fact, sporadic boom periods of railroad construction throughout the latter part of the 19th century, as humorously described by the historian Stewart H. Holbrook, who related the story of a fictional town called Brownsville:

> “First some up and coming individual, or simply a fanatical dreamer, said forcibly that his home town Brownsville needed a steam railroad… the idea grew and blossomed and burgeoned and even soared meanwhile taking on all of the beautiful hues of the sky in the Land of Opportunity. It also dripped with gold, gold for all of Brownsville, soon to be a mighty metropolis, teeming with commerce.”

Eventually, an application was made to the state for permission to build the Brownsville Railroad. This type of scene was enacted many times over across the US during every bout of railroad fever.

The US had more than its fair share of crooks in its railroad history. A group of "robber barons" emerged from the early railroad companies, often using dishonest methods of speculation to gain control of profitable lines. It was a time of wild risks and gambles. In one famous incident—a takeover battle for the Erie Railroad—three railroad barons, led by Jay Gould, holed up in a hotel in New Jersey with several million dollars in cash, protected by armed guards to evade the jurisdiction of the New York courts, which had found in favor of their rival, Cornelius Vanderbilt. (Gould and his associates did eventually win the battle for the Erie Railroad—see p.228). Such events, while not commonplace, were part and parcel of the colorful period of railroad speculation in the US.

The final bout of speculative building in the US was in the early 20th century and involved a series of tramways called "electric interurbans." These were a hybrid of trains and trams that connected towns up to 50 miles (80 km) apart with cheaply built single lines sited next to existing highways. There was a remarkable period of expansion of these lines from just 2,000 miles (3,200 km) at the turn of the century to 9,000 miles (14,400 km) by 1906, and 15,000 miles (24,000 km) by the outbreak of World War I. By then, it was possible to travel all the way from Wisconsin to New York using a series of interurbans. It would have been a cheap ride, costing a maximum of 10 cents for each leg of the journey, but it would have been slow, for the interurbans averaged around 30 mph (48 km/h) at best. Sadly, according to one historian, "the interurbans were a rare example of an industry that never enjoyed a prolonged period of prosperity," and most investors lost all their money. The demise of the interurbans was swift both because they were inherently unprofitable, serving sparsely populated areas, and because they faced competition from the growing use of motor vehicles. Already at the start of World War I, systems were closing and they were all but wiped out by the 1930s, when their vehicles and tracks needed renewing and there was no money for such investment.

All the manias across the world left their mark. Numerous investors lost their shirts, but many of the lines were built. As with other industries, the manias had their roots in genuine need, and many of today's lines worldwide owe their existence to these excesses.

"The Tournament of Today" This US cartoon from 1883 highlights the plight of downtrodden, exploited labor at the hands of the robust railroad monopoly, supported by prominent industrialists W. H. Vanderbilt, Cyrus W. Field, and Jay Gould.

The Iron Giant A steam engine is lowered onto its truck, with large driving and smaller leading wheels visible. Strong enough to carry engines, train wheels and trucks withstand immense rotational and torsional forces.

WHEELS AND TRUCKS

The wheels of a locomotive are mounted on a chassis known as a truck (see below) and are designed to keep the train's wheelsets—two wheels joined by an axle—aligned with the tracks. Each wheel tapers slightly from the inside outward, which helps steer the train around curves (see opposite), and is fitted with a projecting rim or "flange" on the inside edge. Ordinarily, this should not touch the track and is a safety feature to prevent the train from derailing. Wheelsets are variously sized and perform subtly different functions: large driving wheels are powered by the pistons of the locomotive, while smaller, unpowered leading and trailing wheelsets support the weight of the engine and enable the train to pass through junctions and bends in the line.

Trucks

Each leading and trailing wheelset is mounted on a frame beneath the carriage. The strength and rigidity of the structure, or "truck," enables the wheelsets to resist torsional forces when the train turns. Most trucks fix wheelsets in place in an inflexible frame, but "steerable" trucks allow the axles to rotate laterally around a pivot between the two wheelsets, increasing the stability of the train around bends. Modern trucks also house the train's braking and suspension systems.

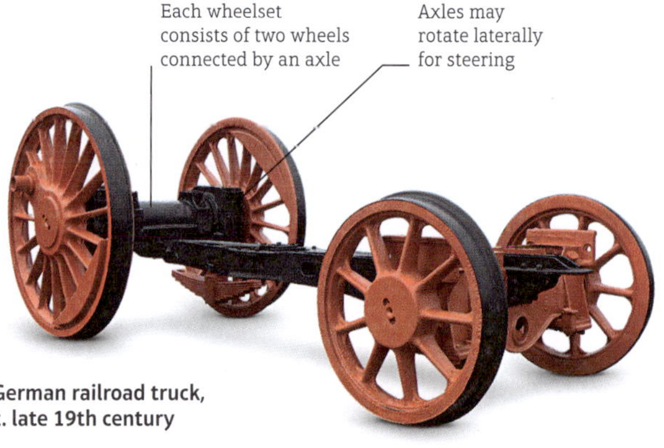

German railroad truck, c. late 19th century

How it works

The flanged wheel was invented in 1789 by English engineer William Jessop. The raised rim on the inner wheel edge prevents derailment and does not touch the rail during normal running; unless the track is poorly maintained. The conical edges of the train wheels allow the wheelsets to slide across the heads (tops) of the rails, enabling the train to follow curves. Railroad engineers observed that the characteristic side-to-side swaying action of a train in motion was due to its tapered wheelsets wobbling up and down the railheads in order to "hunt" for equilibrium. They termed this movement "hunting oscillation."

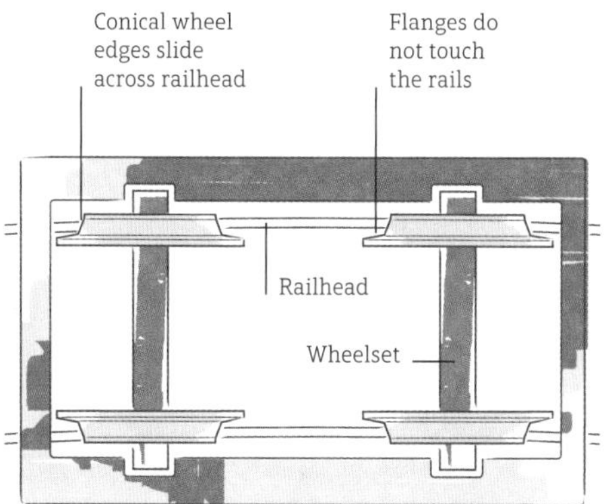

Top view

Negotiating curves

On a curved track, the train's outer wheels have to travel slightly farther. To compensate, the wheelset slides across the railhead, allowing the outer wheels to use the larger radius of their inner edge. The inside wheels meanwhile slide onto the smaller radius of their outer edge. This action allows the train to lean into the bend, much like a cyclist leaning into a corner.

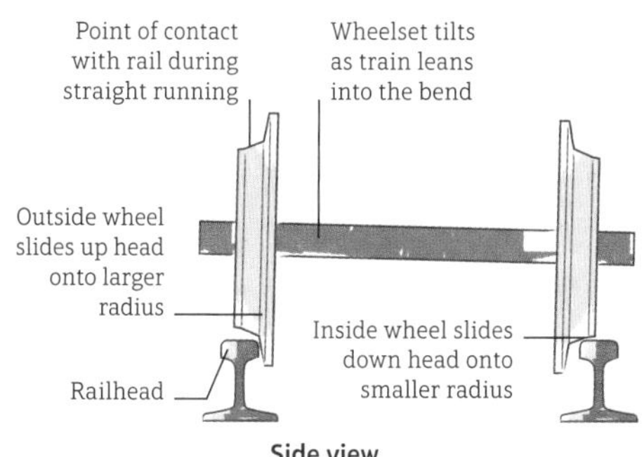

Side view

THE FIRST RAILROAD WAR

The potential of the railroads for warfare soon became apparent. The American Civil War was the first conflict in which the railroads were used extensively to transport troops and provisions.

Since their advent, railroads quickly proved their usefulness in a series of conflicts the world over. Shortly after its opening in 1830, the Liverpool and Manchester Railway (see pp.26–29) was used to carry a regiment of troops from Manchester to the docks in Liverpool en route to quell a rebellion in Ireland. The 31-mile (50 km) trip took just under two hours, rather than the two days it would have taken by foot, and the troops arrived in a much fresher state. Around this time, revolutionary fervor was brewing in Europe, and by the late 1840s, rulers across the continent were using the railroads to help crush these revolts. The first major movement of troops by rail took place in 1846, when a contingent of 12,000 Prussian soldiers was sent to put down the Krakow rebellion of Polish nationalists against their Austrian rulers. The Prussians suppressed the uprising, with considerable bloodshed. Then, two years later, Czar Nicholas I of Russia, the most reactionary of the mid-19th-century monarchs, sent 30,000 troops on the newly built Warsaw–Vienna railroad to help his ally, Emperor Ferdinand I of Austria, to put down another nationalist rebellion—this time in Hungary. Again, the result was a defeat for the revolutionaries.

After this, the scale of troop movements around Europe increased. In the winter of 1850, Austria used the railroads to send a 75,000-strong army, along with 8,000 horses and untold equipment, from Vienna to Hungary. Due to poor weather and the fact that trains traveled along a single track line, the move took longer than expected—26 days for a mere 150-mile (240 km) trip—demonstrating

Also known as *Borsig 1*, this locomotive had three axles and a driving axle

Moving troops This Belgian-built locomotive, one of the first on the Warsaw–Vienna line, was used to transport troops for quashing a rebellion in 1848.

In 1846, Prussian troops covered a total of 200 miles (340 km) in just two days to subdue a Polish nationalist rebellion

that an enormous amount of planning was still needed to use the railroads effectively. Three years later, the French organized a massive movement of troops during the Crimean War, in what is now a disputed territory between Russia and Ukraine. Most of the army of 400,000 men dispatched to fight in Crimea traveled to the Mediterranean seaports on the railroad being built between Paris and Marseille. Although the line was not finished, troops were able to use long sections of it, greatly reducing the travel time. In fact, it was during the Crimean War that the first railroad line intended specifically for military purposes was built. This was the work of the British, who fought alongside the French, and who had struggled to bring men and supplies up to Sevastopol, which they were besieging, from the port of Balaklava 8 miles (13 km) away. The hilly road was little more than a dirt track, and a bottleneck soon built up in the port. To relieve it, a group of navvies (see pp.84–89) was sent from Britain to build a line between the port and the camp outside Sevastopol. They were a wild bunch, causing mayhem on their journey by getting drunk and trying to catch apes in Gibraltar, but they were very effective builders. The Grand Crimean Central

The Grand Crimean Central Railway During the Crimean War, the chaotic scene of war supplies building up in the port of Balaklava prompted military authorities to build the world's first military railroad in 1855 to ensure matériel could reach the troops at the front line.

The Western and Atlantic railroad delivered an army of

100,000

men to General Sherman's forces at Atlanta

Railway—an overblown name for a short narrow-gauge railroad powered partly by horses and partly by steam engines—was built remarkably fast (seven weeks) in 1855. It proved to be of enormous value, enabling troops and provisions, including heavy guns, to be hauled up the hill to support the assault on Sevastopol. The railroad made it possible to bring an unprecedented number of guns to bear on the town, which eventually succumbed under the barrage, effectively ending the war.

A war on wheels

It was during the American Civil War that railroads came of age as strategic assets. The long-brewing conflict had its roots in the differences between the northern and southern states. The North was industrializing and developing its economy on the basis of manufacturing, but the South remained primarily agricultural (cotton was its principal export) and depended on the labor of enslaved people. The trigger for the war was the inauguration of Abraham Lincoln as president in 1861. Lincoln opposed the expansion of slavery; the southern states, fearing the complete abolition of slavery, seceded from the Union by the spring of 1861, thus starting the war. The Civil War was a bloody affair, claiming the lives of 620,000 soldiers. The battles between the Southern Confederates and the Northern

American Civil War Railroads were vital to both sides in this conflict. Here, federal troops of the Massachusetts Regiment board a train out of Jersey City in 1861, bound for the front line.

Federal Army were fought on an unprecedented scale. Throughout history, even wars that raged over long periods typically featured only a handful of battles. However, during the four years of the war between the states, more than 10,000 military encounters took place, of which nearly 400 were significant enough to be considered full-scale battles—which means a battle was fought every four days. Moreover, the war was fought over an area even bigger than Europe, a vast territory that was made accessible by the railroads.

By the outbreak of the war, US railroads extended over more than 29,826 miles (48,000 km). The lines covered most of the eastern states and much of the Midwest, so both troops and matériel could be carried rapidly around the country. Both sides understood the importance of the railroads, but the North made better use of them. Even before the war started, Lincoln ensured that the key railroads were taken under government control and that military traffic was given priority. The outcome of the first major land battle of the war—at Bull Run, Virginia, a small river just 20 miles (32 km) south of Washington, DC—was determined by the clever use of the railroads by the Confederates. The battle started as an attempt by the Federal Army to bring the war to a rapid close by capturing Richmond, the Confederate capital. The Federal Army attacked the enemy alongside Bull Run and initially gained the upper hand. However, they found themselves defeated by a counterattack, made possible by the quick arrival of Confederate reinforcements via rail from the Shenandoah Valley in the west. This was an important lesson for both sides, and from then on, most of the war's major battles took place at or near railroad junctions or stations.

A feat of engineering

The Federal Army launched the Peninsula Campaign—another effort to capture Richmond—in March the following year, and brought "the war's wizard of railroading" into action. This was Herman Haupt, a great engineer whose background made him the

In the line of fire This locomotive of the Richmond & Petersburg Railroad was one of the many casualties during the American Civil War. Railroads were attacked and destroyed to deal a strategic blow against the opposition.

ideal person to harness the railroads for war-time use: he had graduated from West Point, the US Army training college, but then became a professor of mathematics and engineering and had been appointed superintendent of the Pennsylvania Railroad, one of America's most important lines.

Haupt established two main principles regarding the use of railroads in war. First, the military should not interfere with the operation of services, since it was vital to keep to reliable railroad timetables. Second, it was crucial to ensure that empty freight cars were returned to their place of origin and not used as warehouses (or even offices by senior personnel), because running out of wagons in wartime could mean the difference between success or failure in battle.

Haupt's first task in the Peninsular Campaign was to repair the Richmond, Fredericksburg, and Potomac Railroad, a 15-mile (24 km) vital artery that connected the two capitals, Richmond (Virginia), and Washington, DC. The Confederates had wrecked the line in order to damage the Federal Army's capability, and they had

> **"Haupt has built a bridge... and there is nothing in it but cornstalks and beanpoles."**
>
> ABRAHAM LINCOLN, MAY 28, 1862

done a particularly thorough job, twisting the rails so that they could not be used again and burning down bridges. Several miles of track had been put out of commission, but in response, Haupt performed what seemed to be a miracle. He rebuilt the railroad within two weeks, making it possible for a full complement of up to 20 trains per day to run on the line. His greatest achievement came in May 1862 when he rebuilt a 400 ft (120 m) trestle bridge high over the Potomac Creek in just nine days, even though his soldiers were untrained in railroad construction and he had only poor, unseasoned wood at his disposal. This achievement was lauded by Lincoln when he visited the site: "I have seen the most remarkable structure that

Rapid repairs Under the supervision of Herman Haupt, army engineers repaired wrecked railroads, including this bridge on the Orange and Alexandria Railroad in 1865, in record time.

Military railroads During the American Civil War, hundreds of miles of new railroads were built in order to ensure there were rapid supply routes to the front. Here, General Herman Haupt oversees construction work at the Devereux Station of the Orange and Alexandria Railroad in 1863.

human eyes ever rested upon." However, the president only saw the bridge from the embankment and did not venture over it.

Strategic warfare

Haupt's talents also included devising methods to destroy the enemy's railroads, a task that proved to be just as important as repairing existing lines and building new ones. Thanks to Haupt's principles, troop movements by rail were carried out without any major mishaps. The greatest movement of the war was when about 25,000 men were needed to defend Tennessee after the defeat of the Federal Army at the Battle of Chickamauga in Georgia. The defeated army had retreated to Chattanooga, a rail hub in neighboring Tennessee, and needed reinforcements. In an extraordinary operation, involving seven railroads and two ferry trips, the reserve troops traveled 1,200 miles (1,950 km) in just two weeks to relieve the siege of Chattanooga. The town then became a crucial stage for the Federal Army's invasion of the South, which ended the war. That final push was also dependent on the railroads. When General Sherman left Chattanooga on his march toward Atlanta, which signaled the end of the conflict, he relied on the railroads for supplies. As he wrote after the war, with military precision:

> “That single stem of railroad (The Western and Atlantic) supplied an army of 100,000 men and 35,000 animals for the period of 196 days from May 1 to November 12, 1864. To have delivered that amount of forage and food by ordinary wagons would have required 36,800 wagons of six mules each… a simple impossibility in such roads as existed in that region of country. Therefore, I reiterate that the Atlanta campaign was an impossibility without these railroads…”

The most famous episode of the war—immortalized in *The General*, a 1926 Buster Keaton film—occurred on the railroads. A group of 21 Federal soldiers led by James Andrews penetrated enemy lines at Marietta, a town near Atlanta, Georgia, and stole a train hauled by a locomotive called *The General*, with the intention of wrecking the Western and Atlantic Railroad. A Southern conductor, William Fuller, furious at the hijacking of his train, pursued the hijackers, first on foot and then on a gandy dancers' handcart (a device used for track maintenance). He eventually commandeered a locomotive and, evading the obstacles placed on the line by Andrews, caught up with *The General* when it ran out of fuel. The raiders fled into the countryside, but seven, including Andrews, were caught and hanged, while the rest escaped to the North. This, however, was a sideshow. The lesson of the war was clear: railroads were now invaluable military assets, and so they have remained, even playing a vital role in the Ukraine-Russia conflict that began in 2022.

The General Buster Keaton heroically lifts a railroad sleeper out of the path of an engine in hot pursuit of his hijacked locomotive *The General* in the film of the same name.

SIGNALS IN THE STEAM AGE

In the earliest days of the railroads, trains ran up and down single tracks and signaling was not a necessity. As rail traffic and speeds increased, however, train safety grew to be a major concern, and signaling became essential to prevent collisions. Hand and arm signals were soon replaced by flags and lanterns, and in 1832, the first elevated wayside signaling was introduced. By the 1860s, mechanical signals were in general use, but no single system was agreed upon. Semaphore signals were widely adopted in Britain but were not standardized until 1923, while ball signals were common in the US. Color light signals came into use from the 1950s.

Signaling tokens

The block system is a safety mechanism in train signaling, which allows only one train to enter each "block" of a railroad at a time. In the 19th century, tokens provided evidence that a block was free. In the original "staff and ticket" system, the signalers gave the train driver a token or "staff" to allow entry to a block. At the other end, the staff was given up, allowing a train to proceed in the opposite direction. If a second train followed the first along the same "block," both carried written permission or a "ticket." Later systems were operated by means of tokens inserted in a trackside machine.

Ball tokens, India

Signaling staff Some hand signals persisted, despite the invention of other signaling techniques. In this c.1910 photograph, the staff of the Lancashire and Yorkshire Railway in the UK can be seen demonstrating a variety of hand signals.

Early signal systems

As railroad networks became more complex, the companies that ran them largely relied on timetabling to maintain train distances and prevent accidents. However, signals indicating if a line or "block" (section of the line) was clear were crucial in case of timetable alteration or train breakdown.

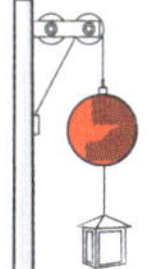

Ball signal (1837)
The most common signal on the early US railroads, it gave rise to the term "highball": when the ball was raised, it was safe to proceed, although this was later reversed.

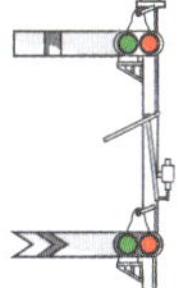

Semaphore (1840)
Widespread after the 1850s, and still in use today, it signaled "danger" in the horizontal position and "all clear" when angled either up or down.

Wood's crossbar signal (1840)
Crossbar signals, in use from the 1830s, indicated on/off (stop/go) with a revolving wooden board. When the crossbar was swung parallel to the line it signaled "clear."

Revolving disc signal (1840)
The disc revolved vertically to signal stop and go, much like semaphore signals. In keeping with most signals of the time, the disc was made of wood and painted red.

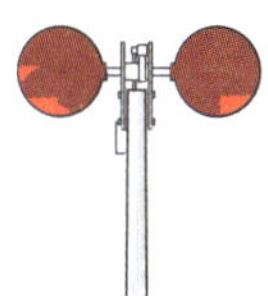

Double disc signal (1846)
Like the crossbar, the double disc rotated on a wooden or steel signal post. Both were short-lived, however, as the "clear" signal was hard for train drivers to see.

HEROIC FAILURES

Before the current system of rail transportation became standard, tracks, wagons, and engines were combined in all kinds of ways that may seem eccentric today.

The railroads as we know them were not the only form of rail transportation that was considered in the latter half of the 19th century. Of the numerous ideas being developed at the time, some might have been successful had they received the proper attention. However, others were patently ill-considered and bound to fail.

The atmospheric railroad

Perhaps the most spectacular failure was the "atmospheric railroad"—a brainchild of British engineer Isambard Kingdom Brunel, the otherwise unimpeachable builder of the Great Western Railway, the SS *Great Britain* (the first propeller-driven iron ship), and the Royal Albert Bridge. His contention was that locomotives were uneconomic because they had to haul themselves as well as their trains (which made uphill travel even harder), and his solution was to remove the engine altogether, creating a train that was propelled by a series of stationary steam engines housed in pumping stations along the track. At the time, locomotives were far from popular—people were afraid of suffocating in tunnels and of sparks setting fire to farmland—so alternatives were welcomed, and in 1844 an Act of Parliament sanctioned Brunel's idea. It was to be tested on the South Devon Railway, a broad-gauge line that Brunel would build from Exeter to Plymouth.

The atmospheric system worked by means of a tube that ran down the center of the track. This functioned like the cylinder of a steam engine (see pp.30–31), having a piston inside it that was connected to the first carriage of the train (the "piston carriage"). The connecting arm of the piston traveled through a slit in the top of the tube,

Brunel's folly A section of Brunel's atmospheric railroad lies reconstructed in the town of Didcot, Oxfordshire. The vacuum tube in the center contained a piston that hauled the trains.

which was kept airtight with a long strip of leather and metal components that opened and closed as the piston passed through it. A steam engine at the side of the track created a vacuum inside the tube, which forced the piston forward, hauling the train along with it. The train then traveled some 3 miles (5 km) until it reached a second engine, which created a new vacuum and propelled the train to the next engine, and so on. A total of eight engine houses were completed for the line, which took it from Exeter as far as Newton Abbot, about 26 miles (42 km) short of the planned terminus at Plymouth—but the final series of engine houses was never built.

The railroad opened in September 1847 on the 11-mile (18 km) stretch of line between Exeter and Teignmouth, and at first it seemed to work well. According to Brunel's biographer:

> “the new mode of traction was almost universally approved of. The motion of the train, relieved of the impulsive action of the locomotive, was singularly smooth and agreeable; and the passengers were freed from the annoyance of coke dust and the sulfureous smell from the engine chimney. In other respects the record of progress is but a checkered one, and exhibits… growing difficulties deepening into ultimate defeat.”

Atmospheric railroad at Dawlish, 1847 The atmospheric railroad had static engines that created a vacuum in a tube between the rails. Engine houses, set up at regular intervals along the route, provided the power for the pressure required to keep the train moving.

It was also fast, with a top speed of 68 mph (109 km/h) and an average of around half of that, which were both remarkable speeds for trains of the period. There were, however, difficulties from the outset. Setting off from a station proved to be a problem, as the train often needed a helping tow from horses or an extra engine attached to a tow rope. The system was also inflexible, as the pipework prevented the trains from being routed from one track to another. The biggest problem, however, was maintaining the vacuum itself. The leather flaps that sealed the pipe failed to be airtight, and there were rumors that they were gnawed by rats. Likewise, the metallic parts of the seal were corroded by salt from sea-spray. Consequently, the atmospheric system was abandoned after less than a year, and the equipment replaced by conventional steam locomotives.

It was an expensive failure. The shareholders of the South Devon Railway were almost £400,000 (in modern terms, around £53 million or $67 million) poorer as a result, which was a huge sum at the time. Much of the money had been spent on the elaborate engine houses, which Brunel had constructed in an Italianate style, their large chimneys disguised as campaniles. Each house cost several times the price of a conventional locomotive, and they were so elegant that one, at Starcross, was later used as a chapel. Also, installing atmospheric traction had been nine times more expensive than the original estimate, and the static engines burned far more coal than expected, costing twice that of conventional traction.

Snowden's system

Brunel's failure was particularly painful since it happened in public, on a commercial railroad, but there were plenty of other disasters that happened in relative privacy. In 1824, for example, British inventor W. F. Snowden designed a train that eschewed the use of steam power altogether. It had a single line of wheels that ran in a U-shaped rail flanked by a pair of flat rails that kept the carriages upright. To propel the train, "industrious laborers" in the leading carriage literally cranked a wheel that

"I could not understand how Mr. Brunel could be so misled. He had so much faith in his being able to improve it that he shut his eyes to the consequences of failure."

DANIEL GOOCH,
BRUNEL'S LOCOMOTIVE ENGINEER,
ON THE ATMOSPHERIC RAILROAD

was connected to a gear that engaged with the toothed edge of one of the rails—thus providing human traction and requiring superhuman stamina on the part of the laborers. Not surprisingly, the idea was never taken up, despite a pamphlet published in 1834 extolling its virtues. However, Snowden's system did highlight a problem that is common to all railroads—that wheels slip in damp conditions and on inclines—a problem Snowden solved by keeping the gear locked in the track. A related idea was to have a rack and pinion (see pp.104–105) in the center of the railroad to aid traction, and such devices are still used on mountain lines today.

Cable railroads

Rope or cable railroads were another attempt at solving the problem of how to haul trains. Again, as with atmospheric railroads, the idea was to have stationary engines placed along the track, but this time for hauling cables attached to the trains. On the Canterbury and Whitstable line in Britain, which opened in May 1830, trains were hauled by rope for 4 miles (6.5 km) out of Canterbury and then by locomotive for the remaining two miles. Several other lines used cables to deal with inclines. Nearly 2 miles (3.2 km) of the

High roller Wagons such as this are operated on the cable railroad at Denniston Incline on the South Island of New Zealand. This line transported coal along a steep incline of 1,798 ft (548 m) from 1879 to 1967.

Rope and steam Propelled both by cables powered by stationary steam engines and moving steam locomotives, the Canterbury and Whitstable Railway was known locally as the "Crab and Winkle" line.

An unusal success This image shows the German suspended railroad, the Wuppertal Suspension Railway, as photographed in 1909. It has run for more than a century and continues to operate today.

Düsseldorf–Elberfeld line in Germany was cable-hauled, as was part of the Brussels–Liège line in Belgium, and the Denniston Incline in New Zealand. The Liverpool and Manchester (see pp.26–29) had cables for the first part of the line out of Liverpool station, as did the London and Birmingham initially for the incline between Euston station and Camden Town. One of London's first railroads, the London and Blackwall, was cable-drawn for its entire 3½-mile (6 km) length. Cables were complicated to operate, however, and as locomotives became more powerful, most of these systems were phased out (although the German one remained in operation until 1927). A cable system was even proposed for the first deep tube line built on the London Underground—the City and South London line, completed in 1890—but given its length of nearly 5 miles (8 km), planners decided to use the new technology of electric power instead, which proved extremely reliable.

Making monorails

Monorails were another great hope of the railroad pioneers, and although a few were constructed—and indeed some still operate today—they have never overcome the basic problems of being expensive to build and being inflexible due to the structural requirements of their rails. The first patent for a vehicle designed to run on a single rail was granted in November 1821 to British civil engineer Henry Robinson Palmer, who described it as "a single line of rail, supported at such height from the ground as to allow the center of gravity of the carriages to be below the upper surface of the rail." The vehicles straddled the rail,

Elevated railroad This experimental railroad was tested on a 508 ft (155 m) track at the 1876 Philadelphia exhibition in the US.

Balloon railroad (below) Many of the more outlandish ideas put forward by 19th-century inventors like this balloon railroad up Mount Rhigi in Switzerland were, unsurprisingly, never built.

rather like pannier baskets on a mule, and were horse-drawn. The idea was to make it easier to transport goods across worksites, and the first monorail was built in the Deptford Dockyard, London, in 1824. The following year, the horse-drawn Cheshunt Railway was built at a brickworks in London. At its opening, it carried passengers—a historic moment, as it predated the world's first passenger railroad, the Stockton and Darlington (see pp.24–25), by three months. Monorails have since resurfaced from time to time, but never with much success. A steam-driven monorail was first demonstrated at the United States Centennial Exposition in Philadelphia in 1876, and although a couple of versions were built, neither lasted very long. The oldest monorail in the world is the Wuppertal Suspension Railway in Germany, which opened in 1901 and still operates today, carrying 25 million passengers a year. From the mid-20th to early 21st centuries, a number of monorails were built in urban areas in Asia, including in Tokyo, Japan, and Kuala Lumpur, Malaysia.

Flights of fancy

Fanciful ideas for new transportation systems continued into the 21st century with futuristic ideas such as a hyperloop, involving carriages traveling at very high speeds in specially made tubes. Like many other previous ideas, this has proved unworkable. Perhaps the strangest of all was the balloon railroad constructed near Salzburg in Austria in the early 1900s. This consisted of a large balloon tethered to a slide running on a single rail up a mountainside. The hydrogen balloon hovered some 30 ft (9 m) above the car, which could carry up to 10 passengers. Once loaded, the balloon was freed, pulling up the car beneath it. To descend, the car's tanks were filled with water. Its inventor, Herr Balderauer, believed that his system would replace the costlier funiculars that were being built across the Alps (see pp.98–103), but perhaps unsurprisingly, it failed to attract investors.

INDIA: DALHOUSIE'S COLONIAL IMPERATIVE

The railroads were critical to Britain's colonial dominance in India, serving as a means of economic exploitation, military control, and administrative consolidation. They demonstrated how infrastructure could be a powerful tool for imperial control.

India was the jewel in Britain's crown during the 19th century, and its colonial rulers were eager to impose their control over the subcontinent. The railroads were vital to this process and were brought to India by the British East India Company—effectively a commercial arm of the British government. The first Indian railroad, which ran from the company settlement of Bombay (now Mumbai), was commercial in aim, prompted by events on the other side of the world: the American cotton harvest was poor in 1846, and this spurred the cloth manufacturers of Manchester to use India as

an alternative source of cotton. However, in order to ensure the steady supply needed to keep their factories running, transportation to the port at Bombay needed improving, so the cotton magnates pressed the British government to build a railroad.

Due to bureaucratic delays—it took months to receive a reply to a letter sent from India to Britain—and indecision on the part of the British rulers, work on the 21-mile (34 km) line between Bombay and Thane, or Tana, did not start until 1850. It was developed as an experiment to assess if it was possible to build railroads in the harsh climate of the Indian subcontinent. The Thane line was not easy to construct. Now part of Bombay's busy suburban network, it originally cut through difficult territory, including a hill and a marsh. Nevertheless, it was completed in three years.

The opening of the line in April 1853 was a momentous affair, not least because it was the first railroad in Asia. Unlike northwest England, where railroads had originated, India was still a nation with little industry, and the sight of powerful locomotives belching fire and steam impressed and frightened the local populace in equal measure. People lined the tracks in the millions to watch the 14-carriage train bearing a rich assortment of VIPs on its inaugural journey, and many spilled onto the tracks, slowing the progress of the train, which nevertheless managed the journey at an average speed of 20 mph (32 km/h)—a very

Oldest Indian locomotive This postage stamp, issued in 1976 to mark the 125th anniversary of railroads in India, shows one of the locomotives built by the British Vulcan Foundry for the inaugural railroad line between Bombay and Thane.

Bombay freight yard, 1862 The main purpose of the early railroads in India was to carry freight, such as cotton bales, from the interior to ports for export to countries such as Britain.

Legendary locomotive
Built in 1855, the *Fairy Queen* lays claim to being the oldest working steam engine in the world still operating. It regularly hauls a couple of carriages on tourist trips on Indian mainlines.

creditable effort. Another, more ambitious, project started simultaneously in Bengal, in the northeast of India. This was a 121-mile (195 km) line stretching from Howrah, on the western side of the Hooghly River, via near by Calcutta to the small town of Raniganj in the coalfields of Burdwan, from which it had previously taken two seasons to cart the coal down to a river for transportation to the rest of the country. Work on the line started in 1851, but a couple of shipping mishaps delayed progress. First, the coaches intended for the line were lost when the ship carrying them sank at Sandheads on the Bengal coast, and then, astonishingly, the locomotives for the line were sent to Australia instead of Calcutta as a result of one of the most expensive clerical errors in history. The locomotives eventually arrived in Calcutta—a year late—but, despite these setbacks, the line, nearly six times longer than the Bombay–Thane railroad, opened in February 1855.

A massive undertaking

The success of these two lines led to a rapid expansion of the railroad system. Unlike in Britain, where the process was unplanned and haphazard, the development of the rail network in India followed a clear plan laid out by the colonial administration. In 1853, Lord Dalhousie, the governor-general, set out a program for the development of India's trunk lines in a 216-page handwritten memorandum. Dalhousie was a hardworking, capable administrator who later claimed to have given India all the necessary "engines of social improvement... Railways, uniform postage, and the Electric Telegraph." His "minute," as he called the memorandum, set out the justifications and guidelines for the railroads of India, whose territory then included what is now Bangladesh and Pakistan.

Dalhousie emphasized the economic benefits that the railroads would bring. They would increase trade between India and the "mother country"—Britain importing cotton and India receiving manufactured goods in return. Railroads would encourage enterprise, increase production, facilitate the discovery of natural resources such as coal and minerals, and encourage overall economic development as they were doing in Europe and the United States, which were now both three decades into the railroad age. However, the core of Dalhousie's argument was not commercial but political. The British administrators and soldiers who ruled the country were thinly spread, and railroads would enable them to travel rapidly to maintain control—an advantage that was worth almost any price.

For his part, Dalhousie was nothing if not a visionary. In his minute, he wrote:

> “the complete permeation of these climes of the sun by a magnificent system of railway communication would present a series of public movements vastly surpassing in real grandeur the aqueducts of Rome, the pyramids of Egypt, the Great Wall of China, the temples, palaces, and mausoleums of the great Moghul monuments.”

An exaggeration, perhaps, but it gives an idea of the tremendous ambition of the scheme.

Challenges faced

Dalhousie's blueprint was given urgency by a mutiny of the army's Indian soldiers that began in May 1857 and threatened colonial rule. The revolt stemmed from a combination of political, social, economic, and military factors. The mutiny—which began with soldiers refusing to bite on musket cartridges covered with tallow made from either beef fat (offensive to Hindus) or pork fat (offensive to Muslims)—had broken out in remote parts of the country. The military realized that instead of bringing vast numbers of British troops over to manage the Indian regiments, it was cheaper to build railroad lines to ensure that troops could be dispatched quickly to deal with insurrections wherever they happened. Although the mutiny put a temporary halt on railroad construction across India, work recommenced at a faster pace when peace was restored in June 1858.

The railroads, in other words, were a nakedly colonial project whose development paid scant regard to the needs of the population. The British decided on the location of the lines and when they would be built. They were designed to serve British interests and would later be seen by nationalists such as Mahatma Gandhi as agents of imperialism. The British government accepted Dalhousie's plan, and the railroads were constructed to the pattern he had devised. Major trunk routes radiated from port cities and centers of colonial administration, such as Calcutta, Bombay, and Madras, and further lines connected other large towns and cities. It was, as one writer suggests, a period of great "romance and excitement," but it was also a time of hardship, particularly for innumerable Indian workers, thousands of

"If we did not rush about from place to place by railroad, much confusion would be obviated."

MAHATMA GANDHI, *THE ESSENTIAL WRITINGS*

Narrow-gauge railroads
The difficult railroad terrain of the northwest frontier, in what is now Pakistan, led to the construction of a miniature 2 ft 6 in (76 cm) narrow-gauge railroad for military purposes. The equipment provided by the French Decauville company had to be carried up the mountains by elephants.

whom died constructing the railroads. The country's diverse and rugged landscape also posed formidable challenges. Bridges, for example, had to withstand far greater pressures than those of Europe, because the monsoon rains made rivers swell to massive and consequently destructive, proportions.

Conquering the Western Ghats

The Western Ghats, a chain of mountains that run down much of the western side of the subcontinent, proved to be an almost insuperable barrier. Although not immensely high—a mere 8,840 ft (2,695 m) at their peak—they rise sharply and ruggedly beyond the narrow coastal lowlands, presenting what at the time was the most difficult section of railroad terrain in the world. It took engineer James Berkley, charged with building a railroad through the Ghats, several years just to find a suitable route, although the mountain section of the line was only 15 miles (24 km) long. When it was finished, the railroad featured two major inclines (see pp.192–193)—the Bhore and the Thul Ghats—as well as numerous tunnels. Berkley devised an ingenious way of overcoming the steep gradient. Instead of building a continuous track, he carved out a reversing section at a bend near the summit, obviating the need for a stationary engine to haul the trains uphill. It was a cheaper and neater solution than a conventional route and was imitated on several other mountain lines, notably in Brazil and the Andes. The system involved driving a train along a narrow line toward a precipice, so it required nerves of steel on the part of the driver, and indeed the passengers.

To create the track bed for the Ghat line, whole sections of the mountain had to be blasted and workers let down on ropes to drill into the face—a perilous

Bhore Ghat reversing incline (above) The railroad reversing station (see pp.192–193) on the Bhore Ghat incline in the Western Ghats, seen here in 1880, was an ingenious way of negotiating the Indian hills, although it involved a hair-raising reverse toward a precipice.

Bridge construction (left) One of the biggest challenges faced by railroad builders in India was building bridges across huge rivers, regularly swelled by snowmelt and monsoons, such as this one at Narmada in Gujarat. The bridge across this river was washed away several times before this more solid structure was completed in 1935.

process. On numerous occasions, the ropes failed or slipped, sending workers down into a ravine from which their bodies were never recovered.

Illness, however, was the biggest cause of death. Numerous deadly diseases, including typhoid, malaria, smallpox, cholera, and blackwater fever, took a high toll on the overworked and undernourished workers, who died by tens of thousands. In Colonial India, the British government considered the lives of Indian workers, offensively referred to as "coolies," to be cheap. As a government report tellingly reads:

> "The fine season of eight months... is favorable for Indian railway operations, but... fatal epidemics, such as cholera and fever, often break out and the laborers are generally of such feeble constitution, and so badly provided with shelter and clothing, that they speedily succumb to those diseases..."

As Anthony Burton, the author of a book on railroads and the British Empire, observes: "the notion that lives—and the inconvenient loss of working time—could be saved by providing proper shelter and decent conditions does not seem to have been considered."

The spread of the railroad in India came at a high cost, but it remained a remarkable achievement as Dalhousie's plan was adhered to long after his departure and death. His belief that the project would be bigger than the construction of the pyramids was borne out. Within 25 years of the opening of the Thane line, India had an extensive network of trunk lines. By the turn of the century, there was a remarkable 25,000 miles (40,000 km) of track—a network that has survived to this day with few closures, and which remains a key part of the infrastructure of a nation in which a highway network was only developed late in the 20th century. The Indian railroads have become synonymous with India itself.

The pillars holding up the Narmada bridge had been washed away in 1863, 1867, and 1871

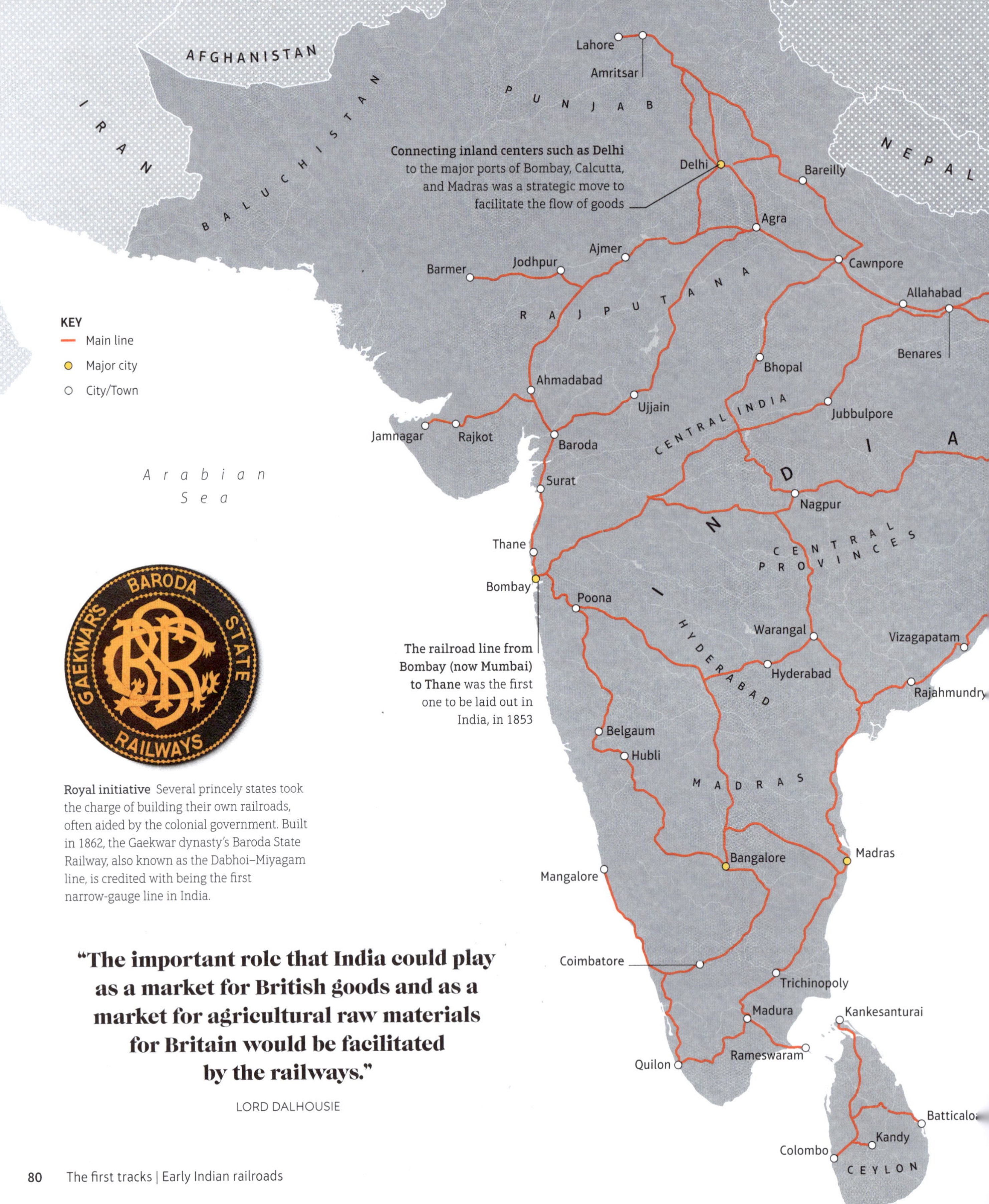

Royal initiative Several princely states took the charge of building their own railroads, often aided by the colonial government. Built in 1862, the Gaekwar dynasty's Baroda State Railway, also known as the Dabhoi–Miyagam line, is credited with being the first narrow-gauge line in India.

> **"The important role that India could play as a market for British goods and as a market for agricultural raw materials for Britain would be facilitated by the railways."**
>
> LORD DALHOUSIE

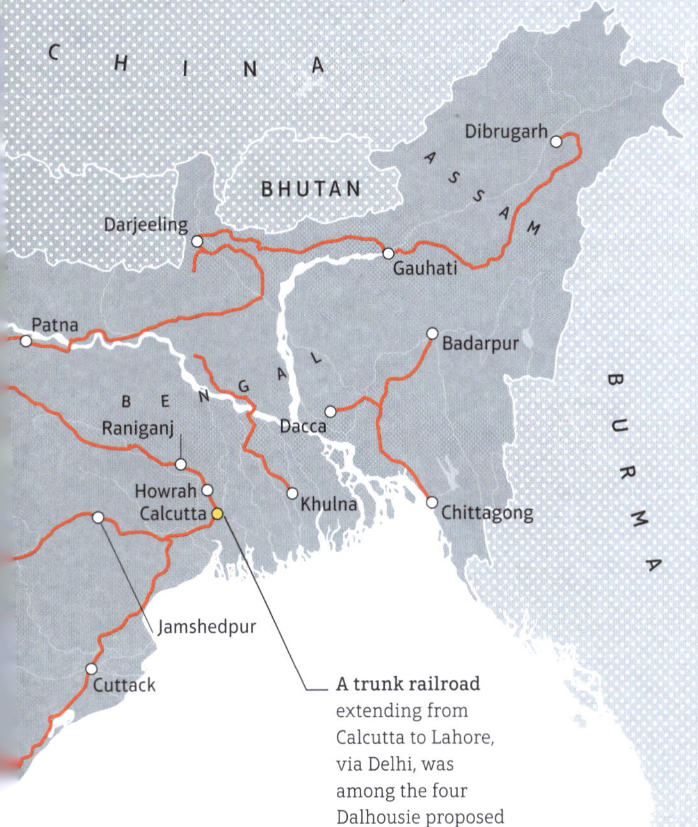

A trunk railroad extending from Calcutta to Lahore, via Delhi, was among the four Dalhousie proposed

Crossing the river A steam locomotive is floated across Yamuna River on a pontoon at Kalpi, northern India, in the late 1800s. The river was later bridged, but before and during this construction, workers had to use improvised measures such as this to transport locomotives over the river.

EARLY INDIAN RAILROADS

Railroad construction took place at a rapid pace on the Indian subcontinent from the 1850s onward. Following Dalhousie's recommendation of a series of arterial "trunk" routes to connect India's major cities, the first lines were built inland from the regional hubs of Bombay on the west coast, Madras in the south, and Calcutta in the east. Smaller regional lines—built in an alarming variety of gauges—fanned out from these main lines, and by the early 20th century India boasted more than 25,000 miles (40,000 km) of track. This map shows the main rail network planned by Dalhousie and built in the colonial era, with city names as they were used prior to the late 20th century.

Into the dark In a life filled with risk and tough conditions, working in tunnels was the epitome of both for the navvies. Accidents were frequent. Here, workers are seen tunneling under Blackfriars Bridge, London, in the 1860s.

THE NAVVIES: DIGGING, DRINKING, AND FIGHTING

Navvies played an important role in establishing the early railroad network that connected towns, cities, and industrial centers. Without their efforts, railroad expansion would have been much slower and more difficult.

The people who built the railroads were a tough bunch—and they needed to be, as they had an arduous job, carried out in remote areas and often in harsh conditions. They were also at the cutting edge of technology, working in a new industry that had developed its own machinery and processes. It was a learning process for all concerned, from the contractors and engineers to those who laid out the embankments and dug the tunnels.

The tracks used by modern, high-speed trains would be quite recognizable to the engineers who built the first lines. After a few early experiments with granite sleepers and wooden rails, the basic design was adopted almost everywhere in the world—iron (later steel) rails laid on wooden sleepers, resting on stone aggregate or ballast (see pp.88–89).

> **"[The navvies] must never be confused with the rabble of steady, common laborers whom they out-worked, out-drank, out-rioted, and despised."**
>
> TERRY COLEMAN, *THE RAILWAY NAVVIES*

A different class of worker

For much of the 19th century, laying the tracks was very labor-intensive. A surveyor drew an approximate line on a map after walking the site, then thousands of workers were hired by a contractor. The workers were called "navvies" because they were thought to have the same skills as the navigators who built the canal system a generation earlier. These navvies were proud of their name, but by no means all the workers on the railroads qualified for it. The laborers came and went, many returning to the farms at harvest time. If they stayed, however, it took a year for laborers to qualify as navvies, who were considered an elite class of worker. To be navvies, they had to work on all the hard tasks, such as tunneling, excavating, and blasting, and not simply shoveling earth; they had to live with the other navvies in camps and

Navvies using a brickmaking machine Although their reputation as volatile, hard-drinking fighters was often deserved, the navvies also carried out long hours of hard labor and had to put up with poor working and living conditions.

follow the railroad as worksites moved along; and they had to match the eating and drinking habits of their fellows—consuming nearly 2 lb (1 kg) of beef and 10 pints or over a gallon (4.7 l) of beer a day. The navvies came from all over Britain and adopted their own particular dress code. According to Coleman, they favored "moleskin trousers, double-canvas shirts, velveteen square-tailed coats, hobnail boots, gaudy handkerchiefs, and white felt hats with the brims turned up." It was not really suitable garb for such hard, manual work, but it demonstrated style. They were known by nicknames that ranged from the eclectic "Bellerophon" or "Fisherman" to the more common "Gipsy Joe" or "Fighting Jack."

Grueling work

To some extent, the skills needed to build the railroads were tried and true. There were similarities with building canals and digging out mines, but in terms of scale, perhaps only cathedral-building compared—although cathedrals took centuries to complete, while railroads took only a few years. The scale and extent of the earthworks alone was unprecedented. The most visible features of the navvies' trade were bridges and tunnels, but the vast majority of their work consisted of moving enormous quantities of earth. Railroads require relatively straight routes and gentle gradients, so the land has to be adapted before the track can be laid. Peter Lecount, an assistant engineer on the London and Birmingham Railway, calculated that building it involved lifting 25,000 million cu ft (708 million cu m) of earth—a greater task than the building of the Great Pyramid at Giza. Occasionally, new techniques were deployed, such as laying embankments through marshy land or crossing large rivers with bridges. Worksites commonly had hundreds of men attacking the earth with their primitive tools and hauling the dirt away in wheelbarrows, or by horse and cart on the flatter sections.

A great deal of gunpowder was used—the fuse-setters and navvies would crouch behind any available cover to shield themselves before returning to prepare the next blast. Safety precautions were minimal and risk-taking was considered manly. Not surprisingly, navvies often died young. In the Kilsby Tunnel on the London and Birmingham, three men were killed as they tried to jump, one after the other, over the mouth of a shaft in a game of "follow my leader." On the Great Western, a man was told to stop cutting under a large overhang of earth, but he ignored the warnings and was buried alive within minutes. Those who survived the numerous accidents—ranging from unexpectedly large explosions to simple falls and collisions—were soon worn out by the hard work and the excessive lifestyle. The 40-year-olds looked 50, and the rare 60-year-olds looked 80. The sheer numbers of workers involved in railroad-building was also colossal—far greater than in any previous industry. In spring 1847, for example, 169,838 men were working on the railroads in England and Wales, out of a total population of 16 million. Initially, the firms employing these men were small, local concerns, but large contractors soon emerged, employing thousands of navvies. These contractors were powerful men such as Samuel Peto and Thomas Brassey, who built railroads all over the world.

Living conditions

Not surprisingly, navvies were rarely welcome in the towns where they were working. They caused a great deal of disruption, and shopkeepers took advantage of the surge in demand to raise food prices. As accommodations were scarce in the remote places where lines were being built, the navvies slept in huts in filthy conditions, sometimes sharing their quarters with pigs and attracting vermin. They often shared beds—one man sleeping while the other worked—and they were accompanied by a retinue of "many women but few wives," as one writer put it. As a result, disease was rife. Riots were not uncommon, particularly on payday, or, as sometimes

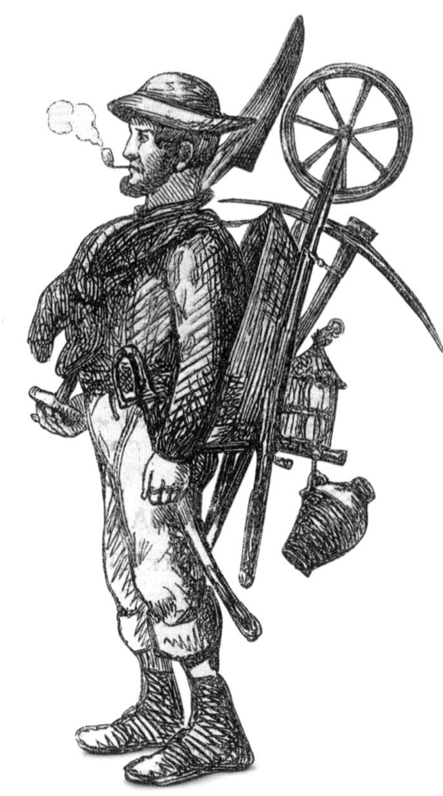

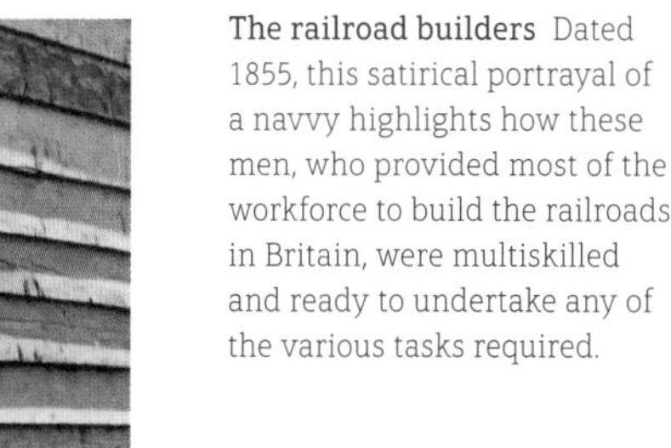

The railroad builders Dated 1855, this satirical portrayal of a navvy highlights how these men, who provided most of the workforce to build the railroads in Britain, were multiskilled and ready to undertake any of the various tasks required.

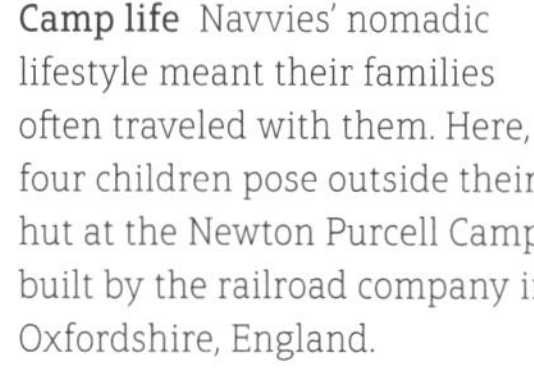

Camp life Navvies' nomadic lifestyle meant their families often traveled with them. Here, four children pose outside their hut at the Newton Purcell Camp built by the railroad company in Oxfordshire, England.

happened, when the navvies had *not* been paid. In 1866, the village of Wiveliscombe in Somerset, England, was terrorized by 70 navvies demanding beer and bread after the local railroad company went bust. A local resident of a Devon village described the chaos when the navvies found themselves without work after the railroad was finished:

> More than a hundred discharged on Monday, and a pretty row there was: drunk altogether and fighting altogether, except one couple fought in the meadow for an hour... the same night the villains stole all poor old xxx's fowls [and] there is not an egg to be got hereabouts.

Similar scenes were played out in other countries. The navvies may have been wild, but they got the job done, so much so that British men found work on many European railroads. In 1841, Thomas Brassey, a contractor, was commissioned to build the line between Paris and Rouen, and a local newspaperman sent to observe construction was greatly impressed:

> I think as fine a spectacle as any man could witness, who is accustomed to look at work, is to see a cutting in full operation with about twenty wagons being filled, every man at his post, and every man with his shirt open, working in the heat of the day, the gangers looking about, and everything going like clockwork. Such an exhibition of physical power attracted many French gentlemen who came on to the cuttings at Paris and Rouen, and looking at these English (actually many were Scottish and Irish) gentlemen with astonishment said *'Mon Dieu! Les Anglais, comme ils travaillent!'* (My God! The English, how they work!)... It was a fine sight to see the Englishmen that were there, with their muscular arms and hands hairy and brown.

There were often labor shortages in the US, and men had to be brought in from other countries to build the railroads. The construction of the Erie Railroad in the late 1830s and early 1850s coincided with a large influx of men from Ireland who were fleeing the famine at home and were eager to work on the railroad. Unfortunately, the men were from two different parts of Ireland—Fardown and Cork—and the former took against the latter in a dispute over lower wages. In the ensuing conflict, the Fardowners set upon the Corkonians in a series of battles that lasted several days. This

Navvy accommodations Toward the end of the 19th century, improved accommodations were provided for the navvies, such as these wooden huts at Barley Fields in Oxfordshire, England.

At its peak, 80,000 men were employed on the Trans-Siberian Railway

culminated with the Fardowners cutting down the rickety structures in which the Corkonians lived, bringing the roofs down on top of them. It is a wonder that they found enough time to build the railroad at all, but construction was unaffected.

Importing labor

In the 1860s, the Central Pacific company was building the line eastward from California on the first transcontinental (see pp.114–121). However, the construction was desperately undermanned, due to both a lack of immigrants and the competition from the lucrative mining industry. One of the line's promoters named Charles Crocker hit upon the idea of taking on Chinese workers but had to overcome resistance from his worksite managers who thought that the workers could not handle such work. They were proved wrong, however; the Chinese were extremely good laborers and received lower pay than their white counterparts, prompting Crocker to organize the recruitment of thousands of men from China. Chinese laborers also worked on the legendary South American railroads, accompanied by the fearsome local workforce, the *rotos* (see pp.190–191).

In Russia, the construction of the Trans-Siberian Railway in the 1890s (see pp.170–177) also meant that a lot of men had to be brought in from afar. The line, which is still the longest in the world, required huge numbers of workers and had 80,000 enrolled at its peak. The local people, mostly tribesmen, were unwilling or unable to work, and as the line progressed farther east into the almost deserted steppe, the shortage of labor was acute. Convicts were drafted in, with 13,500 prisoners and exiles working on the line at the peak of its construction. Laborers also had to be brought in not only from European Russia but from as far afield as the Ottoman Empire, Persia, and Italy.

This conscription of workers continued throughout the 19th century, after which mechanization reduced the need to mobilize such vast labor forces. Until then, however, the railroads were the work of strong men wielding primitive tools. Their legacy can still be seen, not only in railroads that have since been modernized but in the embankments and cuttings that remain where lines have been closed. All over the world, the landscape was transformed by their herculean labors.

Transcontinental railroad The building of the transcontinental railroad in America required many spectacular feats of engineering, such as this impressive wooden trestle at Secret Town, California.

THE PERMANENT WAY

The rails, sleepers, ballast, subgrade, fixtures, and fasteners of a finished railroad line are collectively called the "permanent way." This term dates back to the early days of railroad construction, when a temporary track was laid first in order to rapidly transport materials to the construction site. After the substructure was largely completed, the track was replaced by the permanent "way." The substructure of a track is called the "formation." Since a consistent "grade" (gradient) is required in order for trains to run smoothly, the ground is first prepared to form the "subgrade." The subgrade might also be covered by a layer of sand or stone called a "blanket" before overlaying it with ballast—the granular material placed on tracks for stability and drainage. The "gauge" (distance apart) and alignment of the rails are monitored to ensure that they remain constant throughout straight sections and curves in the line.

Track gauges

The "gauge" of a track is the horizontal distance between the inside faces of the two rails and determines the axle width of trains that can run upon it. While a range of gauges was used when the railroads were built in the 19th century, standardization became necessary as individual lines were connected to form national and international networks. As such, "standard" or "international" gauge (4 ft 8½ in or 1,435 mm) is used for around 60 percent of the world's railroads.

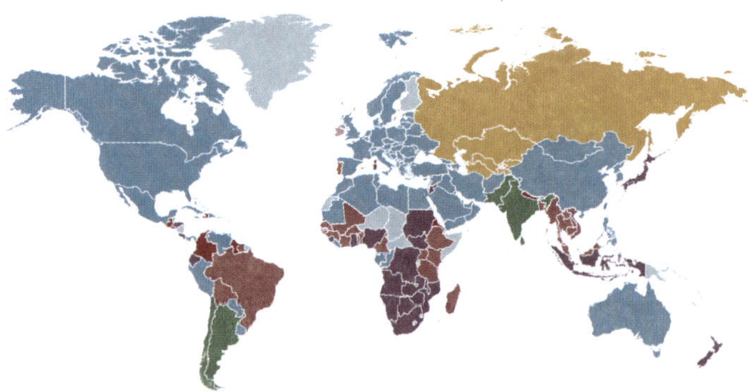

COMMON GAUGES

- 4 ft 8$\frac{1}{2}$ in (1,435 mm)
- 4 ft 11$\frac{4}{5}$ in (1,520 mm)
- 3 ft 3$\frac{2}{5}$ in (1,000 mm)
- 3 ft 6 in (1,067 mm)
- 5 ft 6 in (1,676 mm)
- 5 ft 5$\frac{2}{3}$ in (1,668 mm)
- 5 ft 3 in (1,600 mm)
- 3 ft 1$\frac{2}{5}$ in (950 mm)
- Other gauges

Maintenance of the way Maintaining railroad tracks is essential for safe and efficient train operations. In the early days, this was largely done by hand. Work crews would perform tasks such as replacing worn track components, clearing ditches and culverts, and tamping ballast manually.

Track materials

The earliest railed tracks can be traced back to the 17th century, when pony-drawn wagons made their way down wooden rails. However, a stronger, more lasting material was required to support the large steam engines of the 19th century. The cast-iron rails of the first railroads were succeeded by sturdier wrought-iron rails in the 1820s, while steel—which was stronger still—came into use in the 1850s. Sleepers, also known as ties or track girders, are rectangular supports that transfer weight from the rails to the foundation below. Crushed-stone ballast is still the most common foundation material, but concrete slabs, which are more stable and durable, are increasingly being used.

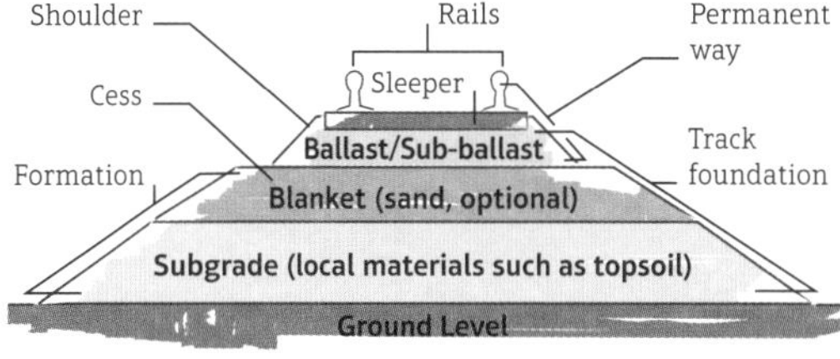

Track structure
Most railroad tracks consist of flat-bottom steel rails fixed to timber or concrete sleepers. The layer of ballast beneath has the benefit of reducing noise from rail traffic but requires maintenance due to displacement from the weight of passing trains.

Cuban sugar mill Early railroads in Cuba were used to transport sugar from the mills to the ports for export. Here, a steam locomotive waits outside a sugar boiling house in Cuba.

CUBAN SUGAR RAILROADS

Cuba was the first country to build railroads in Latin America, but their purpose was very different from those of the United States and Europe.

Few nations remained untouched by the railroad boom of the 19th century, and many were affected in remarkably different ways. The primary role of railroads in Cuba was to transport sugar—a crop that was grown in vast plantations to satisfy the sweet teeth of the developed world—and so they did little to help the general population. Cuba had become a sugar economy somewhat by accident, after an increase in the price of sugar in the late 18th century made its cultivation highly profitable. Relying heavily on the labor of enslaved people, the industry grew rapidly in the early 19th century, but transporting the cane to the mills was expensive because of the island's poor roads. Indeed, in the rainy season, from May to November, the tracks became muddy and rivers flooded, making movement almost impossible. What was needed was a railroad to shift the cane swiftly and cheaply—from the plantations to the mills for processing, and then on to the coast where it could be shipped abroad. Such a line was duly built, and the crop that was brought to Cuba by Christopher Columbus in 1493 found its way back to Europe in unprecedented amounts, making fortunes for Cuba's sugar barons.

Early success

Throughout the 19th century, Cuba was a Spanish colony, but its railroad opened long before that of Spain. Indeed, although Cuba was rural and impoverished at the time, it was

150 years of Cuban rail These commemorative stamps, issued in 1987, mark the 150th anniversary of the opening of the first Cuban railroad line, one of the earliest in the world.

Sugar mill workforce In the 19th century, sugar mills dominated the Cuban countryside. Workers were primarily enslaved Africans, working in both fields and mills.

one of the first countries in the world to build a railroad—by the time its first line opened in 1837, only six other countries had railroads. In 1830, just as the Liverpool and Manchester line was being completed in Britain (see pp.26–29), leading plantation owners in Cuba set up a commission to consider building a railroad network. In 1834, once a route had been established and sufficient funds raised, work started on a 46-mile (74 km) line between the capital, Havana, on the coast, and Güines, inland on the Mayabeque River.

Navigating the bumps

It was a grand and sophisticated operation. The first part of the 16-mile (26 km) route, from Havana to Bejucal, climbed to 320 ft (98 m) above sea level, a very steep gradient for a railroad at the time. The line also had several bridges, the longest of which, across the Almendares River, needed 200 supporting pillars. Moreover, unlike many other early lines, the Cuban railroad was designed to have two tracks right from the start. To supplement the thousands of people enslaved by the railroad company, workers were brought in from abroad to help construct the line. These were largely Irish immigrants who had only recently reached the US, and men from the Canary Islands, which was also under Spanish rule. The new arrivals did not thrive. The Irish in particular suffered, being unused to the tropical climate, which was at its worst during the rainy season. Badly fed and poorly sheltered, large numbers of workers succumbed to the effects of tropical diseases. Many also heavily drank and quickly found themselves in the filthy colonial jails, where they soon perished. The survivors found that

The Cuban sugar railroads
Cuba was one of the first countries in the world to build an extensive railroad system, but its focus was almost entirely on the carriage of sugar cane rather than transporting people.

when their contracts ended, the railroad companies did not fulfill their promise of returning them to the US, and they were left to wander the streets of Havana, penniless and destitute. The Canary Islands immigrants fared little better, even though they spoke Spanish. Their employers considered them more likely to try to escape, so they were treated like prisoners on the work sites. Forced to work up to 16 hours per day, many of them died of exhaustion.

The project ran out of money, but new investors stepped in and the first section of the Bejucal line was completed by 1837, just three years after work had begun. The locomotives and drivers were imported from England, and when the section to Güines opened the following year, the railroad boomed. Although it was primarily intended for freight, passengers flocked to the railroad, too, generating as much revenue as the sugar in the early years. There were two trains a day in each direction—a 30-wagon freight train and a seven-car passenger train.

A period of expansion

The success of the line prompted further railroad construction. The first section of a second line—built to bring sugar, molasses, and rum to the port of Cárdenas—was completed in 1840, after which the system expanded rapidly. A decade after the first line opened, the area around Havana was crisscrossed with lines connecting all the neighboring districts, and the sugar industry thrived as a result. In 1846, Havana alone had 169 sugar mills producing more than 40,000 tons (36,287 tonnes) of sugar and 45,000 barrels of molasses each year. The railroads serving these mills were highly profitable, but they were geared so specifically toward the sugar industry that they provided little support to other industries, or indeed to passengers. They were built purely to help sugar merchants export their produce and so were not treated as commercial enterprises. Unlike in Europe and the US, where every railroad junction soon became a bustling town, the railroads did not stimulate urban development in Cuba.

By 1852, nine companies had built a total of 350 miles (565 km) of track, although the pace of growth slowed down due to a slump in world sugar prices and a clampdown on slavery. However, sugar prices soon recovered, stimulating a second boom in railroad construction.

800,000

Approximate number of enslaved people from Africa transported to Cuba

Hauling sugar Using railroads for transporting sugar cane to ports proved far more efficient and quicker than using carts hauled by animals on the poorly maintained roads.

The Crimean war of 1854–1856 raised prices even higher—sugar was already a global commodity, and the war diverted British shipping from carrying sugar from Asia, creating a surge in demand. The sugar barons found themselves with enormous amounts of cash, which they used to invest in more railroads. Consequently, the amount of track laid reached 800 miles (1,288 km) in 1868, providing this impoverished island in the Caribbean with one of the densest railroad networks in the world. It was bettered only by a few major European nations, and in fact had more miles of track per inhabitant than any other country in the world.

Missing the mark

By the late 19th century, the Cuban railroads had reached a remarkable 5,000 miles (8,000 km) of track, half of which were standard-gauge lines designed to shift sugar out of the plantations and sugar products from the mills. The rest were mainly narrow-gauge tracks, often crudely laid, for hauling cane on the plantations themselves. Unfortunately, however, not only did the railroads fail to serve passengers, but they failed to stimulate the economy, for they remained dependent on British and US technology: no railroad equipment supply industries were ever established in Cuba. If anything, the railroads had a rather damaging effect on the wider economy—they exacerbated the differences between the rich areas, which benefited greatly from their construction, and those that were poor, which became even more neglected. They were also concentrated in the affluent western half of the island. Only a handful of lines were built in the east, where there were few plantations. Crucially, the east-west line connecting the two halves of the island was not built until the 20th century, because it required a government subsidy, which had not been forthcoming. As the authors of a study of the Cuban railroads argue: "the railroad development of the first decades lacked the long-term perspective that would permit the growth of a national grid." In fact, the economic effect of the railroads was quite perverse. By making the plantation owners so rich, they helped perpetuate the slave system that might otherwise have collapsed.

The railroads' dependence on the sugar trade was ultimately their undoing. They were profitable as long as sugar boomed, because there was no other form of transportation. In the late 19th century, however, another collapse in sugar prices rocked Cuba's economy, leading to the takeover of the railroads by British investors. Few lines were found to be viable, so much of the network was shut down. By the early 20th century, the remainder of Cuba's railroads were entirely owned by British and US companies. These monopolized the western and eastern networks, respectively, but the stagnation of Cuba's sugar industry drove the railroads into crisis. While nationalization of the rail network in the late 1950s addressed some of these issues, it did not completely resolve the ongoing challenges, which were tied to broader economic and political factors.

In 2024, only 12 of the 34 large locomotives required for cargo and passenger transportation in Cuba were in operation

Railroad hub The main railroad terminus in Cuba, Havana's Central Station, opened in 1912. It was used for transportation as well as trade.

Imported power (below) Most locomotives on the Cuban railroad system were imported from the US, including this one built by Baldwin, which was the world's largest train-engine manufacturer for a long time.

I. C. R.
HELENA
OLYMPIA
PORTLAND
SALEM
BOISE CITY
CHEYENNE
SALT LAKE CITY
DENVER
VIRGINIA
CARSON CITY
SACRAMENTO
SANTA FE
PRESSCOTT
TUSCON
AUSTIN
GALVESTON
VINTA
LITTLE ROCK
DULUTH
MINNEAPOLIS
ST PAUL
LA CROSSE
MILWAUKEE
LANSING
YANKTON
MONA
SIOUX CITY
DUBUQUE
MADISON
DES MOINES
DAVENPORT
FREEPORT
CHICAGO
DETROIT
OMAHA
COUNCIL BLUFFS
BURLINGTON
AURORA
TOLEDO
LINCOLN
CLARINDA
MARYVILLE
PEORIA
KANKAKEE
ATCHISON
ST JOSEPH
KEOKUK
QUINCY
SPRINGFIELD
INDIANNAPOLIS
LEAVENWORTH
BRUNSWICK
DECATUR
TOPEKA
KANSAS CY
JEFFERSON CITY
ST LOUIS
CENTRALIA
EVANSVILLE
LOUISVILLE
DUQUOIN
FULTON
NASHVILLE
JACKSON
MEMPHIS
GRENADA
DURANT
VIKSBURG
MONTGOMERY
MOBILE
NEW ORLEANS

Going places This 1882 poster for the Illinois Central Railroad depicts passengers waiting for their train. A US map shows this long-distance railroad's route, which earned it the name of "the main line of mid-America."

The spread of the railroads

As train travel increased and the benefits of rail links became evident, it seemed that nothing could stop the spread of the iron road. There was no obstacle—financial, geographic, or social—that could not be overcome by the railroads. Soon mountains were being crossed or tunneled under in territories as far apart as the Austro-Hungarian Empire and India. Rivers were forded and houses demolished to make way for stations in town centers. Even disease-infested jungles were conquered, such as the swamps on the Panamanian Isthmus, although at a terrible human cost. The United States, with its vast western deserts, soon boasted not just one transcontinental railroad, but four—and Canada laid three of its own. Urban transportation, too, was revolutionized. London's Metropolitan Railway, the world's first underground line, opened in 1863, and became the blueprint for many such systems across the world.

Although trains were becoming commonplace, there was little improvement in the quality of services—largely because the majority of travelers had no other means of transportation, so their custom was taken for granted. There were exceptions, of course—prestige services such as those developed by George Pullman, who provided not only far better meals but comfortable overnight sleeper carriages—but by and large rail transportation offered few comforts. Nor was it entirely safe. At first, trains were so few and so slow that collisions were unlikely, but as the tracks filled up and trains traveled faster, accidents became inevitable.

The railroad companies soon became the dominant industry of the day. They were larger than any other business and by their very nature operated across vast areas. Perhaps most enduringly, they liked to demonstrate their importance by building huge stations that became the cathedrals of the age—a source of pride to both the railroad companies and the communities they served.

CROSSING THE ALPS

Trains traversing the rocky Alps appeared to be an impossible dream at the start of the 19th century. However, once the challenge was overcome, the region became home to some of the most spectacular railroads in the world.

Many of the first European railroads ran from cities to ports so that goods could be transferred onto ships. As the network developed, however, it hit a major hurdle in the heart of the continent—the Alps. From the earliest days, the governments promoting the railroads realized that this was an obstacle that would have to be surmounted, but it posed the hardest challenge yet encountered by railroad builders. Engineers had to develop new skills and techniques, excavating far longer tunnels than had previously been achieved and erecting bridges over deep, often seemingly inaccessible ravines.

Semmering sets the tone

The first railroad to cross the Alps was built over the Semmering Pass by the Austrian Empire to connect the imperial

The Semmering Railway
Considered the world's first mountain railroad, the 25-mile (41 km) long Semmering Railway was completed in 1854 after six years of construction.

capital, Vienna, with the Empire's only seaport, Trieste (now in Italy). A circuitous route via the Hungarian plains had been considered, but the transalpine railroad's main backer, Archduke John of Austria, was determined to find a way over the mountains. This was a remarkable challenge, and it took an equally remarkable man to design and build it: Carl von Ghega, an engineer with experience building mountain roads, who had designed the Emperor Ferdinand Northern Railway from Brno to Breclav (both now in the Czechia). In 1842, Ghega was put in charge of the entire Austrian railroad-building program. Believing that an essential part of this program was a link between Austria and the Adriatic, he traveled to the United States to learn about railroad construction methods and how they might be applied to finding a way over the mountains. He returned convinced that it was possible to build a railroad over the Semmering Pass.

Pioneering locomotive An early articulated steam engine, the Engerth locomotive was one of the first to operate on the Semmering Railway.

The mountain pass had been used by travelers on foot and on horseback since the Middle Ages. Although it was the lowest of the Alpine crossings, which consequently remained open the longest in winter, Semmering still rose to more than 3,000 ft (900 m) above sea level, and therefore building a railroad across the range required extraordinary ingenuity and innovation. The Austrian Government backed the project because the revolutions that swept across Europe in 1848 convinced the new Emperor, Franz Joseph, of its necessity—not only to unite distant parts of his disparate empire as they sought to fragment and affirm their national identities but also to create employment at a time of economic depression. Establishing a connection from Vienna to the sea became both politically and economically essential.

New locomotives for a new line

Ghega chose a route through the Alps that started at Gloggnitz in Lower Austria and ran to Mürzzuschlag in Styria. As the crow flies, these two towns are 13 miles (21 km)

At its peak, a workforce of 20,000 people was engaged in building the Semmering Railway

apart, but the railroad covered twice that distance with its curves and switchbacks, the track running across curved viaducts that arched their way over broad valleys before entering long tunnels. In all, the route required 14 tunnels, the longest of which was 4,695 ft (1,431 m); 16 viaducts, several with two levels; and more than 100 curved stone bridges. Avalanche sheds were built to protect the line from falling rock and snow on its perilous path along the mountainside. Even with all these structures, the ascent still rose by gradients of up to 1 in 40 (2.5 percent), very steep for the locomotives of the time; the curves, too, were sharper than those on other lines. To overcome these difficulties, Ghega also worked to develop new designs of engines. In 1851, he initiated a competition, similar to the Rainhill Trials 22 years earlier (see pp.27–28), to find the best locomotive. An engine called *Bavaria* won, but when the line opened, it proved unable to haul heavy loads up the steep inclines. A new locomotive, designed by Wilhelm Freiherr von Engerth, a professor of engineering at Graz University, took its place.

All the construction work was carried out by hand, with the help of gunpowder (the only explosive available at the time). The workforce, made up of Germans, Czechs, and Italians, as well as Austrians, was enormous. Perhaps inevitably, numerous accidents occurred during construction. In the worst single incident—a rock fall in October 1850—14 men lost their lives, and in all, around 700 men died, many from diseases such as typhus and cholera. In one astonishing near miss, the building of the railroad almost changed the course of history. The young Otto von Bismarck, who later unified Germany and became known as its Iron Chancellor, was nearly killed when he came to inspect the line. A gangway over a ravine broke beneath him and he survived only by clinging onto a ledge as he fell.

The first railroad across the Alps The Semmering Railway played a crucial role in creating a link between the Austrian Empire and southern Europe, facilitating trade and travel between the two regions.

New connections

The first freight train traveled over the pass in October 1853, and passenger traffic began the following July. By 1857, the all-important connection between Vienna and Trieste was complete. While the line cost four times its original estimate, it proved its worth as a vital trade link for the Austrian Empire in what turned out

Covered ways (left) Built during the construction of the Fréjus Rail Tunnel, a large section of the Mont Cenis Pass Railway line was enclosed with planked sides and a corrugated iron roof to keep out the snow.

to be its declining years. Moreover, the railroad blended so well into the landscape that it has today been designated a UNESCO World Heritage Site, with the double-layered viaducts singled out as a particularly distinctive feature. After the success of the Semmering, other routes were soon being planned through the Alps. A route under the western Alps was proposed in 1848, but the revolutions of that year and the Italian Wars of Unification delayed its progress. Once Italy was unified in 1861, interest revived and a plan was laid to finish building a line under Mont Cenis, connecting Bardonecchia on the Italian side with Modane in Savoy, which had been annexed to France in 1860 and, more widely, linking the major cities of Milan and Turin in Italy with Grenoble and Lyon in France.

Crossing the Mont Cenis pass was out of the question, given that it reached an altitude of 6,827 ft (2,081 m). However, a temporary rack line (see pp.104–105) capable of climbing steep gradients, the Mont Cenis Pass Railway, was opened alongside the pass road in 1868. The 50 mile (80 km) line was used to speed up the carriage of mail between Britain and India via the Adriatic port of Bari. Worked by British engine drivers, it was the first ever rack railroad based on the fell mountain railroad system, which used a toothed central third rail to help the locomotive up steep hills. However, it proved short-lived and was dismantled in 1871, when the more efficient Fréjus Tunnel replaced it.

The 8½-mile (13.7-km) Fréjus Tunnel, built at a height of 3,684 ft (1,123 m), was the longest in the world at the time.

Technology to the rescue
The construction of the Fréjus Tunnel required groundbreaking innovation, such as this device that used compressed air to help bore through the rock.

Vital connection The Gotthard Tunnel, which forms the summit of the Gotthard Railway, was a crucial link for connecting the north and south of Switzerland. Pictured here is an express train emerging from the tunnel.

Initially, tunneling techniques were still primitive: they involved drilling holes into which explosive charges were placed. Progress was slow at first. Five years after work had started in 1857, less than 1 mile (2 km) had been completed. Then the engineer, Germain Sommeiller, invented a pneumatic rock-boring machine, the pace increased, and the two teams working from each end broke through on December 26, 1870. Thanks to an indirect triangulation, a new method of determining the route that involved teams of surveyors taking bearings on many points on the mountain, the two ends of the tunnel were less than 2 feet (half a meter) out of direct alignment when they met up. The Mont Cenis Railway—the first international railroad linked by a tunnel under the frontier—opened for traffic in October 1871.

The Gotthard Tunnel

The second major tunnel beneath the Alps was the Gotthard, which was also highly difficult to construct because of the terrain. It took from 1871 to 1881 to build and, at 9½ miles (15 km), was slightly longer than the Fréjus Tunnel. Work was faster, thanks to the use of dynamite, but it still took an outstanding man, Swiss engineer Louis Favre, to figure out a method of excavating through the mountain. Favre devised a way to reach the tunnel mouth, at an elevation of more than 3,610 ft (1,100 m). He created tunnels that circled around at a gentle

The Gotthard Base Tunnel links the north and south of Europe

gradient through the rock so that the route spirals up the mountain to reach a point above itself. At Wassen, for example, passengers heading south can see a church spire from below and then, a few minutes later, find themselves viewing it from above. These loops increased the travel time—the line between Lucerne and Chiasso on the Swiss-Italian border is 91 miles (146 km) long, and around a fifth of the route is made up of loops. Sadly, Favre did not live to see his creation completed. In 1879, he suffered a fatal heart attack at the age of just 54 during a tour of inspection of the tunnel. He was not the only fatality: at least 199 tunnel builders died in accidents.

The Swiss touch

After the Gotthard Tunnel opened in 1882, other rail routes were soon carved through the Alps via tunnels, including the Simplon, which at 12 miles (19 km) became the world's longest when completed in 1906, and the Lötschberg, which opened just before the start of World War I. The Swiss developed electric locomotives to pull trains through these tunnels, which would otherwise have filled dangerously with smoke from steam engines (see pp.212–217).

In the first two decades of the 21st century, Switzerland has undertaken the AlpTransit project, a series of ambitious railroad tunnels through the Alps aimed at reducing road traffic over and through the mountains. It plans to replace the first generation of tunnels that had been carved high up the mountains and required trains to climb up through slow loops and curved tracks with "base" tunnels that have been constructed at lower heights. The first AlpTransit project was the 22-mile (35 km) Lötschberg Base Tunnel between the cantons of Bern and Valais in Switzerland, completed in 2007. Then, following a referendum supported by the Swiss people, a further two new base tunnels were completed: the 35-mile (57 km) Gotthard Base Tunnel and the 9¼-mile (15 km) Ceneri Base Tunnel. Indeed, the Gotthard Base Tunnel became the longest in the world, surpassing the 34-mile (54 km) Seikan Tunnel in Japan when it opened in June 2016. While these tunnels are longer than their predecessors, overall they result in shorter and quicker rail trips and accommodate high-speed passenger trains as well as freight.

A towering success

These alpine routes represent the heroic achievements of the railroad builders. They have also proved remarkably safe since completion, with accidents a rarity despite the harsh conditions in which the trains operate, especially during winter. There is also a risk of fires, which have affected several alpine road tunnels with disastrous consequences.

Chamonix-Montenvers Railway Following the success of the first mountain railroads, Alpine trains became popular for tourism. The Montenvers rack railroad, which opened in 1908, took tourists up to France's largest glacier, the Mer de Glace.

CLIMBING MOUNTAINS

The technology that enables locomotives to ascend steep grades of track was invented in the early days of the railroads. John Blenkinsop's 1811 patent for a steam railroad at the Middleton colliery, Britain, used an engine with a geared cogwheel, or "pinion," that engaged with a line of teeth, or "rack," located between the rails. However, it was not until the 1860s that the system was used on a mountain railroad. Rack-and-pinion tracks maintain traction on grades of up to 48 percent, whereas the steepest incline that conventional ("adhesion") trains can climb is around 10 percent, even with assistance from extra locomotives. These specialized tracks also provide essential braking power to ensure that steep slopes can be safely descended.

The Riggenbach and Locher systems

Various rack-and-pinion systems have been developed and adopted since Blenkinsop first proposed his design in the early 19th century. Two such systems are the Riggenbach and Locher systems.

Riggenbach system (1863)
The Riggenbach system was the first of the rack-and-pinion systems to be used widely, but its welded "ladder" arrangement proved expensive to maintain.

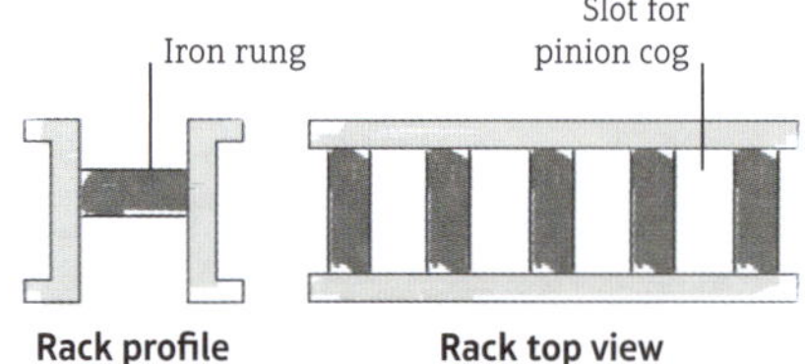

Locher system (1889)
The Locher system was introduced in 1889 and used a horizontal pinion on either side of the rack, enabling trains to climb much steeper grades. It was very stable and allowed carriages to withstand crosswinds.

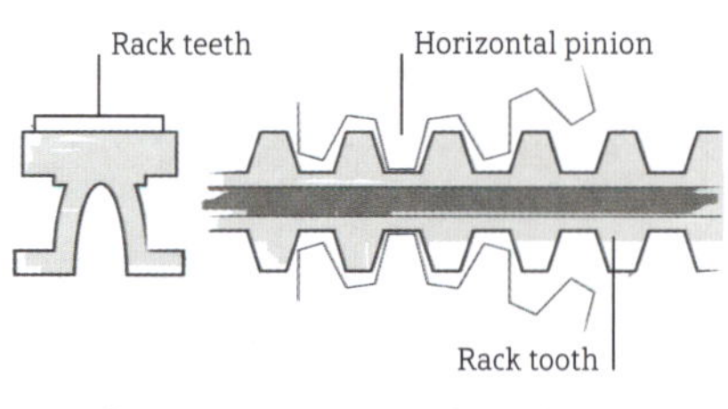

The Cog Railway The 3-mile (4.8 km) Mount Washington Cog Railway in New Hampshire, US, is the oldest mountain rack railroad in the world. It opened in 1868 and climbs more than 3,500 ft (1,100 m) to the summit of Mount Washington, the highest peak in the northeastern US. The line has a ladderlike rack, while the engine's tilted boiler is designed to stay level on the steep grades of the track.

How it works

Rack-and-pinion steam engines have one or more pinions, which are powered by the cylinders via connecting rods. Some designs place the pinion centrally on the axle, between the train's wheels, while others have them mounted on separate axles. Most rack-and-pinion trains have flanged running wheels and so are capable of running on standard rails. Steam-powered trains pushed their carriages uphill, then reversed back down the slope in order to maximize braking power. Today, however, most rack-and-pinion trains are powered by either electric or diesel engines.

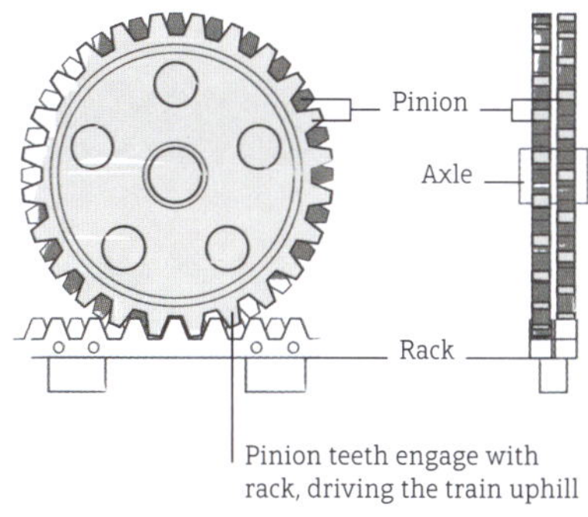

The Abt system (1885)
Designed by Swiss engineer Roman Abt and considered an improvement over the Riggenbach system (see opposite), the Abt system has a rack with two or three rows of teeth—each row offset from its neighbor—to ensure that the pinion is constantly in contact with the rack.

Jungle pathways The Panama Railroad was the first transcontinental line and one of the most challenging to construct, as it traversed a terrain full of jungle and swamp.

THE PANAMA RAILROAD: A DEADLY RUSH FOR GOLD

The rush to California in search of gold helped develop the railroads in Panama. Unfortunately, just like the Gold Rush, the railroads were not always good news for the people.

Although the Panama Railroad was less than 50 miles (80 km) long, its construction had deadly consequences. As many as 12,000 men may have died building it, from a fatal mix of harsh working conditions and tropical diseases. However, for the US, the price seemed worth paying. The railroad linked the Atlantic and Pacific coasts of North America, making it essential to the creation of the US. The railroad was hugely profitable for its owners and shareholders.

On January 24, 1848, demand for transportation across the Panama isthmus became pressing. On that day, James W. Marshall found gold at Sutter's Mill in California, triggering the first Gold Rush. But reaching California from the east coast of America was a huge challenge. The gold prospectors had three options: to sail 15,000 miles (24,000 km) around Cape Horn at the southernmost tip of South America, a voyage that took at least 85 days across notoriously storm-ridden seas; to travel 2,000 miles (3,200 km) overland across the US on wagon trails, a route that took at least six months and was also fraught with perils; or to sail to

During its initial 12 years, the Panama Railroad carried more than $750 million in gold and silver

the mouth of the Chagres River in what is today Panama and cross the narrow isthmus by dugout canoe up the river and on mules over the hills, to Panama City and the Pacific, a 50-mile (80 km) trip that took up to eight days and was also perilous, not least because of the disease-infested jungle. By 1848, various canal and rail routes across the isthmus had already been proposed—and abandoned—by Gran Colombia, the US, and France, respectively; indeed, the Spanish had first considered building a canal in the 1520s, before settling for the Camino Real, the overland mule track that was still in use when the first gold diggers arrived. In 1846, the US Government concluded a new treaty with the Republic of New Granada (Colombia and Panama), which guaranteed the republic's sovereignty in exchange for US transit rights across the isthmus. At the same time, it set the stage for furthering US influence on the state, thanks in no small parts to the economic and military power of the US. Nonetheless, the treaty paved the way for a transcontinental route. A year later, the US Congress subsidized a mail and passenger steamship service up and down the Atlantic and Pacific coasts from New York to the Chagres River and from Panama City to Oregon, enabling people and goods to reach Panama easily.

Setting the stage

New York entrepreneur William H. Aspinwall had won the bid to build and operate the Pacific mail steamships, and, with the onset of the Gold Rush, he set out to build a railroad across the Panamanian isthmus too. To assess the possible routes, Aspinwall traveled to Panama and Colombia with John L. Stephens, a lawyer and writer who had traveled in Central America. They established the Panama Railroad Company, which was granted an exclusive 49-year concession to build a railroad, highway, or canal across the isthmus, as well as 250,000 acres of public land. On the back of this, Aspinwall raised $1 million by selling stock in the company. An astute businessman, he also persuaded the US Congress to pay an annual fee of $250,000 (around £55,000 at the time) to transport mail over the isthmus. Meanwhile, the demand for a passenger train service had become evident: by the end of May 1849, 55 ships had landed more than 4,000 passengers at Chagres, all eager to reach California.

The route was first surveyed by US Army colonel George W. Hughes, who was misleadingly optimistic about the

as employees of the company, and the 41-year-old Totten, ultimately proved to be the hero of the venture.

Initial hurdles

Totten and Trautwine were set to begin work on a route starting from the estuary of the Chagres River, when they found that George Law, the entrepreneur who had won the contract to convey US mail along the east coast, had bought all the suitable land. They were forced to move the terminus, and found a new site further north at Manzanillo Island. They had to start construction by building a causeway to the mainland and then use land known ominously as the Black Swamp. To lay rails over the swamp entailed bringing down tons of limestone rock from an abandoned quarry at Bohio, way up the Chagres River, to build a solid base for the tracks. Once on firm land, at Mount Hope, they were able to use their first rolling stock—a locomotive and string of wagons. However, less than 1 mile (2 km) up the river they encountered further swamps and had to sink yet more tons of rocks. Another problem soon emerged: building wooden bridges was futile as they decayed within months in the tropical climate.

Canoeing on the Chagres (above) Before the railroad was built, travelers seeking to cross the Panama isthmus had to endure a perilous boat journey along the Chagres River, often in stifling conditions.

railroad's construction. His survey indicated that the terrain would be simple for railroad construction but failed to mention the deep swamps, thick jungle, and dangerous hills the route would have to cross. Aspinwall believed the railroad would need to be just 20 miles (32 km) long, from the furthest navigable point up the Chagres River to the Pacific Ocean. He contracted experienced American civil engineers George Totten and John Trautwine to build the railroad, but they soon realized the disastrous errors of the survey—for a start, Hughes had overestimated the length of the navigable passage on the Chagres—and withdrew from the contract. However, both were eventually rehired

Visionary pioneer (right) William Henry Aspinwall was the driving force behind the Panama Railroad and played a key role in facilitating transcontinental trade and travel during the Gold Rush.

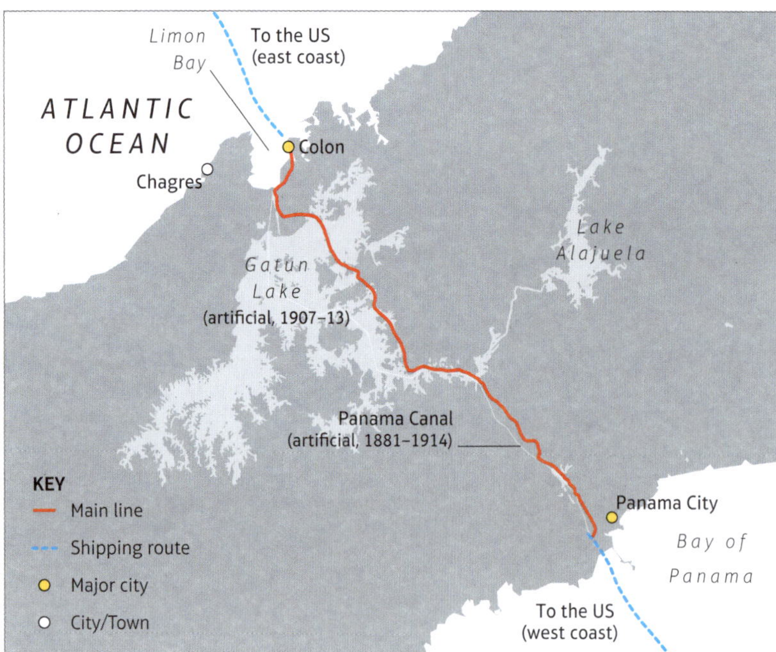

The 1855 Panama Railroad The construction of the line connecting the Atlantic and Pacific oceans took five years and involved 17,500 men, many of whom succumbed to disease in the sweltering, humid conditions.

The railroad builders were also unprepared for the weather. Annual rainfall was around 11 ft (3.5 m), and it poured constantly in the wet season from June to December. The Chagres River could rise 50ft (15 m) in a couple of hours. Not only was this hazardous for men working semi-submerged in the water, but it resulted in a climate teeming with tropical diseases and insect life. Tarantulas, scorpions, centipedes, wood ticks, and insects such as ants—white, red, and black—could be deadly, and malaria-carrying mosquitoes posed a permanent threat. The swamps were also infested with alligators.

Laying the tracks

The workers were a veritable foreign legion, turning up from all over the world and often known only by nicknames or numbers on a payroll. Few records were kept, and it is not known exactly how many men died. However, it has been reckoned that at one point, one in five of the workers was dying every month. Another estimate suggests that one man died for every railroad sleeper along the route. Whatever the actual mortality rate, the railroad's doctor, J. A. Totten (George's brother), found it difficult to dispose of the bodies. His solution, wrote historian Joseph L. Schott in his book *Rails across Panama*, was to

> “pickle the bodies in large barrels, keep them for a decent interval to be claimed and then sell them in wholesale lots to medical schools all over the world… the bodies brought high prices, and the profits from the sale of the cadavers made the railway hospital self-sustaining during the construction years.”

Relations within the international workforce were often fraught. One day, a gang of French laborers stopped work, hoisted the Tricolore, sang the Marseillaise, and refused to discuss their grievances except in their native tongue, which foxed their Irish foreman. The company chairman, who spoke French, refused to negotiate except in English. He resolved the stalemate by cutting off their rations: the French laborers went back to work, their grievances unknown to this day.

Moreover, in Aspinwall's view, the whole region was lawless and subject to banditry at the hands of the Derienni, gangs who stole the gold transported from California and often killed their victims. To combat the Derienni, Aspinwall hired Randolph (Ran) Runnels, a famous Texas Ranger who had hung up his guns after a religious conversion, but had seen in a prophecy that he would be called upon to take up a mission in a "strange land… with a great river full of demons and monsters." In Runnel's mind, Panama fitted the description, and he set up a mule express business as a front for a vigilante force, called the Isthmus Guard. In early 1852, the Guard captured the Derienni while they were relaxing, dancing, and gambling, and hanged 37 of them by the seashore.

Mounting challenges

As if terrible conditions, disease, a restive workforce, and lawlessness were not trouble enough, the company ran out of funds when only 8 miles (13 km) of track had been laid; its stock value fell, and construction ground to a halt. Meanwhile, shipping magnate Cornelius Vanderbilt had started work on a rival route through Nicaragua. Fortunately for the Panama Railroad Company, this route was as plagued by problems as their own.

The great turnaround in the railroad's fortunes came in December 1851, when two steamships arrived at the mouth of the Chagres River carrying a thousand passengers desperate to reach California. Hearing the toot of the whistles on Totten's locomotives, they demanded carriage over the existing section—anything to avoid part of the ghastly mule ride. To deter them, Totten asked an exorbitant fee of 50 cents per mile and $3 for each 100 lb (45 kg) of baggage. To his surprise, they accepted. Soon, so many people were lining up to use the railroad that the income from fares enabled Totten and engineer James Baldwin to push rapidly ahead to a limestone quarry, enabling them to transport stone by rail to strengthen the line. The company was able to then raise another $4 million in stock on the strength of the demand.

It was not all plain sailing even then. In the summer of 1852, many of the workers and their bosses died in a mysterious epidemic. At the same time, renewed banditry saw Runnels carry out more mass hangings. Then Totten's request to use iron instead of wood for the bridge over the Chagres triggered a row with a new company director in New York (Stephens's death had deprived Totten of his major supporter). Totten was sacked and the remaining 21 miles (34 km) of the railroad entrusted to an engineer named Minor C. Story. Regarded as a boy wonder

Inspection run Given the difficult conditions under which the railroad was built, inspections of the track were frequently carried out using handcarts.

Over the river The engineers working on the Panama Railroad had to ford several rivers, with key bridges, such as this one over the Chagres at Gamboa, facilitating the railroad's route.

in the railroad construction business, Story had no idea of the conditions in Panama. He employed the materials he had used successfully in New England, but his wooden bridges collapsed in the tropical climate and he fled, in Schott's words, "bankrupt financially, tarnished in reputation, and broken in spirit." After a year, Totten was recalled and recruited more workers, from Europe, India, and China. Stories of disaster befell the project, among them a train hitting a bull on the tracks and toppling into a ravine. Nevertheless, by the end of 1853, Totten had completed the crucial iron bridge and the way was almost clear for the run to Panama City.

Around this time, a tragic episode took place among a group of Chinese laborers, who had proven to be reliable workers. The laborers relied on a regular supply of opium to maintain their morale. When an accountant in New York cut off the supply for being too expensive—and criminal—more than a hundred of the Chinese workers committed suicide, hanging themselves from trees, walking into the water weighed down with stones, or asking Malay laborers to slay them with machetes.

Glory days

By now the railroad, although still incomplete, was profitable. In 1854, its 31 miles (50 km) received over $1 million in fares from more than 30,000 passengers, and on January 27, 1855, the two groups of men working from opposite ends of the line joined hands. For 15 years, the Panama Railroad's monopoly of transit across the isthmus—and from the east to west coast of America—made it prodigiously profitable. It paid for its construction within four years on receipts boosted by a scale of charges set up by a group of clerks drunk on its success and ready to exploit its monopoly position: once the railroad was complete, it charged $25 in gold for a first-class fare, making it by far the most expensive railroad journey in the world at the time, mile for mile. In its first 12 years, it transported more than $750 million in precious metals and more than 500,000 bags of mail without loss, although the cost of maintenance—including the replacement of rotting pine railroad

sleepers with hardwood *lignum vitae*—dented profits. The Panama Railroad Company's glory days continued until 1869, when the completion of the first transcontinental railroad across the US (see pp.114–121) took business away, but 10 years later, the shareholders made a handsome profit when the directors of a French group with plans to dig a canal across the isthmus paid $20 million for the stock.

Totten stayed on as the railroad's chief engineer until 1875, overseeing improvements and maintenance. Immediately after the railroad's completion, he had devised a scheme for a canal with locks across the isthmus. When French diplomat Ferdinand de Lesseps, the man behind the Suez Canal, embarked upon his project for such a canal, Totten was appointed chief engineer. Totten also found time to build a daunting mountain railroad in Venezuela. Yet his achievement is recognized only by a modest plaque at the station in Panama City. As Schott writes,

> "the brief obituary in the *New York Times* stated that he was a retired engineer. It failed to say that he was the man directly responsible for building the first transcontinental railroad the world had ever seen."

Jungle power Traveling through the Panama Railroad required powerful locomotives, such as this elegant engine named *Toulon*.

CROSSING AMERICA

Railroads were mostly regional in 1830, and the concept of a transcontinental railroad, connecting the eastern and western parts of the US, remained a distant dream.

Chinese transcontinental railroad workers A shortage of workers led the Central Pacific Railroad to recruit thousands of men from China to work on the line that would link the two coasts of the US.

Theodore Judah was a driven man, determined to realize his dream: he believed that the US needed a railroad running across its vast landmass to connect east and west. The son of a clergyman, Judah played the organ as a hobby and came across as rather earnest. Nicknamed "Crazy Judah" in his day, "he was never considered an entirely normal man," according to Oscar Lewis in *The Big Four*. Judah was, however, an experienced railroad engineer who had laid out the route for the spectacular Niagara Gorge Railroad in the State of New York and the Sacramento Valley Railroad, the first in California.

Judah was not the only dreamer: building a transcontinental US railroad had been the ambition of various railroad promoters ever since the first train had chugged down the Baltimore and Ohio Railroad in 1830 (see pp.32–39). Such a railroad was seen not only as economically beneficial but also as a way of bringing together the different regions of the US, which stretched across a landmass of nearly 3,000 sq miles (5,000 sq km); without the railroad, it is possible that the US might not have become and remained united.

Founding and early history

It was Judah, however, who almost single-handedly persuaded Congress to pass a law creating a railroad that would link the existing tracks in the east with California, 1,800 miles (3,000 km) away. He traveled to California to survey a possible route through the Sierra Nevada, a mountain range that reaches 14,500 ft (4,420 m) above sea level. Many doubters argued it would be impossible to traverse the range. His breakthrough came at a meeting in the upstairs room of a modest

grocery store in Sacramento, where Judah had organized an event to attract potential investors. A group of four enterprising and ultimately very lucky men—Leland Stanford, Charles Crocker, Mark Hopkins, and Collis P. Huntington, all small-town merchants with ambition—decided to back his crazy endeavor. The Big Four, as they became known, founded the Central Pacific Railroad company, which won the contract to build the line heading eastward from California. In 1862, President Abraham Lincoln signed the Pacific Railroad Act—an act all the more remarkable given that the Civil War was in full swing and Washington in a state of war. The legislation came with a generous bonus: to ensure the railroad was built, the companies that built it would receive government subsidies of between $16,000 and $48,000 for every 1 mile (1.6 km) completed, depending on the difficulty of the terrain. Moreover, they would be granted all the land extending up to 10 miles (16 km) to one side of the track. Despite the government funding, Judah still needed more money to finance the project.

Sadly, like many railroad pioneers, Judah did not live to see the fruits of his labors. He fell out with the Big Four over their efforts to extract as much money as they could from the scheme by fraudulent activity, and headed back to New York. At the time, the only route back to the east coast was via Panama (see pp.106–113), where Judah unfortunately contracted yellow fever and died at the age of 37. Meanwhile, the Central Pacific encountered various difficulties, from winter snow to a lack of funds caused by the corrupt activities of the Big Four. Few local people were willing to work for the company

"I am going to California to be the pioneering railroad engineer of the Pacific Coast."

THEODORE JUDAH

Moving homes Building the railroad across the vast plains of the western US required the creation of small towns that were moved as sections of the railroad were completed.

because mining and gold-digging were more lucrative, so thousands of Chinese laborers were shipped across the Pacific to provide manual labor. Progress was slow at first, but by 1867, the railroad over the Sierra Nevada at the Donner Pass (7,085 ft/2,160 m) was completed. This was the toughest engineering challenge of the railroad, and subsequent progress on the plains was far easier. When the Civil War ended in 1865, the Union Pacific Railroad, which had the contract for the other end of the track starting in Council Bluffs, Iowa, began to make good progress. Boosting the Union Pacific's construction, many ex-Civil War soldiers joined the teams of railroad-builders, providing a disciplined workforce supplemented by formerly enslaved people.

Like the Central Pacific, the Union Pacific was deeply corrupt and became a vehicle to enrich its backers, notably Thomas C. Durant, the company's vice president, and his cronies. Both companies came up with a simple scheme to purloin the public purse: they created separate construction companies, which were given contracts to construct the line at inflated prices, creating profits for these companies, which in turn paid out generous dividends to their proprietors—who just happened to be the owners of the railroad companies. In this way, all the main railroad backers became multimillionaires at the government's expense.

Challenges during construction

Building a railroad in the sparsely populated west of the US required a remarkable level of organization, and as many as 10,000 workers at its peak. The railroad was constructed in stages: first, an advance party surveyed the route; then graders smoothed out the route, shifting huge amounts of rock and earth, laying the embankments and building the bridges; these were followed by the tracklayers, who put down the sleepers and rails.

The workers lived in camps that moved forward with the railroad, creating virtual towns, which became known as "hell on wheels." They were infamous for their spartan accommodations and saloons. Fights were frequent, both with fists and with guns, and the danger of shoot-outs in these townships was constant. The workers also risked attack from Indigenous Americans, who were justifiably incensed at the land grab. The railroad men responded with force to the raids and massacred countless Sioux and Cheyenne people, including women and children, in reprisals, although they established a better relationship with the Pawnee, allowing them free rides on the railroad and establishing an alliance with them against the Sioux.

Fifteen tunnels were blasted through the Sierra Nevada mountain range by the Central Pacific Railroad

Groups of workers fought among themselves too. The government contracts had been set up in such a way that the two companies were competing to build the most track, as no meeting point had been specified. At one stage, the two lines passed each other on a mountainside: the Irish laborers of the Union Pacific were blasting rock, which tumbled down on the Chinese workers of the Central Pacific below. Enraged, the Chinese started a fight that was ended only by negotiations between the companies. The Central and Union also negotiated a truce over where their respective tracks should meet. This was at Promontory Summit in Utah, where, on May 10, 1869, Stanford and Durant took turns to bang in a golden spike. A momentous occasion, it was marked by celebrations across the US as the news spread rapidly by telegraph. In Chicago, there was a 7-mile (11 km) parade, while in New York, the event was marked by a 100-gun salute. In Sacramento, 30 locomotives assembled for the occasion tooted their whistles in a tuneless concert.

Ceremonial spike
The transcontinental line's completion was marked by the hammering in of a golden spike (above) at a ceremony at Promontory Point, Utah, on May 10, 1869.

Despite the corruption and construction problems, it had taken only six years for the line to be completed, rather than the expected 10 years—although, in fact, the tracks were not quite continuous across the US until the bridge over the Missouri between Council Bluffs and Omaha was completed in 1872.

The "wedding of the rails" at Promontory Summit is considered the day on which the country was united. There were numerous events around the nation to mark its 150th anniversary in 2019. The importance of the achievement cannot be overestimated. A journey that would have taken six months on precarious wagons through a harsh climate—baking in the summer, freezing in winter—could now be achieved in about a week. It triggered the settlement of the West, and immigrants flowed there.

"If he'd of lived, he'd of been a great man. A man like James J. Hill."

F. SCOTT FITZGERALD, *THE GREAT GATSBY*

Expansion of the railroad

Soon, other transcontinental railroads were under construction, both in the US and in Canada. The next two lines opened in 1883—the Southern Pacific (the name of the ocean was used by nearly all the companies), which ran to Los Angeles in California, and the Northern Pacific, which terminated at the other end of the western seaboard in Seattle, Washington. Generous government grants of land stimulated this

Spartan stations On the US railroads in the West, stations such as the Santa Fe depot in Longford, Kansas, were basic buildings usually containing a waiting room and a restaurant.

Laying tracks The work of building the railroads was labor-intensive and there was little mechanization. Here, workers laying tracks for the Northern Pacific Railroad take a short break to pose for a photo (c.1872).

intense bout of railroad construction, as well as a conviction that the lines would bring profits through the anticipated influx of immigrants.

A fourth line was built without any government support, thanks to the tenacity of a remarkable one-eyed frontiersman, James J. Hill. Known as the "Empire Builder," he was probably the greatest North American railroad-builder. Hill was a strange-looking fellow, lithe and short with a huge nose, a small mouth, and deep-set eyes. He had lost sight in one eye as a result of an archery accident in his youth. He was also a remarkable wheeler-dealer, who for 30 years pursued his vision of building a line that would open up the vast prairies of Montana to settlers and made it possible to export grain to the Far East. Moreover, his line the Great Northern Railway—which in 1893 linked St. Paul, Minnesota, to Seattle, Washington—was built to a higher standard than those of his rivals, with gentler gradients and without the tight curves that make trains slow down.

To complete the "set" in the US, the Atchison, Topeka, and Santa Fe Railway crept quietly westward, funded by real estate offices that sold the land that had been granted to it by the government. The railroad, which linked up with existing California lines in 1884, became the most successful of the transcontinental lines by carrying freight to the port at Los Angeles. Indeed, freight was the mainstay of most of these lines although the flow of immigrants proved profitable too, and the lines competed to attract them to the areas served by their routes. The railroads promoted themselves to potential settlers, even opening offices in Europe to attract new migrants so that they could cash in on their vast land holdings. All kinds of dubious claims about the fertility of the land and the mildness of the climate were made to entice desperate people seeking a better life—many of whom gave up after their first winter of heavy snowfall or summer of drought.

Canada's rail network

Canada, then a British colony, was determined to build a transcontinental line too. This was for commercial reasons, but also to unify the disparate parts of the country—notably British Columbia, which had threatened secession. If anything, the achievements of the builders of the first Canadian line, the Canadian Pacific Railway, were greater than those of their rivals south of the border. As ever, the man in charge, William Cornelius Van Horne, was a remarkable character who took a hands-on approach. He traveled from site to site and was not averse to walking over rickety trestle bridges to show his workers that they must be equally fearless.

It was 2,700 miles (4,300 km) from the developed regions of Ontario to the Pacific Ocean, half as far again as the distance covered by the first US transcontinental, and the terrain was certainly no easier. The route of the Canadian Pacific ran to the north of the Great Lakes and,

Canadian Pacific Railway logo The first Canadian transcontinental railroad, named the Canadian Pacific Railway, was incorporated in 1881.

although the initial sections were relatively flat, the granite shelf of the Canadian Shield required considerable blasting through hard rock. There were also two mountain ranges, the Rockies and the Selkirks. The line was initially built at a very steep gradient of 1 in 22 (4.5 percent) to reach the mountain heights, but these steep stretches were later replaced by spiral tunnels. The tough conditions took a high toll on the more than 30,000 workers who helped build the railroad, many of whom were Chinese. Between 600 and 4,000 Chinese workers died while working on the railroad. Construction started in 1881 and the "last spike" was driven in 1885. The line opened without fanfare on Van Horne's instructions, in 1885.

It was another 30 years before the completion of the next Canadian transcontinental, the Canadian Northern Railway, which took a more northerly route through the mountains. It was built gradually, in sections, with the aim of attracting settlers to the vast prairies of western Canada. The rivalry between the first two lines then prompted the decision to build a third, the Grand Trunk Pacific/ National Transcontinental Railway, built in two sections east and west from Winnipeg. This was the hardest of the three to build, and was in many ways unnecessary, since for hundreds of miles it ran parallel to the first Canadian transcontinental.

As a result of all this frenzied construction, there were no fewer than five transcontinental routes across the US by the end of the 19th century, and the three Canadian transcontinental railroads were all completed by the end of World War I. However, Canada had overreached itself, given its sparse population, and later, two of these railroads were declared bankrupt soon after their completion—a fate also suffered by several of the American transcontinentals. Nonetheless, these lines continued to operate, providing vital links within their respective countries, and were instrumental in stimulating population growth and economic development: the railroads had conquered the West. Most of the tracks still survive today, playing a vital role in transporting freight.

Carriage interior Early trains carrying immigrants to the West were crowded, as shown in this 1888 engraving of a sleeping carriage on the Canadian Pacific Railway train.

The construction of the Canadian Pacific Railway was a major endeavor that involved thousands of workers, including up to 17,000 Chinese immigrants

Crossing chasms This image from the 1870s features a train crossing a trestle bridge over a gorge on the Canadian Pacific Railway. The bridge, one of several over deep chasms along the line, was wooden.

NORTH AMERICAN TRANSCONTINENTALS

The first railroad to cross North America was the Pacific Railroad—a combination of the Union and Central Pacific lines that linked Chicago and California. The fledgling United States of America was unified for the first time, opening up the country to further settlement and exploitation. The success of the first route spawned a profusion of alternatives—as well as three lines across Canada—which have together helped the North American rail network become the most extensive in the world.

Prince Rupert was the west coast terminus of the Grand Trunk Pacific Railway, a transcontinental line built from 1906–1914 to compete with the Canadian Pacific Railway

Prince Rupert
Dawson Creek
Grande Prairie
Edmonton
Calgary
Kamloops
Vancouver
Seattle
Portland
UNIT
Promontory Point
Salt Lake City
Sierra Nevada
San Francisco
Las Vegas
Los Angeles
Phoenix
San Diego
PACIFIC OCEAN
MEX

In 1863, Central Pacific Railroad started laying tracks from Sacramento, eastward. The line was extended to San Francisco in 1869, six months after the ceremony marking the completion of the line at Promontory Point

Founded in 1865, the Southern Pacific Railroad initially ran from San Francisco to San Diego, reaching New Orleans by 1883

Central Pacific The crew of a freight train pose for the camera at Mill City, Nevada, on the Central Pacific Railroad in 1883. The train features the classic American "cowcatcher" for clearing the track ahead.

KEY
HISTORIC MAIN LINE:
Southern Pacific
Union Pacific
Great Northern
Central Pacific
Canadian Pacific
Other main lines
Major city
City/Town
The Canadian Pacific Railway built a transcontinental line extending from Vancouver to Montreal, which opened in 1885
CANADA
UNITED STATES
ICO
Hudson Bay
Lake Superior
Lake Michigan
Lake Huron
Lake Ontario
Lake Erie
Gulf of Mexico (Gulf of America)
ATLANTIC OCEAN
Churchill
Saskatoon
Moose Jaw
Regina
Winnipeg
Moosonee
Bathurst
Amherst
Halifax
Montreal
Ottawa
Duluth
Sault Ste Marie
Toronto
Rochester
Boston
Providence
New Haven
New York
Buffalo
Minneapolis
St Paul
Milwaukee
Chicago
Detroit
Philadelphia
Atlantic City
Baltimore
Washington, D.C.
Pittsburgh
Indianapolis
Cincinnati
Newport News
Denver
Kansas City
St Louis
Amarillo
Birmingham
Atlanta
Savannah
Fort Worth
Dallas
El Paso
Mobile
Jacksonville
Baton Rouge
Houston
New Orleans
Galveston
San Antonio
Corpus Christi
Tampa
Miami

GOING UNDERGROUND

An important milestone in the history of transportation, London's underground railroads changed the city's infrastructure and helped relieve the city's increasing traffic congestion.

Building a railroad underground was the radical idea of Charles Pearson, solicitor to the City of London, who realized in the 1840s that something had to be done about the congestion and chaos of the city's streets. The world's first metropolis, London was booming, thanks to the Industrial Revolution. In the first half of the 19th century, its population had grown from 1 million to 2.5 million. As it had expanded, the city's traffic problems had become unmanageable, with pedestrians, hackney carriages, and horse-drawn buses all competing for space on the roads.

Pearson realized that while central London was crowded with slum housing, people could not live far from the center as walking was the only way to get to work. His solution was to build railroad lines that extended beyond the city boundary; the central section of the railroads, however, would have to be built beneath the city streets so that houses would not have to be demolished. Pearson hoped these railroads would allow people to move out to better conditions than existed in the inner city "rookeries," with gardens and fresh air.

A serial campaigner, who fought for universal suffrage, civic rights for Jewish people, and penal reform, Pearson is best remembered for his groundbreaking achievement as pioneer of what became known as the Underground. He first set out his idea in 1845, in a pamphlet proposing a glass-roofed railroad down the Fleet valley between King's Cross and Farringdon.

The 1840s were a period of intense railroad construction as railroad mania took hold. A central station for the whole capital was proposed at Farringdon, on the edge of the City of London, but in 1846, a commission ruled this out because of the destruction it

Traffic congestion By the mid-19th century, congestion and frequent traffic jams in the streets of London led to the proposal of underground railroad to ease the strain on surface transportation.

"Cut and Cover" construction In the 1860s, a section of the Metropolitan District Railway was built by the navvies to link London's mainline stations. The "cut and cover" method used during construction caused significant disruption.

would cause in the City. Instead, the mainline stations were located on the edge of the central area. Ironically, this aggravated congestion as passengers pouring off the trains tried to get around the center of the city. Pearson's vision of an underground railroad to link the stations was the obvious solution. He obtained funds from the City of London and existing railroad companies, then merged with another group of entrepreneurs who had received parliamentary approval for their scheme in 1853. Unusually among railroad pioneers, Pearson did not seek any personal financial gain from the project.

The first Underground line

The Metropolitan Railway Company was founded in 1854, but it was not until early in 1860 that work started on a line to link three of the mainline stations—Paddington, Euston, and King's Cross—with the City, using a new method known as "cut and cover," which involved digging a trench, laying the railroad, and covering it with a tunnel. This technique was disruptive at ground level and meant that the railroad usually had to follow the line of existing streets. Interestingly, one house that had to be demolished on the route of the line, at 23 Leinster Gardens, was recreated as a facade in order not to ruin an elegant terrace, the open track behind the facade serving as a vent for the steam trains.

2,000 navvies built the first underground line by hand over two years

An artist's impression This 1860 image of the first underground railroad shows a tunnel larger than reality and features a broad gauge train, which was only in use for the first few months after the line opened in 1863.

Although the building of such a line was unprecedented, there was only one major mishap, when the Fleet River burst its banks and flooded the works to a depth of 10 ft (3 m) in June 1862. Despite this, the 3½-mile (6 km) line opened in January 1863, only a few months behind schedule, at a cost of £1 million (around £160 million/$270 million in today's money). Sadly, Pearson had died the previous September and missed the banquet held at Farringdon station to celebrate its opening.

There had been doubts as to whether people would venture onto this new type of railroad. Not only were the stations gas-lit and dark, but the trains were also hauled by steam engines that belched out smoke and steam, despite being equipped with special condensing equipment. However, 30,000 Londoners braved what *The Times* had warned would be "dark, noisome tunnels" to travel on the world's first subterranean railroad on the first day, January 10, 1863. The Metropolitan Railway, which gave its name to underground systems all around the world, was an instant success. It provided cheap laborers' trains early in the morning. After, came thousands of office clerks who could afford the more expensive fares charged later in the morning. Throughout the day, the trains attracted all types of traveler in the three available classes.

The Metropolitan Railway sought to ban smoking at first, on the grounds that the locomotives already created a foul fug, but after a complaint in Parliament, the railroad was forced to allow smokers on the trains. Indeed, the air was sometimes so filled with smoke and fumes that chemists near the stations enjoyed a roaring trade in Metropolitan Mixture (strong smelling salts), sold as a panacea for passengers overcome by the fumes. In general, though, one of the reasons people were attracted to the system was that it was safe. No severe accidents

As of 2025, London's Underground network has 11 lines and 272 stations

occurred during its crucial early days, and indeed very few have happened throughout its history. Within a dozen years of the opening of the first line, no fewer than 70 million people were traveling annually on what had soon become known as the Underground.

Expanding the Underground

The Metropolitan Railway began to expand almost immediately. It built two extra tracks between King's Cross and Farringdon, called the City Widened Lines, which were then extended farther south into the City. Other promoters were eager to get involved, and the Metropolitan District Railway (later the District line), run by James Staats Forbes, a rival of the Metropolitan's chairman, Edward Watkin, was selected to build new lines. The two were already in competition before they set out to expand the Underground: Forbes ran the London, Chatham, and Dover Railway, while Watkin was a director of its competitor in Kent, the South Eastern Railway.

For the next 30 years, the rival railroads expanded the Underground system rapidly into north and west London. They had rather different conceptions, which is why the Metropolitan line extends far beyond central London into the Metroland developed in the 1920s and 1930s, while the District line reaches only as far as the more suburban Wimbledon, Richmond, and Ealing. Nevertheless, thanks to the dynamism of this duo, the Underground network soon spread well beyond the existing city boundaries, and, wherever the lines were built, new housing and businesses soon sprang up. Despite their achievements, the Metropolitan and District railroads never reconciled their differences and remained in dispute over who should complete the Circle line, which links nearly all of London's main-line terminals, until its completion in 1884. The two companies ended up running the line jointly, but remained in competition: the Metropolitan ran the clockwise trains and the District the counterclockwise ones. Hapless visitors to London had to choose between the two companies' ticket offices and could end up going the long way around the Circle if they unwittingly bought the wrong ticket.

The Tube

In 1890, the first deep "tube" line, bored out of the London clay rather than being built by the cut and cover method, was completed. The City and South London Railway ran under the Thames River between Stockwell and the

Underground inspection
The Metropolitan Railway opened an extension in October 1868. Here, the future British Prime Minister William Gladstone and other dignitaries can be seen on a tour of inspection a few months before the line's opening.

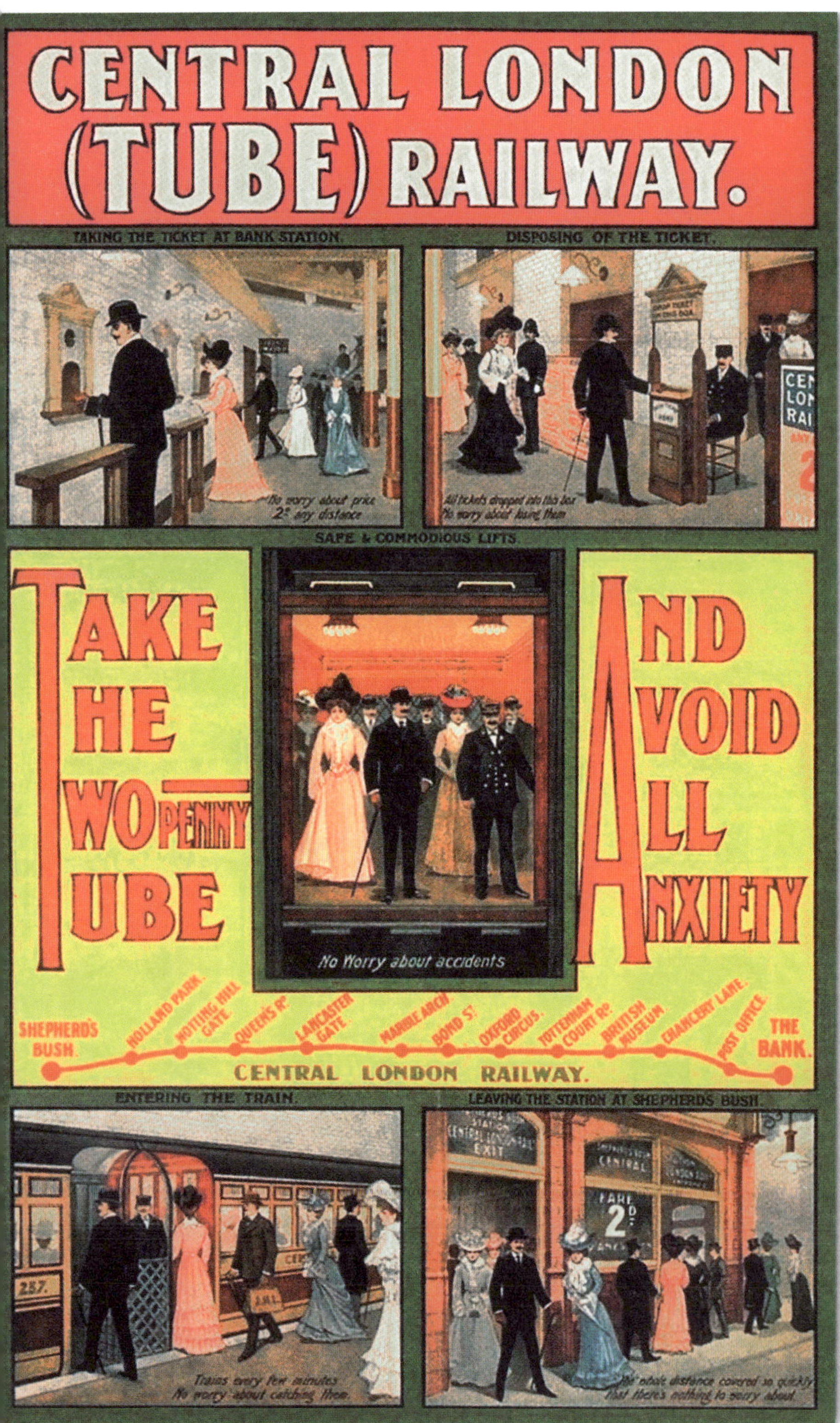

Popular travel This vintage poster from c.1905 was published to promote the efficiency and comfort of the Underground. The line was widely welcomed by Londoners as it provided a cost-effective alternative to the congested roads.

City. As there was inadequate ventilation in the underground tunnels, the trains were powered by electricity rather than steam after a plan for a rope-hauled system was abandoned. The line was dubbed the "tuppenny tube" as two pence was the fare for all journeys, and it too was an instant success—despite the fact that the trains operating the service had only tiny windows and were known as sardine boxes. Other Tube railroads soon followed. Both the Waterloo and City line and the Central line, the most successful of the early lines, had opened by 1900.

Endorsing the Underground

Promoters continued to develop the Underground. Charles Yerkes, an American with a prison record who had once run Chicago's tramways, turned out to be a transportation visionary. He brought together several lines, both existing and proposed, under the auspices of the Underground Electric Railways Ltd (UERL); electrified the Metropolitan, District, and Circle lines; and built three deep Tube lines in the space of five years—the Piccadilly and Bakerloo lines, and the Hampstead section of the Northern line. By 1907, all the Tube lines through central London, except the Victoria line (opened in 1968 and completed in 1972) and Jubilee line (opened in 1979 and extended in 1999), had been built.

After Yerkes, progress was more focused on marketing rather than engineering. Frank Pick, who started working for the network in 1906 and ran it until 1940 alongside chairman Albert Stanley (later Lord Ashfield), created the public image of the Underground. Pick had an eye for detail, while Stanley was more strategic. Their creation lives on today, a public organization whose achievements have been recognized around the world.

Pick instigated the design of both the red, blue, and white roundel that became the instantly recognizable Underground sign, and the innovative and much-imitated map devised by Harry Beck. A technical draftsman employed by the company, Beck created the map, based on electrical diagrams. Pick also commissioned the Johnston Sans typeface for the organization, advertising posters by artists, and cutting-edge architectural designs for new stations. Stanley persuaded the government to pay for suburban extensions of the system. Together, the pair built up the UERL into an organization encompassing almost all the Underground lines and London's buses, and ran the nationalized London Transport from its creation in 1933 until World War II, a period widely regarded as its heyday.

Although the system was neglected after the war and usage fell dramatically, it has been revived since the 1970s and flourishes today. The London Underground is more than just a transportation system; it is the mechanism that made it possible for London to grow in the way it did. It allowed people to live farther out, but also enabled the center of the city to remain compact and accessible. Today, the Underground is again attracting near record numbers of passengers after the sharp decline caused by the COVID-19 pandemic. Moreover, London's rail network has been greatly enhanced by the construction of the Elizabeth line, previously known as Crossrail, which runs under London in an east–west direction and links up with most of the Underground lines. Its trains, which can each carry up to 1,500 people in their nine carriages are far larger than those on the Tube system. Consequently, the line is part of the national rail network rather than the London Underground.

Legacy of the Tube

Uniquely, the London Underground has become the emblem of the city it serves. Thanks to Pearson and subsequent developers, London became the first city with a railroad beneath its streets, and Britain was once again a pioneer. It was not until the end of the 19th century that other cities started building railroads underground. Budapest, in Hungary, was the second city in the world to develop a metro system, which opened in 1896, more than 30 years after London's. Major cities such as Paris, New York, and Berlin followed in the early years of the 20th century. Now, most major cities across the world boast an underground railroad system and there are nearly 200 metro and subway networks around the world, from Yerevan in Armenia to Los Teques in Venezuela.

Tube shelter Thousands of Londoners used Underground stations to shelter from nightly air raids during the World War II German bombing campaign known as the Blitz (1940–1941), but train services carried on as normal during the day.

Evolving with time Underground stations have evolved over time to become more efficient and effective, while also incorporating art, lighting, and unique design. The Bikás park station in Budapest, Hungary, has a glazed dome, flooding the main access with light.

DEATH ON THE RAILS

From catastrophic crashes to groundbreaking safety reforms, rail travel was not always as safe as it is today. In fact, it took several generations to finally tame the "iron horse."

There were many hazardous elements surrounding this strange and inherently dangerous beast of iron. In the words of an old-time railroad man: "Accidents don't happen by accident." Besides the trains themselves—especially their brakes—faulty signaling, defective tracks, human error, and organizational blunders were all culprits. Today, because of the knowledge that train travel is usually perfectly safe, any rail accident attracts an inordinate amount of attention from the media and public distorting public perception of the risk. However, no such attention was ever paid to the fate of the earliest railroad workers, who put their lives on the line, literally. In Britain in the 1860s, 800 workers were killed every year, 10 times the number of passengers who perished. The number of fatalities among both workers and passengers has declined steadily and significantly since then, but working on the railroads, particularly on the track, can still be a dangerous occupation.

Impact of railroad accidents

The sheer metallic brutality of railroad accidents often took more than a physical toll on those involved; they also caused mental anguish, which would now be identified as post-traumatic stress disorder. An early sufferer, British novelist Charles Dickens, described his feelings after he was involved in an accident at Staplehurst in Kent in 1865. At first, he behaved impeccably, nursing the sick and dying. He was, he said, "not in the least flustered at the time," but when he clambered back into his carriage, he could not stop shaking. Recounting the incident later also provoked the same reaction: "In writing these words, I feel the

Montparnasse derailment
This extraordinary accident at the Paris Gare Montparnasse in October 1895, caused by a late train speeding toward the terminus, resulted in only one death, a passerby.

"To this hour, I have sudden vague rushes of terror... which are perfectly unreasonable but quite insurmountable."

CHARLES DICKENS ON THE STAPLEHURST ACCIDENT, 1867

Armagh rail disaster
On June 12, 1889, a packed train with inadequate brakes slid backward down a steep hill and collided with an oncoming train. It remains Ireland's worst railroad disaster—89 people died, mostly children, and hundreds were injured.

shake and am obliged to stop." Dickens never fully recovered from the trauma, remaining frightened of rail travel for the rest of his life, and dying—in a strange coincidence—on the fifth anniversary of the accident.

The only positive outcome of an accident is when it triggers improvements in safety measures or procedures, a process often ghoulishly dubbed "tombstone technology." This was evident as far back as 1842, after the first major disaster in France at Meudon on the line from Paris to Versailles (see p.44). Most of the deaths were caused not by the crash itself but because the compartments were locked—to deter interlopers who had not paid for their tickets—so passengers were unable to escape from the wrecked train. Thereafter, compartments were left unlocked. Similarly, an appalling crash at Armagh in Northern Ireland in 1889 spurred on legislation that greatly increased the railroad inspectorate's enforcement powers, and introduced better braking systems. Many of the fatalities in the Armagh crash were children, which heightened the tragedy and prompted such a strong legislative reaction. However, a famous contemporary wit, the Reverend Sydney Smith, suggested that it would take the death of a member of the nobility to really effect change: "We have up to this point been very careless of our railway regulations. The first person of rank who is killed [he suggested a bishop, a breed for whom he had a particular loathing] will put everything in order and produce a code of the most careful rules."

On average, one person is killed per 3 billion miles (5 billion km) of railroad traveled

Even today, a safety inspector believes that "the railway gets safer and each incident enables us to improve still further." In the past few decades, installing powered doors, which passengers cannot open, has helped eliminate the problem of people jumping on or off moving trains—a form of idiocy that caused half of the deaths and injuries at stations reported by British Rail in the 1980s. But tombstone technology has not always been applied. Wooden coaches had long been known to increase the risk of fire in the event of an accident, but as late as 1928, a crash near Bristol, England, involving these old-fashioned carriages resulted in 15 deaths when inflammable gas ignited.

Even then, wood-framed coaches were not entirely abandoned in Britain until after 1945. Technological faults can also combine with other conditions to cause tragedy. In India, the deadly Bihar rail disaster of 1981 is thought to have been caused by flash flooding combined with a brake failure. The train derailed and plunged into a nearby river, killing nearly all of its approximately 800 passengers. This was one of the worst accidents in railroad history.

Structural defects and human error

Sometimes a train itself may be faultless, but other structural defects can spell doom. Using steel instead of iron has made rails stronger, but the "fishplate" joining rails can be weak. It was a faulty fishplate that caused an accident at Brétigny-sur-Orge near Paris, France, in the summer of 2013, killing seven people. Often, the rail tracks are only as safe as the structures that support them. Most famously, the first rail bridge over the Tay River in Scotland, built in 1878, was not designed to withstand really high winds. It collapsed a year after it was built, plunging a passenger train into the river below. As the poet William McGonagall put it:

> “Beautiful bridge of the Silv'ry Tay!
> Alas I am very sorry to say
> That ninety lives have been taken away,
> On the last Sabbath day of 1879
> Which will be remembered for a very
> long time”

Some accidents are beyond human control. The deadly earthquake and tsunami of Boxing Day 2004 devastated the coast of South Asia. It also caused the world's worst rail disaster when 1,700 passengers were killed on a coastal railroad in Sri Lanka. Other types of railroad "accident" are all too human, and deliberate. Acts of railroad sabotage have been common, not least in the repertoire of British Army Colonel T. E. Lawrence, also known as Lawrence of Arabia (see pp.266–271). Many saboteurs, such as the French railroad men who wrecked their own tracks in the latter stages of the German Occupation in World War II, are regarded as heroes. Crimes such as members of the French Communist Party causing a crash that killed 21 people on the major line between Paris and Lille in 1947 are widely regarded as acts of terrorism. More recently, in the early years of this century, terrorist attacks at stations and on trains as far apart as Madrid, London, and Mumbai demonstrate the vulnerability of railroads to attack by those with evil intent.

Just as pilots are blamed for aircraft crashes, so engineers (called engine drivers in the UK) are always in the spotlight. Fatigue, often after 12 or more hours at work, was the biggest problem before legal limits were introduced. This fatigue syndrome affected not just drivers but other workers as well, such as the overworked signal repairmen who caused the Clapham disaster in London in 1988 by wiring an electrical circuit wrongly. Back in 1879, a

Tay Bridge disaster This 1879 engraving from *The Illustrated London News* depicts steam launches and a divers' barge being used to search for survivors among the wreckage of the Tay Bridge after it collapsed.

time when the companies were fighting any attempt to limit working hours, a parliamentary inquiry reported the case of a guard who had been on duty for 19 hours and consequently failed to apply the brake on his train. And of course drivers are not immune to personal problems. The cause of the worst disaster on the London Underground—when 43 people were killed in 1975 after a train smashed into a brick wall at the end of the line at Moorgate—remains unknown, as it is unclear why the driver, who was among the dead, failed to stop. The most frequent cause of railroad accidents, killing thousands over the decades, is trains overspeeding. Nowadays, there are many more controls preventing drivers from speeding, and warning systems to notify them if they do. However, even on modern trains, speeding remains a problem, as seen in the appalling accident that killed 79 people in the summer of 2013 just outside Santiago de Compostela in northwest Spain. One driver who died while traveling too fast went on to become a cult figure in American folklore and folksong—Casey Jones. A crack engineer (driver) on the Chicago Fast Mail, Jones "took his farewell trip to the promised land" when he crashed into a stalled train in the fog in April 1900 while trying to make up lost time. Jones was killed on impact, but he saved the lives of all his passengers and crew by slowing the train at the last moment. *The Ballad of Casey Jones* states:

> "Casey smiled, said, 'I'm feelin' fine,
> Gonna ride that train to the end of the line.
> There's ridges and bridges, and hills to climb,
> Got a head of steam and ahead of time.'"

Train crashes are increasingly rare, especially in industrialized countries. In fact, it is car, rather than train, drivers, who remain the most likely cause of accidents on the railroads, particularly at level crossings. In the US, this problem is much worse than elsewhere because there are more than 200,000 level crossings across the country. In 2023, 247 car drivers and passengers were killed in such accidents across the US. In three-quarters of the cases, an official report attributed the disaster to "the impatience of the driver of the vehicle involved," a tendency that improvements in the design of level crossings and modernization of the warning signs can do little to improve. Train drivers have to sound their horn at every road crossing, however minor, which is why in the US trains are heard so frequently. Cumbersome trucks also pose a threat. On a line in rural France

The railroad hero Following his death, Casey Jones became the subject of a popular song commonly known as *The Ballad of Casey Jones*, but the sheet music, published in 1909, named it *Casey Jones, The Brave Engineer*.

Indian train disaster India has been the site of many major disasters on its intensively used tracks, such as this accident in the eastern state of Odisha in June 2023. It involved a passenger train colliding with a goods service, resulting in the death of just under 300 people.

2,192

Total number of level-crossing accidents across the US in 2023 resulting in 247 fatalities

in 1997, a diesel train scythed a slow-moving gasoline tanker in two, killing 13 people. It was the worst recent rail accident in France, a country proud of the safety of its trains.

Poorly managed operations

Railroad management has always been a legitimate target for blame. Operations were initially haphazard, because no one knew anything about the dangers of railroads. As writer-engineer L. T. C. Rolt put it: "When we consider operational methods in the early days of railways the remarkable thing is that there were not more serious accidents." Organizational danger has grown over the past few decades, mainly due to the outsourcing of rail work and maintenance, and the increasing prioritization of performance, punctuality, and cost. These kind of institutional inadequacies led to the most serious accident of modern times in Europe. In June 1998, 101 passengers were killed after the locomotive on a German high-speed train separated from the carriages, which then derailed. At the time, the Germans were desperately trying to catch up with the French, who had taken the lead in Europe in high-speed rail travel, and had taken short cuts to achieve the right balance of suspension, wheel design, and track flexibility. Deutsche Bahn had been warned of the problem but chose to ignore it, perhaps due to a combination of pride and an unwillingness to delay the introduction of high-speed travel.

Arguably the worst systemic problems in modern railroads—including several fatal accidents—were caused by the privatization of British Rail in the 1990s. It was replaced by 94 separate organizations, many run by inexperienced executives. Track maintenance was also outsourced to various companies, and it was shortcomings in this area that led to a crash at Hatfield, north of London, in 2000. Four passengers were killed and 70 were injured. Investigations into the crash revealed that the cause was a fractured rail, which exposed the failings of the private maintenance companies. Train speeds in Britain were temporarily reduced to a mere 20 mph (32 km/h) on many parts of the network for more than a year, which had repercussions for passengers and train companies alike. As a result of the accident, track maintenance was partially renationalized in 2002.

In the 21st century, as in the 19th century, railroads and passengers are vulnerable to both natural and unnatural disasters. However, thanks to modern technology, trains are statistically the safest way to travel on land, and also eco-friendly.

A dangerous job Before brakes were controlled solely from the engine, many trains had brake vans, with screw brakes hand-operated by brakemen. The train driver coordinated the braking with signals from the engine whistle.

STOPPING THE TRAIN

During the early days of railroads, a train's brakes were simple wooden blocks, applied to the wheels by turning a lever at several points along the train's length. As speeds increased, however, a more effective way of braking was required to stop trains over a shorter distance, and various attempts were made to create a brake with one point of control, operated by the driver. In 1875, a competition was held in Britain to find the best solution. The clear winner of these Newark Trials was the Westinghouse automatic air brake, which was widely adopted in the US. Britain initially used the less successful vacuum brake, but air brakes have since come into standard usage worldwide.

Brake blocks

The first simple brake blocks were soon developed to become "continuous" brakes. In this system, brakes were located on every carriage and were controlled from the locomotive engine by ropes, chains, or pipes running the length of the train. The wooden block was suspended by a lever, or levers, between the brake cylinder and the wheel. As technology progressed, the block was more often made from cast iron, which is still used widely, although modern railroads also use a wide variety of composite materials.

Brake block on a freight train

Air braking systems

During the late 1860s to early 70s "battle of the brakes", air brakes could bring a train travelling at 84 kph (52 mph) to a halt in half the time taken by vacuum brakes: the braking distance for Westinghouse's automatic air brake was 251 m (825 ft), compared to 467 m (1,533 ft) for a vacuum brake – a considerable safety advantage. Today, air, or pneumatic, brakes are the standard system used by railways around the world. These brakes use compressed air to apply a brake block to the wheel.

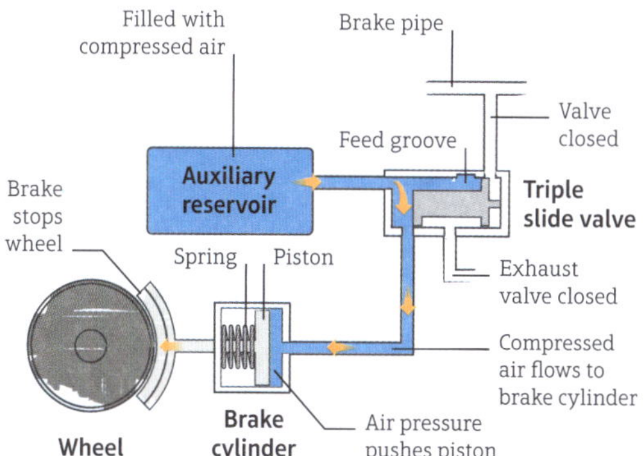

Air brake application
A pump compresses air for use in the system. The driver controls the air with a triple valve. When this is applied, compressed air is released into the brake pipe and air pressure forces the piston to move against a spring in the brake cylinder, causing the block to be applied to the wheels.

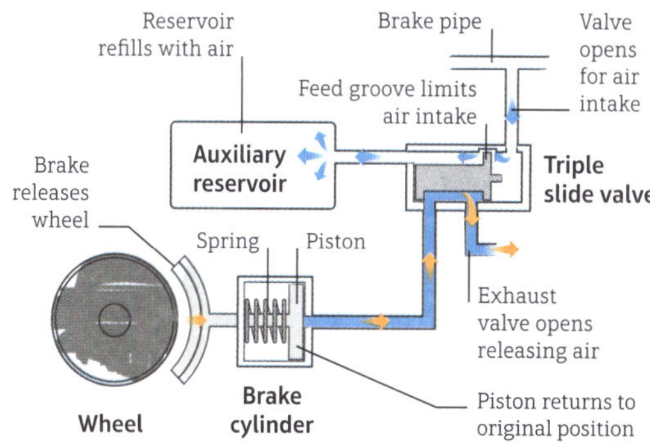

Air brake release
When the driver releases the brake valve, air leaves the brake pipes. As air escapes from the exhaust, a spring in the brake cylinder pushes the piston back, causing the brake blocks to disengage from the wheels. Meanwhile, the auxiliary air reservoir refills.

THE RAILROAD EXPERIENCE

Traveling on trains was not a comfortable experience in the early days, but innovations over time made rail travel smoother, faster, and more relaxing.

Across Europe, railroad coaches were primitive with no amenities and were based on horse-drawn stagecoach designs. Compartments seated six people facing each other, with doors on both sides. Carriages were made up of what was effectively a room supported on two axles, with a basic suspension system. Originally, most of the superstructure was made of wood, which was a fire risk and provided scant protection in the event of an accident.

Tiered ticking system

On the Liverpool and Manchester Railway, and on other early lines, there were different ticket prices. Passengers willing, or able, to pay a little more could obtain a place in the mail carriage, which had only a couple of comfortable seats and offered more privacy. At the other extreme, there was the discount option of riding in a charabanc-style wagon with sides open to the elements. As passenger travel became more popular, a hierarchy developed. Cheap tickets were available for boxlike wagons, which had holes in the floor for drainage, but often no seats. They were used on many railroads throughout Europe and gave people an awful experience of rail travel. Fortunately, these open wagons were soon considered too dangerous, as well as horribly uncomfortable, and were phased out. To replace them, compartment-style carriages were built for second- and third-class passengers, with less space for people's legs and much harder seats than first-class carriages.

Liverpool and Manchester train ticket Passenger train carriages on the Liverpool and Manchester line had standard fares for first, second, and third class. Special passes, such as this ivory token, were also issued to directors of the Railway, granting them free access to the company's trains.

The truly affluent had the option of bringing their own conveyances. The aristocracy simply arrived at the station in their personal horse-drawn coach, which was then lifted onto a flat wagon and held down with chains, rather as motorists later put their cars on motorail services that achieved popularity in postwar railroads across Europe. The upper classes could thus avoid soiling their petticoats or pantaloons by sitting on cushions used by the masses, though even they could not escape the smoke and ashes that enveloped all early travelers. The dilemma facing passengers when the weather was hot was whether to open the window and risk wrecking their clothes from the cinders, or keep it closed and swelter. An infuriated English social reformer and abolitionist, Harriet Martineau, reported that sparks had burned no fewer than 13 holes in her gown during a journey in the United States.

A rough ride

In the early days, the ride was bumpy whatever vehicle class passengers were traveling in. The springs were weak, or nonexistent, and the primitive track, made up of short rails, was uneven. Worse, the couplings between the coaches were not

Humming with activity The intensive use of the railroads by people of all classes can be seen in this 19th-century painting, which shows a platform at Paddington Station in London.

Cramped journeys French artist Honoré Daumier's 1864 painting, *The Third-Class Carriage*, captures the cramped and dismal reality of third-class train travel, a common experience for millions of immigrants arriving in the US.

rigid, but involved an arrangement with chains. Every time the train set off or slowed down, passengers were thrown about. There was no brake mechanism to prevent the carriages from bumping into one another and despite the padded seats in the superior coaches, complaints from the more well-to-do travelers about their uncomfortable journey were frequent and sustained. Luckily, the slowness of the trains reduced the severity of these rough rides, but it was not unknown for the chains to break, leaving some poor passengers stranded. This explains why the last coach of the train was soon fitted with a red light—its absence would warn signalers that the train was not complete.

The compartment system made it easy for passengers to get on and off, but its main disadvantage was that people could not move within the train, so had no access to toilet facilities or refreshments. When trips grew longer, trains had to stop at intermediate stations for "comfort breaks"—not an expression used in the 19th century—and meals. That was already the case across the Atlantic, where the design of coaches was different from the outset. Interestingly, some of the first American carriages were based on canal-boat, rather than stagecoach, designs. These early carriages were more practical and usually more comfortable than their European counterparts. They were longer and were open plan rather than fitted with compartments, which reflected the American ethos of equality. (Equality, of course, only among white passengers. Black passengers were segregated until the second half of the 20th century.) Some carriages even had seats on the roof, open to the elements, but this idea was soon abandoned.

Rail travel in the US

American carriages were similar to long omnibuses: they could accommodate up to 50 people on two-by-two seats with reversible backs, which were reasonably comfortable. Right from the start, there was a little annexe with a hole that opened straight out onto the tracks to serve calls of nature. Relief was only partial. The wheel sets were relatively close to each other, which meant that the ends of the coaches swung to and

Travel in comfort (right) For those who could afford it, train trips could be a luxurious and pleasurable experience, as illustrated by this c.1890 poster advertising a reclining chair route. These innovative seats offered passengers the ability to swivel and recline to their preferred position.

fro, inducing dizziness and even vomiting, especially among children. The problem was not helped by the fact that there were only four wheels on the early vehicles, but happily this soon changed. Four-wheel vehicles gave way to six and then eight, greatly improving stability.

Novelist Charles Dickens, an experienced rail traveler in Britain, visited the US in 1842 and was pretty dismissive of what he found. Traveling on the Boston and Lowell Railroad, he was dismayed by the lack of class differentiation: "There are no first and second class carriages as with us; but there is a gentlemen's car and a ladies' car: the main distinction between which is that in the first, everybody smokes; and in the second nobody does." He noted, too, that there was a "Negro" car, which was "a great blundering clumsy chest." Dickens particularly took against the American habit of spitting—a fellow author described the central corridor through the train as "an elongated spittoon." Poor Dickens also recoiled when his fellow passengers tried to strike up friendly conversations with him about subjects such as politics, blithely oblivious to the famed English reluctance to talk to strangers and fastidiousness about topics of conversation.

Heating in winter was provided by a pot-bellied stove, which was not only a terrible fire risk when there were mishaps but also according to Dickens filled the air with what he called "the ghost of smoke." The stoves were ineffective, making it too hot for those immediately next to them, but giving no warmth to those farther away. Lighting, too, was inadequate. Initially, there were lanterns with candles kept alight by the conductors. The lanterns were placed just above each seat but gave out little light. Much better kerosene lamps replaced them by the 1860s. They hung from the roof and gave adequate lighting for the whole carriage, but they too were a significant fire hazard.

Onboard interactions

Thanks to the open-plan arrangements, American trains attracted hawkers walking along the carriage, offering

2,800 miles

(4,506 km)
Combined length of track in the US in 1840

Coal-fired heating Early train heating systems, reliant on coal-burning boilers, were inadequate and frequently caused smoky conditions in passenger carriages.

Dining cars As long-distance rail travel became more frequent, train companies introduced dining cars, elevating the culinary experience for passengers by offering high-quality meals.

books and magazines to read, as well as drinks and snacks. The first hawkers were self-employed young men who had spotted an opportunity to make money, but later they were officially sanctioned. Many worked for the gigantic Union News Company. They would pass through the trains offering the day's newspapers, magazines, candy, soda pop bottles, and cigarettes. They announced their arrival in a falsetto voice, compressing their wares into a single word such as "candycigarettescigars" or "newspapersmagazines." Another British writer, Robert Louis Stevenson, traveling a few years later than Dickens, was much impressed by these young men and was amazed that he could buy "soap, towels, tin washing-dishes, tin coffee-pitchers, coffee, tea, sugar, and tinned eatables, mostly hash or beans and bacon." It was, he noted, much more entertaining than a ride on a British train. But the vendors were not universally welcomed as some ran scams. The favorite was to sell cheaply bound novels for twice the normal 25 cents, with the promise that one of them contained a $10 note.

Carrier to display newspapers and magazines

Newsboys Young men selling newspapers and magazines became a standard feature on American trains and did a steady business with bored passengers.

The American open-plan model created another difference from Europe: conductors went through the train checking and selling tickets and generally policing the passengers. They were a fearsome bunch and some, who were often on the same train every day or week, became well known to their regulars and even beyond. The doyen of them was Henry Ayers, or "Poppy" as he was generally known, described as "a huge, genial teddy bear of a man, weighing nearly three hundred pounds… [who] hovered over his passengers with benevolent menace." Ayers achieved fame because he had a fierce dispute over the use of the emergency cord with his driver on the Erie Railroad. The driver refused to acknowledge that the conductor had ultimate control over the train. By winning the argument, Ayers established railroad practice that remains universal to this day, and went on to serve the Erie for 30 years. His favorite tale was that he convinced an old lady who had left her umbrella at her station that he had organized to have it sent on by telegraph. The truth was that lost items were dumped in the baggage car,

"It is hard to make railroading pleasant in any country. It is too tedious."

MARK TWAIN,
THE INNOCENTS ABROAD, 1869

so Ayers simply retrieved the umbrella and presented it to its grateful owner at the next station.

More amenities

Some of the Trans-Siberian Railway services (see pp.170–179) were billed as "luxury," with staff instructed to empty spittoons and keep carriage temperatures at a balmy 57°F (14°C). In practice, however, customer service was not a strong point. Delays were standard, and at stations peasants rushed out to cook soup on the platforms, further delaying the train. For everyone else, the dining cars served meals by Moscow time, regardless of the line's seven time zones: toward the east, passengers had to eat breakfast at 2 p.m., while dinner was served at 3 a.m. sharp.

In the early days, train travel in the US was more comfortable than in Europe because people had the freedom to move about their carriages. There was also an outside area on the last coach, which afforded some much-needed fresh air in the summer.

At first, the connections between the cars were too difficult for passengers to negotiate safely, but they soon improved, so people could walk through the whole train. European carriages began offering the same facility for their passengers only in the last quarter of the 19th century, when trains with corridors were introduced, but the layout was different. Instead of an American open plan, the corridor was a passageway at one side of the carriage—at first external and used only by rail staff or intrepid passengers, but later internal. Introducing a corridor marked a significant step forward in passenger comfort, since facilities such as toilets could now be provided and passengers could have access to a refreshment car. This meant that trains no longer had to make intermediate comfort stops. Although corridor trains became the norm, compartment-type carriages lingered well into the last quarter of the 20th century on some European local and commuter services.

Double-decked cars The concept of double-decker cars was explored by some railroad companies, but tunnel clearances proved a major obstacle to their widespread adoption.

POINTS AND PASSING LOOPS

Points, or railroad switches, are track arrangements that allow one set of rails to connect with another. The mechanism consists of a pair of movable tapered sections of track, known as points, which can be pushed into one of two positions, enabling a train to remain on its course or to divert to another line. A common function of points is to control access to a passing loop, or turnout—a length of track that briefly diverges from a line, allowing a train to be temporarily housed while another train passes by. A loop is a type of siding, which is any low-speed section of track that branches away from a running line. Sidings can also be used for marshaling, storing, loading, and unloading vehicles, and for holding maintenance equipment.

Sharing the line

Passing loops allow multiple trains to run on the same routes. They are used primarily at stations to let trains vacate the main line so that express services can pass through, or on longer stretches of track to enable freight trains to be passed by faster passenger services. Safety signals ensure that only one train occupies a passing loop at any one time.

Complex mechanism At busy parts of the railroad, immensely complicated networks of tracks are built up, which require sophisticated switching equipment and careful monitoring by signalers.

Moving points While points were normally controlled from signal boxes, in freight yards they often had to be operated by a railroad worker pushing or pulling levers on the ground.

Changing tracks

The key component of a modern railroad is the points mechanism, which was patented by English engineer Charles Fox in 1832. The mechanism is activated by a lever connected to a pull rod, which moves the points from one track to the next. Most points are now electrically operated, but pneumatic versions are also used on some networks, particularly underground lines.

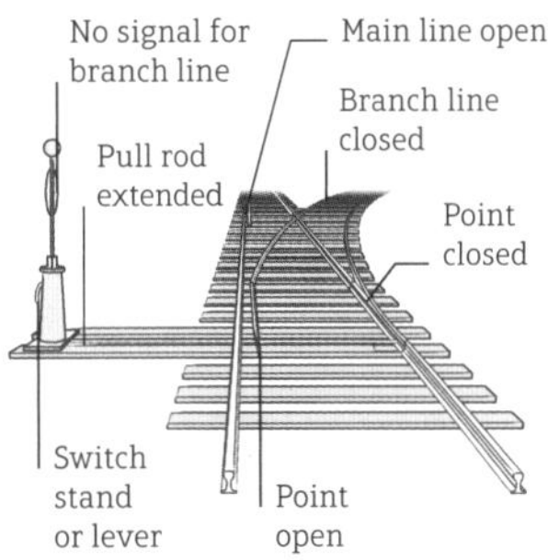

Staying on track
The points are set to keep the train on the main line. The lever is thrown, extending the pull rod to slide the movable rails across the track, drawing the left-hand point away from the track and bringing the right-hand point parallel to it.

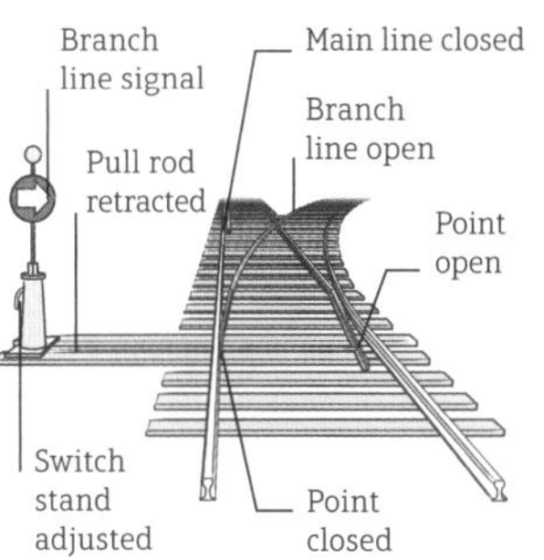

Switching to the branch line
The points are set to divert the train onto the branch line. The lever is adjusted, retracting the pull rod to bring the left-hand point flush with the main track and the right-hand point away from it. The signal indicates the right-hand branch is open.

Control room Signal boxes at stations or other busy sections could consist of dozens of levers, each manually operated and equipped with interlocking frames. These ensured that the levers could be moved only in accordance with the signaling system.

5112

Built for steam The raw power and elegance of the steam engine is captured in this picture of a locomotive pulling away from the platform at Chester Station, England, in 1944.

TEMPLES OF STEAM

The final 70 years of the 19th century are commonly known as the railroad age. But it would perhaps be more apt to call it the "railroad station" age. Stations were a highly visible presence for travelers and the first glimpse of a new place for visitors.

Railroads were a revolutionary intrusion into people's lives. They introduced a whole new world of speed, noise, and bustle. But the vast majority of travelers were oblivious to the marvels of engineering that had gone into building the lines, the bridges, viaducts, and other structures. The station was the passengers' point of contact with the iron road. Architects had to hit the right note—the stations needed to be solid and reassuring, laying a balm of soothing normality over an unprecedented, and therefore alarming, experience. Moreover, the buildings had to reflect the importance of the railroad company responsible for the station and its recognition of the town or society it served.

It took only a decade after the launch of the railroads in 1830 for a quartet of stations to be built worthy of the term "Temples of Steam." The progenitors were the two men who pioneered the modern long-distance railroad, Robert Stephenson and Isambard Kingdom Brunel. Stephenson ensured that both terminals of the railroad he built between London and Birmingham would be worthy of his engineering achievement. Stephenson's architect, Philip Hardwick, built a Grecian-style building at Curzon Street in Birmingham, which is now being restored as the terminus of the high-speed line being built connecting the city with London. At Euston, in London, he constructed a Great Hall of elegant grandeur, with the world's first boardroom upstairs, but unfortunately the heavy Doric arch in front of the station overshadowed the graceful proportions of the Hall.

Brunel could not be outdone by Stephenson. In the early 1840s, his own design for a terminus at Bristol was unexceptional, but 10 years later he worked with a distinguished architect, Matthew Digby Wyatt, to produce Paddington Station in London. Brunel's innovative

> **"Railway termini are our gates to the glorious and the unknown."**
>
> E. M. FORSTER, AUTHOR, 1910

Classical style The Great Hall at Euston station, built in 1849, was typical of the desire of railroad companies, such as London & North Western, to demonstrate their importance and grandeur. It was demolished in the 1960s to make way for a new expanded station.

glass-roofed train shed was complemented by Wyatt's station buildings and 165-room Great Western Royal Hotel, a handsome Renaissance building and the largest hotel in the country at that time. The hotel and the separation of the station buildings and train shed served as a model for many others—most effectively at St. Pancras in London, where the neo-Gothic hotel and glass-roofed train shed, at the time the longest single-span roof of its kind in the world, struck a dramatic contrast.

Local elements

Stations often showcased the character of a town or city. Railroad companies and their architects continued to emphasize solidity, but styles varied as every country reflected its "inner self." Scots went in for Highland style; Germans chose a heavy, Teutonic look; while Spanish and Portuguese stations recalled their ancient Moorish past. Americans went furthest in providing a variety of styles. As railroad historian Lucius Beebe remarked: "Passengers were set down in storybook settings, Grecian temples, Moorish arches, French chateaux, the tombs of Egyptian dynasts, Turkish mosques, Palladian porticos, Gothic castles, and Italian palazzi." The Antwerp Central station in Belgium is thought to reflect so many different architectural styles as to be unclassifiable; conversely, Flemish architectural style can be seen in the early-20th-century Dunedin station in New Zealand. Reactionaries hated the new station buildings. The 19th-century British art critic John Ruskin was appalled at their pretensions to architectural beauty since they represented industry, which, for him, was inherently hideous.

The grandiose Temples of Steam formed only a minute proportion of the thousands of stations built around the world during the 19th century. The smaller ones were often delightful examples of local architecture, sometimes standardized by the railroad company itself, such as the handsome villas spread over much of western France. In Russia, on the Trans-Siberian Railway, there were five classes of stations. Those of the highest class were built of brick and had heated waiting rooms, while the lowest were little more than huts to shelter waiting passengers from the elements.

The beautiful Antwerp Central station in Belgium is known as the Railway Cathedral for its domed central hall, iron arches, and stained-glass windows

American stations were generally built in the middle of the city. Thousands of small towns owed their very existence to the railroad, which often ran down the main street. Stations were at the heart of the community, full of "retired gentlemen, idlers of all kinds, champion talkers, crackerbarrel philosophers." Although there was powerful opposition to lines and stations near some city centers, in Europe, historic York allowed its ancient city walls to be breached to admit the iron horse, while in Cologne the station abuts the city's historic cathedral. However, if a station was not built in the center, it stimulated the creation of a new, important part of town. Railroad companies also created their own towns, simply by locating the enormous workshops needed to build and maintain the trains there.

The shape and size of stations outside Europe and the United States often reflected the tastes of imperial masters or European immigrants, notably in Canada where there was a remarkable mix of French and Scottish heritage. In India, the station and its associated buildings, such as the engine sheds, formed part of an elaborate social and industrial complex, planned by the British colonists. The most impressive example of this is the massive Victoria Terminus (now renamed the Chhatrapati Shivaji Terminus) in Mumbai, completed in 1888. In South America, however, architectural roots varied. Argentinian stations, usually built with British money, reflected their financiers' tastes, but in neighboring Uruguay, locals built stations in their own style. Stations could also fall prey to triumphalism: when the Prussians retook Alsace and Lorraine from the French in 1871, they imposed their own design on a new station at Metz in Lorraine, complete with statues of Teutonic warriors.

Stations take center stage

Railroad stations provided the stage for poignant scenes of farewell and reunion, especially during wars. The departure to the Western Front of waves of soldiers from Waterloo Station in London and the Gare de l'Est in Paris left a lasting impression. Between 1938 and 1939, millions of children were evacuated from cities across Europe, helped onto trains by their distraught parents. The emotional power of the station was not lost on movie producers either, from the tear-jerking family reunion at a small

Chhatrapati Shivaji Terminus, Mumbai This station, pictured here in 1910, was known earlier as Victoria Terminus. Modeled on St. Pancras Station in London, it is still in use today.

Grand Central Seen here in 1930, the majestic concourse at Grand Central Station in Manhattan, New York, looks remarkably similar today, thanks to a loving restoration.

country station in *The Railway Children* (1970), to the highly charged meetings in the station café featured in the romantic classic *Brief Encounter* (1945). One of the earliest movies to feature a train, *Arrival of a Train at La Ciotat* (1896) made by Auguste and Louis Lumière, depicted a train heading directly toward the camera, causing some of the audience to flee in terror. Artists were inspired by stations, too, such as Claude Monet, who painted a whole series of canvases at the Gare Saint-Lazare, just below the Parisian café where he and his Impressionist colleagues used to meet.

Stations also created new markets. Two major companies, WHSmith in Britain and Hachette Book Group in France, were founded to cater for travelers' needs for reading matter—and so gave birth to the "railroad novel." However, the glory of a major station could be marred by the inadequacy of the catering. Before the arrival of special dining or buffet cars on trains, passengers had to rely on meals snatched at stations. The owners of these establishments exploited their monopoly. However, Europe led the way in station food, especially France. In Ian Fleming's novel *Goldfinger*, James Bond stayed at railroad hotels because, "It was better than an even chance that the Buffet de la Gare would be excellent." Today, the Train Bleu restaurant at the Gare de Lyon in Paris is justly famous, as is the Grand Central Oyster Bar & Restaurant at Grand Central Station in New York. The St. Pancras Bar & Brasserie in London's St. Pancras has the longest champagne bar in Europe.

By the end of the 19th century, station architects—and the companies behind them—were confident enough not only to design afresh but also to use architecture to express a political, social, or national vision. The modernist station with exciting clean lines designed by Eliel Saarinen for Helsinki, Finland, in 1919 announced not only the arrival of the modernist movement but also proclaimed Finland's newly declared independence from Russia (1917). And after World War I, the French gloried in local Norman and Breton styles in a number of provincial stations, while at Perpignan in French Catalonia, they erected a statue of Spanish surrealist artist Salvador Dalì. Even the new station at Milan, Italy, in 1930 was Mussolini's statement of fascist grandeur.

Postwar reconstruction

World War II destroyed many great stations, but postwar reconstruction programs included the last true Temple of Steam, the Roma Termini in Rome, Italy. As the automobile usurped the train, however, stations became neglected. The train services in many countries were scaled back, with some routes and stations permanently closed. A few stations were rebuilt, but others were demolished—such as Penn Station in New York. In Brussels, Belgium, the North-South connection railroad network cuts through the heart of the city to link the stations to the north and south. Some disused stations were converted for other purposes, such as the Gare d'Orsay in Paris, which now houses the Musée d'Orsay, a national art gallery, or Manchester Central Station in Britain, which is now a convention and concert venue. In the US, stations, such as St. Louis in Missouri, survived by becoming shopping, hotel, and entertainment complexes.

Today, many of the stations that survived destruction during the automobile boom of the 1960s are now flourishing, with their architectural heritage preserved. St. Pancras Station in London is a splendid example of the renaissance, not just of trains but also of their stations. Until the end of the 20th century, it was best known as a decaying architectural masterpiece, which had been saved from demolition in the 1960s but housed only a derelict hotel and a grimy set of platforms. Today, thanks to a substantial renovation completed in 2007, it is a world-beater. The neighboring King's Cross station has also been given a remarkable makeover with a latticed roof attached to one side. In Spain, the magnificent Madrid Atocha station, from which high-speed trains operate, underwent a rather unique rebuild; originally designed by Spanish architect Alberto de Palacio Elissagne in collaboration with French engineer Gustave Eiffel, during the 1990s, its striking main hall was converted into a huge botanical garden, complete with turtles. Stations such as St. Pancras, Grand Central Station in New York, Kyoto Station in Japan, the Berlin Hauptbahnhof in Germany, and Toronto Union Station in Canada are no longer used simply by travelers passing through, but have become destinations in their own right.

***The Gare Saint-Lazare: Arrival of a Train*, 1877** Impressionist artists such as Claude Monet were captivated by the railroads, in particular the potential of depicting steam pouring out from engines.

RAILROAD SIGNAL TELEGRAPHY

The telegraph transformed railroad signaling, making it possible for train operators to send messages ahead of trains for the first time. American inventor Samuel Morse devised the earliest experimental telegraph, and the Cooke and Wheatstone needle telegraph, a later model, first entered commercial use in 1840 when it was adopted by the Great Western Railway in Britain. The system gained wider acceptance after its dramatic role in apprehending British murderer John Tawell in 1845; he had been seen boarding a train at Slough, and this information was telegraphed ahead to Paddington Station, where he was arrested. In 1844, Morse's telegraph transmitted the words "What hath God wrought" from Baltimore to Washington, DC, and brought about a revolution on the US railroads.

The needle telegraph

Inventor William Fothergill Cooke and scientist Charles Wheatstone patented their five-needle telegraph in 1837. It consisted of a receiver with needles that were moved by electromagnetic coils to point to letters on a board. Each letter was communicated via two currents flowing down two wires, causing the receiving telegraph's needles to swing to the left or right. Six letters were omitted—C, J, Q, U, X, and Z—a limitation that caused confusion when identifying the murderer Tawell (see above), who was described as wearing a "KWAKER" (Quaker) coat.

Cooke and Wheatstone five-needle telegraph (1837)

Reading the message The five-needle telegraph was popular with users as it did not require any knowledge of codes: two of the five needles pointed to one of 20 letters laid out in a diamond pattern on the receiver to spell out words. Over time, the system was simplified to two needles and then to a single needle, mainly to reduce the cost of replacing wires as they deteriorated. However, systems with fewer needles required complex codes, so telegraphy became a specialized job.

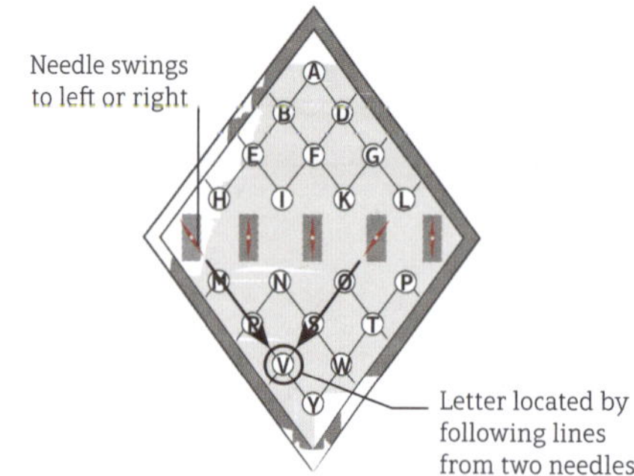

Ready repair The telegraph facilitated the communication required to keep railroads running smoothly, and ensuring that it remained in working order was essential. Here, a linesperson repairs a telegraph pole at King's Cross station, London, in 1929.

Morse's telegraph

Invented in 1835, Morse's first telegraph used a pencil point attached to an electromagnetic pendulum. His partner Alfred Vail suggested using a lever and armature to print a code of dots and dashes—the precursor to Morse code. This system, patented in 1840, was adopted in the US both for railroad signaling and general use, with lines built alongside new railroads. It was cheaper and simpler to use than the needle telegraph, especially once adapted to an audio system.

Transmission key and sounder Messages were passed from one railroad station to another using Morse code sent by key systems, such as this one.

MONOPOLIES AND RAILROAD BARONS

Early railroad entrepreneurs were innovative and visionary, but they were no strangers to unfair business practices and a certain disdain for the paying passengers.

Big money takes over (right) A cartoon from an 1882 edition of *Puck* magazine depicts Jay Gould, William Vanderbilt, and others as "robber barons" dividing up the vast profits made from the US railroads.

Builder's plate (right) Founded in 1845 by Joseph Wright in Saltley, Birmingham, UK, the Midland Railway Carriage and Wagon Builders supplied rolling stock—from wagons and carriages to locomotives—for railroads across the world.

Accustomed as we are to the notion of national railroads and large rail monopolies, it is hard to imagine today that the early railroads were made up of hundreds of small companies, each serving its own immediate area. Local entrepreneurs created these railroads, largely from a desire to improve transportation for their own goods. However, as the railroads expanded, they became more ambitious in scope, and economies of scale became evident. People found it convenient to travel long trips on one train, and it was more profitable for the companies to operate in this way. Carrying goods over a longer distance was relatively cheaper, as loading and unloading them was expensive.

Lines gradually grew longer. In Britain, the London and Birmingham Railway was one of the first railroads more than 100 miles (160 km) long and a civil-engineering project far larger than any before it. Robert Stephenson, son of George Stephenson (see pp.22–29), was appointed chief engineer in 1833 and the railroad, London's first main line, opened in 1838. Other, longer, railroads soon followed, such as the Great Western from London to Bristol, constructed by Isambard Kingdom Brunel between 1835 and 1841 at a cost of £6.5 million ($32.5 million at the time), and the London and Southampton, completed in 1840. In the United States, both the pioneering railroads—the 136-mile (219 km) Charleston and Hamburg, which opened in 1833, and the Baltimore and Ohio, whose first section ran from 1830—were ambitious projects that extended far inland from the Atlantic Coast port cities they served.

Building railroad empires

The men who managed the railroad companies were generally enterprising and progressive, and could see the benefits of far-reaching railroad networks. As the railroads became established, these men dreamed up ever-grander schemes, and railroad promoters raised finance for their construction. These longer railroads began to sprout branches, and the companies grew. Given the advantage of large networks, it was inevitable that railroad companies should come together first to provide joint

CASTLE MONOPOLY
TAX STEALS
LAND GRANTS
FRIENDLY
JUDGES
LOBBYISM
PUBLIC
CLOSED
CLOSED
MANUFACTORY CLOSED
PROTECTION
CORPORATIONS
TELEGRAPH MONOPOLY
STOCK JOBBING
CONGRESS
R. ROAD MONOPOLY
INCOME
UNJUST TAX
TAX-PAYER
HEAVILY TAXED

services. Even as they extended their reach, the railroad companies remained distinct until competition between them made the creation of monopolies attractive and they began to merge—a process that accelerated when railroads fell on hard times, and rivals took over their struggling competitors.

Railroad giants

Amalgamated railroad companies soon became the biggest enterprises in the world. In many respects, they prefigured the growth of capitalism. Before the railroads, there were no large companies in any industry, with the exception of quasi-government organizations such as the Dutch East India Company. Factories were still just small buildings where goods were made, owned by local entrepreneurs and supplying their immediate area. These firms employed local people and were part of the local community. The railroads were a totally new and different sort of enterprise. They stretched for hundreds of miles and across many different localities. Then, they demanded a new style of management with complex organizational structures. Furthermore, the companies needed bosses with vision and great ability, able to see the bigger picture as well as being industrious. The first larger-scale, amalgamated, companies emerged in Britain. These companies were powerful and self-important, as testified to by the grand stations they erected in major cities (see pp.146–151). The first mega-company to spring from the dozens of smaller railroads was the Midland Railway, facilitated by entrepreneur George Hudson (see pp.54–55). In 1844, Hudson created the Midland by amalgamating three smaller companies: the North Midland Railway,

Bustling station Large terminus stations, such as this one in Bradford (Forster Square), built by the Midland Railway, often also incorporated a goods depot and a hotel.

Royal travelers Queen Victoria and Prince Albert used the railroads to tour Britain and can be seen here with the railroad entrepreneur (and cheat) George Hudson at Cambridge in 1847.

the Midland Counties Railway, and the Birmingham and Derby Junction Railway, all of which converged at Derby. The new, combined railroad created the core of a line that ran all the way from London to York, offering a more convenient service to its passengers, with fewer changes of train. Hudson had also built the Newcastle and Darlington Junction Railway, which he now linked to the rest of his network via York so that he had control of more than 1,000 miles (1,600 km) of railroad. He continued to consolidate this network throughout the 1840s by taking over other smaller Midlands lines. In 1842, Hudson cleverly created the Railway Clearing House, an organization that enabled all the railroad companies—of which there were now more than a hundred in Britain—to collect revenues from each other when passengers used more than one company's trains on a journey. Until then, passengers had been obliged to change trains and buy a new ticket at each stage of the journey. Despite Hudson turning out to be a cheat, the ticket-sharing scheme long outlasted his downfall and the collapse of his railroad empire.

The captain of mergers

Despite the obvious advantages of amalgamation, British politicians were reluctant to let the railroads merge, fearing that monopolies would exploit the public. However, the financial weakness of some railroads forced the government to accept the idea, especially at times of economic downturn, so throughout the mid-19th century, companies continued to merge. One of the merger beneficiaries, the London and North Western Railway (LNWR), was, for a while the world's biggest company, employing 15,000 people at its peak. The LNWR was created in July 1846 by the amalgamation of the Grand Junction Railway, the London and Birmingham Railway, and the Manchester and Birmingham Railway. This created a network of 350 miles (560 km). The core route connected London with Birmingham, Crewe, Chester, Liverpool, and Manchester. Its brilliant manager, Captain Mark Huish, was a former Indian Army officer who shrewdly negotiated takeovers, managed the company in an innovative manner, and introduced novel accounting methods essential for the company's size. Although it was smaller than rivals such as the Midland, the LNWR offered the best route between London and the main towns of northwest England. Once it was in a position of strength, the LNWR bullied rivals into mergers or disadvantageous deals to run on their tracks. But the bully-boy tactics did not always work. Two small railroads that combined to run on a shorter route between Birmingham and Chester than their big rival were warned off by Huish: "I need not say if you should be unwise enough to encourage such a proceeding, it must result in a

Brass Thunderer whistle preferred by railroad guards for its loud tone

Train away! Whistles such as this c.1910 one from London and North Western Railway were a key tool for platform staff to ensure that trains were sent on their way safely and on time.

Railroad entrepreneur Swiss statesman and railroad magnate Alfred Escher lobbied for the privatization of railroads in Switzerland. He is considered the driving force behind the Gotthard line, having secured the cooperation of Germany and Italy to build this transalpine line and even presided over its construction from 1871–1878.

general fight…" To his alarm, they resisted the threat, fought a three-year battle through the courts, and, surprisingly, won. However, this was an exception. For the most part, the big bullies effectively quashed their smaller rivals.

Monopolies in Europe

In continental Europe, major networks were created from the plethora of companies that had started running rail services. In France, six big regional companies were formed between 1858 and 1862 with government support. The most ambitious, the Paris–Lyon–Méditerranée (PLM), soon extended into Switzerland and Italy, creating an international network. The Rothschild banking family owned the PLM, along with a second French company, the Nord, and it looked as if the Rothschilds would become the dominant force in European railroads. They also controlled the Austrian Südbahn, including the Semmering Railway (see pp.98–103), and had concessions on various Italian lines. After unification, however, Italy prevented them from expanding their empire. Instead, four big Italian companies were formed, but the poverty of the country and its difficult terrain, with the Apennines running down its spine, made it hard to make a profit. Italy suffered a railroad crisis every few years and, unwilling to allow foreign takeovers, in 1905 became one of the first nations to nationalize its railroad system. In the early days of Swiss rail, meanwhile, the plutocrat Alfred Escher (see p.55) oversaw the explosion in rail construction from the 1850s and became so powerful that he was nicknamed "King Alfred."

The "Big Seven"

The American railroads soon eclipsed all others in scale. The distances to be covered were huge, so big companies such as the Erie Railroad and the Pennsylvania Railroad emerged early in railroad history. When the first transcontinental was completed in 1869 (see pp.114–121), the Union Pacific and Central Pacific railroads became the railroad giants. After them, a series of American railroads earned that accolade as railroad barons consolidated the network.

By 1900, seven companies controlled most of the US railroads. Many of their proprietors became infamous, among them Jay Gould and his son George, J. P. Morgan, Edward Harriman, and the Vanderbilts. William, the younger Vanderbilt, showed off the attitude of the new railroad barons to their passengers when asked why a popular fast train was no longer operating: "The public be damned! … I don't take any stock in this silly nonsense about working for anybody but our own," he is alleged to have replied. Daniel Drew, one of these "robber barons"—a term applied by *Atlantic Monthly* in 1870 to the new breed of capitalists—was also one of the biggest rogues. As the Erie's company treasurer, he agreed several times for the company to borrow money against newly issued shares, and then used his position to profit from selling these shares.

> **"We hear now on all sides the term 'Robber Barons' applied to some of the great capitalists."**
>
> *ATLANTIC MONTHLY*, 1870

One of the most successful of these barons, J. P. Morgan forged a railroad empire by taking over ailing companies and reorganizing them. Unlike Drew, he actually improved his railroads. So too did Edward Harriman, known as the "greatest rail baron in America." He made money on the stock exchange and invested in railroads. He boosted his assets by purchasing rolling stock, improving tracks, and establishing good management. His first major acquisition was the Illinois Central Railroad. After the Panic of 1893—the last of a series of major 19th-century recessions caused by boom and bust in the business cycle—he added the massive Union Pacific to his set. Harriman made it profitable by straightening out bends in the track—many of which had been added by the builders to take advantage of government subsidies—and reducing gradients. By the turn of the century, Harriman controlled more track than any individual in the history of US railroads.

End of the track

The advent of the automobile brought about the decline of the railroads, and empires were broken up or bailed out by the government. In the US, one last pair of barons emerged in the 1920s: the Van Sweringens. The reclusive brothers were property developers who bought a railroad for its development potential and ended up with an empire that included the Erie, the Chesapeake, and Ohio Railroads, and the Pere Marquette Railroad. Following the 1929 crash, their empire fell apart faster than they had built it up. With their demise, the era of the railroad barons came to an end.

Railroads everywhere
The extent of the US railroad network, which eventually reached over 250,000 route miles (402,336 route km), is well illustrated by this busy scene in the small junction town of Hornellsville in western New York State in 1876.

BUILDING BRIDGES

As the railroads expanded, railroad bridges were erected to enable lines to follow the most direct routes possible. Engineers devised a range of architectural and engineering strategies for overcoming the obstacles of local geography—from vaulting brick viaducts spanning valley floors to iron suspension bridges that dangled tracks above rivers and gorges. Concrete and steel are now the materials of choice, but the ingenuity of modern designs is no less impressive than the elegant blends of function and form deployed by the early railroad builders.

The Tangiwai disaster

New Zealand's worst-ever rail bridge disaster occurred on Christmas Eve, 1953, when 151 lives were lost in the catastrophic failure of the Whangaehu River bridge near Tangiwai, in the center of the North Island. A mudflow from a nearby volcano weakened the supporting pier of the beam bridge (see opposite), which gave way under the weight of an express train.

Wreckage of railroad carriages on the banks of Whangaehu River

Railroad trestle bridge Despite their rickety appearance, trestles were an incredibly safe method of fording rivers and valleys. The bridge pictured here was used to haul timber to a nearby lumber mill in Minnesota.

Types of bridges

Different types of railroad bridges have been developed to meet geographical and economic constraints. While there are multiple variations on—and combinations of—each design, the basic types of bridges can be grouped into four categories: beam, arch, cantilever, and suspension.

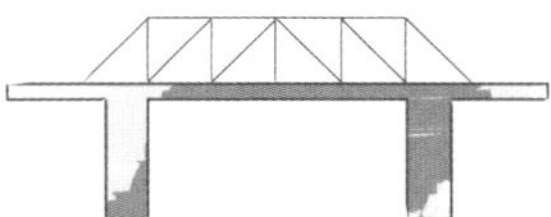

Through-truss beam

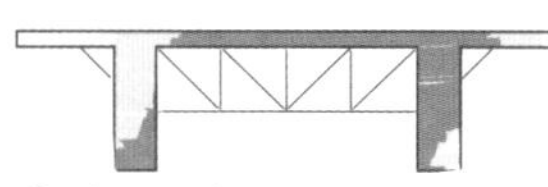

Deck-truss beam

Beam bridge

The simplest of all bridges, a beam bridge, consists of a "beam" or girder laid across a gap, supported at each end by piers and often strengthened by a truss. A through-truss design uses iron or steel struts joined together in triangular sections to form the load-bearing superstructure, which carries the railroad track beneath. A deck truss uses the same arrangement of struts but supports the beam from below.

Through-arch

Arch bridge

A classic arch bridge supports the railroad from below, but in the more sophisticated through-arch design, the top of the arch rises above the deck, suspending the railroad from vertical cables or struts.

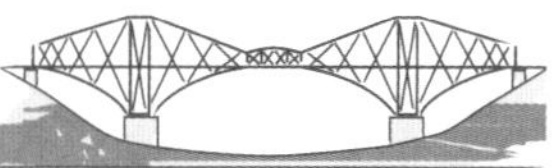

Cantilever

Cantilever bridge

Built from sections that are supported at one end only, cantilever bridges have the advantage of not needing "falsework" (temporary supports) in construction, so are ideal for wide crossings.

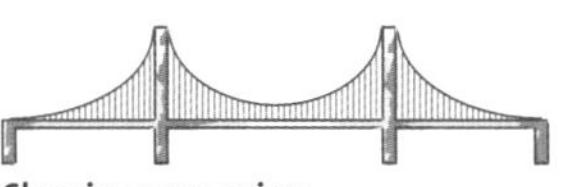

Classic suspension

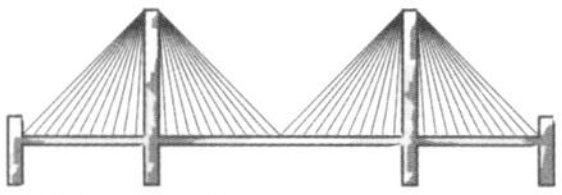

Cable-stayed suspension

Suspension bridge

Well-suited to long crossings in exposed, windy locations, suspension bridges make use of cables to support the deck. The classic design stretches a cable laterally between one or more towers, with vertical suspension cables to support the deck. A cable-stayed bridge suspends the deck directly from one or more towers via a series of angled suspension cables.

THE PULLMAN PHENOMENON

The Pullman Car transformed train travel, introducing a level of luxury and comfort not seen before.

The name of engineer George Pullman is still used to refer to the sleeping carriage he developed for rail passengers. He was the American "genius of the bed on wheels," who destroyed all his competitors to establish a monopoly in the United States by the end of the 19th century. As with many such legends, the original idea was not his, but Pullman made it his own.

The first sleeping carriages were developed in the US, where travel times were longer and trains slower because of the sharper curves and steeper gradients of the tracks. At first, trains simply stopped for the night and passengers stayed in local hotels and inns, which was unsatisfactory and inefficient. The first sleeping carriage, introduced on the Cumberland Valley Railroad in Pennsylvania in 1839, did not afford a comfortable night's sleep. The sleeping accommodations consisted of a couple of carriages, each with four sets of three-tiered berths. They were no more than hard upholstered boards, which were then folded away during the day.

A few years later, the New York and Erie Railroad devised an equally uncomfortable solution. Two carriages, known as "diamond cars" for the shape of their windows, were equipped with iron rods that could be used to link facing seats to create a basic bed. The cushions were made of horsehair cloth that penetrated all but the thickest clothing and were invariably infested with a variety of insects. As if that were not bad enough, the condition of the track, with its short, badly laid rails, made the experience akin to "sleeping on a runaway train," according to one early passenger.

Rise of the sleeper carriage

By the 1850s, several railroads advertised improved sleeping accommodations based on an idea by Webster Wagner, an employee for the New York Central.

Luxury on wheels George Pullman's trains had excellent facilities for both night and day travel. This 1876 engraving shows the luxurious interior of a Pullman parlor car on the Pennsylvania Railroad between New York and Philadelphia.

Sleeping on the train The long distances needed to travel across America led to the development of sleeping cars. The sleeping car pictured here is by the Cumberland Valley Railroad, the first company to provide this facility.

He went on to found the Wagner Palace Car Company, a rival to Pullman. Wagner developed the idea of a coach with a single tier of berths and bedding closets at each end. Several other competitors emerged, building sleeping carriages to a variety of designs. But it was Pullman who transformed nighttime train travel, making it comfortable and respectable.

Pullman had already achieved success in the business of moving houses, quite literally. Several low-lying houses in New York State were in the way of a planned extension to the Erie Canal, so Pullman, along with his father, contrived to move them to higher ground by putting them on dozens of wheels. Pullman then moved to Chicago, where he started a railcar business in 1858, building two carriages for the Chicago and Alton Railroad that provided upper and lower sleeping berths.

The radical aspect of Pullman's design was that the upper berth was suspended from the ceiling by ropes and pulleys. When not in use, it could be hauled up to the ceiling, leaving plenty of seating space during the day. Curtains around the berths created privacy, but these carriages were still crude affairs. Candles for lighting and a wood stove for heat were a fire risk given the large number of curtains. Each carriage accommodated 20 people, but while both blankets and pillows were provided, sheets had to be brought by the passengers. Soon the carriages plying between Bloomington, Illinois, and Chicago, filled up every night. The only problem was dirty footwear. The conductors had to convince the passengers to take off their boots at night so that they didn't soil or damage the bedding. There was a great reluctance to do so, presumably because of fear of theft, so for many years every Pullman carriage carried notices politely requesting, "Please take off your boots before retiring."

Hotel on wheels

In 1861, in association with local authorities, Pullman supervised the raising of many Chicago buildings in an attempt to

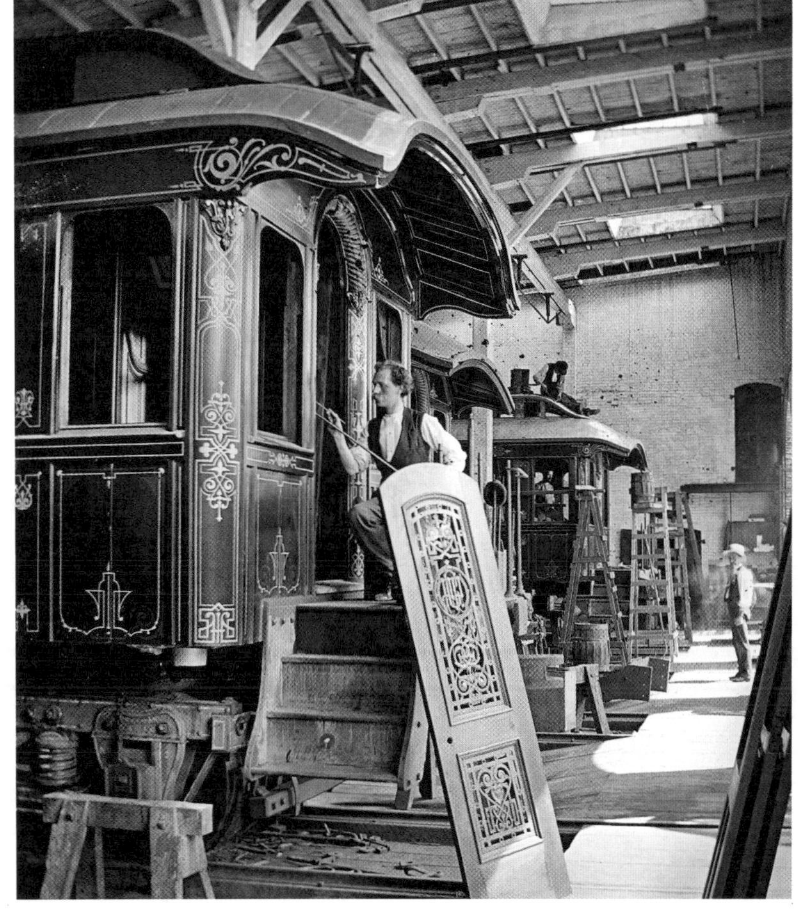

Service and repair Pullman cars were built and maintained to the highest standards to ensure passengers traveled in the best possible accommodations. The exterior of train cars were hand-painted in the Pullman Detroit Shops.

"It is considered tolerable that (women) should lie with the legs of a strange, disrobing man dangling within a foot of their noses."

KARL BAEDECKER, GUIDEBOOK AUTHOR, DESCRIBING PULLMAN'S COACHES improve the city's street sewerage system. His most spectacular feat was saving the four-story Tremont House Hotel, the tallest building in Chicago at the time. The hotel was in line for demolition, but Pullman devised a clever plan to save it. He put the whole building on 5,000 jacks, then a team of 1,200 workers turned the screws 180° each time Pullman gave the signal. They successfully raised the hotel by 6 ft (1.8 m), while the house band inside continued playing and the hotel guests continued eating their lunch.

Perhaps this inspired Pullman to create a moving hotel for rail passengers. In 1863, he set about building what he claimed would be the finest and most luxurious sleeping carriage ever, in a bid to attract the rich and famous. His new carriage, called the *Pioneer*, cost $20,000 to build, perhaps four times the cost of any other railroad vehicle at the time. Mary Todd Lincoln, the First Lady, saw it on a visit in early 1865 and was enchanted by the style and elegance of the luxurious train, with its hand-carved seats and panels and thick pile carpet. When she was called upon to organize the funeral of her assassinated husband a few months later, she recalled the vehicle, and it was used as the hearse for the funeral procession along the Chicago and Alton Railroad.

Pullman day coach The classical furniture and fittings of a Pullman car interior lent an air of solidity and comfort to affluent passengers during their travels.

Collaboration with other railroads

Soon Pullman began building vehicles for other railroad companies. Before long, many other railroad companies, such as the Michigan Central, the Burlington, and the Great Western, were attaching luxurious Pullman carriages to their trains. Pullman's company also sold the tickets for the berths, which cost 50 cents more than the railroad's own sleeping accommodations. Passengers were carried in comfort in Pullman sleepers to almost every part of the US. The carriages were all built to the same design, equipped for both day and night travel, and served by Pullman's employees. It was a great business model and highly profitable as Pullman did not have to pay any of the costs of hauling the trains or using the tracks. Oddly, despite the luxurious surroundings, the Pullman carriages were inferior to those in Europe in one key respect: they did not provide the same level of privacy. Pullman's design

Dining in style Pullman trains were advertised as the epitome of comfortable travel, with dining cars offering the same level of service as a restaurant.

was open plan, with makeshift folding seats, pull-down berths, only curtains for privacy, and nothing to stop a loud snorer from keeping the whole carriage awake. In Europe, compartments were retained, containing up to six beds on three levels, although a few open-plan carriages were introduced for third-class passengers, notably on the Trans-Siberian Railway (see pp.170–179). The open-plan design survived in the US until the second half of the 20th century and can be seen in several famous movie scenes, notably the Billy Wilder classic comedy *Some Like It Hot*, starring Marilyn Monroe. Although the carriages were popular, some commentators disapproved of such close-quarters living arrangements.

Dining aboard a Pullman

In 1867, Pullman developed a combination sleeping-and-eating car, with a kitchen at one end and removable tables set between the seats at mealtimes. Although this was not the first time that meals had been provided on board trains, the quality was undoubtedly superior to anything that had gone before. Sugar-cured ham was 40 cents; a Welsh rarebit, 50 cents; and steak with potatoes, 60 cents—cheap even at the time. Pullman was a great publicist and introduced his first hotel carriage on a trip around the eastern US from New York to Chicago that took seven days. Next, he put self-contained dining cars on trains. The first was called *Delmonico*, after an eminent restaurateur of that name. Pullman tried it out on the Chicago and Alton, his home railroad on which he always tested his ideas. It was another great success, and Pullman subsequently both built dining carriages for other railroads and operated them himself on some lines. The selection of meals on the best trains was sumptuous.

Life as a Pullman attendant

While Pullman's customers greatly enjoyed the quality of service, it was a terrible idea to die on one of his trains. Pullman ruled that if a passenger passed away, the corpse had to be put off at the next station, regardless of whether the town had an undertaker, leaving the traveling companions of the deceased to deal with the situation. Fortunately, most of the attendants were more compassionate than Pullman and would ensure the body was dispatched at one of the larger towns, where funeral facilities were more likely to be available.

Later, Pullman devised simpler carriages, which were cheaper but still clean and comfortable with good service. Whatever the level of luxury, the attendants (called porters) were always Black and male, and all known as "George." At first, they were not paid and relied on tips to earn a living. Although this changed later, tips remained a key part of their wages. To make it even harder, Pullman sent inspectors incognito, to ensure that the attendants carried out their tasks properly. These inspectors would "mislay" jewelry, and the female ones would even make romantic overtures to tempt the attendants into breaking the rules. Attendants who failed to respond appropriately were sacked instantly. Despite the many indignities, being an attendant was stable and reasonably well-paid work, so was much sought-after.

The Pullman legacy

By the early 1870s, Pullman had become, according to one railroad historian, "the foremost industrial name in the United

Devastating strike Pullman's anti-trade union stance and an attempt to cut workers' wages led to a devastating strike, which spread to other rail companies. On July 6, 1894, rioting workers set fire to 600 freight cars at the Panhandle Chicago yard.

The hotel carriages on the Chicago–Omaha service in the 1870s offered a choice of 15 seafood and fish dishes, together with 37 meat courses, including a huge variety of game

States." He was to remain so for more than 20 years. Pullmans were introduced in Europe and Asia, too, but it was the dining-carriage concept that really caught on. Pullman's influence spread outside the US, though railroad companies tended to provide their own sleeping carriages or use those of Pullman's rival. Pullman carriages also spawned the trend for luxury that was continued by the Palace on Wheels in India, the Blue Train in Africa, and most famously the Orient Express (see pp.180–185).

The Pullman name lives on in the town he built east of Chicago to house the workers at his factory. The factory is long abandoned but the houses survive. The housing, however, was a source of friction between Pullman and his employees. When the economic panic of 1893 reduced demand for new carriages, Pullman announced redundancies in the factory but refused to reduce the rents on the houses he provided for them. A bitter strike ensued and spread across the country after 250,000 rail workers joined the action in sympathy. Violence broke out in several cities across the US and while the strike eventually collapsed, it left a long and bitter legacy. Pullman's reputation was so tarnished among workers that when he died, his family arranged for his remains to be placed in a lead-lined mahogany coffin, which was then sealed inside a block of concrete for fear that it would be dug up by angry trade unionists. This extreme measure underscores the severe consequences of his labor policies, despite his company's role in providing services on trains.

COMPAGNIE
INTERNATIONALE
DES
OITURE-LITS
44

Linking Europe and Asia The Orient Express, launched in 1883, ran the length of continental Europe, linking Paris and Istanbul with a luxury sleeper service.

Railroads come of age

By the last quarter of the 19th century, the iron road had become so profitable that many railroad companies were using their profits to create new lines. It was an adventurous period that saw the construction of many extraordinary railroads, including the Trans-Siberian—a 5,771-mile (9,288 km) line between Moscow and Vladivostok, which remains the longest railroad in the world.

Railroad technology was now tried and true, and promoters were driving it to its limits. In South America, several lines were built through the Andes to help exploit the region's mineral wealth—becoming not only the highest railroad lines in the world at the time but also the most spectacular, cutting through mountains and running along perilous cliffs and precipices. In India, the British desire for a cooler climate in summer led to the construction of a series of narrow-gauge hill railroads that climbed slowly but surely up the steep inclines far quicker than the road traffic ever had. One of the most ambitious ideas was to run a railroad line across the whole of Africa, from Cape Town to Cairo. Cecil Rhodes, the prime minister of Cape Colony (in what is today South Africa), had hoped to link the whole continent by a railroad that traveled through only British colonies but was stymied by difficulties with construction, lack of finance, and the unwillingness of the British government to support the scheme.

It was also a time in which services were greatly improved to encourage passengers (particularly the wealthy) to use the trains. The most notable luxury service was the Orient Express, which crossed the whole of Europe from Paris to Constantinople (now called Istanbul). In the US, competition between railroads led to the launch of rival services between New York and Chicago, offering the red-carpet treatment to their passengers. And farther south, in Florida, the "overseas express" to Key West—one of the most astonishing railroads ever built—was completed by Henry Flagler. It was an exciting time for planners and passengers alike.

THE TRANS-SIBERIAN RAILWAY

One of the most famous and ambitious railroad networks in the world, the Trans-Siberian is a symbol of Russia's objective of modernizing its infrastructure and strengthening its military and economic connections across its vast territory.

When Princess Maria Volkonsky sped across Russia from Moscow to join her husband in exile in 1827, it took 23 days before she saw the churches of Irkutsk, the capital of eastern Siberia, looming out of the snowy atmosphere. That was extremely fast by contemporary standards, and she had traveled night and day on the trans-Siberian Trakt—a crude road that was easier to travel in winter.

Siberia had long been equated with exile. It was a distant part of Russia, a huge region encompassing all Russia east of the Ural mountains. A spartan land, its sparse population was concentrated on a few river and road arteries, and was mostly employed to maintain the Trakt or protect the territory. They were supplemented by two types of exiles: people convicted of crimes sent to Siberia as an alternative to prison or execution; and political exiles like Prince Sergei Volkonsky, Maria's husband, who had been involved in a failed coup attempt in December 1825.

In the early 19th century, it could take up to nine months to travel from Moscow to Irkutsk by road

Need of the hour

The terrible transportation situation between Siberia and European Russia provided the impetus to build the Trans-Siberian Railway, which was by far the most ambitious railroad project ever attempted. Russia had first established a base on the Pacific as early as the 17th century, but its control of the land between the Urals and the ocean was maintained only tenuously. Indeed, Russia's ability to retain its vast Eastern territory began to look even more fragile in the mid-19th century, as the development of efficient steamships in the 1840s and the completion of the Suez Canal

in 1869 made it easier for its European rivals—France, Britain, and Prussia—to access the Pacific. The completion of the first American transcontinental railroad, also in that year, followed in 1885 by its Canadian equivalent, raised fears among the Russian elite that an invasion from the East was imminent.

There had been discussions about a possible trans-Siberian line as early as in the 1850s, and a succession of plans and projects were presented to the Russian government over the following decades. Some of the tales of these schemes may have lost accuracy in the telling. A favorite is the idea that a British gentleman going by the name of Mr. Dull was the first to suggest a trans-Siberian railroad. The truth is more prosaic, or, rather, duller. The individual was, in fact, Thomas Duff, an adventurer who went to China and returned to St. Petersburg in 1857, where he knocked on the door of the transportation minister, Constantine Chevkin, and suggested the construction of a "tramway" from Nizhny Novgorod, 265 miles (426 km) east of Moscow, to the Urals. The line would be horse-drawn, and

The trans-Siberian Trakt
Before the Trans-Siberian Railway, the main route through Siberia was a primitive road known as the Trakt, seen here as it reached the outskirts of Irkutsk.

The tea route Beginning in the 17th century, tea was transported from China to Europe via Siberia and the railroad would expand and strengthen this trade route. Here, tea sellers can be seen lining up to buy tea in the Transbaikalia region.

some of the four million wild horses that roamed western Siberia could be enlisted to provide the traction. Duff was quietly shown the door, as was a succession of both Russian and foreign entrepreneurs. Even Nikolay Muravyov-Amursky, the governor-general of eastern Siberia, who had managed to establish Russia's control over previously disputed territory and who wanted to build a line connecting the Pacific Ocean with the Siberian interior, had no better luck than Duff. Neither did three English adventurers (about whom little is known except that they were called Sleigh, Horn, and Morrison), nor Peter Collins, an adventurer from New York, who was reportedly the first American to cross the entire breadth of Siberia. Collins also suggested a line in eastern Siberia, from Chita, 250 miles (400 km) east of Lake Baikal, to the navigable section of the Amur River, which flows into the Pacific.

Despite rejecting all these suggestions, controversy raged within the Russian government throughout this period about the need for a trans-Siberian line. While there were many reasons not to build the line—such as the expense and the technical difficulties of creating a railroad 5,750 miles (9,256 km) long between Moscow and Vladivostok—the supporters of the project eventually won the argument on both military and nationalistic grounds. The military motives for the line were both defensive and offensive. It would not only allow a much quicker response to any attack on Vladivostok, but it would also make

> **"Unite the rich yields of Siberian nature with the network of Russian railroads."**
>
> CZAR ALEXANDER III'S INSTRUCTION TO HIS SON, NICHOLAS ALEXANDROVICH

it easier for Russia to establish control over its vast, but at the time very weak, southern neighbor, China.

Early beginnings

In 1886, the czarist government, despite being ruled by the very conservative Alexander III, took the radical step of deciding to build the line. The immediate catalyst for the decision seems to have been a fear that large numbers of Chinese were infiltrating Transbaikalia, the region around Lake Baikal. In fact, this had little basis in reality, but somehow it was the crucial trigger point that finally made the government decide to give the go-ahead to the plan.

Finding the money and getting the unwieldy Russian government behind the railroad delayed the start of construction for five years. Finally, however, the czar sent his son, the future Nicholas II, to Vladivostok, where on May 31, 1891, he wielded a shovel to fill a wheelbarrow with clay soil, which he emptied onto an embankment of what would become the Ussuri line. However, there was still no agreement on how to complete the work, or how it could be funded. What the project needed was someone with vision and drive. That person was Sergei Witte, and he was briefly transportation minister in the Russian government, but was finance minister by August 1892. Normally such posts were held by people of limited vision, with an interest only in keeping the purse strings tight—not so with Witte. A math graduate, he both managed the country's finances with acumen and ensured that there were plenty of funds for work on the Trans-Siberian Railway.

Born in the Georgian capital, Tblisi, Witte came from a minor aristocratic family that had fallen on hard times, and he had to work as a railroad clerk—a very lowly task for a man of his birth and ambition. His ability was soon recognized, however, and he was swiftly promoted to manage a railroad company, and then obtained a senior government post in St. Petersburg. When he became finance minister, work on the railroad had come to a halt due to a famine in the Volga region and lack of funds. Witte's masterstroke was to create a Committee for the Siberian Railway, headed by the young Czarevitch (heir to the Russian throne) Nicholas, which effectively guaranteed that the project would enjoy the continued support of the monarch. Witte thus became the father of the Russian railroad. He took a constant interest in its progress, ensured that money was available, fought off any resistance

Developmental agenda Czar Alexander III, the second last Russian czar, gave the go ahead for the construction of the Trans-Siberian Railway, hoping that it would cement the nation's hold over its vast eastern lands.

Memorabilia The Trans-Siberian Railway was depicted as a source of pride in many artworks, such as this memento, which Czar Nicholas II presented to his wife, Alexandra Feodorovna, in 1900.

Silver egg bearing an engraving of the Trans-Siberian Railway route

Across the water Crossing the vast rivers running through Siberia was the most difficult task for the builders of the Trans-Siberian Railway. This metal-truss railroad bridge that runs across the Kama River near Perm, was constructed between 1905 and 1915.

to the project within government, and appeased the Chinese, who were highly suspicious that the line would be used against them.

Unprecedented challenges

The difficulties facing the railroad's builders can hardly be exaggerated. Although the terrain the line had to cross was not as difficult as the Alps (see pp.98–103) or the Andes (see pp.186–191), nor as barren as the American deserts (see pp.32–39), the sheer length, the extreme temperatures, and the absence of a local labor force made the railroad's construction an unprecedented challenge. To illustrate the scale of the task, the 5,750-mile (9,250 km) route was 2,000 miles (3,200 km) longer than the Canadian transcontinental—and the US equivalent was not only shorter overall; it required only 1,750 miles (2,800 km) of new track, since a great deal of railroad had already been laid in the east. By contrast, Russia's railroads at the time reached only as far as the Urals, and so the Trans-Siberian Railway needed an entire 4,500 miles (7,240 km) of new track.

> **"We must give the country such industrial perfection as has been reached by the United States of America."**
>
> SERGEI WITTE, FINANCE MINISTER IN A MEMO TO CZAR NICHOLAS II, 1899

Although there were no enormous mountain ranges in the way—the Urals and the Siberian ranges were relatively easy to get through—there was no shortage of other difficulties. In the vast steppe, neither stone for ballast nor wood for sleepers could be sourced locally, so materials had to be brought from afar, mostly by river. The rails, too, had to be transported from factories in the Urals and eastern Russia, as did the steel for the bridges, which had to ford the massive Siberian rivers. Then, two-thirds of the way from Moscow, was the biggest obstacle of all—Lake Baikal, Russia's biggest lake by volume and the deepest in the world. The northern shore was too much of a detour and the southern one was lined with steep cliffs right to the water's edge, which meant that a shelf for the railroad had to be blown out of the stone.

Construction begins

Time was at a premium, with the czar intent on seeing the project completed within a decade. As a result, the surveys of the route were cursory, carried out only on a narrow belt that had been drawn thousands of miles away by St. Petersburg bureaucrats who had never been to Siberia and had only inaccurate maps. The ethos behind the construction was to "muddle through," since it was reckoned that building the perfect railroad would simply take too long. That strategy worked well in terms of ensuring that the job was done on time, but the result was a very basic track that could carry only a handful of trains per day and was dogged with technical problems in its early years.

For construction purposes, the railroad was divided into three main sections, each of around 1,500 miles (2,400 km)—

the western, the mid-Siberian, and the far eastern—and it was the latter where most difficulties were encountered. Work started first on the western section in 1891, from Chelyabinsk, the easternmost point of the existing railroad, and the main difficulty was a lack of local workers. It was estimated that some 80,000 people would be needed to build the first two sections, so workers were recruited not only from western Russia but as far afield as Persia, Türkiye, and even Italy. The work was onerous, but well paid—agricultural workers could get far more than they did on the fields, but even then they would often return to their villages at harvest time to help their relatives. Oddly enough, the main shortage of material on this section was wood—the local timber was deemed unsuitable—and supplies had to be brought in from western Russia.

Labor shortage

Construction on the mid-Siberian track began in 1893, and the labor shortage was so acute that it proved necessary to call on an obvious local source of workers—people convicted of crimes who had been exiled to Siberia. This proved to be an excellent decision, for they were eager workers, not least because a year of their sentence was remitted for every eight months they worked on the railroad, and they had access to tobacco and even occasionally alcohol in the work camps. Conditions were harsh for the workers, but they were generally better than those of other 19th-century railroad projects—largely because workers were in short supply and their employers had to keep them happy and, indeed, alive. In the summer months, between May and August, the hours were long, with men being expected to work from 5 a.m. to 7:30 p.m., broken only by a lengthy lunch period of an hour and a half. In the winter, work was confined to the daylight hours, but since the line was quite far south—roughly on the same latitude as London, Berlin, and Prague—this still meant a seven- or eight-hour day in midwinter. The work was

Careful construction Here, workers can be seen laying track in the Krasnoyarsk region, where progress was relatively rapid, thanks to the flat terrain. Supplies would be delivered along the newly built tracks.

Crossing Lake Baikal Before the completion of the line around Lake Baikal, two icebreaking ships were imported from the UK to ferry trains across the frozen lake. From 1900 to 1904, the *Baikal* and its backup *Angara* linked the two sections of the line on either bank of the lake.

dangerous, too. The death rate was calculated at around 2 percent, which was less than on other projects such as the Panama railroad (see pp.106–113) and the never-completed Cape to Cairo railroad (see pp.202–209), but it is still shocking by today's standards. The most perilous work was constructing the major bridges, particularly in winter, when men had to perch high above the rivers with no safety equipment and were dangerously exposed to the elements. Often men became so cold that they fell unconscious and plunged to their deaths in the icy waters.

The two western sections were completed by 1899, enabling trains to reach Irkutsk, but the eastern section proved more difficult. Witte agreed to a fateful change in plan—to run the eastern section through Manchuria, part of China, rather than building the planned Amur Railway, which would have kept it throughout on Russian soil (the Amur line was eventually built between 1907 and 1916). The Manchurian route was shorter, but it was dangerous politically. Although the Chinese government acquiesced to the arrangement, the railroad would prove politically troublesome and eventually lead to the Russo-Japanese war, which broke out in 1904, soon after the completion of the line.

Nearing completion

After the opening of the Chinese Eastern Railway in November 1901, there was still one section left to be built. This was the 110-mile (180 km) long Circum-Baikal Railway, along the southern shore of Lake Baikal, which proved to be the hardest section to build. Work did not start until

Russo-Japanese war The construction of the Trans-Siberian Railway facilitated Russia's occupation of Manchuria, which ultimately prompted Japan's successful attack on Russia in 1904–1905.

1895 and, because of the need to create a shelf alongside the cliffs, it did not finish until 1905. Until then, passengers traveling east of Irkutsk had to take a train ferry across the lake in summer, or a sleigh over it in winter. In fact, it was not until 1916—when the Amur Railway, which required the erection of the longest bridge on the line at Khabarovsk, was completed—that the whole trip from Moscow to Vladivostok could be undertaken entirely by train on Russian soil.

Shaping history

Even the most optimistic promoters of the railroad could not have anticipated the impact that it would have on Siberian—and indeed Russian—history, and it has not all been good. Not only was the line the catalyst for the Russo-Japanese war, but it played a key role in several other conflicts, most notably two world wars. Also, the czarist regime that created it paid a heavy price. By concentrating so many of its limited resources on the project, the government neglected other areas of spending, and this imbalance helped trigger a failed revolution in 1905 and then a successful one that led to the overthrow of the monarchy in 1917. This also led to the execution of Nicholas II and his family at Ekaterinburg, which, ironically, is one of the main stations on the western section of the line. Nevertheless, the project must be counted as a success, despite its cost, and the sometimes unusual conditions endured by its early passengers (see p.138). The Trans-Siberian remains the main artery between Siberia and the rest of Russia. It is a double-track, electrified line and is heavily used by both freight and passenger trains. It remains the longest railroad in the world, and arguably the most important.

Around the lake The Circum-Baikal Railway skirts Lake Baikal. Given its proximity to the icy lake and the rocky terrain of the shoreline, most of the route is laid out in tunnels and platforms carved out of the rock. Today, however, the main Trans-Siberian line follows a route through the hills, farther from the lake.

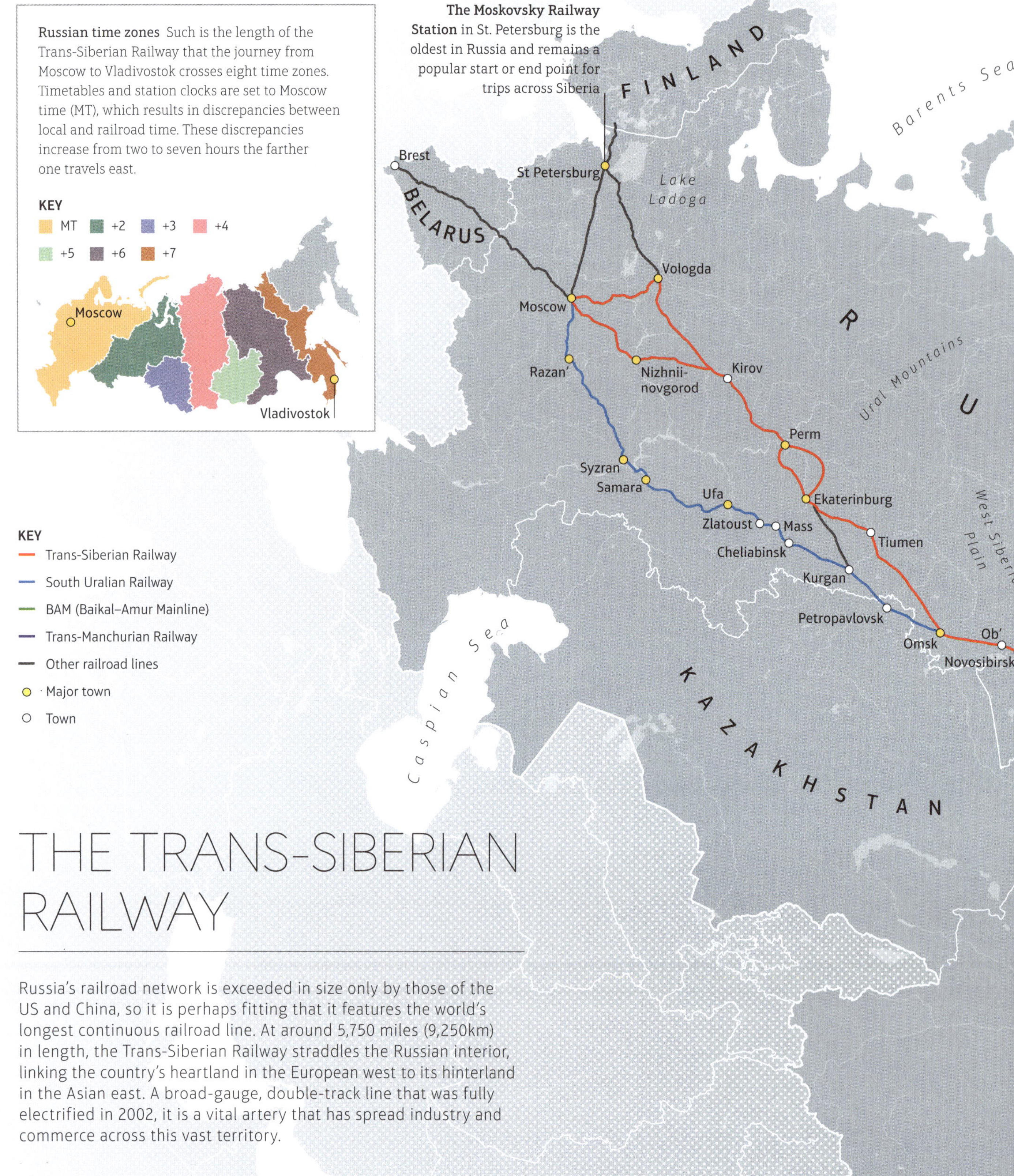

THE TRANS-SIBERIAN RAILWAY

Russia's railroad network is exceeded in size only by those of the US and China, so it is perhaps fitting that it features the world's longest continuous railroad line. At around 5,750 miles (9,250km) in length, the Trans-Siberian Railway straddles the Russian interior, linking the country's heartland in the European west to its hinterland in the Asian east. A broad-gauge, double-track line that was fully electrified in 2002, it is a vital artery that has spread industry and commerce across this vast territory.

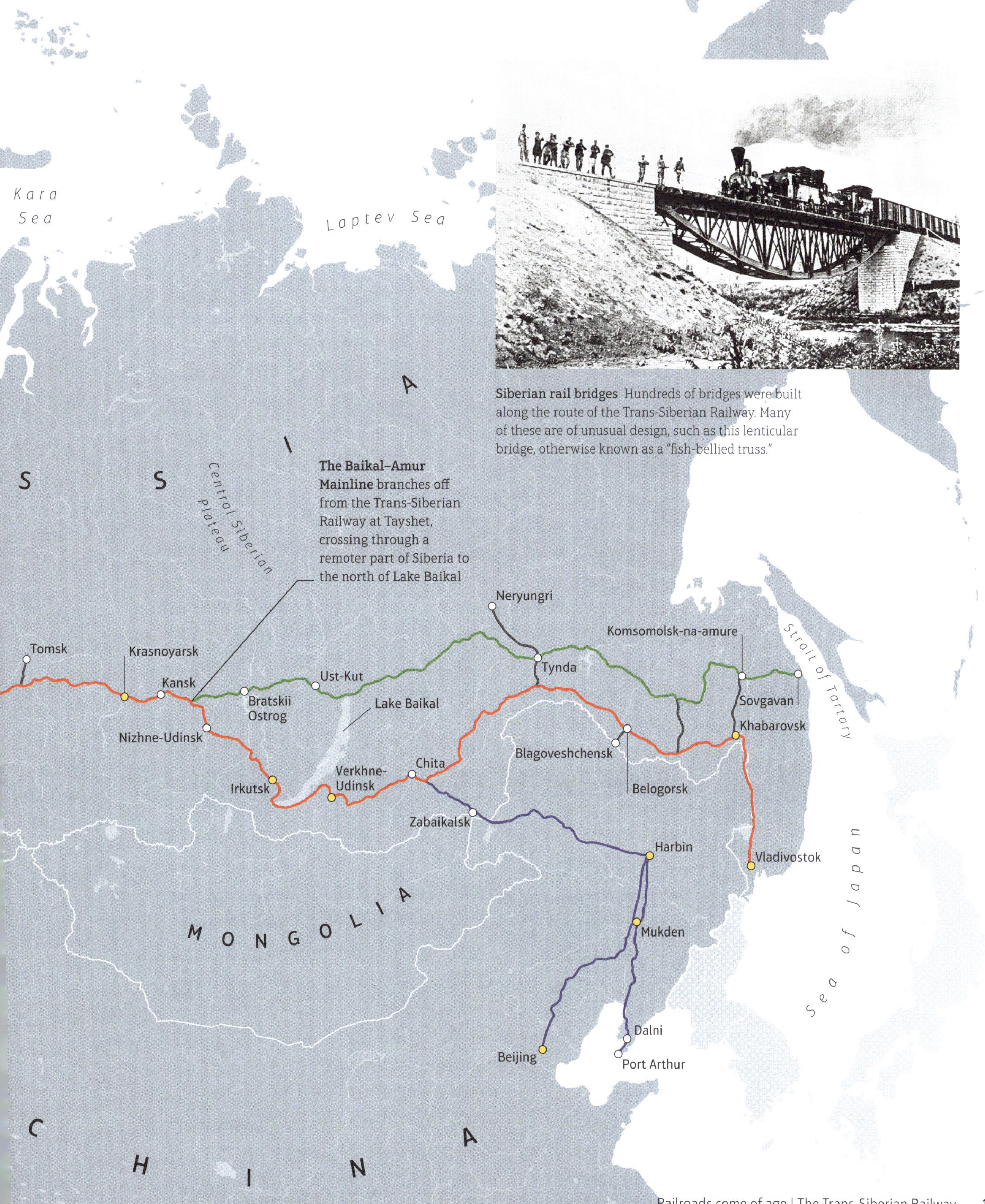

The Baikal–Amur Mainline branches off from the Trans-Siberian Railway at Tayshet, crossing through a remoter part of Siberia to the north of Lake Baikal

Siberian rail bridges Hundreds of bridges were built along the route of the Trans-Siberian Railway. Many of these are of unusual design, such as this lenticular bridge, otherwise known as a "fish-bellied truss."

THE ORIENT EXPRESS

The Orient Express was the most exciting and exotic train service in the world, crossing the whole of Europe and entering territories that were little known to Western Europeans.

While there never was a murder on the Orient Express like that described in Agatha Christie's novel, there is no doubt she chose a fitting setting for her classic whodunit. Indeed, the service was one of the wonders of the age, and like so many railroad innovations, it owed its existence to the tireless efforts of one individual, in this case, the Belgian engineer Georges Nagelmackers. Nagelmackers was the founder of the Compagnie Internationale des Wagons-Lits, a popular service that offered compartments instead of the open-plan carriages of Pullman's sleeping cars (see pp.162–167). However, Nagelmackers' real genius lay not in the trains he built but in the routes he established. He wanted a Europe *sans frontières*, one that travelers could cross quickly and in style in his well-appointed trains. To that end, in 1870, he created a service that ran from Ostend, on the North Sea coast of his native Belgium, more than 1,000 miles (1,600 km) south to Brindisi, on the tip of the Italian heel. The venture proved successful, and with the East and the Balkans opening up as the Ottoman Empire declined, he saw that a service linking Europe and Asia would also be profitable. So he began work on his Orient Express—a roughly 1,864-mile (3,000 km) passage from Paris to Constantinople (now Istanbul), bridging east and west and crossing six countries en route.

Mitigating challenges

Dealing with the railroads of six diverse nations was no easy task, and Nagelmackers had to use all his skills as a negotiator to solve a whole range of problems. Most importantly, he had to ensure that each country had locomotives that could haul his trains and that the tracks were of standard gauge (see p.88). Other issues included the width of the route's tunnels, and arcane matters such as the security of wine lockers. He was also a great publicist and generated huge interest in his venture, not least because the route passed through the Balkans, an area that was still recovering from numerous wars, having struggled for independence from both the Ottoman and Austro-Hungarian empires.

Fit for royalty

In readiness for its first outing, Nagelmackers had created a train that *The Times* correspondent Henri Opper de Blowitz described as having a level "of comfort

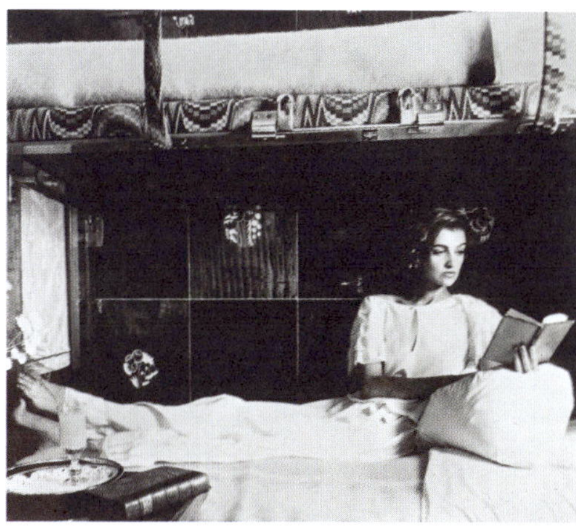

Sleeping compartments Most passengers on the Orient Express traveled in compartments with bunk beds (above). More affluent travelers had the choice of comfortable rooms, with a plush double bed and luxury furnishings (left).

Luxury on rails Although it bears the original name—which still evokes the glamour and elegance of early 20th-century travel—the Venice-Simplon Orient Express is an occasional luxury train that runs on various parts of the European rail network. It is shown here at the Newcastle Station in England on December 17, 1984.

and facility hitherto unknown." There was a smoking room, a ladies' boudoir, and a library, and each compartment (or coupé) had a miniature drawing room in the style of Louis XIV, complete with a Turkish carpet, inlaid tables, and plush red armchairs. In the evenings, the compartment walls could be folded down to reveal beautifully upholstered beds. The *cabinet de toilette* had a mosaic floor, and a special coach at the rear of the train had cubicles for showers that were supplied with hot and cold water—certainly a railroad first.

According to one account (and numerous tales were published), the *piéce de résistance* was the dining room:

> "[It] had a ceiling with embossed leather from Cordoue [Cordoba], walls lined with tapestries from the Atelier des Gobelins, founded by the Sun King, and drapes of finest Gènes [Genoa] velvet."

The tables were covered with white damask cloths and intricately folded napkins, and ice buckets filled with champagne bottles were at hand—and if the five-course meal were not enough, iceboxes full of exotic foods and cold drinks were available at the end of each carriage. Nagelmackers was a stickler for detail and set out a series of rules to maintain high standards. Attendants had to be smart at all times and on special occasions had to dress like footmen from the time of Louis XIV, complete with blue silk breeches and buckled shoes. Even the engine crew had to dress up on occasion, often in white coats that were highly impractical in the driver's cab.

The maiden journey

The inaugural train, for press and VIPs, left the Gare de L'Est in Paris on the evening of October 4, 1883, and was scheduled to take three and a half days to reach Constantinople. At Strasbourg, Vienna, and

The Orient Express This map shows the two principal routes of the train service between Paris and Constantinople (Istanbul), with the northerly route originally terminating at Varna in Bulgaria and requiring a ferry to reach Turkey (now Türkiye).

Feasting in fashion This c.1885 illustration of a dining car on the Orient Express depicts the comfort and luxury the line afforded its more affluent passengers.

Budapest, the train was met by brass bands and local dignitaries, while at Tsigany, in Hungary, a Romani orchestra came aboard and serenaded the passengers all the way to the border with Romania. The only drawback was that the track was incomplete. The bridge over the Danube River was unfinished, so the crossing from Romania to Bulgaria had to be made by ferry, and even then the line reached only as far as the port of Varna, where passengers had to take a ship to Constantinople. This last section of the journey was, according to Blowitz, through a land full of "brigands" who had recently attacked one station and "garrotted the stationmaster and his subordinates in order to get hold of the money they expected in his till," and fled only when they were disturbed by workmen. To deal with this, Blowitz and his companions armed themselves with revolvers, although they never had occasion to use them. They arrived at Constantinople precisely 82 hours after their departure from Paris and were met by Sultan Abdul Hamid II, with whom Blowitz conducted a newspaper interview, the ruler's first.

> **"Peasants in half a dozen countries would pause in their work in the fields and gape at the glittering cars and the supercilious faces behind the windows."**
>
> E. H. COOKRIDGE, *THE ORIENT EXPRESS*

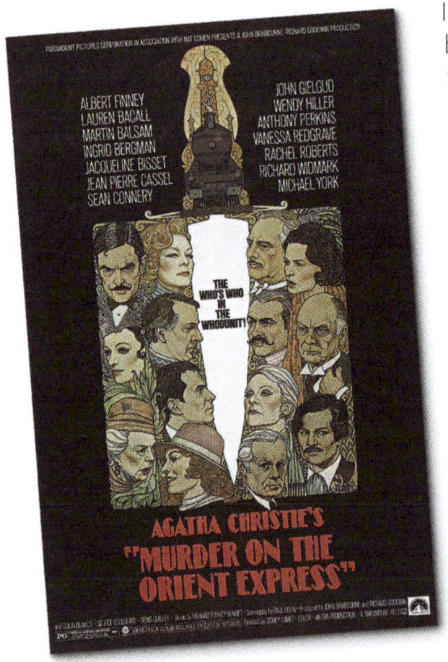

Inspiring literature (above) One of British author Agatha Christie's bestselling titles, *Murder on the Orient Express* (1934) has been adapted for film several times.

It was another six years before it became possible to take the train all the way from Paris to Constantinople. The trip took just under three days, leaving Paris on a Wednesday at 7:30 p.m. and arriving at 5:35 p.m. on Saturday in Constantinople. The service became popular, attracting a wide range of travelers as it was quicker and more convenient than traveling by ship. Subsequently, a variety of other routes were opened, running trains that bore some variant of the name "Orient Express." Several connecting train services were also introduced, including one from London via a train ferry.

Expanding tracks

Inevitably, when war broke out in 1914, the Orient Express was suspended. The war ended in November 1918, and by that spring, a second line was opened—the Simplon Orient Express, on which Agatha Christie's tale is set. Using the Simplon Tunnel between Switzerland and Italy, this second line was a more southerly route via Milan, Venice, and Trieste, and soon became the more popular route linking Paris and Constantinople. A third line was added by the 1930s (the heyday of the Orient services)—the Arlberg Orient Express, which ran via Zurich and Innsbruck to Budapest, with sleeper cars continuing on to Bucharest and Athens. The outbreak of World War II in 1939 again interrupted the service, although the German Mitropa company ran trains through the Balkans until Yugoslav partisans destroyed the line.

Beneath the glitter

While there were no recorded murders on the Orient Express, there was at least one mysterious death—when a US agent allegedly fell from a train at the height of the Cold War in the 1950s—and there was no shortage of mischief. Sleeping car attendants were regularly called on to hire prostitutes, not just for ordinary passengers, but for princes and even bishops who found that a train offered more privacy than a brothel. Indeed, many men took the train simply for these services alone. There was plenty of spying, too, given that the trains linked east and west. Between the wars, "King's Messengers"—effectively couriers for the British Foreign Office—traveled in compartments where they guarded their diplomatic bags with their lives—and later claimed that they were immune to the wiles of the spies sent to entrap them.

Fading glory

For all its luxuries, however, the service did not remain exclusive for long. On the contrary, although there was only one class of carriage in the original service, which cost 300 Francs (the equivalent of two weeks' average wages at the time), second- and third-class carriages were opened for poorer people who used it for shorter, mostly domestic journeys. In these packed carriages, as one writer put it, "the pulse of Old Europe beat, with its almost medieval characters: the tramp, the peddler, the gypsy-musician…." Indeed, although the service continued to operate even after the Iron Curtain divided Europe, communist countries increasingly replaced the luxurious Wagon-Lits cars with more spartan carriages run by their own railroad networks.

By 1962, the Orient Express and the Arlberg Orient Express had stopped running, leaving only the Simplon Orient Express, which was replaced by a slower service, the Direct Orient Express, which ran daily trains from Paris to Belgrade and twice-weekly services from Paris to Athens and Istanbul. The service to Istanbul finally came to an end in 1977, killed off by the ubiquitous spread of the automobile. A service called the Orient Express stuttered on between Paris and Vienna, and between Budapest and Bucharest, but that ended with the opening of the high-speed line between Paris and Strasbourg in 2009 (a service called the Venice-Simplon Orient Express still operates between London and Venice, but it is a separate entity, privately run for luxury passengers on an occasional basis). By the time of its swansong in 2009, the original Orient Express was an anachronism—a relic that had perhaps done well to last as long as it did.

Creative cross section The Orient Express captured people's imagination and inspired detailed examination, such as this 1896 illustration of the workings of the dining car.

Higher ground Traveling aboard the Peruvian Central Railway's Lima–Huancayo train affords tourists an unparalleled view of the Andes. The Lima–Huancayo line is the highest railroad in the Americas and its construction dates back to 1870.

THE MOST SPECTACULAR RAILROADS IN THE WORLD

Henry Meiggs was a scoundrel who made good by building railroads. Despite his questionable beginnings, the impact Meiggs had on the development of railroads is undeniable.

When Meiggs arrived in Chile in 1855, he was a 44-year-old outcast who had fled San Francisco amid accusations of fraud, but by the time he died 22 years later, this handsome, larger-than-life character had been honored with the unofficial title of "Don Enrique." By then, he had conquered some of the world's most difficult railroad terrain—the seemingly impossible slopes of the Andes—for which he also earned the nickname "Yankee Pizarro," after the Spanish conqueror of the Inca empire.

In his youth, Meiggs demonstrated a remarkable capacity for hatching imaginative schemes, but he was never entirely honest—if a venture failed, he was not above lying and manipulating others to avoid being exposed. He had an early success in the timber business, setting up his own company in New York City and relocating to San Francisco during the Gold Rush. After that he went into property and developed land near the Golden Gate, but he soon fell into debt and avoided bankruptcy only by raising cash with illicitly obtained warrants.

When his fraud was discovered, he fled to Chile, where his devious reputation preceded him. The only work he could find was overseeing a gang of laborers building the

Commendable career This 1870 medal commemorates the construction of the Callao to La Oroya line in Peru by US entrepreneur Henry Meiggs.

railroads, but he proved to be so efficient that he was soon given charge of entire railroad projects.

Early success

Two of his predecessors, a New Englander named William Wheelwright and Richard Trevithick (see pp.20–21), had dreamed of building lines inland from the west coast of South America, but it was Meiggs who finally constructed them. This achievement opened up vast deposits of copper, silver, and minerals for exploitation and made fortunes for those who took advantage of the mining boom.

To help him with construction, Meiggs engaged engineers who shared his own daring outlook on the fearsome terrain. His first major success came with the laying of a 90-mile (145-km) line from the Pacific coast to San Fernando, which involved bridging the Maipo River, previously a major obstacle separating north and south Chile. On completing the line faster than his contract required, Meiggs successfully bid for the most important route in the country—from Valparaíso, on the west coast, to Santiago (the capital), a mere 55 miles (89 km) inland as the crow flies, but in practice 115 miles (185 km) due to the mountainous terrain. Wheelwright had begun the route, but after spending a million pesos (or tens of thousands of dollars), only 4 miles (6.5 km) had been completed by the time Meiggs took over. To finish the route, the Chilean government

15,681 ft

(4,781 m)
Height above sea level of the Galera station in Peru

Moving guano (above) The large flocks of seabirds on the Peruvian coast were a great source of wealth, as their droppings—called guano—were a superb fertilizer. Whole railroad lines were developed to transport this valuable resource.

Building bridges (left) The railroads built by Meiggs in South America included sophisticated engineering projects, such as this metal bridge on the Valparaíso and Santiago Railway.

borrowed money from Barings Bank of London, and Meiggs negotiated a speedy deal with the Minister of the Interior, promising to complete the route in three years for six million pesos—so long as he received an additional half million pesos if he finished early, plus an extra 10,000 pesos for every month gained. Backed by a workforce of 10,000 men, Meiggs completed the line in just two years and three days, a triumph that proved his astonishing capabilities both as a contractor and a negotiator.

Peruvian exploits

Having thus "conquered" Chile, Meiggs moved on to even bigger schemes in Peru, a country that was just striking rich, thanks to its enormous deposits of guano, or bird droppings, which made an excellent fertilizer. Understandably, Peruvians wished to use their newfound wealth to build a railroad system that would unify the country, just as the Belgians had done 40 years earlier (see p.44), and as the Canadians (see pp.119–21) and the Italians (see pp.46–47) were doing at the time. For that reason, Meiggs was welcomed with open arms—or open palms, in the case of the ruling class, who demanded huge amounts of money in bribes.

Meiggs's big opportunity came as the result of an episode that was typical of Peru's dramatic political history. In 1868, Colonel José Balta, the type of buccaneering army officer often found in South America at the time, was elected president. Immediately after his election, Peru suffered a devastating earthquake, and Meiggs cannily donated $50,000 (£7,300) to the government, or rather to Balta personally, ostensibly for crisis relief. Balta had already upset the local oligarchy by giving a French company a monopoly on the sale of guano, and now he used money raised by the deal to pay another foreigner—Meiggs—to build Peru's railroads. And so, in the three years following Balta's election, Meiggs signed six contracts to build over 1,000 miles (1,600 km) of railroads, on terms that were highly favorable to him. The result was that, having had a mere 61 miles (98 km) of track in 1861, Peru boasted 947 miles (1,524 km) by 1874, and nearly 2,000 miles (13,200 km) by 1879, two years after Meiggs's death.

Taming the mountains

Meiggs built two lines in Peru, and both are wonders of the railroad world. The first runs from the southern port of Mollendo to Arequipa, Peru's second-biggest city, and then up to Lake Titicaca and the mining area of Juliaca. Meiggs estimated that it would cost him 10 million soles to build it (around $300 million or £237 million today), then told the government that it would cost 15 million, and proceeded to build it for 12 million, even completing it early. The second line, the Central Peruvian, rises from Callao, the port of Lima, up through the steepest and highest sections of the Andes, following precipitous llama paths to the copper mines of Huancayo and the fabled silver mines of Cerro de Pasco.

Unfortunately, the lines were built at a time of great financial turmoil. As the country's guano ran out, so the supply of money from the government dried up, and Meiggs was forced to use his own bills of exchange—the so-called "Billetes de Meiggs." Sadly, too, Meiggs died during construction, but by then he had shown how it was done and had conquered the steepest slopes. He followed the British idea of zigzagging railroads uphill (see pp.192–193), but did so on an unprecedented scale. In India, the British lines reached 2,500 ft (760 m)—Meiggs's trains scaled mountains over 14,000 ft (4,250 m) high and zigzagged 25 times in a matter of 100 miles (160 km).

Being a foreigner, Meiggs was an easy scapegoat for Peru's economic woes, one journalist even writing that "the ruin of Peru is the monument [to] Henry Meiggs."

Billetes de Meiggs In the 1870s, Henry Meiggs effectively created a form of currency to finance his railroad projects in Peru. Around a million soles' worth of banknotes known as Billetes de Meiggs were put in circulation.

However, he was mostly considered a hero, and one of the country's highest peaks was soon named after him.

Meiggs's "railroad army"

His success was due not only to his ability to find the best route for a railroad but also to his formidable organizational skills and his ability to bring out the best in his workers. One Peruvian journalist described his "railroad army" battling the elements:

> "The "army" (distributed along the line in 11 camps), consisting of Don Enrique's engineers and laborers, was attacking the Andes. The scouts went ahead to determine the best and least costly route; the advance guard followed in their tracks, staking out the exact route to be followed; next came the main body, leveling the barriers, making fills and cuts and piercing tunnels; lastly, there was the rear guard, putting down ties and laying rails."

Meiggs was famously generous to his workforce, particularly the *rotos*—the much-feared Chilean working class. According to James Fawcett, in *Railways of the Andes*, a typical *roto* was notorious: "for his hardihood, his skill in the handling of the

Vintage locomotive This antique steam locomotive, dating back to 1926, has pride of place in Lima's Parque de la Amistad. This park celebrates Peru's rich railway history.

sharp, curved, disemboweling knife that all his tribe carried, his hatred of any sort of discipline, his love of cane sugar as a beverage, and his addiction to gambling." Meiggs succeeded by treating his workers as valued employees rather than enslaved people, and he was even more successful with the 5,000 Chinese workers he hired and who were normally treated worse than the *rotos* (see p.87). According to one observer, quoted by Fawcett: "some of them were fat, the only fat Chinese in the country! Meiggs fed them well with rice and beef in plenty and a good breakfast of bread and tea before starting the day's work."

Toward the end of his life, Meiggs wanted to return to the US, claiming that he had repaid his San Francisco debts, but the governor of San Francisco vetoed a bill that was passed to exonerate him from his offenses. In 1977, a century after Meiggs's death, the California Supreme Court quashed the indictment against him, declaring that he "had gone to a higher court," but his death was not the end of his family's influence. His nephew, Minor C. Keith, went on to complete a railroad his uncle had started in Costa Rica. Its major source of income was carrying bananas. Keith went on to found United Fruit, the colossus that dominated the sale of bananas for a century.

For his railroad-related accomplishments, Henry Meiggs had a 17,575 ft (5,362 m) high mountain in the Peruvian Andes named after him

Global workforce Railroad construction workers were brought over from many parts of the world to help in the building of the lines in South America. Here, workers can be seen flanking a stretch of railroad track near Lima, Peru.

GOING UPHILL

The first railroad lines were laid along the flattest routes possible, but the requirements of industry—particularly mining—soon demanded that trains could travel uphill. The earliest solution was the "incline"—a pair of parallel tracks that enabled a descending train to haul an ascending train uphill by means of a chain that connected the two via a pulley. This worked particularly well on the short sections of track that were used to draw raw materials up from pits and quarries, and variants were powered by horses or stationary steam engines. The basic premise lies behind modern-day funicular railroads, and other engineering solutions, such as spiral loops and switchbacks, have also been developed.

Spiral loop

Building a railroad track on a spiral allows a train to gain elevation in a much shorter length of track than would be possible with a conventional curve. Spiral loops also avoid the inconveniences of reverse travel and interrupted movement that are necessary when climbing switchbacks, the other railroad engineering method by which traction trains climb hills (see opposite). Popular in challenging terrain, such as mountainous regions in which level ground is limited, spirals are set at a constant grade and degree of curvature and allow the track to pass over itself as the line ascends.

Brusio spiral viaduct, Switzerland To allow trains to navigate mountains, railroads employed various techniques, including this 469 ft (143 m) loop with a gradual ascent.

Switchbacks The railroad linking Ecuador's coast with its capital, Quito—at 9,350 ft (2,850 m)—crosses the Nariz del Diablo escarpment via a series of switchbacks. By this method, trains gain height in a short length of track by entering a dead-end siding and then reversing to climb the next switchback.

Funicular railroads

One of the first funicular railroads—a form of cable car operating on similar principles to a railroad incline—opened in 1862 in Lyon, France, and featured a four-rail track layout on which two cars traveled on separate parallel tracks. The development of passing loops allowed later designs to economize on the space and materials used. First came a three-rail layout, in which cars shared a central rail—then came a two-rail layout in which the cars shared both rails on either side of the passing loop.

How it works
Two- and three-rail funiculars contain a passing loop at the halfway point. Each car has "blind" (flangeless) inner wheels and double-flanged outer wheels to prevent them from switching rails.

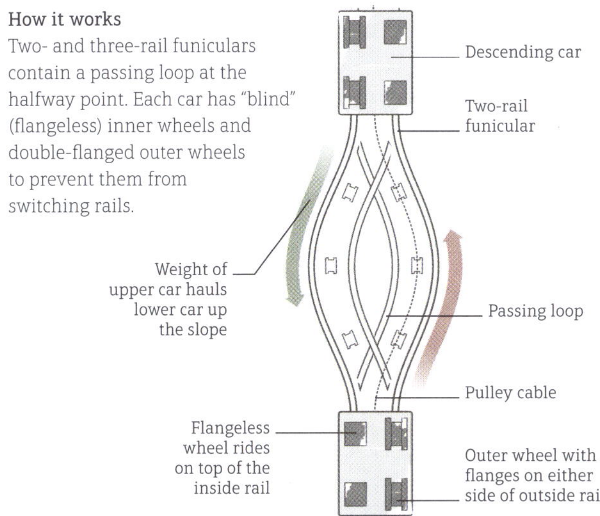

Stoosbahn, Switzerland—the steepest funicular in the world

HENRY FLAGLER AND THE OVERSEA RAILROAD

US industrialist Henry Flagler spent the last 30 years of his life building a railroad line and establishing Florida's tourist industry. His final triumph was the construction of the world's most ambitious "oversea railroad"—a line stretching from the US mainland across the Florida Keys to its southernmost tip, Key West.

Oversea expansion Flagler's remarkable railroad proved to be a great attraction and opened up the resort of Key West to thousands of visitors. Pictured here is a train traveling over the Florida East Coast Railway's Key West extension.

For decades before his great Florida adventure, Flagler had been a key partner in the creation of J. D. Rockefeller's gigantic Standard Oil monopoly. According to Flagler's biographer, David Chandler, Rockefeller readily admitted that Flagler was an inspiration. Indeed, Flagler had contributed more than Rockefeller to the organization of Standard Oil and was wholly responsible for the clever legal structure that protected it against antitrust lawsuits. However, Flagler craved an outlet for his colossal creative energies, and that was just what he found in Florida, which he explored in 1883 while on honeymoon with his second wife, Ida.

Flagler's vision

At the time, Florida was still a young state eager to sell its land rights, and Flagler saw that even underdeveloped St. Augustine, the oldest European settlement in the US, was attracting plenty of wealthy tourists. Sensing a golden opportunity, he gave up his daily involvement in the Standard and set about building a chain of hotels along the east coast—the first of which, the 540-room Ponce de León, opened in St. Augustine in 1888.

Designed by the architects of the Metropolitan Opera and New York Public Library, the Ponce de León was the height of luxury and immediately attracted many visitors. However, the local railroads were a deterrent, for they ran on a variety of gauges (see pp.88–89) and so travel required frequent changes of train. What was needed was a reliable railroad that would link the town directly to New York,

Beyond railroads Henry Flagler not only built railroads but also established a new tourism industry in Florida by constructing several hotels along the coast, including the Ponce de León.

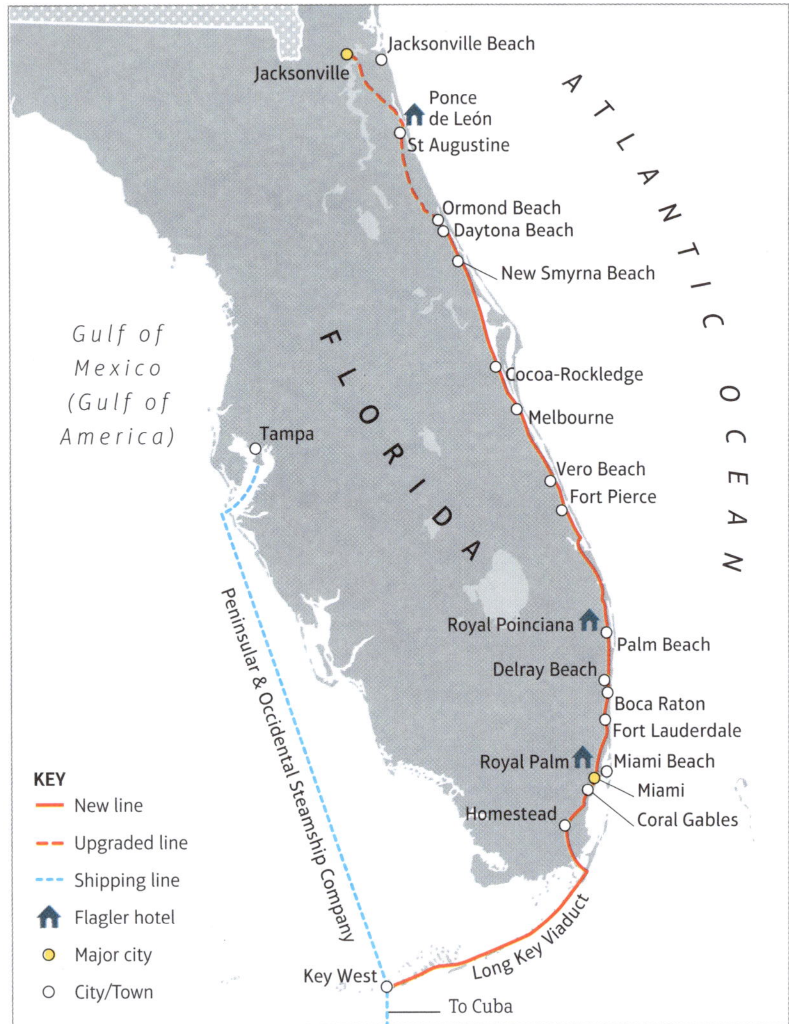

Florida's East Coast Railway
Completed in 1912, the railroad line linked a series of villages, sparking the growth of thriving towns and cities along Florida's Atlantic coast.

so Flagler bought up the existing lines and converted them to standard gauge. As he noted: "the average passenger will take a through car ninety-five times in a hundred in preference to making a change." Another problem was that the lines ran only to Daytona, a beach about a third of the way down the coast—beyond that, Flagler would have to lay his own tracks.

Flager's next port of call was Palm Beach, a natural harbor that he explored in 1893. As always, he inspected the site incognito, to avoid attracting attention, and then returned openly to buy the land he wanted. Within months, he opened the 1,100-room Royal Poinciana hotel, which Chandler called "the largest resort hotel in the world... equipped and staffed in the most luxurious manner imaginable," and extended the railroad south to reach it. The guests did full justice to the luxury of the accommodation, with a hundred private railroad cars arriving each winter for the George Washington Birthday Ball—an event at which the most powerful men in America, including Flagler himself, dressed in the most elaborate drag costumes, complete with fishnet stockings, powdered wigs, and strings of diamonds. Another great draw was an annex called the Breakers, which proved so popular that Flagler turned it into a casino.

Connecting Florida to the Keys

To foster local industry, Flagler also established a "Model Land Company," which, in Chandler's words, "did more perhaps to actually building up the Florida East Coast than any of his other undertakings." He encouraged people to plant vegetables, citrus fruit, and pineapples, and when an unprecedented snowstorm wiped out the fledgling industry in the winter, he secretly spent a fortune helping the affected farmers.

> **"I regard [the Over-Sea Railroad] as second only to the Panama Canal in its political and commercial importance to the United States."**
>
> ELIHU ROOT, US SECRETARY OF STATE

He even arranged a link-up with weather forecasters, and if a serious drop in temperature was predicted, his engine drivers sounded six long blasts on their whistles as they thundered through the orange groves, calling on farmers to hurry out with their "smudge pots"—oil-burning heaters that prevented frost from forming on the fruit trees.

Another consequence of these cold snaps was Flagler's decision to extend his railroad south, for only 60 miles (100 km) away the climate was warmer and better suited to farming. Extending the railroad also entitled him to land grants, and on the basis of these, he accumulated over two million acres of territory, including Biscayne Bay, a beautiful spot protected from the Atlantic by a barrier island and watered by the little Miami River. At the time, the area was "mostly swamp, and was filled with mosquitoes, snakes, mangrove thickets and Spanish Bayonet" (a nasty type of cactus), but Flagler tamed it and brought water and electricity to the town he established there. The locals wanted to call the town "Flagler," but Flagler declined the honor, preferring to name it after the river. Thus Miami was born. The following year, he set about building another luxury hotel, the Royal Palm, which was as popular as the Royal Poinciana. The railroad arrived at Miami in 1896, completing a 500-mile (800 km) line that ran south from the neighboring state of Georgia through Jacksonville and the resorts Flagler had built. Anyone glancing at a map would consider Miami as the end of the line, but Flagler kept on going, running the railroad on bridges out to sea, away from the mainland and over the Florida Keys—an archipelago that sweeps southwest from Miami to Key West, far out in the Gulf of Mexico (Gulf of America). "There is an impelling force within me," he told a friend, "and I must carry out my plans"—and the result was his 128-mile (206 km) "oversea railroad."

Challenges and innovations

In one respect, Flagler was lucky. By the time his plans were ready, US President Theodore Roosevelt had authorized the construction of the Panama Canal, making Key West a potentially vital

Work locomotives Construction locomotives and work trains were loaded onto barges and ferried across to the Florida Keys to facilitate the building of the railroad. Here, workers prepare the track for the arrival of one such locomotive in 1906.

A grand celebration The arrival of the first passenger train in the Florida Keys, with Flagler and his large party on board, was met by huge crowds celebrating the completion of the railroad.

transportation hub. As for getting the work done, Flagler simply found the right man for the job and left him to it, ignoring the question of cost, even though there were no more grants to be had. His chosen engineer was Joseph Carroll Meredith, who had already built massive docks at Tampico on the Mexican coast. However, before he started on the offshore part of the route, Meredith had to lay 91 miles (146 km) of railroad through the Everglades, an ordeal in which every kind of danger and annoyance was encountered, from apparently bottomless swamps and uncharted lakes to snakes, alligators, mosquitoes, and obstacles that only the biggest dredgers in the country could move. Then he faced the 37 miles (60 km) of the "oversea" railroad itself, a route demanding 17 miles (27 km) of bridges and 20 miles (32 km) of embankments—a feat of engineering that has rarely been equaled. The Long Key viaduct alone measured 2½ miles (4 km), and was second only to the 7-mile (11-km) Knights Key viaduct, which rested on 366 concrete columns and had a swing bridge to allow ships to pass through it. Without dry land for accommodations, the 4,000 workers were housed on enormous barges, which contained all the facilities needed for survival, including vast quantities of fresh water. However, there was still a high casualty rate, both from accidents and disease, and a hospital was built in Miami to treat the afflicted. The elements also caused havoc, not least in 1906, when a hurricane sank an accommodations barge, causing at least 70 deaths, and delaying construction for a year.

An enduring legacy

The whole Florida East Coast Railway project was completed at a cost of $20 million ($750 million in today's money) in less than seven years. This was largely thanks to the loyalty of Flagler's men, one of whom told a reporter "there isn't one of us who wouldn't give a year of his life to have Mr Flagler see the work completed." And see it he did, opening the line to the public on January 22, 1912, tearfully exclaiming: "my dream is fulfilled, now I can die happy." He had never expected to see the project completed, predicting 20 years earlier that it would take 30 years to finish, and accurately forecasting: "I have

"But that any man could have the genius to see of what this wilderness... was capable and then have the nerve to build a railroad here..."

GEORGE W. PERKINS OF J. P. MORGAN, ON FLAGLER'S ACHIEVEMENTS only 20 more years to live." The line's completion was celebrated by the introduction of the Havana Express, a regular through service that arrived at Key West only 52 hours after leaving New York, giving passengers the luxury of strolling across the quay to take a ship to Cuba, a mere 90 miles (45 km) away. Flagler, his life's work accomplished, died a happy man the following year.

Sadly, however, the line never prospered. It failed to attract many passengers and proved to be unreliable due to the bad weather. Consequently, the railroad went bankrupt in 1932, and the offshore track was destroyed on Labor Day 1935, during the worst storm of the century. Nevertheless, Meredith had built his railroad well. Highway 1, which replaced it, was constructed on the roadbed that Flagler had financed. Indeed, Florida, the Sunshine State, has much to thank him for. When he started work, it was one of the poorest states in the Union—today, it has one of the strongest economies in the country.

Streamlined service In 1939, the Florida East Coast Railway introduced a daily streamlined passenger train between Jacksonville and Miami, named after its founder, Henry M. Flagler.

HAULING FREIGHT

The workhorses of the railroads, freight locomotives require high power output rather than speed and offer efficient and reliable solutions for long-distance movement of cargo. The use of containers to convey goods has increased demand for freight trains, and rail is still the most effective method for moving bulk cargo, such as coal, grains, and liquids.

Santa Fe Southern No.92 (1953)
Santa Fe Southern's No.92 is a GP7-class built by Electro-Motive Division (EMD) at General Motors. It is a diesel-electric "switcher" used to shunt trains at rail yards. No.92 was one of the first locomotives to use the "hood unit" design, in which a narrow body is surrounded by external walkways.

Union Pacific No.25408 *Caboose* (1959)
Common on US and Canadian railroads, cabooses were the last carriage on a freight train and housed the crew. Thought to be named after the Dutch *kabuis* ("ship's galley"), their use has declined as automatic signaling reduced the need for crews. The pictured model has a cupola for watching the train's cargo.

Norfolk and Western No.522 (1962)
No.522 was the first of a series of the GP30 class from General Motors to be put into service by the Norfolk and Western Railway. It achieved a power output of 2,250 bhp (1,680 kw) through its diesel-electric engine.

B&O No.7402 (1964)
One of 24 Baltimore and Ohio SD35-class diesel-electric locomotives, No.7402 was powered by a 16-cylinder engine that yielded a power output of 2,500 bhp (1,900 kw). Its two three-axle trucks are typical of low-speed, high-weight freight trains.

B&O No.3684 (1966)
No.3684 is a General Motors GP40-class diesel-electric, a versatile locomotive that could be used for "manifest" freight—hauling a range of different units in a single train—as well as heavy loads. It was the first engine capable of a power output of 3,000 bhp (2,240 kw) to be used by the Baltimore and Ohio Railroad.

Deutsche Reichsbahn V100 (1966)
The East German V100 diesel-hydraulic was first tested in 1964, and 1,146 locomotives of several versions were built between 1966 and 1985. The pictured model yielded a power output of 1,184 bhp (883 kw).

Norfolk and Western No.1776 (1970)
With a power output of 3,600 bhp (2,680 kw), No.1776 was one of 115 SD45 diesel-electrics produced by General Motors for the Norfolk and Western Railway. It was painted in a stars-and-stripes livery to mark the 1976 bicentenary of the US Declaration of Independence.

SBB Cargo TRAXX F140 AC (2003)
Built by Bombardier, the TRAXX class is a modular family of trains that can be adapted for a range of functions and is the most economically successful train ever produced. The pictured model is of an electric freight train operated by SBB Cargo of Switzerland.

Inaugural trip Railroad engineers stand ready to despatch the first train on the Salisbury–Umtali line, which opened in May 1899, as part of Rhodes's vision for the Cape to Cairo railrail.

CAPE TO CAIRO: THE RAILROAD THAT NEVER WAS

A continuous line from Cairo to the Cape of Good Hope—linking Britain's colonies in Africa—was the most ambitious and improbable of all railroad dreams, and it failed, but only just.

Construction started on a through-rail route from Cape to Cairo in the 1880s, and most major lines were completed by the 1920s, although hundreds of miles of transfers via lakes and rivers were necessary to complete the journey. However, even the project's most optimistic protagonists had accepted that maritime interruptions would be necessary. Indeed Cecil Rhodes, the godfather of the idea, stated that the project was never for a railroad that depended on traffic all the way through, but one that would "pick up trade all the way along the route" and, crucially, would run entirely through British Imperial territory.

The idea represented the various impulses behind the British Empire in the late-Victorian era. It combined private megalomania, commercial and financial greed, and military necessity, although it received little support from London. Whether the project is viewed as a failure or as a partial success, the imperialists, contractors, and engineers who worked on it built thousands of miles of railroad that are still vital for the African continent today. The route incorporated separate lines to both the Atlantic and Indian oceans and, as a by-product, created a number of new towns and cities. Lusaka, now the capital of Zambia, was described in railroad historian George Tabor's *The Cape to Cairo Railway & River Routes* as no more than a "lion-infested

Through Africa The back cover of the British South Africa Company's *The Story of Rhodesia* (1936) bears a map of Africa with the British colonies marked in red. Cecil Rhodes hoped to build a railway line running through these colonies, across Africa.

SALISBURY UMTALI
NOW WE SHANT BE LONG TO CAIRO
No

Construction of the Cape to Cairo Work started on southern Africa's first railroad at Cape Town in 1859. By the time the tracks reached the Congo River in 1918, the dream of a trans-African railroad had been abandoned.

siding," and Gaberone, the future capital of Botswana, was a "remote watering hole on the edge of the Kalahari desert."

An idea is born

The idea of an all-British railroad through Africa was first suggested in 1876 by the explorer and journalist H. M. Stanley (of "Dr. Livingstone, I presume" fame), in letters to the *Daily Telegraph* newspaper. Stanley's idea was set in motion by the unbridled ambition of Cecil Rhodes, an imperial and political megalomaniac who made his fortune from the lucrative diamond trade of southern Africa (present-day South Africa). Rhodes was supported throughout the project by Charles (later Sir Charles) Metcalfe, an unusual blend of aristocrat and consulting engineer, who had been a friend since the pair were students at Oxford University.

Executing the vision

To carry out his ambitions, Rhodes required someone with the engineering skills to build a railroad over thousands of miles of virtually impassable country. That person was British railroad engineer George Pauling, head of family-owned engineering contractor Pauling & Co, which already had a decade of experience building railroads overseas when it was established under that name in 1894. The firm also included George's brother Harry, four cousins—Harold, Henry, Willie, and Percy—and his brother-in-law Alfred Lawley. In every respect, George was a larger-than-life character. He was a very big man who professed that he was "never able to reduce my weight below 16 stone [220 lb]". This was perhaps not surprising given his enormous appetite—on one occasion, he consumed 300 bottles of German beer with two friends while stuck for 48 hours on a railroad line; on another, he ate a thousand oysters in one sitting. As his banker Baron Frédéric Émile d'Erlanger put it (Pauling relied on the d'Erlangers' financial backing, as Rhodes depended on the Rothschilds'), he was "endowed with a physique that made light of any feat of strength and enabled him to defy fatigue or illness."

Pauling's stamina was combined with a readiness to build rough-and-ready lines, leaving bridges to wait until later. He knew that his work would prove to be durable, and it was this confidence that ensured his promises of apparently impossible speeds of construction would be kept. His financial success came from his capacity to identify almost at a glance the shortest and cheapest route for a line. Although he based his estimate on an initial outside survey and charged a fixed fee per mile, he profited greatly from his ability to find shortcuts.

The first railroads had opened in the Cape Colony, at Africa's southern tip, in 1863. To save money, they were built to a narrow gauge of 3 ft 6 in (1,067 mm), which became known as "Cape Gauge." Development of the lines was limited by financial constraints, and the narrow gauge resulted in speeds that never

About 30,000 to 40,000 laborers were employed at various points throughout the construction of the railroad to link the Cape of Good Hope to Cairo

Integrated transportation Steamship companies ran services linking with rail timetables to ensure that their passengers could quickly reach inland destinations.

averaged more than 35 mph (56 km/h). It was the 1872 diamond rush at Kimberley Mine, roughly 600 miles (965 km) to the north, that sparked more ambitious railroad-building plans, adding a solid financial rationale to the young Rhodes's imperial ambitions.

The rails reached Kimberley by 1885 while Rhodes, still only in his thirties, was busy building up a diamond monopoly through his company, De Beers Group. This first stage of the line was no easy feat, with a climb of more than 3,500 ft (1,000 m) to the dry, dusty uplands of the Karoo. Pauling ensured that the pace of construction was far faster than the eight years it had taken to lay the first 75–100 miles (120–160 km) from Cape Town to Worcester. Progress was easier on the plateau of the Karoo, and Pauling's men could advance as much as half a mile (1 km) a day. Pauling pushed ahead despite opposition from the region's Afrikaner population, who hated the railroad as a symbol of British imperialism and as "an invention of the devil." But Pauling had an unexpected trump card to play. His family had welcomed in a couple of stranded Afrikaners who had been turned away by English hoteliers, thus ensuring the permanent gratitude and support of President Paul Kruger of the neighboring South African Republic.

The "Rhodesian" section

By 1890, Rhodes, a politician as well as an entrepreneur, had become Prime Minister of Cape Colony. A year earlier, he had founded the British South Africa Company, which was to control the two countries later named after him—Northern and Southern Rhodesia (now Zambia and

4,200 miles

(6,759 km)
Distance from Cape to Cairo as the crow flies

Zimbabwe). He planned to lay rails north to the Zambezi River and, eventually, to the Nile Valley. The first step was Mafeking, 96 miles (154 km) to the north of the existing end of the rails at Vryburg; the line was opened to traffic in October 1894. The next step was the 600 miles (965 km) to Bulawayo. Pauling made good his promise to build the railroad at an amazing speed—more than a mile a day—and the line arrived at Bulawayo in 1897 to a banner reading "Our two roads to progress: Railroads and Cecil Rhodes."

The next step was to connect the Cape line from Bulawayo to Salisbury (now Harare in Zimbabwe), the capital of Southern Rhodesia. Two links were required: one connecting Salisbury to Beira on the coast of Portuguese-controlled Mozambique, and another running directly from Salisbury to Bulawayo. Construction was delayed by tension between the British and Portuguese authorities, which culminated in a diplomatic incident involving British forces and a Portuguese gunboat. The discord was resolved by a treaty between the two sides, and construction was permitted to proceed in 1892. Even by 19th-century standards, it was a very risky project, crossing both swamp and forest terrain. In the first two years of construction, more than half of the white men died of fever, as did virtually all of the 500 Indian immigrant workers, who had even less immunity to the local diseases. However, this did not deter Pauling & Co's project manager, Alfred Lawley, himself an excellent engineer, from achieving what Tabor describes as an "amazingly successful 2-feet [61 cm] gauge miniature line, almost 'thrown together'... on the rough and ready earthworks," even though "at times it ran like a fairground switchback." The line would be improved a year later in 1899, when it was widened to the "Cape Gauge." The first train reached the Rhodesian frontier in February 1898 carrying the slogan "Now we shan't be long to Cairo." By 1902, the Bulawayo stretch of line was connected to Beira on the Indian Ocean, creating a continuous link of more than 2,000 miles (3,200 km) to Cape Town on the Atlantic.

The northern line

There was considerable progress on the northern section of the railroad, which stretched south from the Mediterranean coast of Egypt. There had been railroad lines in Egypt since the mid-1850s, but financial and political problems ensured that they did not stretch into Sudan, the country's southern neighbor. In 1898, a major and entirely unexpected breakthrough took place when Major General Sir Herbert Kitchener, commander-in-chief of the British-controlled Egyptian army, arrived with an army to recapture Khartoum, the capital of Sudan. The city had been captured 15 years earlier by the Mahdist Army, who had killed General Charles Gordon and all the British inhabitants. To reach Khartoum from Egypt, Kitchener needed a railroad to convey the troops south from Wadi Halfa on the Nile, in order to bypass hundreds of miles of unnavigable sections of the river. Experts dismissed the idea as impossible, but Kitchener found his equivalent of Pauling in a much more orthodox character—a brilliant and experienced young French Canadian railroad engineer by the name of Percy Girouard.

Girouard identified a route that included a 250-mile (400 km) shortcut across the desert to Abu Hamed instead of following the winding Nile River, which took nearly 600 miles (1,000 km) to reach the same point. It was not easy terrain, as the young Winston Churchill—who combined the roles of journalist and officer

Victoria Falls tram The Bamba tram, which links the local railroad station with Victoria Falls, remains a popular tourist attraction to date.

in Kitchener's army—explained: "it is scarcely within the power of words to describe the savage desolation of the regions into which the lines and its constructors plunged." Kitchener took the long view and decided that the line should be built using the "Cape Gauge," in view of the possible link up with Rhodes's line. Girouard established a veritable "railroad town" at Wadi Halfa on the Nile, as well as a railhead—a mobile town complete with a station, stores, and a canteen—and reached halfway to Khartoum in a mere six months, coincidentally on the same day that Pauling reached Bulawayo.

Battle of Omdurman

The line reached Atbara near Khartoum nine months later, in time to enable Kitchener to avenge Gordon at the Battle of Omdurman in September 1898. The battle was a virtual massacre that cost around 50 British lives, while the army of Mahdist Sudan perished. As Churchill pointed out, such a war "was primarily a matter of transportation. The Khalifa [the Mahdi's official title] was conquered on the railway." The conquest had a major political repercussion for the British Empire. Joseph Chamberlain, the imperialist Colonial Secretary, later told a reporter: "you will live to see the time when a railroad will be built through that country to the Great Lakes, the Transvaal, and the Cape." Back in the south of the African continent, just before the Boer War broke out in 1899, Pauling had promised to fulfill Rhodes's dream to build a yet-more-ambitious line. He committed to extending the tracks from Salisbury to the Zambezi River at Victoria Falls and then on to the Congo border at Likasi—more than 1,000 miles (1,600 km) of track. It was projected that this track would take 14 years to lay. However, plans were delayed for three years by the war.

The railroads, commanded by the ubiquitous Girouard, proved to be vital for British communications during the conflict but required a high proportion of British troops in order to guard the lines against

Winning move In order to retake its former colony from local rebels, the British built a 560-miles (900-km) railroad across the Sudanese desert. It allowed the British Army to reclaim lost territories after defeating the Mahdist Army at the Battle of Omdurman in 1898.

Victoria Falls Bridge Cecil Rhodes commissioned this magnificent bridge over the Zambezi to enable trains to travel between the countries known today as Zimbabwe and Zambia.

attack. The first stretch of the new line was relatively simple, and the 300 miles (480 km) of track across open savanna countryside arrived at the Zambezi in 1904. Soon the Zambezi Express from Cape Town was providing a regular service to the north. The seemingly impossible task of crossing the 650 ft (200 m) span of the Victoria Falls was achieved when the Cleveland Bridge & Engineering Company of Darlington in northeast England built a bridge to specifications set out by the British engineer George Andrew Hobson. It took five months to build and was then shipped to the heart of Africa, where it was constructed in situ.

Completion of the railroad

The next extension of the line had a sound economic object: the enormous reserves of coal at Wankie, and the equally staggering riches of copper in the so-called Copper Belt at Broken Hill. Both areas were in Northern Rhodesia, and the route to reach them required a bridge even longer than that at Victoria Falls. Designed by Hobson, the structure that crossed the Kafue River had 13 steel spans and was completed in 1906 in a mere five months. Pauling and his colleagues had become even more adept at managing these huge construction

"Build the bridge across the Zambezi where the trains, as they pass, will catch the spray of the Fall."

CECIL RHODES

Kafue bridge A ceremony to mark the opening of the 1,400 ft (427 m) long Kafue bridge was held in 1906. The bridge was built for Mashonaland Railways, which later merged into Rhodesian Railways.

projects, and completed the 281 miles (450 km) from Kalomo, the existing railhead 50 miles (80 km) north of the Zambezi, to Broken Hill (now Kabwe) in just 277 working days. The impetus behind the project, however, had been greatly reduced following the death of Rhodes in 1902, at the age of just 48. His successor was Robert Williams, a Scottish mining engineer who lacked Rhodes's imperial vision. However, after three years of negotiations, Williams obtained concessions from the Belgian authorities to continue the railroad into the recently annexed Belgian Congo. The line finally left British-controlled territory in 1909 on its way north to the Katanga region—which had even bigger deposits of copper and other minerals than Northern Rhodesia—rather than east to Tanganyika, which was part of German East Africa at the time. It eventually reached Bukama, 450 miles (725 km) farther along the Congo River, in 1918, the year before a defeated Germany was divested of its East African territories.

By the end of World War I, the idea of a grand imperial railroad all the way down the spine of Africa was abandoned in the wake of other far-reaching political changes, such as the demise of the Ottoman Empire. Instead, efforts were concentrated on building the shortest route to export the Congo's minerals to Europe; to this end, the Benguela Railroad in Angola was extended to Lobito Bay on the Atlantic. This difficult route of more than 800 miles (1,200 km) would not be complete until 1929. Till then, a tenuous—and somewhat roundabout—rail link did indeed run from the Cape to Cairo, using ferries to cross lakes and the Nile River. A few hardy travelers succeeded in traveling along the entire route—that, surely, could count as a success for Rhodes's vision, given the monumental scale of the task of crossing the continent.

A link to the ocean In the early 20th century, the Benguela Railroad was built as a branch line off the main Cape to Cairo route in order to connect it with the Atlantic Ocean at Lobito in Angola.

CAPE TO CAIRO

A Victorian imperial ideal with the goal of opening the African continent up to commerce, Cecil Rhodes's ambitious plan for a north–south railroad across British colonial Africa was never fully realized. The challenges of the terrain, local opposition, and a lack of finance to meet the huge material demands of laying iron rails across mountain, jungle, and desert meant that, by the close of World War I, pragmatism had overcome idealism. Africa's abundant natural resources of diamonds, gold, and copper became the main destination of its railroads. This map shows the sections of the Cape to Cairo line that were completed between the 1880s and the 1920s, and its connecting railroads.

Railroads came much later to some regions in Africa, including Liberia, where the first railroad started in 1950 mainly for transporting iron ore

Making way While the dream of a railroad running from the Cape in South Africa to Cairo in Egypt was never fully realized, many sections of the line were built. Large numbers of local people were called upon as construction workers, invariably with few tools at their disposal apart from picks and shovels. In this 1914 image, laborers can be seen clearing a path through the dense Congo forest for this line.

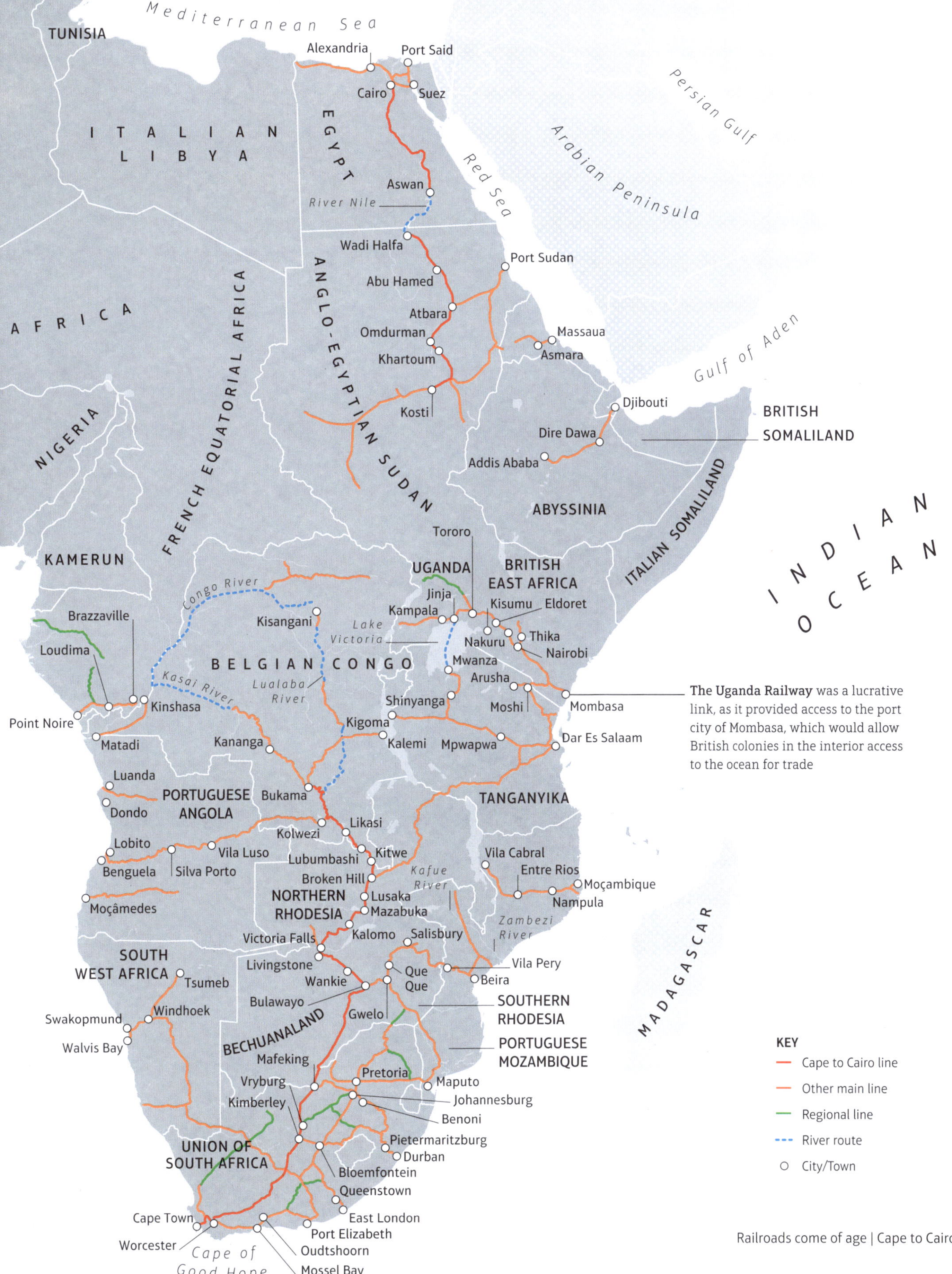

The Uganda Railway was a lucrative link, as it provided access to the port city of Mombasa, which would allow British colonies in the interior access to the ocean for trade

ELECTRICITY LIGHTENS THE LOAD

It was not until the last years of the 19th century that electric power was introduced on the rails. This technology would go on to challenge and eventually topple the supremacy of steam.

Steam locomotives were almost universal on the railroads by the end of the 1830s, once horses had been seen off the tracks, and they remained the dominant form of traction well into the 20th century, when electric power took over. Although it has numerous advantages over steam—electricity is cleaner and more efficient, allows for faster acceleration, and is ultimately cheaper—it requires greater initial capital investment, as power has to be provided either by an external delivery system, most commonly an overhead wire or third rail, or by an internal system such as an onboard power generator—technologies that demand a high initial outlay. However, once its benefits had been observed and the technology was improved, electricity superseded steam.

Britain was, again, a pioneer with electric trains, as it had been with the steam engine (see pp.22–29), although it lost out in the technological race once electricity was more widely adopted. As early as 1837,

a chemist from Aberdeen, Robert Davidson, made the first electric locomotive. It was battery-powered, as was a second version named *Galvani* (after its galvanic cells, or batteries) that was exhibited at the Royal Scottish Society of Arts Exhibition in 1841. This massive, 7-ton (6.3-metric ton) vehicle managed to haul a load of 6 tons (5.4 metric tons) at 4 mph (6.4 km/h) for a distance of 1½ miles (2.5 km) and was tested on the Edinburgh and Glasgow Railway the following year. However, the perennial problem of batteries running out of power—which still limits their use in transportation today—meant *Galvani* was not very practical. Railroad workers also opposed it, fearing electric trains would ruin their livelihoods, and destroyed the engine.

The first electric trains

German industrialist Werner von Siemens developed the first electric-hauled passenger train in 1879, and exhibited it on a 985 ft (300 m) circular track in Berlin, Germany. The train ran for several months, using a third-rail system to reach a speed of 8 mph (13 km/h). Britain's first electric passenger railroad, the narrow-gauge Volk's electric railroad (named after its inventor, Magnus Volk), was completed in 1883 and, remarkably, still survives today, running 1 mile (1.6 km) along Brighton's seafront. A low-voltage electric generator originally supplied a 50-V current to the small engine via the two running rails. Later the voltage was increased and the gauge widened from a narrow 2 ft (60 cm) to 2 ft 8½ in (82.5 cm).

Some fascinating early experiments with electricity took place elsewhere. In Ireland, brothers William and Dr. Anthony Traill used hydro-electricity from a waterfall to power a railroad for visitors to the Giant's Causeway, a local tourist attraction. They built the 9¼-mile (15 km) Giant's Causeway, Portrush, and Bush Valley Railway on a 90 cm (3 ft) gauge, and installed turbines and dynamos to provide the power. However, electricity generation was unreliable when the railroad opened in 1887, and steam engines were used to supplement the electric power.

Siemens's first electric passenger train Werner von Siemens's train was exhibited at the Berlin Trade Fair in 1879, to the excitement of visitors. Over a four-month period, more than 86,000 passengers took a trip on it.

Reliability improved once the supply was converted to overhead wires rather than the third rail, which was also hazardous to people crossing the line—in 1895, a cyclist was killed when he touched the live rail. Traills' railroad was ahead of its day in ecological terms, and many lines, especially in mountainous regions, have since been powered by more sophisticated forms of hydro-energy.

Trams jump a step

The exception to the near universal adoption of steam for railroads at their inception were the tramways—omnibuses that used tracks through towns so that they would not get stuck on muddy roads. Steam engines trundling through towns would have been not only dangerous but also impractical, as they operated poorly at slow speeds and they had to stop and start a lot. Consequently, horse-drawn trams were the norm until electric tramways began to emerge—skipping a technological step. The first commercial electric tram line opened in Lichterfelde, a suburb of Berlin, in 1881, and was built by Werner von Siemens, who had exhibited the first electric train two years earlier. In 1883, the Mödling and Hinterbrühl Tram—the first regular service in the world powered from an overhead line—opened near Vienna, in Austria.

In the US, electric trolleys (the American name for tramways) were pioneered in 1888 on the Richmond Union Passenger

Changing times Electric trams rapidly replaced their far less efficient and slower horse-drawn predecessors, as is evident in this scene outside the New York Metropolitan Opera House in 1905.

Map of the electric railway This late-19th century map shows the underground and overground electric railway lines connecting the City to South London. The underground route extended from the City to Stockwell, across areas, such as Borough and Kennington.

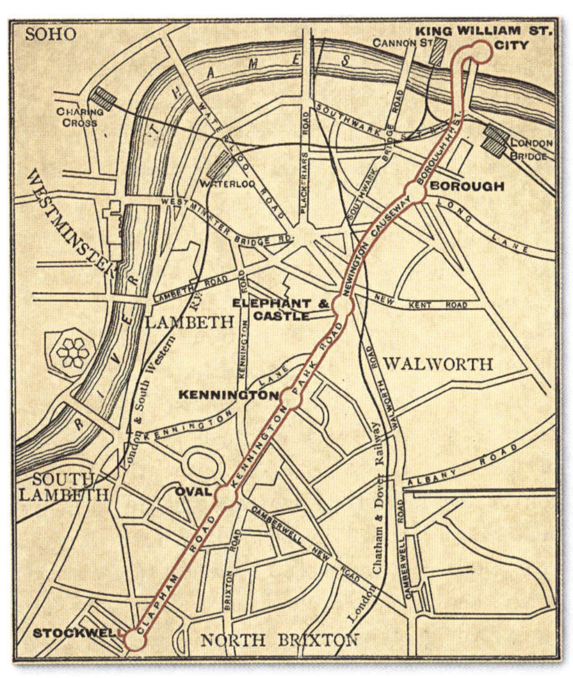

Railway in Virginia. The new technology encouraged rapid expansion and in just over 10 years, trolley cars had become almost universal across the country: there had been just 3,000 miles (4,800 km) of horse tramways prior to electrification, while by 1905, there were more than 20,000 miles (33,000 km) of electric tramways, and the trolley car became the most common form of urban travel. Although there was a potential hazard associated with trams powered from overhead lines, which occasionally resulted in electric shocks, in practice this seems to have been rare.

Going underground

Elsewhere, the increasing use of tunnels, especially in urban areas and through mountainous regions, stimulated the need for electric locomotives. Despite the success of London's Metropolitan Railway, which opened in 1863, it soon became apparent that steam engines in tunnels caused dangerous levels of smoke, leading local authorities to prohibit their use within city limits. Britain developed the first underground railroad, with a line using electricity. The City & South London Railway, the world's first deep-tube line, opened in 1890. Bored through the London clay, the whole railroad was below ground.

The City and South London Railway was 3¼-mile (5.1-km) long

At first, cables were suggested as an alternative form of traction but proved unworkable in such a long tunnel and, in the end, electricity was used. Small engines provided the power, and at times they could not cope with the heavily loaded trains on the line, which had proved to be an instant success. As a result, it was not unknown for trains to fail to make it up the incline at King William Street, the terminus for the line in the city, and to have to roll back for a second attempt. Nevertheless, electricity became the power supply of choice for all underground railways and soon the power units were fitted under the passenger cars, eliminating the need for a separate locomotive. The early lines of the London Underground were all converted from steam to electricity in the first decade of the 20th century.

Electrification becomes the norm

The mountains and tunnels of Switzerland made it an obvious site for electric-powered trains. In 1896, the first commercial electric trains ran on the Lugano Tramway and, by 1899, a 25-mile (40 km) stretch of main line between Burgdorf and Thun had been electrified. It was on its mountain

Tunneling under the mountains Electric traction allowed for the construction of far deeper tunnels, as there was no longer the need for ventilation shafts. The electrified Simplon Tunnel was the longest railroad tunnel in the world when it opened in 1906.

routes, however, that Switzerland pioneered electrification. The Simplon Tunnel line was powered by electricity when it opened in 1906, and the St. Gotthard line demonstrated the advantage of electric traction when it was introduced in 1920. In a test between the systems, two steam engines struggled to climb up the steep gradients pulling a 200-ton (181-metric ton) load at 20 mph (32 km/h), while one electric locomotive hauled a load of 300 tons (272 metric tons) up at 30 mph (48 km/h). After that, electrification became the norm in Switzerland and began to spread rapidly across Europe. The Swiss success with electricity, combined with a coal shortage after World War I and an abundance of cheap hydro-electricity, drove its progress. Italy, which had already electrified a couple of its mountain lines, and France both drew up ambitious plans to electrify many of their main lines. Technical problems combined with the resistance of railroad managers who still favored steam held up France's program. Italy, however, rapidly expanded its electrified services, driven by Mussolini, the nation's dictator after 1925, who saw electric trains as epitomizing modernity.

The US was the first country to electrify a main line when, in 1895, it opened the Baltimore Belt Line of the Baltimore and Ohio Railroad—a connection from the main line to New York through a series of tunnels around the edges of Baltimore's downtown. A 1903 decision by the New York State legislature to outlaw the use of smoke-generating locomotives in Manhattan and south of the Harlem river boosted electrification in the US.

The Baltimore Belt Line was a 4-mile (6.5-km) long electrified railroad

As a result, electric locomotives began operation on the New York Central Railroad in 1906. In the 1930s, the Pennsylvania Railroad electrified all its lines east of Harrisburg, Pennsylvania.

Challenges persist

Despite the obvious advantages of electrification, the conversion of railroads to electric power around the world remained patchy. This was partly because railroad managers were resistant to change but also because it was hard for them to know which of the plethora of incompatible systems to choose. Many different kinds of electric technology were used: as well as various delivery systems, there was a wide variety of voltages, different phases (one-, two-, or three-phase), and types of current—DC (Direct) and AC (Alternating). Even today, there are numerous systems in operation, which hampers the integration of services, especially across national borders.

The most difficult choice that promoters of electrification had to make was whether to use a third-rail or an overhead system. For the most part, overhead was used for main-line railroads, while urban, metro, and suburban systems were generally equipped with a third rail. Sir Herbert Walker, the general manager of Britain's Southern Railway from 1923 to 1937, was a great pioneer of electrification in the country. He decided on the use of a third-rail rather than an overhead system—indeed, on the Brighton line, he replaced the existing overhead with a third-rail system. Nowadays, this is seen as outmoded and inefficient, as it relies on low voltages and DC current. However, with a network of more than 1,000 miles (1,600 km) of suburban and regional railroad equipped with a third rail, it would now be prohibitively expensive to convert to overhead operation. The London Underground is unusual in that it operates on a four-rail system—one of the only ones in the world (the fourth rail helps to increase the total voltage available).

It was not until after World War II that new railroads were almost invariably powered by electricity and the majority of existing main lines in Europe were electrified. Oddly, however, despite its early adoption of electric-powered trains, very little of the US rail network is electrified today—a few passenger lines in the northeast and some commuter services—while most mainline trains are powered by diesel engines. The US chose diesel over electric power when modernizing their lines, as it was cheaper in the long run and did not necessitate costly investment in wires or third rails to adopt. As of February 2024, about 94 percent of the total broad-gauge network in India had been electrified. In most modernizing Asian countries, electrification is now standard, and all high-speed trains around the world are electrically powered.

Third-rail experiment
While most tram systems used overhead wires to capture the current, there were experiments with a third rail. However, as this cutaway shows, having an electrified track on the ground posed a shock risk for pedestrians.

GOING ELECTRIC

In the 19th century, electric trains were seen as a cleaner alternative to smoke- and soot-belching steam locomotives. The first electric trams appeared in the 1880s, with electric trains following in the 20th century. Cheaper diesel-electric engines arrived in the 1930s.

NER No.1 (1904)
One of two Class ES1 electric locomotives run by North Eastern Railway (Britain), No.1 featured a "steeplecab"—a centrally mounted cab—and could be powered by overhead lines or an electrified third rail.

DB Class 160 "Bügeleisen" (1927–1934)
German national railroad Deutsche Bahn operated a fleet of 14 Class 160 electric shunting locomotives between 1927 and 1983. Its distinctive appearance led to the nickname "Bügeleisen" (clothes iron), due to the placement of the cab behind the engine.

English Electric No.788 (1930)
A small locomotive used for shunting at the English Electric engineering works, No.788 drew its power from rechargeable batteries. This class was used for a range of light industrial applications in Britain.

Pennsylvania Railroad No.4935 (1943)
Nicknamed "Blackjack," No.4935 was a GG1-class electric passenger locomotive that was later pressed into freight service. Industrial designer Raymond Lowey's distinctive streamlining hides a powerful locomotive with concrete ballast for greater traction.

SNCF BB9004 (1954)
The BB9004 was a high-speed electric locomotive built for French national railroad SNCF. In 1955, it set a world speed record of 205 mph (331 km/h) on the same day that another SNCF engine, the CC 7107, achieved the same feat. The record was not beaten until 2006.

Conrail No.2233 (1963)
This general-purpose GP-30 diesel-electric locomotive was one of the "second generation" of diesel engines, and was first unveiled by the Electro Motive Division of General Motors. In the 1970s, No.2233 joined the fleet of Consolidated Railways, which arose out of the wreckage of six failed railroad companies.

Pennsylvania Railroad No.4465 (1963)
No.4465 was an E44-class electric freight locomotive built by General Electric. A versatile and reliable engine, the E44's six traction motors could produce a top speed of 70 mph (112 km/h).

BR Class 92 (1993)
Designed to haul freight trains through the Channel Tunnel between Britain and France, the dual-voltage BR Class 92 were built by Britain's Brush Traction and Swedish-Swiss ABB Traction. Assembled in the UK between 1993 and 1996, these locomotives are operated by GB Railfreight/Europorte 2 and DB Schenker/Cargo.

JRF Freight EH200 DC (2001)
The EH200 class is an electric freight locomotive built by Toshiba for JR Freight, Japan's main cargo carrier. With a top speed of 70 mph (110 km/h) and a power output of 6,061 hp (4,520 kw), it is primarily used for hauling oil tanks and working steep grades of track.

THE PEOPLE WHO RAN THE RAILROADS

Railroads needed massive numbers of people to keep them running. Once the tracks were laid and the labor force of navvies had dispersed, a whole range of new personnel was required.

From their inception, many railroads were responsible for the largest workforce in their country. This included drivers, firemen, porters, conductors, engineers, track workers, signalers (known initially as policemen), and level-crossing keepers. During the early days, and in many countries well into the 20th century, this workforce was almost exclusively male, and it was only during and after the world wars that women began to be employed on the railroads in any number.

When the Liverpool and Manchester Railway opened in England in 1830 (see pp.26–29), it was not only the first commercial passenger railroad line in the world, but it also introduced many standards and practices that other railroad companies all around the world would adopt. Strict discipline and attention to detail were vital in order for the trains to run on time and to ensure the safety of the new railroads, so employees were expected to follow military-style rules and wear smart uniforms.

Since the armed services were the only contemporary organizations comparable in size and scale to the railroads, inevitably their ex-personnel became a major source of trained, well-disciplined labor. Indeed, many of the first workers who took up posts as porters, drivers, firemen, and track workers were former soldiers or sailors.

Recruiting for railroads

As the railroad business boomed in the mid-19th century, running the increasingly large companies required new skills and new types of professional workers, such as specialist engineers, accountants, lawyers, and managers. Many of these workers were also recruited from the armed services, but this time from the officer ranks. This enhanced the military character of the early railroads, and issuing "orders of the day"—setting out the daily tasks to be undertaken—became a popular practice at this time. However, the railroads were not solely the domain of military men;

Railway lamp Metal lamps such as this one were used by guard and track workers to alert the driver of any potential hazards.

Ready for service Railroad station personnel pose together in this 1889 picture, showcasing the number of staff required for busy stations. Each member played a crucial part in daily operations.

white-collar jobs such as ticket-office clerks were snapped up by anyone with a modicum of education, and the rapidly expanding industry was so different from any other that training mostly consisted of learning on the job.

In many countries, the structure of the railroads simply reflected the dominant social or political hierarchy. When India was under British colonial rule (pre-1947), the laborers and untrained workers were locals, but managers were predominantly white Europeans, or Eurasians with an Indian mother and a European father. Recruiting people to work on the railroads was more difficult in parts of the world where the tracks traversed inhospitable and sparsely populated territory. On the Trans-Siberian Railway, completed in 1916 (see pp.170–179), some of the local workforce consisted of people convicted of crimes who had been sent east to Siberia as punishment, but the railroad company could not afford to be too selective in its recruitment. Thus, many of the watchmen hired to guard property at night had been banished to Siberia for robbery, and passengers were often served by conductors and ticket clerks who had committed violent crimes.

Discipline and duty

The rules of the railroads were strict, and workers would be sacked instantly for serious offenses, such as falling asleep

By 1880, there were more than 400,000 people employed in the railroad industry in the United States

on the job, or have their wages docked for more minor transgressions, such as "deserting" their post to fetch a cup of tea. It was hardly surprising, however, that some people fell asleep at work: workers toiled for up to 20 hours a day, six days a week. Furthermore, some of the restrictions placed on railroad workers were notoriously harsh. Drivers on delayed trains received no extra pay, or time off in lieu, even if they worked several extra hours. Employees could be sacked without warning, but they were required to give employers three months' notice if they wanted to leave. A London and South Western Railway Company employee who failed to give the required notice was prosecuted and sentenced to three weeks hard labor in a case that served as a warning to others.

Discipline was largely the domain of special police forces, employed by individual railroad companies. A railroad policeman's duties included keeping order at stations, on the railroad, and in the local area around the railroad; removing trespassers; and ensuring staff adhered to company rules at all times. Most policemen carried a truncheon as a weapon, but equipment

Penn station luggage, 1901
Porters were a vital part of the early railroads. They handled various duties, including carrying the passengers' luggage.

such as watches, flags, lamps, shovels, and wheelbarrows was also issued and frequently used.

Perks of the job

In most countries, working for the railroads was highly regarded, especially at the beginning of the railroad age. Even untrained workers earned relatively high wages—railroad laborers could earn twice as much as farm laborers. The relatively good pay, strict rules, and the smart uniform gave the new industry prestige and afforded its workers a certain level of respect. Corporate loyalty was also strong as working for the railroads offered long-term stability, a permanent job in a world where that was a rarity, particularly in rural areas. Many men spent their whole working lives in the railroad industry, and jobs were often kept within families for several generations. Railroad companies were usually keen to employ multiple members of the same family because they saw it as another way of fostering loyalty. The companies also devised other ways of retaining employees: many jobs required working in remote areas so accommodations, at times with reasonable rent, were also a common perk for railroad workers. In towns, too, where workers had to start very early, accommodations were often provided near depots and stations. Providing cheap, convenient housing meant that workers would be reluctant to leave their jobs since it would make them, and their families, homeless. Moreover, the most efficient and loyal workers were rewarded with the best homes. As Frank McKenna puts it in his history of railroad workers, "from the earliest days, the companies used housing policy as a means of staff control and for the preservation of company loyalty." Free or concessionary fares for employees and their families were also a widespread benefit in kind that still exists today.

The railroad companies, therefore, took a paternalistic approach, controlling their employees with a firm but seemingly generous hand. However, railroad work was often very dangerous (only mining and fishing had a higher casualty rate), although most employers did not feel inclined to address the problem. The most hazardous jobs were shunting and coupling or decoupling wagons, as this involved working on the track right next to moving trains, but all track workers faced a high risk of being hit by a train. Moreover, in the early days of the railroads, individual carriages didn't have brakes, so when the driver stopped the locomotive, the carriages simply bumped into each other to stop. On average, more than five times as many workers were killed in railroad accidents as passengers. In Britain in the first half of the 1870s, for example, there was an average of 782 worker deaths per year. In the US, the number of fatalities was even greater, with more than 2,000 dying in 1888 alone, a toll that belatedly led to the sponsoring of the Railroad Safety Appliance Act in 1893, which gradually began to reduce the number of accidents.

High risk Railroad shunting posed a significant risk to workers, who could be crushed while coupling locomotives and wagons in the confined space between the tracks.

Worker welfare and trade unions

Eventually, the loyalty of the railroads' employees was simply pushed too far. Concerns over safety, wages that hadn't kept pace with other industries, and autocratic management led rail workers to join together to form trade unions, which could coordinate campaigns for improvements to pay and conditions. The traditional loyalty that workers felt toward the railroad companies began to erode. In Britain, trade unions started to be organized

in the 1860s. In 1867, workers on the North Eastern Railway went on strike over working hours—they wanted the company to agree to a maximum 10-hour day or 60-hour week, which does not seem unreasonable by modern standards. However, the company reacted aggressively by employing strikebreakers and sacking the strikers, so the protest action collapsed.

However, trade unionism could not be held back for long in an industry dependent on the constant presence of thousands of people and gradually organized labor movements gained a foothold over the ensuing couple of decades. Membership of unions grew quickly, and employers had to take notice. The unions were able to wrest a few concessions from the railroad companies, principally over the long hours and lack of overtime pay, but the companies were far from happy about it. In Britain, matters came to a head on the small Taff Valley Railway, a line serving several coal mines in South Wales. The Amalgamated Society of Railway Servants union had successfully negotiated a 60-hour-week in 1890, following a brief strike, but the Taff Vale Railway Company still failed to recognize the union officially. This provoked a second strike by the workers in 1900, but the company decided to sue the union. In 1901, the strike was judged to have been illegal and the union was ordered to pay £42,000 (US$210,000 at the time) in compensation to the company, a judgment that made any further industrial action in Britain impossible. This incident provoked a bitter public reaction and as a result the Conservative government was heavily defeated in the 1906 general election.

Climbing the ladder During the latter part of the 20th century, health and safety at work became a serious issue. As trade unions grew, the welfare of workers became a major concern at last.

The new government, led by the Liberals, introduced the Trades Disputes Act, which effectively gave unions immunity from being sued in such circumstances. This resulted in a rapid growth of union strength.

Other countries followed a similar pattern. In the US, railroad workers began to organize into trade unions in the 1860s, but this was strongly opposed by the railroad companies. Railroad workers were involved in three major strikes in the last quarter of the 19th century, and although all ended in defeats for the workers, union membership nevertheless increased and the rail companies were forced to recognize them. The US public largely supported the workers' desire for basic rights, and in the early years of the 20th century, trade unions grew across the rail industry, and they remain relatively strong in the 21st century. Similarly, in the Netherlands, railroad companies were initially resistant to any legislation that would restrict the number of hours that employees worked. So in the late 1890s, brotherhoods began to form, and in 1901 they coalesced into a single trade union, the Federatie van Spoorwegorganisaties. The union's first strike, in January 1903, was in support of dockworkers and immediately won concessions, but a second strike in April over working conditions resulted in mass sackings. Eventually, though, hours were reduced and workers' wages increased.

"The great object... is, to place the two rival powers of capital and labour on an equality so that the fight between them, so far as fight is necessary, should be at least a fair one."

BRITISH PRIME MINISTER
HENRY CAMPBELL-BANNERMAN
ON THE 1906 TRADES DISPUTES ACT

Railroad control center
As railroads modernized, individual signal boxes next to the line were replaced by computerized equipment that can oversee lengthy sections from a remote building.

Shift to automation

Today, railroads require far less labor. Signal boxes have been replaced by control centers covering vast regions; electric and diesel trains require only a single driver, as firemen are no longer necessary (although in some countries, such as the US, two people are still required to be in the drivers' cab at all times); stations no longer employ porters; ticket sales and collection are often now online; and machines have replaced people for some track safety and maintenance tasks. Some modern metro systems are even "driverless," with trains controlled by computers. The days when the railroads were the largest and most prestigious employers are largely over, although Indian Railways remains the ninth largest employer in the world with 1.2 million workers. However, with more than 620,000 miles (1,000,000 km) of railroads around the world, a significant, skilled workforce remains vital to build, maintain, and operate the world's growing railroad networks.

THE WRONG SIDE OF THE TRACKS

By the 1840s, the rapidly expanding railroad system was attracting many new businessmen, entrepreneurs, and investors, all hoping to see generous returns for their money, if not always by honest means.

Compelling characters John Sadleir was immortalized by several writers, including Charles Dickens and Anthony Trollope, who are believed to have based on him the characters of Mr. Merdle in *Little Dorrit* and Melmotte in *The Way We Live Now*, respectively.

From the 1830s onward, railroads became potential sources of huge profit. People and goods could be transported farther, faster, and for less money than ever before. Those local merchants who had invested in the earliest railroads, such as the Liverpool to Manchester line (see pp.26–29), reaped the financial rewards. Further railroad expansion was needed, and many people saw it as an opportunity to make money.

Cashing in

In 1859, investigative journalist, D. Morier Evans, stated in his book *Facts, Failures and Frauds*: "It is with the railway mania of 1845 that the modern form of speculation may be said to begin and the world has not yet recovered from the excitement caused by the spectacle of sudden fortunes made without trouble." It was finance capitalism at its most primitive, with George Hudson (see pp.54–55) typical of those who, in Evans's words, were "pioneering new lines through every difficulty" and establishing the various ways in which he and his successors could defraud the public. Hudson embezzled a fortune and ruined many investors along the way, including the famous English literary family, the Brontës.

By modern standards of corporate governance, the promoters responsible for some of the world's railroads were dishonest. Yet many of these, such as Henry Meiggs (see pp.186–191), made innovative contributions to the development of the railroads. Even George Hudson belonged to the class of railroad promoters who cared passionately about railroads, as well as feathering their own nests. So perhaps the worst scoundrels were those who contributed nothing to the actual development of the railroads. John Sadleir, a successful Irish financier and Lord of the (British) Treasury, who issued £150,000 (around $750,000) worth of forged shares in the Royal Swedish Railway Company, belonged to the latter category.

Government takes control

While Sadleir was eventually ousted for his crimes, his railroad fraud ensured that the Swedish government assumed responsibility for its country's rail system from then on. In this, the Swedes were typical of many European governments whose control over their railroads was far more complete—and more honest—than that of the British. The French, for instance, operated a system of controlled regional monopolies. Nevertheless, there remained opportunities for those involved to enrich themselves, and some politicians made handsome, if completely unethical, profits from the railroads. In Prussia (later a part

The Railroad King George Hudson was a highly successful early railroad developer in England, but his downfall was rapid when it was discovered he had used fraudulent methods in developing his empire.

THE RAILWAY KING!
DOWN UPON HIM!

of Germany), Chancellor Otto von Bismarck had no qualms about instructing his banker to buy shares in the railroads he was proposing to nationalize—a process that made him a tidy profit, but that would now be deemed illegal insider trading.

The fight over Erie

Perhaps inevitably, it was the US, with the biggest rail network in the world, that provided crooks with the greatest opportunities. The battle for control of the Erie Railroad in the late 1860s really laid bare the world of railroad speculation—the varied characters, the complex legal dealings, and the level of political involvement. The battle was immortalized by Charles Francis Adams, a grandson and great-grandson of presidents and himself a railroad man, in his book *Chapters of Erie* (1871). The Erie Railroad had never been profitable, he explained, but industrialist Cornelius "Commodore" Vanderbilt saw an opportunity to create a monopoly of the tracks to Lake Erie and make some money. However, he came up against a formidable trio of directors and speculators—Jay Gould, who had acquired a reputation as the most sinister and corrupt of railroad barons, and his two associates, Daniel Drew and Jim Fisk. The Gould gang issued masses of stock—and bonds convertible into stock—in order to dilute Vanderbilt's holdings. The ensuing battle spread to the courts and the politics of New York State. When the battle reached the State legislature at Albany, Vanderbilt looked like winning the hearts, minds, and pockets of the legislators, but Gould got there first—at an estimated cost of $1 million (around £150,000). In the end, Vanderbilt gave up.

Corruption and profiteering

Russia, too, was ripe for corruption. During the railroad boom in the latter part of the 19th century, many lines were built by

What a carve up! Entrepreneurs Cornelius Vanderbilt, Jay Gould, Russell Sage, and Cyrus W. Field are shown dividing up the United States' railroads in 1882, as European royalty watch from across the Atlantic Ocean.

Borki train disaster Train crashes, such as this one in Russia in 1888, added to the unpopularity of the railroad companies who were, at times, perceived as putting profit before safety.

private enterprise with the government guaranteeing a generous rate of return on their investment. This proved highly lucrative. Russian railroad baron, Samuel Polyakov, manipulated the companies he ran to ensure that he owned all the shares, thereby reaping all the dividends. Polyakov also amassed shares in other railroads, which he used as collateral against loans from foreign bankers, betting on the expected rise in share value. While these activities might just have been on the right side of the law, he also artificially inflated costs of railroad construction in return for bribes to state officials, usually paid with railroad shares. And he was not the only one. In *A History of Russian Railways* J. N. Westwood writes: "Many other important civil servants and even members of the royal family… received bribes in the form of shares from railway promoters." This corruption was endemic at all levels—even conductors, who were poorly paid, would often allow a passenger to travel for a "consideration," usually around half the proper fare.

German philanthropist Baron Maurice von Hirsch died both respected and respectable, yet he was also a railroad profiteer. Today, his fortune, most of which he made on the Constantinople-to-Vienna railroad, would be counted in billions. Hirsch was awarded a concession by the Sultan of the Ottoman Empire, Abdulaziz, to build lines in the open country, which did not touch any towns. This left gaps that had to be filled, which Hirsch did—expensively—and he was reckoned to have made several million pounds from the construction contracts alone. To make matters worse, the lines were built so shoddily that they required extensive improvement. Hirsch increased his profits by issuing "loans" to himself at cheap rates, then selling them on to banks at a profit. (The banks then sold them to the public for even more.)

"A man who has never gone to school may steal from a freight car; but if he has a university education, he may steal the whole railroad."

THEODORE ROOSEVELT

From pickpockets to poker players

Every aspect of railroad promotion, construction, management, and operation attracted its own type of crimes and criminals. Unsurprisingly, given the crowds, stations were favorite haunts of pickpockets and other opportunistic rogues. In 1853, David Stevenson, Goods Manager of the London and North Western, Britain's largest railroad company stated "We are at our wits' end to find out the blackguards. Not a night passes without wine hampers, silk parcels, drapers' boxes or provisions being robbed; and if the articles are not valuable enough they leave them about the station."

William Robson stole £27,000 ($132,000) from the Crystal Palace Company in 1855

In the US, card sharps proliferated on the railroads, including the infamous Alice Ivers Tubbs, better known as "Poker Alice," a petite, blue-eyed beauty whose winning combination of card skills and feminine wiles made her a very successful gamester.

Forgers at the fore

Access to the files of a railroad company also provided rich pickings for forgers and fraudsters. None was more successful than Leopold Redpath, a British clerk at the Great Northern Railway (GNR), the company that owned the tracks between London and York. Redpath was assisted in his deception by the fact that the company had numerous kinds of stock, bearing various rates of dividend, and therefore intricate calculations were required to determine the level of payments to which the owners of the certificates were entitled. Redpath forged share certificates in which he was both buyer and seller or, more cunningly, added the figure "1" to genuine documents bought by him, transforming, say, £250 to £1,250. In total, Redpath is believed to have embezzled an astonishing £220,000 (about £18 million/$23 million in today's money) through forgery and speculation on the company's stocks and shares (which was also forbidden). Interestingly, although he used his ill-gotten gains to live a comfortable and luxurious life, Redpath also became a philanthropist; as Evans summarizes:

> "never was money obtained with more wicked subtlety; never was it spent more charitably. A greater rogue, so far as robbery is concerned, it were difficult to find; nor a more amiable and polished benefactor to the poor and the friendless. It is certain that he spent in acts of high benevolence much of the money that he gained by robbery."

Ultimately, it took the revelation of anomalies in the affairs of another business, the Crystal Palace Company, to prompt a similar investigation at the Great Northern Railway. This led to the discovery of Redpath's deception and resulted in his conviction in 1857. Redpath was not alone, however; his defense counsel revealed that when Redpath joined the Northern "he found... a widespread system of speculation and of trading in stocks and shares under other people's names—names not infrequently entirely utterly fictitious." It is impossible to know how many similar frauds occurred during this time but have remained undetected, but it is very likely that there were many more.

The great train robbery

One railroad crime from this era stands out for its cunning execution—the theft of £12,000/$60,000 of gold bullion (around £1 million or $1.2 million in today's money)

Picking pockets This historical illustration that was published in *The Boy's Own Paper* (1879–1880), a British newspaper for boys published by the Religious Tract Society, depicts a pickpocket stealing from a likely inebriated passenger in a station waiting room.

in 1855 from a South-Eastern Railway train traveling from London to Folkestone, Kent. It was largely an inside job involving Messrs. Burgess, a guard; Tester, a clerk; and Pierce, a ticket-printer and fraudster; together with Edward Agar, a long-time professional thief. The plan was devised by Pierce and Agar: the gold was bound for France and would be transferred from the train to the ship at Folkestone. On the way to Folkestone, it was carried in a guard's van in safes with two separate locks and was then weighed at the docks to ensure that nothing had been stolen. The gang managed to acquire impressions of both sets of locks and enough lead to counter the weight of the gold. They were able to board the train, open the safes, extract the gold, and replace it with the lead, all before the train reached Folkestone. The scheme unraveled only when Agar was arrested for an unrelated crime. He asked Pierce to provide for Fanny Kay, the mother of one of his children, but Pierce failed to do so. Kay then revealed the plan to the railroad company and Agar confessed, implicating the other three to reduce his own sentence.

Thus the early commercial railroads attracted a wide range of crooks and cheats, forgers and fraudsters, speculators and schemers from every echelon of society, all looking to line their pockets while emptying others'. As Samuel Smiles put it in his 1857 biography of George Stephenson: "Folly and knavery were… in the ascendant. The sharpers [card sharps] of society were let loose and jobbers and schemers became more and more plentiful. They threw out railway schemes as lures to catch the unwary."

Inspiring films Railroads captured the imagination of the public, inspiring novels and even movies. Set in Victorian England, this 1978 movie is based on the great train robbery of 1855.

Agony Point The fourth loop on the Darjeeling Himalayan Railway, named Agony Point, also has the tightest curve along its route. It is located just north of Tindharia station, on the steepest part of the line.

INDIAN HILL RAILROADS: CLIMBING OUT OF THE HEAT

There were many reasons to build railroads—from carrying passengers and freight to uniting villages, towns, and nations. The Indian hill railroads, however, owe their existence to a very particular phenomenon—the British colonists' dislike of the hot Indian summer.

Since their inception in 1853, the railroads in India had quickly become a vital part of the way of life in the subcontinent, used by both the Indians and the British, though British segregation policies mostly prohibited even affluent Indian passengers from first-class compartments. As the railroad network grew, the British realized that it could also be the answer to the nagging question of how to avoid the oppressive heat during the summer months.

Mountain railroad The logo of the Darjeeling Himalayan Railway shows the difficult terrain that had to be overcome to build the railroad.

Leaving the towns in the summer for cooler areas in the hills had long been a habit of the colonists, but it was a long and arduous journey. Building the Indian hill railroads, which would climb perilously steep inclines to link the hill towns with the plains below, seemed the obvious, if ambitious, solution. Such a venture seemed impossible at first, however, as the hills in question—which included the foothills of the mighty Himalayas—had gradients that appeared too steep to tackle. Yet as the 19th century wore on and railroad engineering became more and more sophisticated, it was soon felt that no

mountain, ravine, or river could present any serious obstacle to the iron road's inexorable progress.

Darjeeling Himalayan Railway

The first, and still the most famous, hill railroad to be built in India was the Darjeeling Himalayan Railway (DHR). It linked Siliguri in the plains of the Himalayas (400 ft/122 m above sea level) with Darjeeling in the Lesser Himalaya mountain range (6,710 ft/2,045 m above sea level), climbing nearly 1¼ miles (2 km) in its 55-mile (88 km) journey. Construction began in May 1879, just months after the mainline railroad had reached Siliguri, and it aroused great interest in India. In March 1880, Lord Lytton, the British Viceroy of India, traveled on the first completed stretch of track, cheered on by huge crowds. The line was completed in two years, which is truly remarkable considering the challenges the engineers faced. For most of its length, the DHR ran alongside a newly built road, but while the first 7 miles (11 km) was a gentle incline, after that the gradient became much steeper, up to 1 in 23 (or 4 percent). This level of incline can be problematic for a railroad without extra support, such as a rack or a cable, but the DHR engineers avoided this by building a lighter, narrow-gauge railroad. Later they also added loops, in which the track passed over itself, and switchbacks, in which it reversed back on itself, to reduce the sharpness of the gradient further. One of the four loops on the DHR was named Agony Point because of the perilous tightness of the bend and its proximity to the precipice of the hill.

"That was the most enjoyable day I have spent in the earth."

MARK TWAIN, AFTER A TRIP ON DHR IN 1896

A successful start

Perhaps surprisingly, the DHR was extremely profitable right from the start. Not only did it transport British residents eager to escape the summer heat and tourists who immediately flocked to see the wonderful scenery, it also carried vast amounts of tea down the hills. In fact, the arrival of the railroads helped the local tea industry to thrive. Although the railroad was very slow, rarely reaching speeds of more than 15 mph (24 km/h), it was still much faster than the bullock carts that used the road. As with the mainline Indian railroads, the hill railroads also had a military function: building railroads deep into the Himalayas enabled the British to establish control and create garrison towns that would protect the most remote parts of the subcontinent.

In the early days, the mail train left Siliguri at 8:25 a.m., and passengers were treated to an unparalleled experience as the train climbed up through the cloud and early morning mist, steadily navigating the steep gradient to find

Darjeeling station Soon after its completion in 1891, Darjeeling station was used primarily by the British in India to enable them to spend the hot summers in the cooler climes of the Himalayan foothills.

the warmth and blue skies of Darjeeling. An early description in *Railway Magazine* in 1897 recounts an amazing climb up the Himalayan foothills:

> “And now we approach the culminating wonder of the line. At one place, we have been able to count three lines of rail below us which we have just traversed, and to see three more above us, up which we are going to climb, making in all seven lines of track (counting the one we are on) visible at one time, nearly parallel with each other at gradually rising heights on the mountain side. But now the wheels groan with the lateral pressure caused by a tremendous series of curves, and for a few breathless seconds, the train seems transformed into a veritable snake, as we pass 'Agony Point' and in so doing traverse two complete circles of such incredibly small diameter that the train, if at rest, would stretch round more than half of the circumference of one of them.”

Today, the DHR, along with other hill railroads, is a designated UNESCO World Heritage Site, honored for its innovation and socioeconomic impact. It is also still a functioning railroad, carrying both local passengers—there is even a special school train, which transports children to schools in local towns—and countless tourists. The trains can be heard anywhere on the mountain up to Darjeeling, thanks to the loud horns that sound constantly, even managing to drown out the trucks and buses. If they are lucky, passengers can see Mount Everest in the distance, although the frequent mists and clouds make this relatively rare (this author spent a week there without so much as a glimpse of

On the doorstep The Darjeeling Himalayan Railway, seen here in the town of Kurseong, passes through towns and villages so close to homes and shops that people can hop directly onto the train.

Everest). Incredibly, some of the original steam locomotives supplied by the British company Sharp, Stewart & Co. are still running, although they spend much of their time in the workshop at Tindharia, a third of the way up the line. The line has suffered from subsidence and landslides over the years, but after a lengthy closure in the 2010s, it is now operating fully again, and new "vistadome" coaches have been introduced to give tourists a better view from the train.

Nilgiri Mountain Railway

The next hill railroad project in India was the 3 ft 3⅜ in (1 m) gauge Nilgiri Mountain Railway (NMR) from Mettupalayam to Udhagamandalam (more commonly known as Ooty) in Tamil Nadu, a state in southern India. It had initially been proposed as a garrison line way back in 1854 at the start of the Indian railroad age, but construction did not begin until 1894. The NMR was even steeper than the DHR, as the railroad had to climb more than 1 mile (1.6 km) from the plain to the summit, over a distance of 29 miles (46 km). Consequently, it took much longer to build than the Darjeeling line and entailed far more major structures, including 108 curves, 16 tunnels, and a staggering 250 bridges. It did not open fully until 1908. The steepness, which at some points reached

Challenging construction The Nilgiri Mountain Railway was constructed in a rugged forested region, which involved cutting tunnels and building bridges through rocky hills. Manual labor was used to lift the racks and rails, as well as to remove rocks and boulders.

Vintage locomotive The NMR's *Blue Mountain Express* continues to operate with vintage steam and diesel locomotives, preserving its old-world charm.

1 in 12 (or 8 percent), was too great for a locomotive to manage on its own and consequently for the first 17 miles (27 km), between the towns of Mettupalayam and Coonoor, the line used a rack-and-pinion system to navigate the steep gradient. This involved installing a third rail in the middle of the track, with teeth similar to those on a gear mechanism. A special toothed wheel on the locomotive then locked in to the rail, enabling it to grip and help pull the train up the hill (see pp.70–71). Given the steepness of the line and its sharp curves, it was a very slow journey, taking five hours to reach Ooty at the top. As with the DHR, some very old steam locomotives still travel on the line today. In honor of that fact, the NMR joined the DHR as a UNESCO World Heritage Site in 2005, and they became known collectively as the Mountain Railways of India.

Kalka to Shimla

The third famous Indian hill railroad to be completed was the Kalka to Shimla line, opened in 1903. Shimla (or Simla as it was then known) was a much more important center for the British than Darjeeling or Ooty. By the 1830s, it had become a well-established summer residence for the British and was noted for its balls and other social highlights, attended by colonial officers and senior administrators. Although the roads up to the station were widened and improved with the construction of the Hindustan–Tibet highway, which was commissioned in 1850, it was still a four-day journey from the plains up to Shimla. When, in 1863, Shimla became the official summer capital of India, it meant that the whole paraphernalia of government, even the military, was moved between Calcutta and Shimla twice a year.

Due to Shimla's importance to the colonists, it was vital that a railroad should be built up to the town, but it was a far more complicated proposition than the other two hill railroads. As with the DHR and the NMR, the Kalka to Shimla Railway was built to a very narrow gauge (in this case 2 ft 6 in/762 mm) to make it lighter and to save construction time. Nevertheless, the railroad involved the construction of more than 806 bridges and, although many were little more than culverts over streams, several were arched, multitiered structures rising from the bottom of deep valleys.

As of 2025, the Nilgiri Mountain Railway is the only operational rack railroad in India

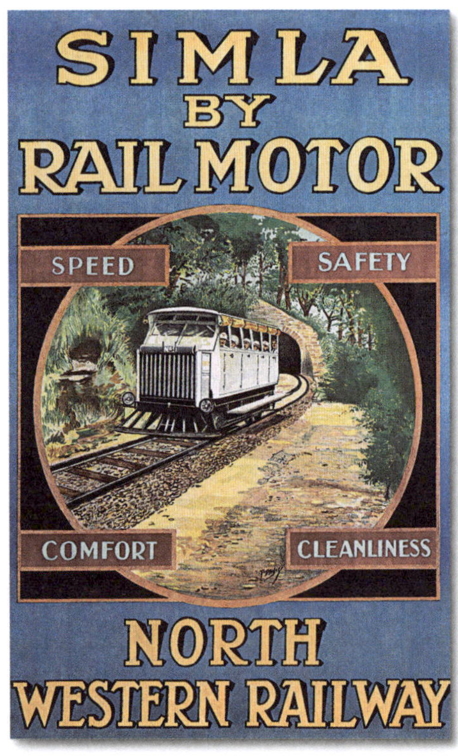

Take the train This poster from 1930 was used to promote a heritage train that runs between Kalka and Shimla.

In fact, there is a sad legend about the longest tunnel on the line (number 33), which is nearly ¾ mile (1.2 km) long. Colonel Barog, the engineer of this tunnel, ordered digging to begin at both ends, but the two sections were not properly aligned so they didn't join up. Barog was fined a nominal amount (1 rupee) by his employers, but many believe Barog's failure plagued him and led him to die by suicide. Another engineer completed the tunnel, but it was named the Barog Tunnel in memory of the original engineer. Despite this mishap, the 60-mile (97 km) line was a feat of engineering and came to be known as the "British Jewel of the Orient." The prolific railroad writer O. S. Nock traveled on the line in the 1970s and was amazed at the difficult terrain that the line traversed. He wrote:

> "The geology of the area is highly erratic. The formation consists of a heterogeneous mass of boulders, clay containing small quantities of sand and other debris, while in other locations it is a solid rocky mass. There is frequent trouble during the monsoon season from slips and subsidence, and these sometimes occur without any preliminary warning because of the peculiar geology and the unpredictable hydrology of the area."

He goes on to explain that he found the use of the word "erratic" by local geologists rather strange until he traveled up the line and saw for himself that the area posed particularly unique difficulties for the construction of a railroad. It was worth it, though. The line is one of the most impressive in the world, with spectacular views of the Himalayan foothills, and in 2008, the line was added to the UNESCO World Heritage Site, the Mountain Railways of India.

Commemorative stamp Issued in 1993 to commemorate mountain locomotives, this postage stamp depicts the Matheran Hill Railway steam engine.

Kalka to Shimla railway (right) As well as more than 800 bridges of varying sizes and complexity, the Kalka to Shimla line also featured 107 tunnels, a figure which has since been reduced to 102.

Other hill railroads

Several other hill railroads were built during this era and are still thriving today. These include the Kangra Valley Railway (opened to passengers in 1929) in the sub-Himalayan region; the Matheran Hill Railway (built in 1907), which ascends the Western Ghats mountain range in south; and the Lumding to Silchar line, built at the turn of the 20th century, lying deep inside the state of Assam, in the Barak river valley of the Cachar Hills. All of them are spectacular railroads, providing a vital connection between remote hill towns and the lowlands. However, Indian hill railroad-building is not just a thing of the past: the Kashmir Railway, which aims to connect the region in the outer Himalayas with the rest of the country, is an ongoing challenge. First mooted in 1898, the proposed route includes major earthquake zones, extreme climates, inhospitable terrain, and is subject to continued conflict between India and Pakistan over territorial rights to Kashmir. These geographical and political difficulties combined to delay the start of building work until the late 20th century, and after numerous technical and political difficulties, the first stage of the Kashmir Railway finally opened in 2025 in a ceremony attended by Indian Prime Minister Narendra Modi.

To the front lines Trains, such as this one carrying British troops in 1915, were a remarkably efficient way of transporting large numbers of soldiers to the front line during World War I.

War and uncertainty

The railroads reached their apogee just before the outbreak of World War I. Trains were now safer, cheaper, and faster than they had ever been and reached virtually every sizable town and village in the developed world. Therefore, it was the railroads that bore the brunt of coping with the huge transportation demands of the war. Not only did trains take virtually all the war matériel to ports for dispatch overseas and to the front, they carried millions of men off to war, and brought the wounded soldiers home in specially adapted ambulance carriages. Indeed, the armies built whole networks of narrow-gauge lines to carry men and supplies right up to the trenches of the front line. Railroads inevitably became targets during the conflict, notably in the Middle East, where Lawrence of Arabia led a series of assaults on the Hejaz Railway controlled by the Ottoman Empire.

After the war, the railroad companies began to realize that they had to look for alternatives to steam locomotion. There had been some electrification before the war, but now diesel was being considered as the main fuel, and both the Germans and the Americans created fast new diesel services in an effort to improve travel times. Attempts were still made to modernize steam locomotives, however, and the fastest-ever speed by a steam engine was reached in 1938 by the British locomotive *Mallard*.

In World War II, the railroads saw their darkest hour—millions of Jewish people and other minority groups were transported by train to the German concentration camps, and thousands of prisoners died while constructing the Burma–Siam railroad. Elsewhere, the railroads played a vital part in the eventual Allied victory over the Germans and the Japanese, notably helping Allied troops swoop through France, Belgium, and the Netherlands after D-Day. However, the railroads were poorly treated after the war—as soon as hostilities ended, services closed in many countries as competition from road transportation and aviation intensified.

Hustle and bustle Irish artist Stanhope Alexander Forbes' 1925 painting entitled *The Terminus, Penzance Station, Cornwall* depicts crowds of people milling about the busy westernmost station of the British railroad network at vacation time.

THE GOLDEN AGE OF THE RAILROADS

Railroads became the most significant means of transportation during the early 20th century. Expanding around the world, iron roads revolutionized the world, spurring economic growth and disseminating information and ideas.

In many ways, identifying a "golden age" of rail is difficult. At various times, there were many incredible railroads in operation, and several companies undoubtedly enjoyed relatively long periods of prosperity, but trouble always seemed to be around the next bend. The problems came in varied forms—safety issues, worker dissatisfaction and unrest, the need for further investment to improve services and cope with new technology, the whims of hostile governments, and, perhaps most crucially, the arrival of new methods of transportation, such as the car and the truck, later the airplane.

A distinct edge

Initially, however, the railroads had a crucial advantage: for nearly the whole of the first 100 years following the opening of the Liverpool to Manchester line in 1830 (see pp.26–29), they were the only feasible form of transportation for many types of trips. Thanks to the railroads, passengers could travel across whole continents, travel between a nation's major cities, commute between town centers and suburbs, and even reach remote villages—and freight, too, could be moved swiftly over great distances. By the beginning of the 20th century, the railroads had become a sophisticated industry—larger and more influential than any other in existence at the time—and in the years leading up to World War I in 1914, they reached the height of their power. It was a time when the automobile was still the province of the rich and the truck was an unreliable contraption, and both had to cope with

Late arrival China was the last of the major nations to join the railroad bandwagon, though it eventually embraced the utility of the iron road, as is evidenced by this c.1910 image of a busy train station.

roads that, for the most part, were rutted, muddy tracks. It was a brief heyday for the railroads, but it was one that had deep and lasting effects.

Global presence

By 1914, virtually every country in the world had entered the railroad age. There were no absolute boundaries to the spread of the railroads, and even the toughest natural obstacles—jungles, mountains, rivers, and deserts—could be overcome by clever engineers. Latecomers, ranging from Costa Rica (1890) to Hong Kong (1910) and Morocco (1911), joined the established railroad nations in Europe and the Americas, extending the iron road across most of the world. The US, Europe, and Asia could boast transcontinental lines. Even some small islands had substantial systems. Sicily, the biggest island in the Mediterranean Sea, had more than 1,500 miles (2,400 km) of line at the peak of its railroad age, and even the Isle of Wight, measuring just 150 sq miles (380 sq km), boasted 55 miles (89 km) of line by the turn of the 20th century. In the Caribbean, the island of Cuba had 64 miles (103.5 km) of railroad by 1849, mostly for carrying sugar.

Most countries embraced the railroads, particularly as their spread seemed so inevitable, but there were some exceptions. China was the last major nation in the world to give in to the incursion of the iron road. Even when the first line was finally built between Shanghai and Woosung in 1876, opposition to it was so strong, partly because it had been financed by foreign interests, that it was dismantled a year later. Gradually the powerful Chinese mandarins, or administrators, were persuaded of the necessity of joining the railroad age, although by 1895 a mere 18 miles (30 km) had been completed. In contrast, today China has more high-speed rail lines than any other country (see pp.336–343).

Rapid expansion

For the most part, and despite their key role in warfare, railroads played an important role in connecting the world in the 19th and early 20th centuries. Thanks to their facility for carrying both passengers and freight in large numbers, railroads began the process of globalization that was carried forward in the late 20th and early 21st centuries by airplanes and information technology. In the latter years of the 19th century and the start of the 20th, railroads across the world grew on average by 10,000 miles (16,000 km) per

By 1914, the iron road spanned 750,000 miles (1,200,000 km)

year, making many towns and villages accessible to the outside world for the first time.

Creating opportunities

The precise impact of the railroad varied across the world, but it was invariably profound. Unlike roads, which need little day-to-day attention, railroads require constant maintenance, such as patrols that ensure the good condition of the track, and investment, such as replacement of rails and signaling equipment. Therefore, once the railroads arrived, they transformed the economy and, inevitably, the character of a region. In fact, the railroads were a revolutionary force in both predictable and unpredictable ways. The most obvious advantage was a reduction in the cost of transportation. Consequently local produce, whether it was crops, minerals, or manufactured goods, could be transported more cheaply to national or global markets. The mail-order industry grew hugely at this time, as the railroads transported all sorts of mail-order goods to the newly connected citizens. The railroads also stimulated international population movement: immigrants arrived in the US by ship but then transferred to trains to fan out across the country. Indeed, many of the tracks were built especially to transport the influx of workers to industrial or agricultural centers, and then to transport away

On-the-fly mail From the 1860s, the US Railway Mail Service set up trackside cranes with mail pouches, which were pulled into moving trains and sorted on board to speed up the process of delivering mail.

Metal rings at both ends of pouch to attach to mail crane

Land of opportunity This painting from 1870 shows German immigrants boarding a train from Chicago to Colorado, where they could carve out a new home for themselves.

the results of their labors. Within countries, too, the railroads were a catalyst for the vast migration of people—the towns became honeypots for people from the countryside who could now relocate far more easily.

British economist Alfred Marshall, writing in 1890, summed up the influence of the railroads and the industrial boom they had stimulated: "the dominant economic fact of our age is the development not of the manufacturing but of the transportation industries." Another important outcome of the railroad boom concerned the workers and industries that supported the railroads themselves. The railroads required a whole set of new skills to enable them to run very large enterprises, so according to the railroad historian Terry Gourvish, "it is not an exaggeration to say that the [rail] industry played a key role in encouraging the growth of occupational professionalism based on specialized work. Engineering, law, accountancy, and surveying all received an important stimulus."

Creating tracks The railroads needed a huge supply industry, such as mills for producing steel rails, to drive its spread across continents.

Banks developed new loan systems in order to provide investment capital, universities stepped up to supply competent engineers and surveyors, and factories of all kinds were built to manufacture the vast array of equipment needed, ranging from huge steel components such as boilers and wheels for locomotives to soft furnishings for seats and panels for train roofs.

Opening up markets

Furthermore, the railroads affected other industries. By making transportation cheaper, they enabled similar factories to be concentrated in particular areas, which enabled the easy transfer of skills and experienced workers. The railroads also stimulated small-time capitalism, empowering many people previously restricted by their geographical isolation. In Mexico, Teresa Miriam van Hoy, the author of a social history of the railroads, found that the railroads introduced local competition in more remote regions since they:

> “prompted the arrival of multiple suppliers, thereby breaking any monopolies or market strangleholds, and provided smallholders affordable access to markets beyond their local community.”

In Russia, the village usurer (money-lender) became redundant because the local peasants were now able to travel to the town market by train to sell their produce and turn it into cash. The new stations, according to one contemporary writer:

> “swarmed with a mass of small traders, exporters, and commission merchants, all buying grain, hemp, hides, lard, sheepskin, down, and bristles—in a word everything bound for either the domestic or the foreign market.”

Many of the lines built, especially in the latter stages of the railroad boom, were unprofitable but nevertheless had a lasting effect on the regions they served. A railroad built in Senegal in 1885 as a way of establishing French colonial rule became a vital lifeline for the economy as, according to one historian of the African railroads, it allowed "the rubber, the cereals, and the peanuts from a rich hinterland to reach the Senegal River and transported [back to] the interior manufactures produced on the coast, such as textiles, foodstuffs and machinery." This story of economic opportunity was replicated across the world.

Bedrock of economies

The railroads not only revolutionized existing industries, but they also helped create new ones: in the US, Birmingham, Alabama, was a sleepy backwater until it was transformed into an industrial center by the Louisville and Nashville Railroad, which provided favorable freight rates, thus enabling the iron ore deposits at nearby Red Mountain to be exploited. The wine industry also developed, and not solely because of the cheaper transportation. In Argentina, wine production centered on the inland town of Mendoza and, as European immigrants arrived by train, they modernized the small existing vineyards and then exported their vastly increased yield via the railroads. Italian favorite Chianti became a regular feature of French and British restaurant tables, thanks to quicker, easier access to wider markets. In other regions, the taste of wine improved notably, thanks to the railroads. As the rail historian and wine writer Nicholas Faith recounts, "in pre-railway days, many wines tasted decidedly resinous because they had been carried on mule-back in hog skins painted with pitch."

It was not only industries and economies that were affected by the railroads. Even the lives of those who could not afford train fares were improved by the

Ice train One strange industry facilitated by the railroads was the transportation of ice in the US. Until the advent of refrigeration, natural ice was harvested in cool northern regions and transported via railroad to the warmer south.

Transporting wheat in Dakar The railroads revolutionized modern commerce. The Dakar station in Senegal became a thriving center of trade, transporting wheat and other commodities.

Luxury ride Train travel in the late 19th century could be a comfortable affair for those who could afford the luxuries of berths, dining cars, and first-class compartments.

railroads existence. In many countries, particularly in South America, Asia, and Africa, the railroad provided the only safe thoroughfare for walkers—provided they did not get in the way of the trains, of course. The railroad lines forded rivers and canyons and cut through mountains far more efficiently than the old mule paths that were circuitous and badly maintained. Pipelines also followed many railroad routes, bringing water to many towns and villages for the first time. Even the station buildings became prominent local landmarks.

Every railroad also had a telegraph system, which allowed faster communication than ever before. Finally, thanks to the iron road, people were free to travel around spreading ideas, and information and newspapers could be distributed easily. Thus, the wider dissemination of democracy, and other political and social ideas, can be attributed—at least in part—to the railroads.

Lopsided development

By 1914, in many countries, the railroad network was virtually complete. Consequently, the railroad companies were able to focus investment on improvements, such as faster locomotives or straighter track. Moreover, they could also devote substantial resources to making life more comfortable for passengers, especially those at the luxury end (see pp.162–167) of the market. These included elegant restaurant cars, comfortable sleeping facilities, and luxurious waiting rooms. At the other end of the scale, however, there were still many rudimentary services. A branch line shuttle might run only a couple of times a day and was not only slow but also subject to regular delays—the passenger cars might be pulled next to freight wagons, which could be shunted off at various stops along the way, slowing progress. The "stoppers" that meandered between mainline towns often used the oldest carriages and made their way in a desultory fashion, waiting patiently for express trains to pass at every siding. Timetables were also subject to all kinds of vagaries and were often designed

Railroad stations were often the most imposing buildings in cities and were frequently used as community meeting places

for the convenience of the railroad company rather than its passengers. The railroads were unchallenged, and the companies took full advantage, with many making healthy profits by charging high fares and bullying their smaller rivals to improve their own position. Worst of all was the grime—steam locomotives were messy beasts, spewing smoke and grit wherever they went.

So while for a short period the railroads were king, their dominance could not last. By 1914, the railroads had done their job as the catalyst for the creation of the modern world. The world would never be the same again, but nor would the railroads. By the end of World War I in 1918, trucks had become more sophisticated and would soon offer viable alternatives to rail freight transportation. Moreover, in the coming years, the car and the truck would become ubiquitous, further reducing the dominance of the railroad for both passengers and freight.

Working in the depot Workers at the Longsight locomotive sheds in Manchester, England, polish a set of locomotives in preparation for the Whitsun holiday rush of 1936. At the time, the railroads were still the most popular means of long-distance travel.

THE FIELD RAILROADS OF WORLD WAR I

The "war to end all wars" put railroads at center stage and showed the strategic value of the iron horse to the world, as trains were used to ferry people and supplies to and from the front.

As strategic assets, railroads came of age during World War I. At the start of the war, they were used chiefly to transport troops as close to the front as possible, after which soldiers still had a long march to their posts, usually burdened with supplies and equipment. However, as the two sides fought themselves to a stalemate on the Western Front, smaller, narrow-gauge lines began to proliferate locally, connecting the main lines with the trenches.

Field railroads in the war

The German army, possibly having anticipated the stalemate, were better prepared than the Allies. They had

Heading for the Eastern Front German troops travel by train to the Eastern Front in 1914. Large troop carriers such as this took the soldiers to the railhead, from which light railroads took them to the front.

stockpiled huge quantities of 2 ft (60 cm) gauge railroad equipment, having devised the concept during a bloody campaign in which they colonized South West Africa (now Namibia) in a three-year massacre that began in 1904. The *Feldbahn*—literally "field railroads"—were very flexible and could be laid quickly to transport troops across the Namibian plains.

The German trains carried both troops and supplies and were powered by little steam—or even gasoline-driven—locomotives which, by virtue of having eight wheels, the leading and trailing pairs of which could swivel and move sideways, were able to cope with short-radius curves of track. They could also be hauled by horses, of which there were plenty in each infantry unit. When they invaded Belgium and France, the Germans took enough 2 ft (60 cm) gauge railroad equipment to lay several hundred miles of track.

Meanwhile, the French regarded themselves as the inventors of the minirailroad, having used the concept extensively in their invasion of Morocco in 1911. And so, as soon as trenches began to be dug in 1914, the French brought some 400 miles (645 km) of narrow-gauge track (manufactured by Decauville) out of storage. The standard French narrow-gauge locomotive was the Pechot double-truck, double-boiler, eight-wheeler, but this was soon supplemented by vast numbers of small, saddle-tank locomotives from the great US engine manufacturer Baldwin.

> **"All the European powers had built up vast armies of conscripts. The plans to mobilize in these millions rested on railroads and railroad companies cannot be improvised."**
>
> A. J. P. TAYLOR, HISTORIAN, ON THE WAR EFFORT'S DEPENDENCE ON RAILROAD TIMETABLES

Mule train French soldiers of the 11th Artillery Regiment complete a 2 ft (60 cm) narrow-gauge railroad near Soissons, France, in 1917. The wagons were hauled by mules.

At the front lines

The Russians—despite the many inadequacies of their army and their preparation for war—had also anticipated the need for railroads, having used the Trans-Siberian as the basis of their transportation system in their war with Japan in 1904–1905. They also made use of these narrow gauge lines, having built a 30-mile (48 km), horse-drawn, narrow-gauge line near Mukden, which had greatly facilitated troop deployment. In 1914, the Russian army had nine railroad battalions, of which three worked on narrow-gauge tracks. Once the Eastern Front, which was longer and more fluid than the Western Front, was established, a staggering number of lines were built. In addition to some 560 miles (900 km) of preexisting track, a further 2,500 miles (4,000 km) were laid, about half of which was used by horse-hauled trains, and most of the rest by steam engines. The Russians had the most need for this adaptable railroad system, since they were fighting both the Germans and the Austrians across a wide swath of Eastern Europe. The Austrians also had a well-developed field-railroad system, especially for their campaign in the south against Italy. In the mountains of the Dolomites, they added to the existing narrow-gauge lines—which were, in fact, slightly bigger than the standard 2 ft (60 cm), as they used a 2½ ft (75 cm) gauge—to keep their mountain troops supplied. As historian John Westwood writes in *Railways at War*:

> “Anticipating war in the Dolomites, the Austrians had realized that it would be hard to build standard-gauge lines on the Italian–Austrian front, so a proportionately heavier task had been allocated to the narrow-gauge lines, which were expected to be quite long. Indeed, in the long and usually fairly static campaign against Italy from 1915 to 1917, three substantial narrow-gauge lines were built by the Austrian army: the line from Auer to Predazzo, for instance, was thirty miles long, and included six tunnels and fourteen big bridges.”

44,000 miles

(71,000 km)
Total length of railroad tracks in Russia on the eve of World War I

The British war initiative

All of this was a far cry from the attitude of the British. British military strategists had expected a fluid war of movement, with troops attacking and counterattacking each other across large areas, and so they were ill prepared when the Western Front became entrenched. According to a report into the British Army’s use of transportation during the war, the authorities could not believe that the stalemate would continue:

> “For the first two years of the war, the British transport arrangements were dominated by the idea that the war would soon revert to one of movement, that it was useless to embark on any large scheme which might be left far in the rear and become valueless before it had materialized, and become of use.”

As a result, the British Army devoted more energy on trying to harness road transportation for the war effort than either their allies or their enemies. It was a hopeless task—what roads there were in rural France soon became impassable, and very often there were none to the front line. A British official report described the situation surprisingly eloquently:

> “... beyond the roads lay a nightmare quagmire of pulverized fields, ruined ditches, and flooded shell holes, threaded by temporary duckboard tracks and communications trenches. Through this muddy wasteland, every single item needed by the troops—food, water, clothing, medical supplies, tools, timber, barbed wire, mortars, machine guns, rifles, ammunition, and yet more ammunition—had to be carried.”

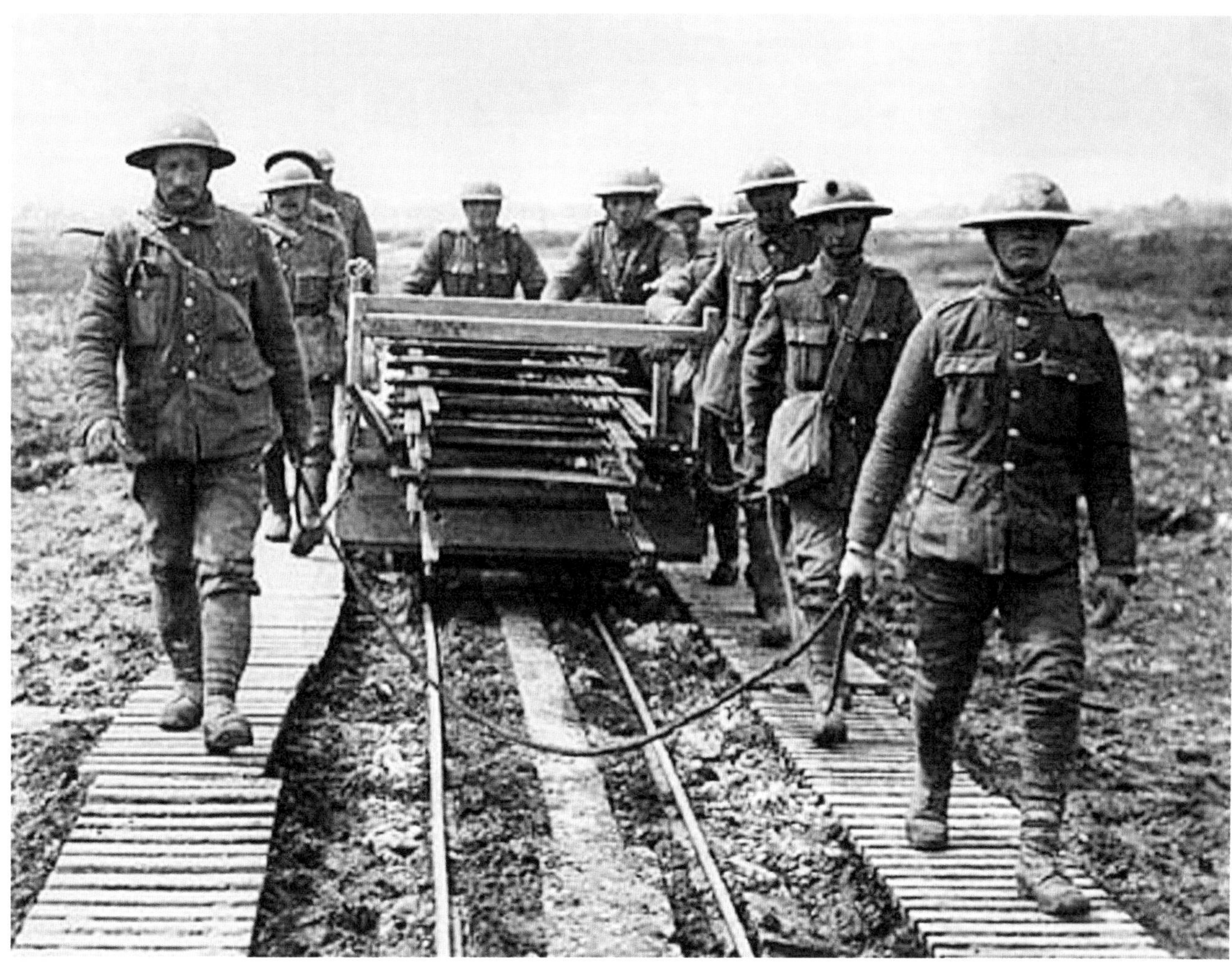

Vital supply line Allied troops lay a light railroad on the Western Front in 1918. The line brought supplies to the front and enabled troops to move swiftly between the trenches.

Rapid expansion (left)
Realizing its importance to the war initiative, the Russian army worked hard to expand their railway network. Here, army engineers can be seen laying a narrow-gauge railway track during the Russian campaign of March 1916.

It was an unedifying and perilous task. Many men died as they wandered off the duckboards in the dark and into flooded shell craters, where they were weighed down by their huge backpacks and drowned.

Narrow-gauge railroad lines were the perfect answer to this logistical problem. Their main advantage was that in the precarious conditions of the front line, they were more flexible and efficient than any other form of transportation. They could be laid easily, with a minimum of ballast and only basic sleepers, and were also very easy to repair if they were shelled or damaged by the constant traffic they had to carry. As the name "field railroad" implies, they could easily be lifted up and used elsewhere if the front line moved. The British, seeing the French success in using light railroads, belatedly began to develop their own in the summer of 1915.

Types of field railroads

The initial British light railroads were crude affairs that were mostly man-hauled, although mules were occasionally used. However, the beasts were reluctant to do their job at times, especially at night, the period when most of the operations were carried out. Far more sophisticated networks were later developed, and gradually two different types of narrow-gauge railroads emerged.

Ammunition train Narrow-gauge railroads proved vital in bringing ammunition to the front and were at times, as in this instance during the 1917 Battle of Langemarck, hauled by converted road vehicles.

The first type mainly ran from railheads to depots near the front line and was worked by gasoline or gasoline-electric locomotives, or even steam engines in some cases. The second type of line—sometimes even narrower than 2 ft (60 cm) gauge, which made it seem almost like a toy train track—was a cruder design that reached right up to the trenches. Often called "tramways," these lines mostly used men or mules for traction, partly because they were so close to the enemy that the noise of the engines might attract attention and possible shellfire. The two systems were supposed to be kept independent of each other, since the lines nearer the front were not sufficiently robust to carry the larger loads used by the lines from the railhead. All the lines were necessarily short, usually between 5 and 15 miles (8 and 24 km) long, and required almost constant maintenance. Derailments were common, particularly when tanks and artillery were being transported, and were usually dealt with by manpower alone—a few men would be called upon to heave the engines or carriages back onto the tracks.

Wartime adaptations

Trains were forced to operate under the cover of darkness, and the only light—if one were used at all, which was impossible near the front—was the size of a small torch. Yet nearly all the lines were single-track, and there was no signaling system, so operations were carried out on a tramway-type system of "line of sight." This meant that the drivers had to stay constantly alert, checking whether there was a train ahead that had unexpectedly halted or broken down. A telegraph system could be used to contact the controller, but only if there were problems. The unsophisticated nature of the system is best revealed by the fact that the drivers had to resort to finding water for their steam locomotives from the nearest shell hole, as there was often no other water source. One madcap scheme inspired by

Compact Simplex These armored gasoline locomotives hauled trains weighing up to 15 tons (14 metric tons) on the narrow-gauge railroads, which often stretched right up to the trenches.

"The Russians had perhaps the greatest need of such lines... given their exceptionally long front line."

JOHN WESTWOOD, *RAILWAYS AT WAR*

the lack of rolling stock was to adapt Model T Ford automobiles to rail use. They were fixed to a rail chassis, but proved too light for the task—they slipped on the rails due to insufficient adhesion, so the idea was abandoned.

Given the poor state of the lines and the frequent use of men or mules, speeds were very slow. There were other limitations. The maximum load of a narrow-gauge train was 30 tons (27 metric tons) and consequently, when supplies were transferred at the railhead, at least 10 such trains were required to take the load from one mainline service. Nevertheless, these little toy-town railroads were infinitely better than any other form of transportation at the front and carried huge loads. An officer of the railroad corps reckoned that one line could carry up to 1,200 tons (1,089 metric tons) of materials each night, representing up to 150 trains each run by a couple of men. Even large guns were carried, often straddling more than one wagon. Toward the end of the war, a new use was found for the lines: field guns were set up on wagons, enabling the gun to be moved after a few shots were fired, thus preventing the enemy from locating them. And it was not only ammunition and supplies that were carried—whenever possible, the trains carried troops to and from the front, saving the men hours of trudging through heavy mud where, in darkness, they risked falling into shell holes.

John Westwood concludes that "all the belligerents, even the Germans, made greater use of the narrow-gauge railways than they had expected." This was partly as a result of the stalemate that lasted for three and a half years on the Western Front, but also because of the state of transportation technology at the time. Field trains were an ideal solution for the logistical problems of the war's muddy battlefields, and they became ubiquitous. It was only when the Germans, at last, broke through the lines in the spring of 1918 and the Allies then counterattacked that the lines lost their purpose. Because of their temporary nature, very few survive today, with just a handful of sections of line in northern France preserved to show what *Les Petits Trains*, as the French call them, achieved in that terrible conflict.

Railroad gun The French deployed eight of these massive 16 in (400 mm) howitzers in World War I to break through heavy fortifications, especially during siege situations.

AMERICAN LUXURY

Passenger services began in the United States in the 1830s, and by 1869 the first journeys across the continent were made. Long-distance travel led to innovations such as Pullman sleeper cars (see pp.162–167) and observatory carriages.

Pullman *Pioneer* (1864)
With its black walnut interior, thick pile carpeting, and plush upholstery, the Pullman *Pioneer* was the most luxurious rail vehicle of its time and would cement Pullman's reputation as the creator of the "hotel on wheels." In 1865, this car was used to carry the body of assassinated US President Abraham Lincoln back to his hometown of Springfield, Illinois.

RDG No.800 (1931)
No.800 was the first electric multiple unit (EMU) to be put into service by the Reading Company on its Philadelphia commuter routes. An EMU train consists of self-propelled carriages—No.800 was powered by 11,000 volts of AC current, collected via a pantograph from overhead lines.

RDG Observation No.1 (1937)
This Budd Company observation car was the tail carriage in Reading Company's flagship *Crusader* train, a streamliner service that linked Jersey City and Philadelphia. It boasted ultra-modern features, including air conditioning, sound proofing, and movable arm-chair seating.

NW No.1489 *Scioto County* (1949)
Named after a county in Ohio, *Scioto County* was built by Budd Company for the Norfolk and Western Railway as a sleeper equipped with 10 roomettes (small, single rooms) and six double-bedrooms. After several refits and spells as a commuter car and snack-bar coach, it was retired in 2001 before returning to service on a heritage line.

Bomx No.130: *Hershey Ware* (1949)
Named *Hershey Ware* by the Baltimore and Ohio Railroad Museum after a restoration, No.130 was a passenger carriage built by Budd Company in Philadelphia. Originally used as a 21-berth sleeper by the Pennsylvania Railroad, it was refitted as a commuter car in 1963 for the New York World's Fair.

NW No.512: *Powhatan Arrow* (1949)
No.512 was a 51-class lightweight steel carriage built by Pullman. It was one of the units that made up the *Powhatan Arrow*, Norfolk and Western's streamliner passenger service that served a 676-mile (1,088 km) route from Norfolk, Virginia, to Cincinnati, Ohio.

Baltimore and Ohio No.1961 (1956)
A Budd Company self-propelled dining car, No.1961 was powered by two underfloor diesel engines. The rear of the car could seat 24 regular passengers, while the eight-table dining area could serve 24 additional passengers from a full kitchen. It was converted for conventional passenger duties in 1963 before being retired in 1984.

WARTIME RAILROAD DISASTERS

Some of the worst railroad accidents, in terms of the number of fatalities, took place during the two world wars—although none involved enemy attack.

It is no coincidence that a high proportion of the world's most serious rail disasters occurred during wartime. The highest death toll of any rail accident in Europe occurred in Romania during World War I. Each of these disasters was wholly or partly caused by the overuse of the railroads due to the demands of war, combined with a compromise of normal peacetime safety standards. Wartime censorship meant that information on these incidents was withheld at the time, and even today the details are sketchy. Consequently,

these wartime disasters have been mostly forgotten by the general populace, despite the high death tolls.

A costly error

The first of this series of tragedies took place during World War I at Quintinshill, near the English–Scottish border. In terms of loss of life, it remains by far the worst train accident in British history, and while the direct cause was a series of mistakes by signalmen, a contributory factor was the enormous pressure placed on the railroads due to the war. The Caledonian main line approaching Carlisle from the north—one of two main rail connections between England and Scotland—was one of the busiest stretches of railroad in the country during the conflict. A huge number of "Jellicoe specials"—freight trains carrying coal for Admiral Jellicoe's Royal Navy—used the line when returning empty from Scotland to England, as well as local and express passenger services. On the morning of May 22, 1915, the two overnight sleeper expresses from London were late, as often happened in the war due to the intensity of traffic. The small signal box at Quintinshill, 10 miles (16 km) north of Carlisle, controlled a section of the main line as well as the sidings on either side of the track, which were used to temporarily accommodate slower freight trains or local services so that faster trains could overtake.

That morning, the sidings were full of empty Jellicoe specials waiting to return to the mines to collect coal. Consequently, the signalers decided to direct a slow local train off the northbound main line and

Heading for the front During World War I, trains were used on an unprecedented scale to shift troops and equipment to the battlefield. Here, French soldiers depart for the Western Front in 1914.

Triple collision at Quintinshill
An express engine lies in the wreckage of an earlier collision between a local service and a troop train at Quintinshill, England, in 1915. A freight wagon (left) has been thrown off the track.

onto the southbound track, in order to allow the sleeper express trains to pass through. Disastrously, the signalmen then forgot that the southbound track was occupied, even though the parked train was within sight of the signal box.

It was just after 6 a.m., and the signalmen were about to change shifts—George Meakin giving way to James Tinsley. However, against the rules, the two men had agreed to swap shifts a little later than scheduled to give Tinsley time to take the local train to the signal box. Tinsley, therefore, was busy filling in the register—to cover the fact that he had not started work until after 6 a.m.—and chatting about the war when he gave the signal "line clear" to a southbound troop train. He had forgotten that the local train—on which he had just traveled—was sitting on the southbound main line. The troop train was carrying 485 soldiers of the Royal Scots, who had just finished their training and were bound for the fighting at Gallipoli in Ottoman East Thrace (modern-day Türkiye). The driver had no chance of stopping when the troop train came down a slight gradient at more than 70 mph (110 km/h). The train smashed into the local service head on with such force that the troop train's carriages were compressed into a length of just

210 ft (64 m)—a third of their original size. To compound the disaster, the old rolling stock that had been commandeered for the troop train was made of wood and acted like a tinderbox—a fire quickly broke out and was fueled by gas-lighting cylinders and coal from the engines. But worse was yet to come.

The northbound express for which the local service had been waiting was unable to stop and plowed into the wreckage from the two earlier trains, which had been strewn across the northbound main line. The death toll from the incident was 227—by far the worst British rail disaster, and nearly twice the total of the second-worst, at Harrow in 1952—but fatalities on the two passenger trains were light, although the figures may have been massaged by the wartime official sources. The two signalmen were jailed for manslaughter, with relatively light sentences given the scale of the disaster—Tinsley received three years and Meakin half that.

Disaster at Ciurea

The Romanian accident, which happened on January 13, 1917, is shrouded in mystery because of its location and the tight censorship of the Romanian and Russian authorities. It bore several similarities with a later disaster at St.-Michel-de-Maurienne in France (see p.263)—a heavily overloaded troop train ran out of control, leading to a fire that killed many of the victims. The accident occurred at Ciurea—in a remote eastern part of Romania near what is now the border with Belarus—and involved Russian troops as well as Romanian ground infantry (GIs) and civilians fleeing a brutal German advance. Romania had entered the war late on the side of the Allies, and after early success was soon overrun by German forces. To escape the enemy, a huge train of 26 carriages packed with wounded Russian soldiers, as well as refugees, left the town of Bârnova bound for Ciurea. A survivor, Nicolae Dunanreanu, wrote of the scramble to get on the train:

> “… everywhere, people—and particularly soldiers—clambered on to the roofs, steps, and buffers, gripping each other in mad desperation. There was not even the smallest corner free, one could not even get both feet on a step, nor a buffer, and these desperate people seeking a relative or fleeing from the enemy who occupied more than half the country could not guess that a greater disaster awaited them.”

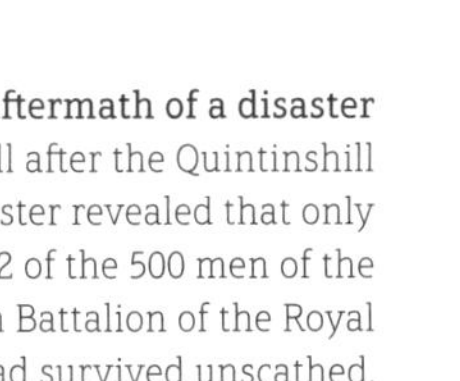

The aftermath of a disaster
A roll call after the Quintinshill disaster revealed that only 62 of the 500 men of the 7th Battalion of the Royal Scots had survived unscathed.

Tragedy at Ciurea, 1917 It is thought that the devastating crash was partly caused by damaged brake pipes.

The two stations were separated by an incline that averaged 1 in 40, but with sections as steep as 1 in 15. It became apparent shortly after starting the descent that the train's brakes were not working properly—it later emerged that passengers had broken the connecting pipes between carriages by stepping on them as they crowded onto the train. The two locomotives did not have sufficient braking power between them, and consequently the train hurtled ever faster down the slope. Despite the efforts of the train crew—who took the emergency measure of putting the locomotive in reverse, and tried to sand the track to increase adhesion—the coaches were derailed as they entered Ciurea station, causing destruction on a vast scale. The final death toll is thought to have exceeded 1,000, although wartime secrecy—and the remoteness of the area in which the accident occurred—meant that no precise figure has ever been ascertained. There is no doubt, however, that it was by far the worst railroad accident ever to occur in Europe.

"The train jumped off the rails like a monstrous reptile of iron and steel, pulling all its travelers to mutilation or on the great journey to beyond."

SURVIVOR OF THE CIUREA RAILROAD ACCIDENT

Catastrophe in France

Later that year, an accident occurred in France that would prove to be the worst railroad disaster within Western Europe. It was caused by elementary mistakes made by railroad officials working under the strain of wartime loads and—crucially—under the orders of the military, who ignored the officials' warnings. A very long train of 19 carriages was being hauled over the Alps on the night of December 12, 1917, carrying more than 900 French troops on their way home for Christmas. The men had fought in Italy and were anxious to get home quickly for their leave. Having traveled through the Mont Cenis tunnel, a crucial link between the two countries, the train waited at Modane on the French side for more than an hour as other services were allowed onto the overburdened line. The train was also being delayed because of the lack of a second locomotive, which was vital not just to provide extra power up the gradients but to assist with braking on the descents. Only three carriages had air brakes, while the rest had either crude, hand-operated brakes or none at all.

As the delay lengthened and the *poilus* (French infantry) became rowdy, the train driver, Girard, came under pressure to proceed down the incline. He refused unless a second locomotive could be found, but the only one available had been allocated to an ammunition train. Girard was overruled by the local military traffic officer, Capitaine Fayolle, who told the driver that he would be thrown into the fortress (prison) if he refused. It was a classic case of military personnel failing to understand the limitations and safety requirements of the railroad. As a result, the inevitable happened. With such a huge load and inadequate braking power, the train began to speed out of control. When the brakes were applied, the friction was so great that they heated up and caught fire. This sowed panic among the passengers, some of whom jumped off the speeding train. Traveling at around three times the speed limit of 25 mph (40 km/h), the train jumped the rails at a bend near the village of St.-Michel-de-Maurienne. Several carriages plunged into the gorge below, while others burst into flames. Relieved of its burden, the locomotive stayed on the tracks—and Girard, who was not initially aware of having lost his load, survived.

At the time, the death toll was announced as 424, but is now thought to have been 457. Other estimates put the number as high as 675, since many of the dead were incinerated in the ensuing fire—which took a day to burn out—and several survivors later succumbed to their injuries in the hospital. But it could have been even worse. Only the quick actions of a stationmaster prevented a train carrying Scottish troops toward Italy from crashing into the debris. Reflecting the sensitivity of such wartime incidents, it was not until 79 years after the accident, on December 12, 1996, that a memorial to the dead was opened at the site of the disaster.

Spain's worst rail disaster

Spain experienced its worst train disaster during World War II, despite the country's neutrality. The accident occurred on January 3, 1944, near the village of Torre del Bierzo in the León province, when three trains collided inside a tunnel. Like the Romanian and French disasters, the cause was a runaway train speeding down an incline, resulting in a fire that claimed most of the lives. The overnight Galician mail express failed to make a scheduled stop at Albares due to a broken braking system.

Number of unidentified dead at St.-Michel-de-Maurienne

135

Disaster in the Alps The remains of a 19-car train carrying over 900 French troops lie at the bottom of a gorge near the village of St-Michel-de-Maurienne, France.

The stationmaster at Torre del Bierzo, the next station down the line, ordered sleepers to be placed on the line to slow the train down, but his efforts were to no avail. The train ran toward a tunnel where it hit another train that was in the process of being moved out of its path. Unaware of the crash, a coal train with 27 loaded wagons then approached the tunnel from the opposite direction and plowed into the wreckage.

The ensuing fire burned for two days, preventing the injured from being rescued and making identification of most of the victims impossible. Strict censorship under the regime of General Franco meant that the accident received very little publicity at the time, and the official RENFE (the Spanish rail operator) file on the accident was lost. There were many illegal travelers on the train heading for a post-Christmas market, and although the official death toll was put at 78, research has shown that the real figure was closer to 500.

Tragedy inside the tunnel

World War II was also the backdrop for Italy's most serious accident, which brought a death toll far in excess of any other rail disaster in the country. Again, wartime conditions were the underlying cause. The accident happened at Balvano, a small town inland from Salerno on the Bay of Naples. The area was under occupation by Anglo American forces that had battled their way up from Sicily, and food and other basics were in short supply. Many townspeople jumped on freight trains illegally to travel into the countryside to obtain supplies, either for themselves or to sell on the black market. One such steam-hauled train left Salerno on the wet and cold evening of March 2, 1944, heading for farms inland in the Apennine mountains. Hundreds of people jumped onto the flat wagons at each successive stop, and sheltered under tarps and whatever else they could find. The train stopped in a tunnel near Balvano, where it was forced to wait nearly 40 minutes for another service to come down the hill. This was to prove fatal for hundreds of the 650

"The faces of the victims were mostly peaceful. They showed no sign of suffering. Many were sitting upright or in positions they might assume while sleeping normally."

OBSERVATION BY A US ARMY COLONEL WHO HELPED IN THE AFTERMATH OF THE BALVANO DISASTER

Headed for disaster A railroad worker at the Balvano-Ricigliano railroad station in Italy points in the direction in which the doomed train was heading. The tunnel where the incident occurred is 1.2 miles (2 km) farther away and not visible here.

or so illegal travelers. Wartime shortages meant that the only fuel available for the engine was poor-quality coal, which emitted a high level of carbon monoxide. The incline in the tunnel caused the fumes to spread downward; the death toll was enormous and has been estimated at between 450 and 500. Those who survived had mostly been in the rear wagons, which were not in the tunnel when the train stopped. The alert was sounded by a brakeman, who ran back to the nearest station shouting "they are all dead," before collapsing from the effects of the fumes. Death had come quietly and quickly.

A safer present

Fortunately, the scale of these disasters is unlikely to be repeated in the modern era. Train technology—such as advances in braking efficiency—and the enforcement of regulations mean that train travel is far safer now. Generally, trains are not as overcrowded as in previous years, and fire is rarely a hazard given that steam locomotives are no longer used. Moreover, carriages are no longer made of wood and are designed and built to be strong enough to withstand the forces of crashes—so even when accidents do occur, the survival rate tends to be higher. Nevertheless, with high-speed trains traveling at around 186 mph (300 km/h) or even 200 mph (320 km/h) every day in many countries that have built high-speed rail systems, the possibility of a tragedy on a large scale remains—as evidenced by the July 2013 accident at Santiago de Compostela in Spain, in which 79 people lost their lives when a train left a high-speed section but failed to slow down sufficiently and consequently derailed.

THE HEJAZ RAILWAY

The military and political value of railroad lines was the catalyst for the construction of a railroad deep in the desert of the Hejaz region of western Asia. This railroad later gained fame in the West through the exploits of Lawrence of Arabia.

Railroads came late to the Middle East. By the end of the 19th century, there were just a few lines operating in the Ottoman Empire. As with many pioneering railroads, the idea for the construction of a railroad in the Hejaz region was mooted long before work commenced. German American civil engineer Charles Zimpel proposed a line from Damascus to the Red Sea in 1864, and numerous similar lines were also suggested in the last third of the 19th century. However, it was the proposal in 1897 by Muhammad Insha Allah, an Indian Muslim teacher and journalist, that attracted the attention of the Sultan of the empire, Abdulhamid II.

Abdulhamid was the conservative leader of the crumbling Ottoman Empire, ruling from Constantinople (now Istanbul). Soon after his accession in 1876, the empire lost two-fifths of its territory, including Bulgaria and Serbia, effectively ending Ottoman influence in Europe. Following this loss, the Sultan resolved to strengthen his hold over the remaining Asian part of the empire, in particular, the Arabian Peninsula. The political influence of the empire was waning, but Abdulhamid hoped to reinforce its religious significance. The proposed railroad offered an opportunity to consolidate his own position as Caliph, leader of all Muslims, as the new line would ensure a fast, cheap way for pilgrims to travel to Mecca. Consequently, funding for the railroad was obtained largely through Muslim support due to its religious significance.

The work begins

Work started on the 3.5 ft (1,050 mm) gauge railroad in late 1900 under the auspices of a German engineer, Heinrich Meissner, who was in charge of the project for eight years. Initially, the line was beset by problems, and progress was slow. The original surveys were unsatisfactory and had to be redone. The

Desert railroads The Hejaz Railway primarily used steam locomotives, sourced from several European nations, particularly Germany, for its operations. This preserved locomotive is now used to ferry tourists along the railroad near Wadi Rum, Jordan.

Building the line (left) The majority of the construction of the Hejaz Railway, including laying tracks, was carried out by military conscripts, who formed the backbone of the labor force.

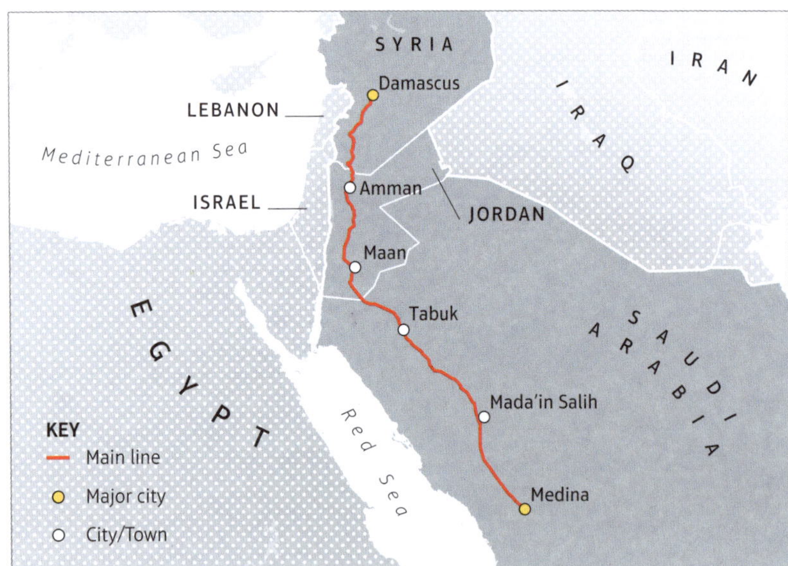

The Hejaz Railway The railroad line ran from Damascus (in present-day Syria) through Jordan to Medina in Saudi Arabia, but it ultimately fell short of its original intended destination, Mecca.

laborers, mostly conscripts, worked in conditions so appalling that it provoked a mutiny. Recognizing the lack of progress, the Sultan took a softer approach and Meissner began to impose a more acceptable regime, attracting experienced foreign workers from Belgium, France, and Germany in particular. In the later stages, however, Christians were not allowed to work on the southern end of the railroad because of religious sensibilities, but by then, trained Turkish Muslim engineers were available.

Three teams were created: for reconnoitering, surveying, and construction. The reconnoitering team, which made a preliminary assessment of the route, experienced the most difficulties: they went into the desert mounted on camels and horses, venturing into unmapped land and facing hostile local people, and so were accompanied by a cavalry detachment. The second team, the surveyors, used the maps created by the reconnoitering group to set out a detailed route for the construction gangs to follow. Construction was carried out by a special railroad battalion with four divisions, each focused on a particular task: the advance party marked out a trace for the track and prepared the earthworks; the second division put down the ballast; the sleepers were laid by the third group; and the rails were tied in by the fourth.

Myriad challenges

Such a disciplined and organized process allowed rapid progress despite the difficulties of the terrain and other obstacles. It was not just the heat, which could reach 122°F (50°C) in the middle of the day (matched by cold nights in winter), or the remoteness of the land, but the sheer scale of the operation: 1,000 miles (1,600 km) of track would have had to be laid to reach the original destination—the holy city of Islam, Mecca.

The scarcity of water was the worst problem faced by the builders of the line, which followed old pilgrimage trails. These had occasional wells and pools where rainwater collected, but, for the most part, the vital liquid was stored in cisterns installed along the line and replenished by wagons transported down the newly constructed railroad. While lack of water was a perennial problem, ironically, flash floods washed away parts of the line in the rainy season. To limit such damage, many sections of the railroad were built on embankments. Sand drifts across the tracks were another obstacle. When construction reached the desert of the southern Arabian Peninsula, there was little vegetation to

> **"The engineers had to build a railway through this precipice, the Batn el-Ghul, the 'belly of the demon.'"**
>
> DOMINICAN FRIAR, TRAVELING ON THE HEJAZ RAILWAY IN 1909

prevent sand being driven onto the railroad by the wind, and it was therefore necessary for the line to be protected by sandbanks made of stone and clay.

The greatest irony was the shortage of fuel. Coal mined in Anatolia (Türkiye) proved too smoky, and so fuel was imported from Wales at great expense, then mixed with the local black stuff. Since steam locomotives can run on oil, the solution was in fact near at hand. As James Nicholson, author of the line's history, puts it, "In view of the fact that the Ottomans at that time also controlled the Eastern Province of what is now Saudi Arabia, they would have been surprised to discover just how easily all their fuel needs could have been met by what lay beneath the sands."

The workers, who numbered 7,000 at the peak of construction, lived in small tents that had to be moved forward constantly as the line progressed. Laborers lived on a diet of bread, biscuits, or rice, with only occasional additions of meat. There were no fresh vegetables or fruit, so vitamin deficiency diseases, such as scurvy, were common. Cholera outbreaks were not unusual and caused widespread panic, with workers fleeing the camps, which delayed progress.

Stopping short

As the railroad approached Medina, plans were still in place to extend the line to Mecca. However, opposition to what was called "the iron donkey" was strong among the local peoples, who did not want to see it reach Mecca. Their objections were not solely stimulated by religion: many local peoples made their living from operating the camel caravans for pilgrims. This resistance culminated in a revolt in January 1908, when Abdulhamid's political position was already weak. As a result, the planned extension of the line to Mecca was scrapped and Medina, the second-holiest city in Islam, became its terminus.

The last stretch of track from AlUla to Medina was the most difficult to lay in terms of the terrain, but work sped up with the arrival of extra workers. The rapid conclusion

Railroad safeguard To protect the railroad line from flood damage, sections of the track were laid on solid embankments, with numerous bridges—built high enough to withstand flash floods during heavy rain—integrated into the route.

Desert revolt Arab soldiers are shown attacking a train on the Hejaz Railway in this still from the film *Lawrence of Arabia* (1962). Despite the notoriety he gained for his exploits, Lawrence insisted it was the Arabs' war.

of the project was partly to ensure that the line's opening coincided with the anniversary of the Sultan's accession to the throne on September 1, 1908. The deadline was met and there were celebrations in Medina, but the Sultan did not attend: his popularity was by this time so low that he feared his absence from Constantinople might result in a coup.

Despite the Sultan's mounting political difficulties, the Hejaz Railway enjoyed eight years of normal operations, carrying many thousands of pilgrims to and from Medina. However, the line's fate was always bound up with regional and, indeed, global political considerations, and World War I was to turn the railroad into a battleground.

Uncertain future

The Ottoman Empire entered the war in 1914 on the side of the Germans. The British were eager to ensure that the Turks did not launch attacks elsewhere and so encouraged the Arabs in the Peninsula to rise against them. The Hejaz Railway was an obvious target, and in June 1916, the Arab people began attacking the line. However, the Arabs needed explosives and better equipment, and that is where British officer T. E. Lawrence—later known as Lawrence of Arabia—entered the fray. Despite ranking only as captain and holding a desk job in Cairo, he persuaded his superiors to send him across the Suez Canal to support the uprising led by Prince Feisal, one of the sons of Sharif Hussein, the Emir of Mecca.

Feisal's irregular troops had already launched several successful attacks on the line when Lawrence joined them in early 1917. He led several more raids, both attacking trains and sabotaging the track. The strategy, an early use of guerrilla tactics, was not to close the line but rather to tie up Turkish troops in its protection. Very few of

Lawrence's troops were killed in these raids—depicted so powerfully in the David Lean film *Lawrence of Arabia*—but thousands of Turks lost their lives and the strategy proved successful. Gradually, Lawrence and Feisal worked their way up the line and gained control of the railroad as the Turks fled north. This meant that Medina, and the Turkish troops defending it, were cut off from the rest of the Ottoman forces. Lawrence and Feisal eventually joined up with the British forces under General Allenby for a final assault on Damascus. Feisal's army, which included Lawrence, was given the task of cutting off the junction that led from the Syrian city of Daraa to the Mediterranean port of Haifa. The last, decisive attack on the Turks in Damascus in September 1918 was successful, but Medina was still occupied by Turkish troops who did not surrender until January 1919, arguably the last action of World War I.

As Lawrence recognized in his account of the battle over the Hejaz, *Seven Pillars of Wisdom*, the Turks were courageous and became adept at repairing the line. Following the war, and the division of the Ottoman Empire into states under British or French control, the operation of the line was split between the two European colonial powers. The Allies and the retreating Turks had destroyed much of the southern section of the railroad, but several parts remained open for traffic.

Reviving desert routes

The eight years from 1908 to 1916 were to be the only time at which regular services operated along the whole railroad. Even then, conditions were uncomfortable for the pilgrims, with overcrowded and slow services. The journey, however, took a few days and was a vast improvement on the old 40-day overland trip. It proved a brief heyday for one of the world's most ambitious railroad construction projects.

The best-used sections were freight services on the branch line between Damascus and Haifa and, until the start of the Syrian conflict in 2011, there had been a regular passenger service linking the capitals of Syria, and Jordan: Damascus and Amman. There is, however, renewed interest in rail in the region. Saudi Arabia is building a network to cater for the Hajj (the pilgrimage) as well as the nation's freight needs. Indeed, the part of the Hejaz Railway that was never completed has now been built as a new 280-mile (450 km) high-speed line, opened in 2018, between Medina and Mecca. There has even been talk of reopening the entire railroad, but this is likely to remain a pipe dream, given that most pilgrims now fly to Mecca.

Battlefield memoir In *Seven Pillars of Wisdom*, T. E. Lawrence recounts his experiences in the desert, fighting against Turkish soldiers on the Hejaz Railway.

War damage A German-built Krauss 0-6-0T locomotive still lies on its side at Hedia Station, abandoned following an Arab attack intended to prevent enemy use of the Hejaz Railway.

STREAMLINERS

In the age of aviation and the automobile, locomotive designers sought to lure passengers back to the railroads with a new generation of high-speed, modern designs. First applied to the marquee passenger expresses of the US, the term "streamliner" came to describe the steam, diesel, and electric locomotives that were sculpted for speed. These trains ran faster than their predecessors, some even setting world speed records. Not only were these speedsters more economical, but their elegant designs also captured the imagination of the public.

The Landi Locomotive Ae 8/14 No.11852 (1931)
Three prototype Class Ae 8/14 electric locomotives were built for the Swiss Federal Railways' (Schweizerische Bundesbahnen, or SBB) Gotthard line in the 1930s. Each of these powerful double locomotives had eight driving axles and could haul heavy trains unaided.

ETAT ZZY 24408 (1933)
Built by French car maker Bugatti, ZZY 24408 was one of several "Autorail Rapide" express railcars used in France. Despite a number of innovations—such as drum brakes, four gasoline engines, oil-damped suspension, and a central cupola for the driver—the model was withdrawn in 1953 due to the expense of its fuel.

Pennsylvania railroad No.4935 (1943)
Nicknamed "Blackjack," No.4935 was one out of 139 powerful electric locomotives built for the Pennsylvania Railroad between 1934 and 1943. They entered service in 1935, hauling express passenger trains on the newly electrified New York to Washington, DC, main line but were relegated to freight service in the 1950s. They had all been withdrawn by 1983.

LNER No.4468 *Mallard* (1937)
A Class A4 Pacific built by London and North Eastern Railways, No.4468 *Mallard* holds the world record for the fastest speed achieved under steam traction. On July 3, 1938, it hauled seven coaches at a speed of 126 mph (203 km/h), thanks to its aerodynamic bodywork and highly efficient steam circuit.

PPL No.4094D (1939)
A "fireless" shunter run by Pennsylvania Power and Light Co., No.4094D had a reservoir charged with steam from an external source instead of a firebox and boiler. It was used in settings where pollution or fire risk had to be eliminated, such as gas power stations or chemical works.

NW No.611 (1950)
With rigid wheelsets and lightweight driving rods to enable its relatively small driving wheels to reach 110 mph (177 km/h), No.611 is a Norfolk and Western J-class steam engine. The railroad's flagship model, this class hauled both passenger and freight trains.

DB Class 602 (1970)
Originally built in 1957 as a diesel-hydraulic VT 11.5 passenger train for the Trans-Europ Express, the Deutsche Bundesbahn's Class 602 was a 1970 refit with 2,200 hp (1,600 kw) gas turbine engines. The new class was capable of 124 mph (200 km/h), but high fuel costs led to its withdrawal in 1979.

Hokuriku *Shinkansen* E7 (2013)
This model of Japanese *Shinkansen* high-speed train (see pp.330–335) was launched in November 2013 in Rifu—a town in the Miyagi prefecture of Japan. These high-speed trains operate at speeds of around 162 mph (260 km/h).

AUSTRALIA'S GAUGE BUNGLE

Plagued by indecision and disconnection, the checkered history of railroads in Australia is a case study of how not to manage a railroad network.

In contrast to many other countries, where the railroads acted as a great unifier and were built in a standardized way that assisted their expansion, the state-run railroad companies in Australia seemed to take an almost perverse enjoyment in making life difficult for freight carriers and people wishing to travel across this vast country. In no other country in the world has the issue of the gauge of the various lines so dominated the history of the railroads and resulted in so much damage to the development of an integrated and viable rail network.

Early railroads

Given that in its infancy Australia was the destination of so many British people convicted of crimes, deported there in the 19th century, it is perhaps unsurprising that its first railroad line was operated by convict-power. In 1836, an 5-mile (8 km) narrow-gauge line was built across the Tasman Peninsula in Tasmania to the Port Arthur prison settlement, enabling visitors to avoid a stormy sea passage. Convicts who had first been press-ganged into building the track were then required to haul the little open-top wagons that plied the line, enjoying a slight rest on downward sections, where they could hop aboard for the ride. Passengers paid the not-inconsiderable fare of one shilling.

Horse power The first line in South Australia started in 1854, and comprised a horse-drawn double-decker tram running between the towns of Goolwa and Port Elliot.

However, this human-powered arrangement could hardly be called a railroad, and it was not until 18 years later that the first proper lines opened.

Gauge confusion

Constructed almost simultaneously, the nation's first lines set a pattern of disconnected services that would plague Australia's railroad system throughout its history. In South Australia, a 7-mile (11 km) horse-drawn line opened in May 1854 between Goolwa on the lower Murray River and Port Elliot, and four months later the nation's first steam service began in Victoria, between Melbourne's Flinders Street Station and Sandbridge (now Port Melbourne).

Both lines were built to the 5 ft 3 in (1,600 mm) broad gauge, as used in Ireland, but a line was opened in New South Wales the following year with the 4 ft 8½ in (1,435 mm) standard gauge. This was the start of Australia's failure to coordinate its railroads, resulting in—according to rail enthusiast and former deputy prime minister Tim Fischer—a veritable confetti of gauges, with 22 different track widths being used across the nation. Following the opening of these first lines, early attempts were made to coordinate the use of gauges. However, these only added to the confusion. Amazingly, the New South Wales line was first converted to the broader width and then back to standard gauge in the belief that this would match neighboring Victoria. However, Victoria and South Australia claimed that, in fact, changing to standard gauge would be too expensive, as they had bought rolling stock in broad gauge. And thus, as a historian of rail transportation in

Gauge conversion Some smaller engine types in Australia, such as the one on the left in the image above, were designed so that they could easily be converted to broad gauge. However, large engines, such as the locomotive on the right, were too wide to ever run on the narrower standard gauge.

Gauge spaghetti Taken in 1930, this picture of a goods yard in Gladstone, Australia, demonstrates that when different gauge trains ran on the same tracks, three rails were needed to guide them, increasing both construction and maintenance costs.

Australia put it, "the glorious bungle began." To exacerbate matters, the three remaining states, Queensland, Tasmania, and Western Australia—all of which were separate British colonies until the creation of the Commonwealth of Australia in 1901—each chose the 3 ft 6 in (1,067 mm) narrow gauge. While this enabled cheaper construction, it also served to add to the gauge confusion.

A disjointed network

In the last quarter of the 19th century, the railroads began to expand rapidly, mostly due to the demand for freight carriage. The overseas export market was the catalyst, with the consequent need to carry ore from the country's mines, and agricultural produce from the vast interior, to Australia's ports. But any attempt to create a national network—or even merely to establish links across state borders—was hampered by the gauge issue. In effect, the six Australian states each built a railroad network resembling that of an individual country, with very few connections and little cross-border traffic.

For example, when the rails of New South Wales and Victoria met at Albury in 1883, in theory linking Melbourne and Sydney, the different gauges meant that passengers had to change trains, and goods had to be transhipped for onward dispatch. The same happened between Sydney and Brisbane, when the lines between Queensland and New South Wales met at Jennings in the same year. Even at borders between states where there was no break of gauge, "huge time-wasting barriers were created to stop any kind of seamlessness," according to Fischer. The only two adjoining states with the same gauge—Victoria and South Australia—changed locomotives at the border because each state had bought different types of engines that could not fit onto the other state's network. This lack

Australia's railroads by gauge Although there have been efforts to reduce the variety of gauges, Australia still employs several different ones, as shown in this 2023 map of Australian Railways.

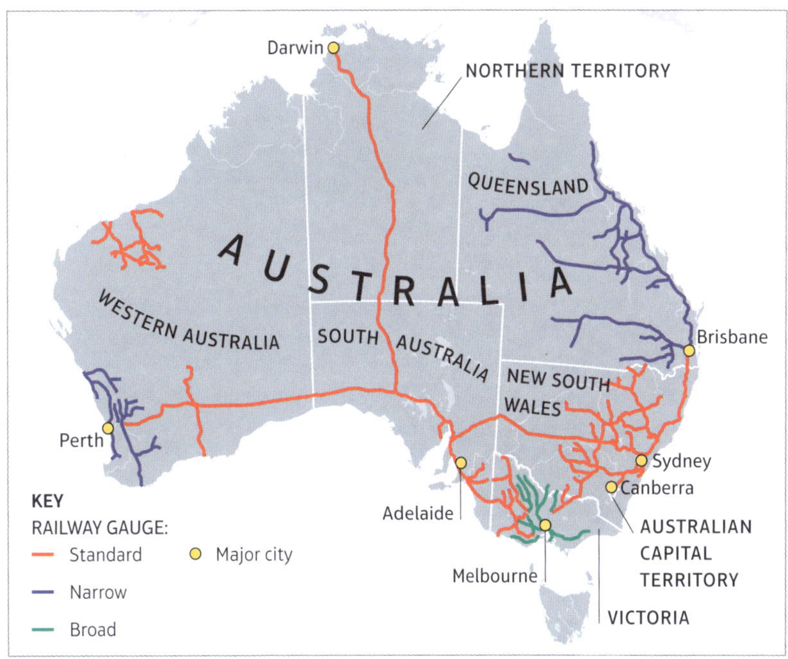

of standardization proved costly, as it hindered savings from bulk-buying of equipment. Coastal shipping took up the slack, handling most passenger and freight traffic between states, even though maritime transportation was a slower method of travel.

Attempts at standardization

The question of whether all the railroads should adopt standard gauge had been debated as early as 1890. However, it was not until Australia became an autonomous nation in 1901 that the gauge issue was addressed by the new federal government. Before then, the various colonial administrations had decided that the cost of standardization would be too high, making differences in gauges—known as "breaks of gauge"—inevitable. In 1917, the government built the standard-gauge Trans-Australian Railway between Kalgoorlie in Western Australia and Port Augusta in South Australia, but several breaks of gauge were required to reach connecting stations—at Kalgoorlie to reach Perth, and at Port Augusta and Terowie to reach Adelaide. Similarly, when the line between Sydney and South Australia was later completed in 1927, breaks of gauge were required at Broken Hill, where the line switched to narrow gauge, and at Terowie to reach Adelaide.

The nationwide rail system had expanded to some 26,000 miles (40,000 km)—relatively small for so large a country—by the end of World War I. As elsewhere, railroads lost market share between the wars as they faced growing competition from road transportation. Starved of much-needed investment from their state owners, the railroads then had to cope with the added loads of wartime

Maiden journey On 22 October 1917, the first passenger train ran on the Trans-Australian Railway from Port Augusta in South Australia to Kalgoorlie in the west, a journey that lasted two days.

matériel, following Australia's entry into World War II in September 1939. The railroads were used intensively for the war effort, carrying both troops and freight, but afterward a pattern of neglect began to threaten their very existence. Facing even greater postwar competition from road transportation, and with the emerging airlines picking off long-distance passengers, there was talk of abandoning the system. In the words of one historian of the Australian railroads: "they might have succumbed to the... critics and become nothing more than streaks of rust across the countryside..." However, the attempt to develop a standard-gauge network would continue for much of the 20th century. The first concerted effort had been made in 1932, with the completion of a standard-gauge railroad between Sydney and Brisbane, but it was not until after World War II that there was a serious discussion about the issue. In the 1950s, a plan was drawn up to create a national network of standard-gauge lines, but progress was slow because of the cost. In 1962, the Sydney–Melbourne route, the busiest long-distance line in the country, was standardized, and eight years later, the Sydney–Perth route was also converted. The Melbourne–Adelaide railroad was converted to standard gauge in 1995, and the Adelaide–Darwin line followed nine years later.

There is no doubt that the gauge "bungle" cost Australia and its railroads dearly. Changing trains is both unpopular with passengers and costly for freight. The Australian experience is in great contrast to that other vast country that developed as a result of immigration—the US—where the railroads were the principal catalyst for growth. However, thanks to the Australian government's program of standardization and modernization—including the introduction of diesel trains and the closure of heavily loss-making branch lines—the railroads survived and, in places, even began to flourish, although they have never been as vital a part of the economy as in many other countries. There is still no high-speed line in Australia, but there is now an attempt to initiate one between Sydney and Melbourne which is the world's busiest air route. A government commission has been set up with the initial

Across Australia The Ghan transcontinental railroad runs from Darwin to Adelaide—a 1,851-mile (2,979 km) journey that has been possible only since 2004, when the entire track was finally converted from narrow to standard gauge.

The distance the Trans-Australian Railway runs without a bend

297 miles

(478 km)

The longest straight track in the world

task of looking at the possibility of a line between Sydney and Newcastle, which are around 100 miles (160 km) apart.

Railroads in New Zealand

The experience of Australia is in sharp contrast to its neighboring country and fellow ex-British colony, New Zealand. Although the origin of the railroads was similar—the first lines were built by provincial governments, with the first one opening in 1863—central government took over in 1876. From then on, New Zealand's railroad system was developed in an integrated manner, using just one gauge.

The government of the dominion of New Zealand deliberately expanded the railroads to provide a unifying force for the sparsely populated nation, which consists of two main islands. As author of a history of New Zealand railroads, Neill Atkinson, put it: "since the late nineteenth century, the state used its expanding rail network to promote not just the development of agriculture, industry, forestry, and mining, but to further policies in areas as diverse as education, town planning, and recreation. Trains ferried school children to the classroom, suburban workers to factories and offices, sportspeople to competitions, and thousands of picnickers and punters to beaches, parks, and racetracks."

Railroad stations soon became the hub of their communities. Each station's "Railway Refreshment Rooms," sold appetizing, cheap food and beverages served "in the legendarily thick New Zealand Railway" cups, bowls, and plates. The railroads became an integral part of the country's economy and culture and were, in the words of a 1938 advertisement for New Zealand Railways, "the industry that made New Zealand—the people's railways for the people's profit." The contrast with Australia could not have been greater.

Social hub (above) The refreshment rooms at provincial New Zealand railroad stations often became the social heart of the townships they served, offering hearty meals at decent prices.

The joy of trains The New Zealand government promoted rail transportation not only for industrial purposes but for leisure activities too.

No 1

Streamlining steam In the 1930s, railroad companies began streamlining locomotives to increase their efficiency and give them a modern look. This scene from 1938 at Stevenage Station, UK, is a study in contrast as a period steam train stands alongside a more modern locomotive (right).

HIGH-SPEED STEAM TRAINS

The crude "tea kettles on wheels" built by pioneers were transformed over the first 100 years of the railroad, as steam-train technology made a leap forward.

Railroads evolved as the work of pioneers such as George Stephenson in Britain and Peter Cooper in the US was steadily built upon to introduce and improve steam technology. The period between the world wars, in particular, saw great engineers of the time turn steam locomotives into sophisticated powerhouses.

Steady but slow

An interesting study undertaken in 1889 by early "trainspotters" E. Foxwell and T. C. Farrer provides a comparative analysis of the speeds of trains across the world. In general, the compilers were greatly disappointed by the slowness of most trains. For their research, the pair included only "expresses," which they defined as averaging at least 29 mph (47 km/h)—hardly speedy travel, but even so, not many qualifying trains were found. There were no such services in several major railroad nations—including India and the whole of South America—and only a handful in Australia. Foxwell and Farrer found that the countries with the highest proportion of fast services were France and the Netherlands, which interestingly used mainly British locomotives. In Germany, an average of 35 mph (56 km/h) was rare, while in Italy there was only one express—a daily service between Milan and Venice. High-speed services in Sweden—then still a poverty-stricken agricultural country—were "poor," but Denmark had several good trains. Hungary, meanwhile, was praised for allowing the Orient Express (see pp.180–185) to average 32 mph (51 km/h), which was faster than in neighboring Austria. In the US, the only trains that qualified as expresses were in the east, including the best service in the world—a train that ran the 40-mile (64 km) trip between Washington, DC, and Baltimore at an average of 53 mph (85 km/h). Otherwise, Foxwell and Farrer were disappointed at the speed of many services in the US, finding that even those with famous names, which often contained words like "Flyer," barely qualified as express trains, averaging only around the 30 mph (48 km/h) mark. The problem, they found, was that tracks in the US often had to go through the center of towns, where the trains had to travel very slowly because of potentially dangerous level crossings.

The scenic route A poster for the London-to-Scotland West Coast line c.1910. Competition with the East Coast line reduced travel times by several hours.

This intrepid pair of timetable-watchers returned to their task a decade later and found that considerable improvements had been made. By the start of the 20th century, France led the way with 20 daily expresses averaging at least 56 mph (90 km/h) and a series of fast international services running from Paris that covered much of Western Europe, including Vienna and Warsaw. In Germany and Britain, too, expresses routinely averaged 50 mph (80 km/h) or more.

Healthy competition

Part of the reason for these increases in speed was a trend that had begun around the time of Foxwell and Farrer's first survey—rival railroad companies would vie for the fastest travel time between two points. The first such contest took place in Britain, in a bid for the best time between London and Scotland. Two parallel lines, the East Coast and West Coast main lines, traveled between these two destinations. The companies that ran these services had a tacit agreement that travel times between London and Edinburgh would be 9 hours by the East Coast, and 10 by the longer West Coast route, which also had to contend with steeper gradients. But in June 1888, the two West Coast companies—the London and North Western and the Caledonian, which together provided a joint service—announced that they would cut the extra hour from their service. A few weeks later, just ahead of the Scottish grouse-shooting season—which started on August 12 and represented a lucrative period for the London–Scotland operators—the East Coast companies (the Great Northern, the North Eastern, and the North British) retaliated. They cut half an hour from their timetable by limiting stopping times, reducing the travel time to 8 hours and 30 minutes.

The North Western (the main company on the West Coast route) responded quickly, vowing to slash the travel time to 8 hours—a full 20 percent reduction on its previous 10-hour schedule. The East Coast companies hit back in this dramatic game of poker, promising a travel time of 7 hours and 45 minutes. As the battle reached its height, people gathered at departure point to see off the rival trains, and their performance was reported in the manner of weekend soccer games. Signalers along the routes took special care not to slow down these prestigious trains, and teams of workers ensured that the tracks were up to standard. Eventually, the East Coast companies peaked with a run of just 7 hours and 27 minutes later that summer, but the contest concluded soon after as the rivals came to agree on a standard travel time at 8 hours and 30 minutes.

A dangerous turn

Seven years later, in the summer of 1895—following the completion of the Forth Bridge, which greatly reduced travel times to the north of Scotland—an even fiercer and ultimately more dangerous race broke out. This time the trains ran by night, and the "race course" was extended to Aberdeen—more than 500 miles (800 km) from London by rail, and about 100 miles (160 km) farther than Edinburgh, the previous terminus. For added excitement, the trains from the two rival lines were forced to share the final section of track after the Kinnaber junction, 38 miles (61 km) south of Aberdeen. The first train to reach this point was the clear winner. The contest lasted for 17 days in August 1895 and attracted huge crowds at the departure and arrival points. Rival companies engaged in various underhand methods, such as not stopping at intermediate points, traveling with just two or three carriages to keep the weight down, and simply ignoring the timetable altogether. By the end, the times were

> **"... the traveling was so curiously smooth that [...] it was difficult to believe we were moving at all..."**
>
> CHARLES ROUS-MARTEN, ON THE *CITY OF TRURO'S* RECORD-BREAKING RUN

incredible, with the East Coast service a mere 8 hours and 40 minutes. The West Coast companies finally managed to beat this by 8 minutes with an average speed of 63 mph (101 km/h). However, the affluent passengers arriving for the season's grouse shooting did not welcome being turfed out of their comfortable carriages at Aberdeen at 5 a.m., rather than 7 a.m., which had been perfectly timed for breakfast.

Concerns over safety and cost caused the contest to peter out. Furthermore, the following summer, a major disaster occurred at Preston on the West Coast line due to excessive speed. An inexperienced driver failed to slow the train as it passed through the station, where a curve demanded a speed restriction of 10 mph (16 km/h). Unlike most trains passing through Preston, the service was scheduled to run through without stopping, and the train jumped the tracks at 50 mph (80 km/h). There was only one fatality, but the accident alerted passengers and the railroad companies to the risks of focusing purely on speed.

Railroad rivalry in the UK

By 1900, the Great Western Railway (GWR), the biggest of the British companies in terms of mileage, was leading the race for speed. In 1904, one of its new locomotives, *City of Truro*, was clocked at 102 mph (164 km/h) on a downhill stretch in Somerset. Although the exact speed is disputed, it is generally considered one of the first times in the world that the 100 mph (160 km/h) barrier was breached. This occurred during a campaign by GWR to establish itself as the premier railroad company in Britain. The company's ambition led to competition with the London and South Western (LSWR) company over traffic from liners sailing to and from the US.

Pioneering speedster The *City of Truro* (below) became the first locomotive to breach the 100 mph (160 km/h) mark when hauling the "Ocean Mails" special service between London and Plymouth on May 9, 1904.

Transatlantic ocean liners had traditionally docked at the English port of Southampton, with passengers traveling onward to London by train. However, to save time, since travel by land is faster than by sea, ships also began docking at the port of Plymouth—over 150 miles (240 km) west of Southampton. Though farther from London, passengers could cover the remaining distance by train, shaving nearly a day off the total trip. The LSWR had traditionally served Plymouth, but now the GWR also wanted a slice of the action. A full-scale war broke out as rival companies ran trains with no particular timetable, simply picking up passengers from ships as they arrived and steaming to London as quickly as possible. This was to have tragic consequences on July 1, 1906, when a special service that had left Plymouth just before midnight attempted to travel through the city of Salisbury at more than twice the 30 mph (48 km/h) speed restriction and came off the rails. Of the 43 people on board, 28 were killed. While these special services were later run with more care, the race between the two companies continued until 1910.

Reaching a compromise

In the US, the race for the fastest time between New York and Chicago lasted many years. It had begun in 1887, when the Pennsylvania Railroad introduced the Pennsylvania Limited—an all-Pullman affair boasting a barbershop, valet, and maid service. Two years later, the New York Central Railroad responded with a train that covered the 436 miles (701 km) between New York and Buffalo (on the Canadian border) in 7 hours, at an average speed of 61 mph (98 km/h). Then in 1902, the Central launched the Twentieth Century Limited express train, which covered the 1,000-mile (1,600 km) distance between New York and Chicago in 20 hours—a reduction of 4 hours on the usual time. In response, the "Pennsy," as it was known, renamed the *Pennsylvania Limited* the *Pennsylvania Special*, and managed to complete the trip in the same time as its Central rival. A battle ensued, with each company repeatedly trying to reduce the travel time in a series of much-publicized initiatives. However, these grand contests proved too costly for either company, and eventually an agreement of a 20-hour travel time was reached.

A final hurrah

Train races of this kind largely died down until the 1930s, when they were revived as a last-gasp attempt to help steam technology see off competition from rival methods of

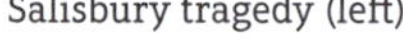

Salisbury tragedy (left)
The Salisbury train derailment led to considerable loss of life and property. This telling image of the aftermath of the 1906 disaster shows the extensive wreckage of the trains and buildings at the platform in Salisbury, Hampshire.

traction. Steam engines had improved remarkably between the wars, thanks to several illustrious engineers. The greatest of these was French engineer André Chapelon, whose rigorous scientific analysis and emphasis on efficiency were widely imitated, leading to radical improvements in locomotive performance. In Britain, a contest broke out in 1937 between the two consolidated companies—Britain's many companies had been merged into just four in 1923—serving the Scottish route. William Stanier, chief engineer at the London, Midland, and Scottish (LMS), built the Princess Coronation class of high-speed locomotives, which are widely recognized as the best British locomotives ever produced. On a specially arranged press trip, the first engine of the class reached 114 mph (183 km/h), a speed that was intended to better the effort of its rival, the London and North Eastern Railway's (LNER) streamlined A4 Pacifics. The LNER claimed that an A4 had reached 113 mph (181 km/h), but when the company learned the record had been beaten, it planned a record run in great secrecy. This was eventually undertaken in 1938 when *Mallard*, a streamlined A4, reached 126 mph (203 km/h) in a specially organized run on a straight section of downhill track south of Grantham. This record for steam locomotives would never be surpassed, although a German Class 05 locomotive had come close three years earlier when it reached 124½ mph (200.4 km/h) between Hamburg and Berlin. In the US, the use of high-speed diesels (see pp.212–219) on prestigious routes spelled the end of steam, and, by the 1970s, steam power in continental Europe had mostly been displaced by large-scale electrification.

Record-breaking run Designed by Sir Nigel Gresley, the chief engineer of the LNER, *Mallard* can be seen here as it charges through the English countryside. On July 3, 1938, it reached a record-breaking speed for a steam locomotive—one that is likely to remain forever.

GOING DIESEL: FROM THE *FLIEGENDE HAMBURGER* TO THE FUTURE

Diesel engines were able to replace steam locomotives in the 20th century as they were far more efficient and flexible, but they have now largely given way to electric propulsion.

Steam engines were dirty beasts—difficult to maintain, temperamental, and inefficient—so a search for alternatives started early. Experiments with electric traction led the way, but once the internal combustion engine had been invented, attempts to apply it on the railroads were bound to follow. The first internal combustion engines tried out on trains were fueled by gasoline, but it did not prove efficient and was expensive, especially for large engines.

German engineer Rudolf Diesel invented and patented the eponymous Diesel engine in 1892. Instead of a spark plug, it used air heated by high compression to ignite the fuel. Two main types of diesel locomotives were devised: one provided power directly; the other, the diesel-electric, used a diesel engine to power a generator, which then provided electricity for propulsion. Both have been used extensively.

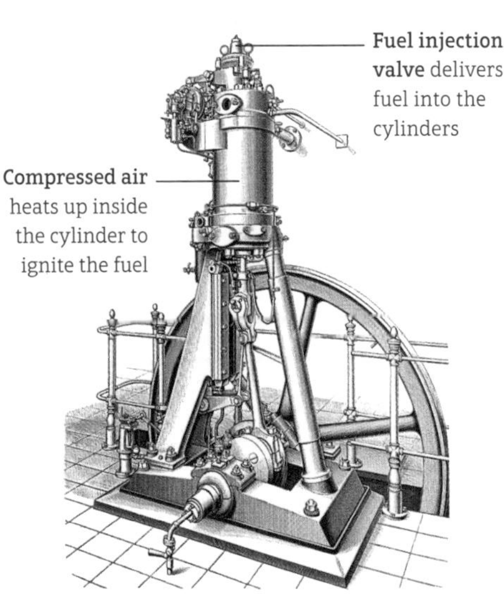

Early experimentation

Following Diesel's invention, experiments with locomotives began almost at once. However, there were numerous technical obstacles to overcome before they could be put into practical use, and, apart from a few running on a small Swedish railroad diesel engines were not introduced until after World War I. Efforts to build functional

The flier from Hamburg The streamlined design of the *Fliegende Hamburger* not only improved the train's speed and efficiency by reducing wind resistance but also created an enduring design style.

The first diesel engine (left) Rudolf Diesel's revolutionary concept took physical form in the third Augsburg prototype, the ancestor of all diesel engines.

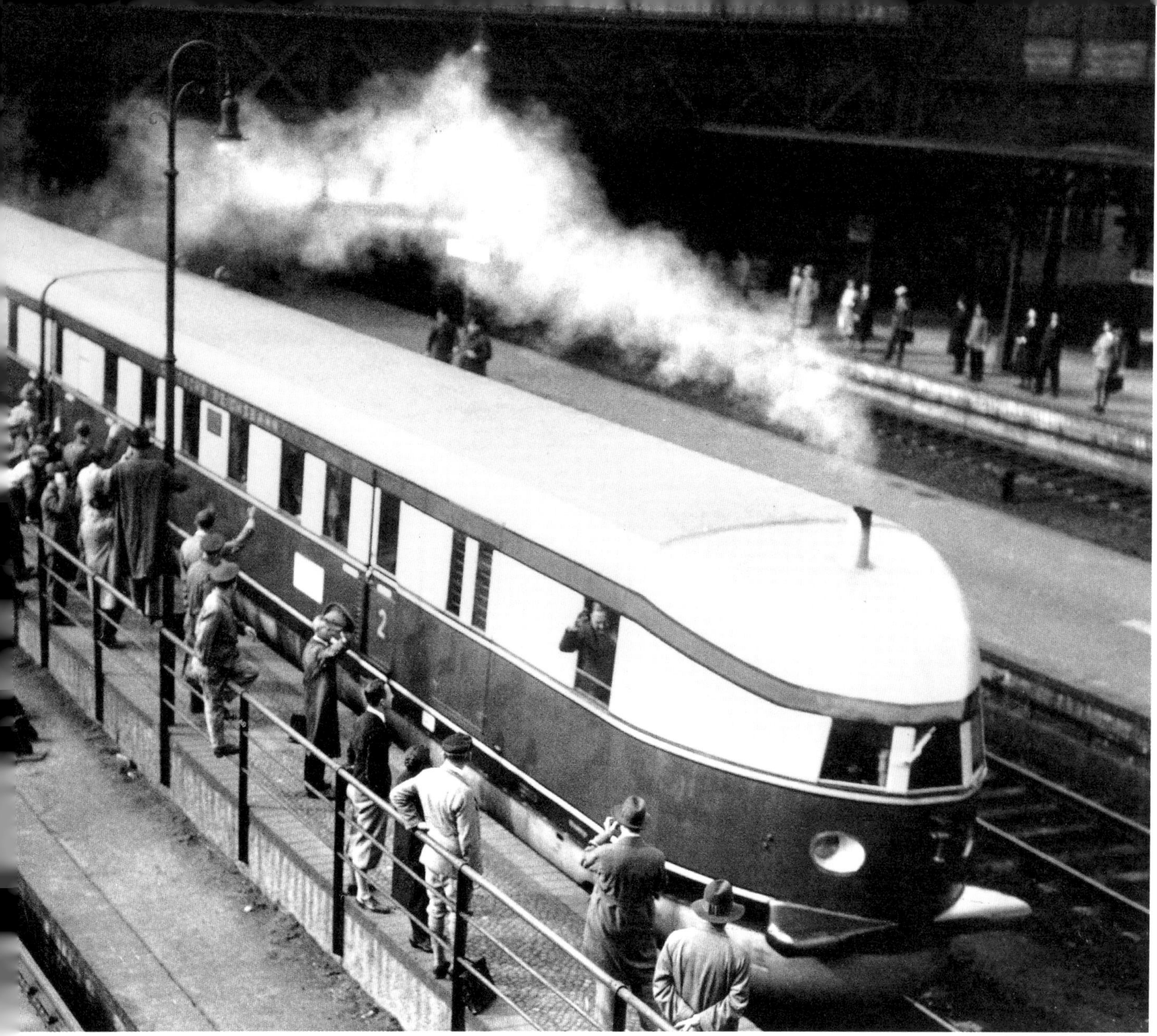

diesel locomotives continued through the 1920s. Despite some success on the US and Canadian railroads, the real pioneer was Germany, which began experimenting with powerful diesel engines for rail propulsion. The result was a two-car unit called the *Fliegende Hamburger* ("Flying Hamburger"), which represented a considerable advance for rail technology in both speed and efficiency. The Germans had, in fact, already established the world's rail speed record with a bizarre-looking four-wheel coach powered by a gasoline aircraft engine with an airplane-type propeller at the back. It was built by BMW and reached 143 mph (230 km/h) on a test run in June 1931, but a host of technical difficulties ensured it never saw regular service. By contrast, the *Fliegende Hamburger* did become a widely used model on several routes, first going into service under this name in the winter of 1932–1933. It covered the 178 miles (287 km) between Berlin and Hamburg in 2 hours and 18 minutes—an average speed of 78 mph (126 km/h)—which required cruising speeds of around 100 mph (160 km/h) to maintain the timetable, making it by far the fastest rail service in the world. The train had a remarkable streamlined design, like a Zeppelin airship, the result of wind-resistance tests in a wind tunnel. Although Hitler preferred cars, which he saw as the transportation of the future, the *Fliegende Hamburger* became part of the propaganda exercise to show the superiority of the "Thousand-Year Reich."

Pioneers and progress

The success of the *Fliegende Hamburger* soon led to the design being used on other services: two years later, a similar service was introduced on the Berlin–Cologne route, with an average speed of 82 mph (132 km/h), and a *Fliegende Frankfurter* ("Flying Frankfurter") service followed. These diesel trains represented a radical technological development, but were laid up in World War II because of fuel shortages and saw service again only briefly after the war.

It was in the US that diesel technology was developed more widely and successfully than elsewhere. Its development took place against the background of a need to compete in a nation where cars, and later planes, were eroding rail's market share. The US railroad companies had been taken over by the government during World War I because of their incompetence and refusal to cooperate with one another. They emerged from state control eager to improve what they offered, by using prestigious trains such as the *Pennsylvania Special* and *Twentieth Century Limited* as their trademark services.

By the late 1920s, however, these services had begun to seem slow, and their operators were desperately seeking a new technology to speed the trains up. This was particularly true for the railroad companies whose services crossed the vast swaths of the West. With car use still not widespread and aviation in its infancy (the first commercial domestic flight, between Boston and New York, was launched in 1927), and planes still posing a safety risk, the railroad companies began to look to diesel as the answer to their problems.

These new diesel trains were a different kind of train to the steam-hauled services. Consisting of perhaps half a dozen or eight cars, they were exclusively for passengers and provided a high degree of comfort. They were built of light stainless steel and alloys, which made them look sleek—especially compared to the heavy, conventional steam trains—and they ran fast between major cities, with limited stops to improve travel times.

While some diesel locomotives had already been introduced by various US railroads, these were confined to shunting since the powerful diesel engines were thought too heavy to be economical compared with traditional steam. Gasoline engines continued to be tried on some trains, such as the three-car *Blue Bird* trains of the Chicago Great Western that ran between the Twin Cities (St. Paul and Minneapolis) and Rochester, Minnesota—but again, they were simply too expensive to operate.

The first of its kind CNJ No.1000, a pioneering commercial diesel-electric locomotive, was originally used for shunting operations in the 1920s.

Novel technology

A key technical breakthrough for diesel engines was made by General Motors, the automobile company, which used alloys rather than steel to give a better power-to-weight ratio. The new, lighter engine attracted the attention of Ralph Budd, the head of the Chicago, Burlington, and Quincy Railroad—the Burlington, as it was known—at the Chicago World's Fair of 1933. Budd, one of the few railroad visionaries of the interwar period, realized the more powerful engine's potential to revolutionize

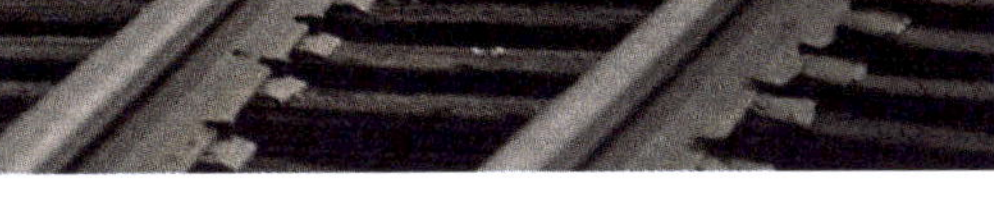

A lighter alternative (left) The lighter diesel locomotives, replacing their steam counterparts, were so much easier to move that they could be pulled along the track by a tug-of-war team.

Marketing modernity The elegance of the new types of trains was highlighted in publicity, such as this brochure from 1934, which suggests that diesel locomotives were far superior to their steam predecessors.

long-distance rail travel. After seeing it at the fair, he commissioned a new type of streamlined diesel locomotive whose sleek and elegant looks were an attraction in themselves. Called the *Pioneer Zephyr* (the name Zephyr, meaning light west wind, came from Chaucer's *Canterbury Tales*, which Budd had been reading), it was launched amid much fanfare in May 1934 with a record-breaking "Dawn to Dusk Run" between Denver, Colorado, and Chicago. The 1,015-mile (1,633 km) trip was covered at an average of 78 mph (126 km/h), remarkable by US standards and almost as fast as the German diesels. However, a lot of special measures had been taken: patrol staff were placed on all 1,689 level crossings along the route to stop car traffic well ahead of the train, and the train was limited to just three carriages to reduce the weight. Famously, Budd reported that the fuel for the train was far cheaper than coal, costing a mere $14.64 (£3)—although, at 4 cents per gallon (3.8 liters), that meant using 366 gallons (1,386 liters) of diesel.

While such fast speeds could not be achieved on regular trips, the train was far faster than any before and became the pioneer for a host of services that transformed American long-distance train travel in the years running up to World War II. A veritable family of *Zephyrs* and other trains sprang up on routes across the expanses of the West and along the East Coast, operated by these elegant new streamlined diesels. The Burlington, spurred on by Budd's enthusiasm, introduced in quick succession the *Twin Cities Zephyr*, between the twin cities and Chicago, and the *Mark Twain Zephyr* to St. Louis.

Legacy of Union Pacific

The Union Pacific's pioneer train went on a nationwide tour in 1934, before entering active service as the *Kansas Streamliner*. Renamed the *City of Salina* in 1936, it could run at more than 90 mph (145 km/h) for long distances, averaging a stunning 92 mph (148 km/h) on its run across the Nebraskan plains. The *pièce de résistance* of the period was the record-setting coast-to-coast journey by the *City of Portland*, a Union Pacific six-car sleeper train, which traveled the 3,250 miles (5,230 km) between New York and Los Angeles in 56 hours and 55 minutes—nearly a day faster than the regular coast-to-coast service. Moreover, the fuel cost was only £20 ($80), compared with £56 ($280) for coal. This was only a trial run, however, and a nonstop coast-to-coast service was strangely never established as passengers had to change trains at Chicago or St. Louis.

These modern diesels later acquired observation cars and other amenities to satisfy their affluent clientele. A fabulous variety of food and drink was offered and for a while the trains became the envy of the world, with the companies competing to provide the best facilities. These services were the apogee of America's rail system—indeed, they were probably the best the world had ever seen—but by the 1950s, as flying became safer and cheaper, they began to be phased out. Diesel remains,

"They really don't run this Union Pacific train, they just aim and fire it."

AN OBSERVER ON
THE UNION PACIFIC *ZEPHYR*

however, the main form of traction on US railroads to this day, with only a very small proportion of electrified railroads. Indeed, the typical image of American rail is of freight trains more than 100 wagons long, being hauled by three or four powerful diesel locomotives.

Diesel goes global

Elsewhere in the world, diesels began to replace steam locomotives soon after World War II. Diesel multiple units, in particular, were a great way of saving money on branch lines. These had engines under the floor of the carriage so that there was no need for a locomotive, and they could be driven from either end, obviating the need to turn around. The French even developed a rubber-tired diesel train called the *Micheline*, which was used extensively on minor routes.

However, electrification was often chosen over diesel. While it is initially more expensive, electric haulage is ultimately cheaper, cleaner, and offers faster acceleration. On many suburban services, steam trains were replaced directly with electric trains rather than diesels. Nevertheless, with Switzerland the only country in the world operating a fully 100 percent electrified network, diesel remains an important form of traction, in particular for heavy freight and on little-used lines where the cost of electrification is not worthwhile. Diesel trains will be with us for a long time yet.

Pneumatic tires In 1932, a brief but unsuccessful attempt to use rubber tires on trains, sponsored by the French firm Michelin, was trialed on the tracks of the London, Midland, & Scottish Railway.

DIESEL POWER MEETS ELECTRICITY

Diesel-electric traction emerged as the economically and functionally superior successor to steam power in the 1940s. Power is derived from a diesel engine (the "prime mover") but is transformed into electricity by a generator that powers motors in the trucks, which in turn propel the train.

Maryland and Pennsylvania No.81 (1946)
No.81, a General Motors EMD NW2-class shunter, was one of the first diesel-electrics to see widespread use. Popular due to its low cost and versatility, this small yet powerful class remains in service in small numbers even today.

GN No.201 (1947)
This RS-2 class diesel-electric switcher was built by ALCO and was one of 20 purchased by the Great Northern Railway (US) to replace its coal-fired locomotives. Its 12-cylinder engine yields a power output of 1,500 hp (1,100 kw).

CNL No.6505 (1949)
The EMD F7 diesel-electric was designed for freight but was also used for passenger trains by some operators. Economical to operate and maintain, the pictured unit runs on the Conway Scenic Railroad (US) heritage line.

SP No.6051 (1954)
One of nine EMD E9 diesel-electric passenger locomotives run by the Southern Pacific Railroad, No.6051 hauled services out of Los Angeles. Capable of a 2,400 hp (1,765 kw) power output, it was retired in 1969 and restored to its original "daylight" red-orange paint scheme.

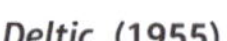

***Deltic* (1955)**
English Electric's *Deltic* was the prototype for the 22 Type 5 *Deltic* D9000 Class 55 diesel locomotives bought for services on the East Coast route from London to York and Edinburgh. They replaced the famous London and North Eastern Railway A4 Pacific steam engines (see p.285).

British railways D200 (1958)
An English Electric Type 4 Class 40, D200 was one of the first wave of diesel-electrics to ply the rails in Britain. With a top speed of 90 mph (140 km/h), the class had been intended for passenger expresses but was relegated to slower passenger and freight services.

Erie Lackawanna No.3607 (1967)
No.3607 was a General Motors EMD SD45, a six-axle diesel-electric freight locomotive with a power output of 3,600 hp (2,680 kw). More than a thousand units were produced between 1965 and 1971, a small number of which are still in operation on US railroads.

NS No.9628 (1996)
Norfolk Southern Railway (US) still operates a fleet of 1,090 General Electric Dash 9-40CW diesel-electric locomotives, the first of which was introduced in 1996. The class is powered by a 16-cylinder engine that is limited to a power output of 4,000 hp (3,000 kw) to improve running costs.

"Gate of death" This image shows the railway entrance of the Auschwitz II-Birkenau concentration and extermination camp in Oswiecim, Poland, which most of the 1.3 million prisoners sent to their deaths passed through.

WORLD WAR II: ATROCITIES ON THE LINE

While the railroads did not have as fundamental a role in the Second World War as in the First, they were still a vital part of the supply line and, tragically, played a key role in some of the worst atrocities perpetrated in the conflict.

Although the railroads' role in World War II was not quite as fundamental as it had been during World War I (see pp.250–255), they were nevertheless a vital part of the logistics of war. With gasoline in short supply and a lack of modernized roads in many conflict areas, the railroads carried troops and supplies far and wide. However, the railroads were also involved in two of the greatest war crimes of the World War II: the Holocaust, which resulted in the deaths of two-thirds of the Jewish population in Europe and millions of other people at the hands of the Third Reich, and the construction of the Burma to Thailand (formerly Siam) Railway, for which the Japanese used prisoners of war. These two events portray a darker side that is often left untold in railroad histories, but vividly, if hauntingly, demonstrates the power of the railroads and their significance to those who controlled them.

Approximately six million Jewish people were killed by the Nazis in the Holocaust, along with millions more from other groups such as Slavs, Poles, Romanies, communists, the disabled, and queer people. Most of the victims were taken to death camps by train.

> **"If I am to wind things up quickly, I must have more trains."**
>
> GERMAN NAZI LEADER HEINRICH HIMMLER, IN A LETTER TO THE NAZI MINISTER OF TRANSPORTATION, JANUARY 1943

Haunting Holocaust

The sheer volume and speed of the deportations would not have been possible without intensive use of the railroads. Any other method of transportation would have presented insuperable problems—to have devoted so many trucks to the task would have damaged the Germans' war effort, and marching victims along roads might have revealed the true horrors of the Nazis' plans to the wider population.

The first of these trains were used principally to move German Jewish people to ghettos and ran between Germany and Poland (and then farther east to Riga in Latvia). The grim dispatch of Jewish people and other sections of the population to the concentration and death camps began in

Sorting prisoners Upon their arrival in Auschwitz-Birkenau, Holocaust prisoners alighted from the train onto a long platform, where military doctors decided their fate. A majority of these prisoners were executed.

the spring of 1942, and the flow intensified over the following two years. These deportations were carried out in a systematic manner on an industrial scale, as part of the "Final Solution" agreed at the notorious Wannsee Conference in January 1942. Efficiency was seen as essential and required the active involvement of numerous German government ministries, including the Reich Security Main Office (RSHA), the Transportation Ministry, and the Foreign Office, as well as the corresponding organizations in other allied or occupied states who were required to hand over their citizens. Many railroad workers were involved, too. The deportations were mostly carried out in freight wagons. Some victims, notably those from the Netherlands and Belgium, were transported in third-class passenger cars, partly to maintain the subterfuge that they were merely being rehomed. Conditions on the trains were appalling: the freight wagons were each supposed to be filled with a maximum of 50 people, but in fact, due to a shortage of wagons, they sometimes carried as many as 150 occupants, which meant standing room only. Trains could haul a maximum of only 55 wagons each, as anything longer would travel too slowly. There was no food or water on the trip and only a bucket latrine. The only ventilation was through a barred window and consequently many people suffocated. In the summer, the temperature could be unbearably hot and victims baked, while in the winter the temperature plummeted and victims froze. The trains were given the lowest priority on the railroad network and consequently trips were often delayed while more important military convoys were allowed through. This meant that the deportees were sometimes held in sidings for days or even weeks and the average time for trips, which should have taken a day or so, was four and a half days. The longest trip involved the deportation of about 1,800 Jewish people from the Greek island of Corfu, who were taken by boat to the Greek mainland and then transferred to a train. The train was held up several times and took 18 days to reach Auschwitz. By then, many of the occupants were already dead. Given the conditions, length of the journey, and the lack of food and water, deaths in transit were common and most trains arrived containing several corpses.

One-way tickets

One of the least-known parts of the deportation process was the fact that the victims were often forced to buy tickets for the journey, a full one-way fare for adults, with children being charged half price. This scheme generated an astonishing amount of revenue, calculated at around 240 million Reichsmarks (around $201 million, or £50 million). At the peak of the process, there were up to 10 trains per week arriving at the camps. For the Nazis, it was the very efficiency of this mode of transportation that made the extermination of so many people possible. The dispatch of trains began to slow down only when the Allies invaded France in the summer of 1944, and the operation ceased entirely as the Third Reich began to fall apart in the spring of 1945. In the 21st century, several railroad companies have apologized for their role in these wartime deportations, including Dutch railroads Nederlandse Spoorwegen in 2005 and French SNCF in 2011.

Scene of the crime

During the Holocaust, the railroads conveyed millions to their deadly destinations. Meanwhile, in Asia it was the railroad line itself that was the scene of another war crime. When the Japanese overran Singapore, the main British naval base in Southeast Asia, in February 1942, they captured more than 80,000 British, Indian, and Australian troops. Along with 50,000 existing prisoners, many were sent to work on the construction of the Burma to Thailand (formerly Siam) Railway, which was intended to provide the Japanese with a vital supply line as they advanced westward, toward India.

As there was no adequate existing road or rail links between the two countries and the sea route was vulnerable to attack from Allied ships and submarines, a railroad seemed the obvious solution. To build the 258-mile (415 km) line, which went through harsh mountainous territory and tropical rainforest, the Japanese used forced labor of up to 330,000 men, mostly made up of press-ganged locals, but also including more than 60,000 Allied prisoners of war (PoWs). The line was started simultaneously from

Inhuman travel conditions Most prisoners of the Holocaust were taken to concentration camps in adapted goods vehicles. Many deportees died en route due to lack of food and water.

Cramped floor space of about 215 sq ft (20 sq m)

Captive labor During World War II, the Japanese used PoWs to build the Burma–Thailand railroad. Here, PoWs can be seen carrying railroad sleepers about 25 miles (40 km) south of Thanbyuzayat, Burma, in 1943.

both ends, Thanbyuzayat in Burma (present-day Myanmar) and Nong Pladuk in Thailand, in June 1942. There was a constant shortage of materials and most of the equipment, including tracks and sleepers, was brought from dismantled branches of other local railroads. The human cost was, however, appalling and the line became known as the "Death Railway." Dutch merchant sailor Fred Seiker described his experience as PoW on the railroad labor force:

> "You carried a basket from the digging area to the top of the embankment, emptied it and down again to be filled for your next trip up the hill. Or you carried a stretcher—two bamboo poles pushed through an empty rice sack— one chap at each end, and off you went. Simple really. But in reality this job was far from easy. The slopes of the embankments consisted of loose earth, clambering to the top was a case of sliding and slithering with a weight of earth in attendance. This proved to be very tiring on thigh muscles and painful, often resulting in crippling cramp. You just had to stop, you could not move. Whenever this occurred the Japs were on you with their heavy sticks, and beat the living daylight out of you. Somehow you got going again, if only to escape the blows."

Working hours were typically 7:30 a.m. to 10 p.m. and the food rations were just 7 oz (200 g) of rice per day, often with no vegetables, let alone meat. Robert Hardie,

a British doctor who was captured in Singapore, described in diaries published posthumously in the 1980s how the Japanese would line up the sick that he was tending and demand that a dozen of them should be sent to the work camp. He wrote: "One is under constant pressure to provide men to work under this Nipponese system: for certain groups of men are given certain work to do in a certain time. If many go sick in a group, the others have to work all the harder and longer." Hardie also recounted the repeated refusals of his captors to provide even basic medical supplies, as well as their indifference to the spread of diseases, such as cholera, malaria, and dysentery. The death rate was particularly high in the final months of the railroad's construction as the Japanese were desperate for the line to be completed.

Stained-glass window The "Humanitas window" at the Death Railway Museum and Research Centre in Kanchanaburi, Thailand, shows emaciated PoWs aiding wounded Japanese soldiers while at gunpoint during the construction of the Death Railway.

A heavy price

Despite the weakness of the men due to starvation and disease, their sheer numbers and the pressure from their Japanese guards ensured that the line was completed remarkably quickly, in just 12 months. On October 17, 1943, the two sections of the line met, 11 miles (17 km) south of the Three Pagodas Pass at Konkoita in Siam. By this time, the death toll was estimated to have reached more than 100,000, a figure that included a quarter of all the Allied prisoners. The railroad immediately became a vital part of the Japanese line of communication after their navy lost control of the South China Sea during the summer of 1942. However, as an essential bridge to the Burmese railroad system was never completed, the supply route still entailed transporting goods via ferry. The story of the Burma to Siam Railway reached a wider audience through the 1957 David Lean film *The Bridge on the River Kwai*, which was based on a book by Pierre Boulle. The story refers to Bridge 277, built over a stretch of river that was then called Mae Klong. The tale is largely fiction, since it shows the bridge ultimately being destroyed by sabotage. In reality, the bridge remained in working condition, despite the men's attempt to undermine it by mixing the concrete poorly and encouraging termites to use wooden supports as nests. Although the film was criticized as unrealistic and failing to depict accurately the appalling conditions which the men lived and died under, it nevertheless helped to ensure that the memory of this terrible project lasted longer than the line itself. Much of the railroad was damaged during the war and it never fully reopened. A few sections, such as the line between Kanchanaburi and Nong Pladuk, did operate in the 1950s, but most of it was abandoned, submerged under water by the Vajiralongkorn dam, or reclaimed by the jungle. Today, a tourist train runs along a surviving 81 mile (130 km) section, while other parts have been converted to a walking trail. Three large cemeteries honoring those who lost their lives building the line can be found along the route, with an Australian-built memorial and museum at Hellfire Pass, and several smaller memorials.

The Bridge on the River Kwai This acclaimed film is set against the backdrop of the construction of the Death Railway and portrays the cruel working conditions the PoWs endured.

High-speed trains Nothing better represents the ability of the railroad to adapt to the modern age than the high-speed network built in China since the 2000s. Here, a variety of high-speed train models are on show at the main depot in Wuhan.

The iron road today

In the immediate postwar years, the railroads suffered a period of decline. The car had become the preeminent form of passenger transportation, and the truck dominated the freight business. Superhighways and highways were being built across the world. The plane had also become affordable, and both international and domestic services were proliferating globally. Railroad closures started with branch lines and rural tracks then spread to the main lines themselves. In the United States, the decline of passenger railroads was particularly swift, and for a while, it seemed as if they would barely last into the 21st century.

Then everything changed. The oil crisis of the mid-1970s, together with congestion on the roads and environmental concerns regarding exhaust emissions, suddenly brought the train back into fashion. In 1964, Japan's high-speed "bullet" trains were introduced, which traveled faster than any car. Networks of similar lines were built in France and Germany, and later in China, Spain, and numerous other countries. Moreover, when the long-mooted 31-mile (50 km) Channel Tunnel linking France and Britain was finally given the go-ahead, it was built to carry trains because a railroad was the only practical way of traveling in such a long tunnel. It was connected to London with a new 68-mile (109-km) high-speed rail line, Britain's first. To relieve the congestion on Europe's Alpine roads, a series of rail tunnels have been built under the mountains. In 2006, China completed the highest railroad in the world—the Qinghai–Tibet line, which offers an easier journey than the dangerous road. China currently has the largest high-speed network in the world.

The railroads are therefore booming in the 21st century. Light rail systems, metros, high-speed lines, and newly electrified tracks are being built across the world. The 19th-century invention has found new friends in the 21st century and is enjoying a renaissance, thanks to its ability to transport the masses quickly and cheaply.

BREZHNEV'S FOLLY

What started out as an attempt to relieve congestion on the Trans-Siberian Railway and to explore the potential of a previously uninhabited part of Siberia became a nightmare for the Soviet government as costs mounted because of the difficult working conditions.

Of all the many madcap schemes in the history of the railroads, one takes the prize for being not only the craziest but also the most costly, both financially and in terms of the loss of human life. That winner is the 2,300-mile (3,700 km) Baikal–Amur Mainline (BAM), a branch off the main Trans-Siberian (see pp.170–179) that dwarfed the original railroad both in difficulty and cost. It was one of the most ambitious of numerous megaprojects dreamed up by the Soviet regime to demonstrate the superiority of Communism (others included the space program and a plan to reverse the flow of several Siberian rivers, which was fortunately abandoned). The idea behind the BAM was to provide an alternative route to the existing Trans-Siberian, which ran from European Russia to the Asian Pacific Railway.

The Baikal–Amur Mainline took about three-quarters of a century to complete and cost a total of $14 billion (£11 billion)

Lofty ambitions

The Soviet regime first mooted the railroad as a strategic alternative in the 1930s Stalinist era, following disputes with China and Japan over a section of the Trans-Siberian that crossed Chinese territory to reach Vladivostok. Even the Amur Railway, a longer route over exclusively Russian territory that was eventually completed in 1916, a decade and a half after the opening of the Trans-Siberian, was considered too close to the Chinese frontier and therefore vulnerable to attack. To counteract the perceived threat, Stalin's government passed a secret decree to construct a new line running parallel to the existing Trans-Siberian but around 500 miles (800 km) farther north. No details of the route were set out other than the start at Tayshet, where the line diverged from the Trans-Siberian, and the terminus at Sovetskaya Gavan, on the Pacific Ocean 800 miles (1,300 km) north of Vladivostok.

The face of BAM The Soviet leader Leonid Brezhnev was determined to see the Baikal–Amur Mainline completed and drafted in thousands of young people to help build it.

Glory to the constructors of BAM Railway! Brezhnev's decision to finish building the BAM in the 1970s was a monumental propaganda exercise, intended to inspire a new generation of workers with the ideals of Communism and gain their support for the regime.

СЛАВА СТРОИТЕЛЯМ БАМА!

The land crossed by the proposed new railroad was virtually uninhabited, as most of the population of Siberia had settled within 100 miles (160 km) of the Trans-Siberian, so the reasons for undertaking this vast project were dubious, even given the potential of Sino-Japanese conflict. The Soviet government had started publishing five-year plans setting out its economic targets, and its Second Five-Year Plan, for 1933–1937, emphasized the economic advantages of building the BAM.

> **"[BAM] will traverse little-investigated regions of eastern Siberia and bring to life an enormous new territory and its colossal riches—amber, gold, coal—and also make possible the cultivation of great tracts of land suitable for agriculture."**
>
> SECOND FIVE-YEAR PLAN, 1933–1937

"More beets, more sugar"
A propaganda photo from Stalin's second five-year plan emphasizes growing sugar beets for the production of sugar. It was believed that construction of the BAM could provide access to large tracts of land for agriculture.

Harsh conditions

Surveyors were dispatched to the Siberian wastes to prospect the land. Working under a reign of terror, several were executed for not doing their job properly in the view of the regime, while others were forced into construction gangs. These were made up of prisoners—mainly political—sent to the Gulags (the government's corrective labor camps) by Stalin's increasingly repressive regime. Tayshet became infamous as a camp for prisoners working on the railroad after Alexandre Solzhenitsyn described it in *The Gulag Archipelago*. Published first in the West in 1973, the book drew the world's attention to the atrocities that took place in Soviet forced labor camps under Stalin. Hundreds of thousands of prisoners were sent to these camps and forced to work on the line in appalling conditions—far worse than those endured on the Trans-Siberian. Russians knew that being sent to the "Bamlag"—the camps of the BAM Gulag—was effectively a death sentence, as prisoners were subjected to unendurably harsh conditions and systematically starved.

The northern latitude of the route meant that most of the terrain it traversed was permafrost—a leftover of the freezing temperatures of the Ice Age—which presented particular difficulties for track-laying. Once railroad workers started digging through the insulating surface layer of soil to the permafrost, ice that had been frozen for millennia thawed and did not refreeze, even in winter. Instead, the land turned marshy and unstable. Waiting for the ground to settle would have delayed work by years, so tracks were laid regardless, resulting in rail breaks and

derailments. Disturbing the permafrost also led to an increase in seismic activity in the region.

Slow progress

In addition to the issues of permafrost and earthquakes, the mountainous region north of Lake Baikal posed insurmountable difficulties. Weather conditions were extreme, with only 90 frost-free days a year, and winter temperatures as low as −76 °F (−60 °C) meant that mechanical equipment did not work and special cold-resistant steel had to be used for the rails. These factors, combined with a starving labor force, meant that by the outbreak of World War II, when work was halted, only a couple of short sections at each end had been completed.

Remarkably, as soon as the war ended in 1945, work resumed on this vanity project, which Stalin seemed intent on completing. The workforce was now made up of Japanese and German prisoners of war (PoWs), who were treated more harshly even than the prewar domestic convicts. It is estimated that of 100,000 German PoWs sent to the Ozerlag camp near Lake Baikal, only 10 percent survived to be repatriated in 1955; the Japanese prisoners suffered similar rates of mortality. A conservative estimate of the death toll of the two groups is 150,000—and all for nothing, since barely 450 miles (725 km) of the line had been completed by the time work was again halted following Stalin's death in 1953.

The demise of Stalin and his repressions might have signaled the end of the BAM project. Nikita Khrushchev, Stalin's successor, showed no interest in the railroad, and the Gulag camps that had provided its labor were closed. By the 1960s, however, interest was revived, with a series of ostensible new reasons to build it: the line would relieve congestion

Forced labor German and Japanese prisoners of war were used as forced labor to build the BAM, and many died in the terrible conditions.

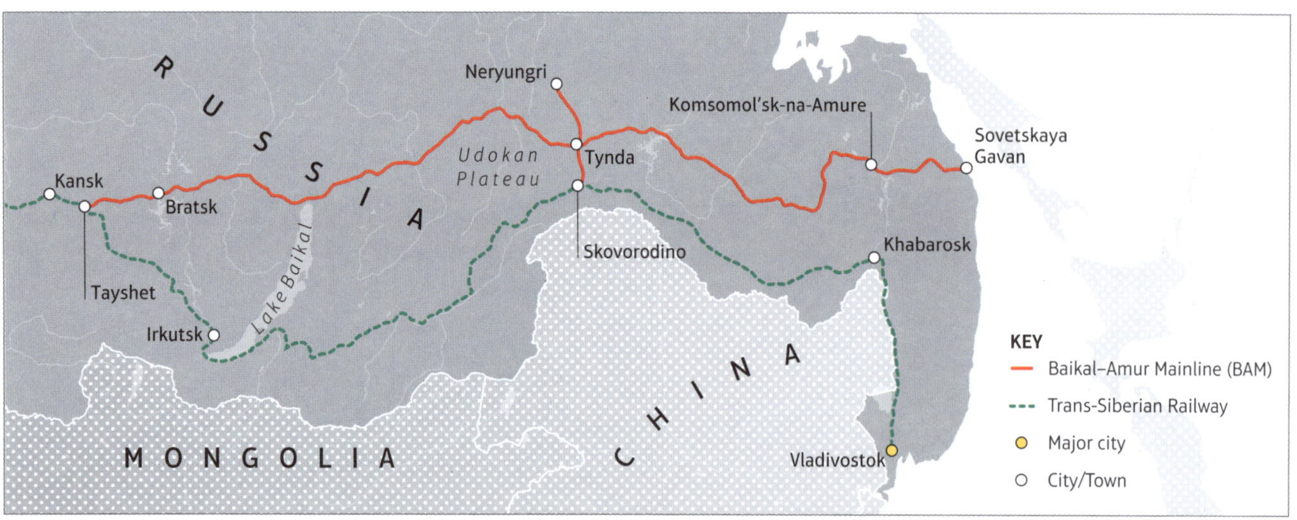

Two major railroads This map traces the routes of the BAM and the original Trans-Siberian.

Workers' prize Idealistic young Komsomol workers on the BAM were rewarded with medals and praise, as well as material goods such as cars and housing.

on the Trans-Siberian, open up gas fields in western Siberia, and provide a new route for burgeoning container traffic between the Far East and Europe. Moreover, vast copper deposits had been discovered at Udokan, 250 miles (400 km) east of Lake Baikal.

Promoting socialism

It was Leonid Brezhnev, the uninspiring and deeply conservative leader whose stern demeanor characterized Soviet rule in the 1970s, who decided to restart the scheme. Now a new type of cheap labor was to be used: volunteers of the "All-Union Leninist Youth League" (the Komsomol). The project was turned into a propaganda exercise run by the Komsomol, not only to demonstrate the advantages of the Communist way but also to enthuse a whole generation of young people with that ideal. By helping to build the line, the volunteers' thinking was that they would become lifelong supporters of the regime. Building the BAM became a rallying cry for Socialist propaganda as well as a path to victory over the obstacles that nature and the elements posed against humankind, making it a struggle that had to be won, at whatever cost—and that cost was to prove enormous.

In 1972, after much secret preparation, the Komsomol announced that work on the railroad would restart immediately and the BAM would be completed in 10 years (later extended to 1984). The project was given priority over other Soviet schemes and a nationwide appeal for volunteers was issued. While some young people may have turned up at the recruitment offices for idealistic reasons, there were practical incentives too: volunteers were promised priority allocation of housing and cars, both of which were in short supply in Soviet Russia, and for those interested in a political career, working on the BAM was essential for their CVs. The pay was good, too, compared with jobs back home. However, even those who started off with genuine enthusiasm were soon disillusioned. They were well treated, but once they discovered the sheer scale of the project and the incompetent way in which it was being run, it dawned on them that the railroad was no advertisement for the Communist system—quite the opposite. They realized, as geologists and other scientists had long known, that creating a railroad in northern Siberia was not a good idea.

Erratic progress

There were innumerable practical difficulties. The recruits were given little training for what was a skilled task, no detailed route had been prepared, and the physical conditions were even worse than expected. Attempts to continue work in winter, because of the ideological need

"BAM will be constructed with clean hands only!"

LEONID BREZHNEV, 1974

for rapid progress, were counterproductive. Although work was stopped when temperatures reached −4 °F (−20 °C), even above that temperature bulldozers stopped functioning and axes shattered. Any lessons learned from previous attempts to work in the permafrost seemed to have been forgotten, and once again whole sections of track gradually sank into the morass, while station and warehouse buildings constructed on shaky foundations collapsed.

Conditions on completed sections of the line were so bad that trains had to go extremely slowly and derailments were frequent. One 117-mile (188 km) section between Tayshet and Tynda that was one of the first to open took eight hours to traverse. With the tunnels also proving far more difficult to dig out than expected, the completion of the line was inevitably delayed: the 10-year target had always been a fantasy. The 9-mile (15-km) Severomuysky Tunnel, east of the Baikal, caused almost insuperable problems. When digging began in 1977, water from an underground lake flooded it. Although an ingenious solution was eventually found—

Resuming construction Abandoned after the death of Stalin, work on the BAM resumed when it was perceived as a key project to open up the lands of Siberia to new settlers.

liquid nitrogen was injected into the tunnel walls, freezing the water while the tunnel was lined with a concrete shell— it took 26 years to complete. In the meantime, two very steep bypasses were built, both adding considerably to the travel time. Nevertheless, the Communist authorities—intent on using the line for propaganda purposes—stuck to the 1984 opening date with a ceremony that featured the hammering fast of a golden spike to tie in the final rail. It was a complete sham. No foreign journalists were invited, as it would have been obvious that the line was far from complete.

Continuing the construction

In the end, the BAM was officially opened three times. Brezhnev had died in 1982, but Mikhail Gorbachev, who came to power in 1985, continued with the scheme. It was by then soaking up 1 percent of the nation's total annual GDP. Seven years after the first ceremony, Gorbachev announced that the line was open and boasted that it would form a new link between Russia and Japan. Even then, the intractable Severomuysky Tunnel was still not complete and several sections could accommodate only slow trains used to supply materials for constructing the line. Russia's post-Soviet president Vladimir Putin announced the line's completion in 2001, and the troublesome tunnel finally opened in 2003.

Unfulfilled promises

The BAM has nowhere near lived up to Brezhnev's expectations. The promise of opening up a vast agricultural region was always a delusion, since the Siberian climate is so harsh. It did not relieve pressure on the Trans-Siberian, since it is the section west of the junction at Tayshet, which is shared with the BAM, that is under greatest pressure. Nor has it provided a practical alternative route between Asia and Europe.

Downfall of Communism

Just as the Trans-Siberian contributed to the downfall of the czarist regime, the BAM and the excessive resources devoted to it helped bring down Communism. Most of the half a million Komsomol volunteers and other workers who built the line returned to their home towns deeply skeptical of the ideals of Communism and its grand

Golden moment On October 1, 1984, engineers marked the completion of the BAM at Kuanda station by placing symbolic "golden" links on the track.

> **"We intend to invest in the mainline's expansion and... this should inspire our veterans, should demonstrate that their efforts were not wasted."**
>
> VLADIMIR PUTIN, JULY 8, 2014

Carting cargo Despite its fraught history, the BAM is slowly coming into its own, especially in terms of hauling freight.

projects. Indeed, many were infuriated that the cars and housing they had been promised were denied to them, a failure that led to demonstrations in the post-Soviet era, with ex-BAM workers demanding that their vouchers for volunteering be redeemed.

Far from carrying people to the promised land of a 21st-century future, as the slogans had promised, the BAM clearly went nowhere. The BAM became, in the Soviet era, the butt of popular jokes, symbolizing failure and the powerlessness of the Soviet leaders. American historian Christopher J. Ward wrote in *Brezhnev's Folly*, a history of the line:

> “By repeating ad nauseam claims of BAM's economic, social, and cultural significance, the Komsomol, the Communist Party, and the Soviet government held an unwavering belief that the USSR's youth needed this message to avoid a loss of collective faith. Ironically, however, the realities of the railway helped to intensify such a loss of faith in the Soviet political and economic system in general.”

Racing toward redemption

Today, however, there are a few signs that the railroad may have been worth at least some of the effort. Russian Railways, the state-owned company, has increased container traffic on the line, which is now carrying more minerals from Siberian mines too, and there has been further recent investment, including the construction of the 2½ miles (4 km) Kuznetsovsky Tunnel to give better access to the Pacific, as well as improvement of parts of the line that were slow due to steep gradients. In 2023, during the Russia-Ukraine conflict, Ukraine claimed responsibility for two explosions aimed at the Severomuysky tunnel. However, despite the slight uptake in usage and the military potential, the BAM will still go down in history as one of the most misguided civil engineering projects ever attempted and forever be known as “Brezhnev's folly.”

RAILROADS LOST AND FOUND

Almost as soon as the railroads were built, sections started to become redundant and were closed. Some lines, built by companies to meet a need that turned out not to exist, were never profitable and were soon abandoned when industries vanished.

In Britain, 200 miles (320 km) of track had already closed by World War I, either due to the lines never being viable or because of competition from rival routes. The first significant closure was the 17-mile (27 km) line between Great Chesterford and Six Mile Bottom in Cambridgeshire, built by the Newmarket and Chesterford Railway. It was closed in 1851 after a more direct route was created. Unusually, the line closed outright rather than being kept open as a freight route, a viable and potentially profitable alternative for many early lines. Other countries simply built too many railroads. France had more railroads than it needed, thanks to government support for railroad construction in the 1860s, and many of the lines did not survive into the 20th century. Ireland, despite enduring the terrible famine of the 1840s that resulted in the death of 3 million people and the emigration of more than 2 million, built a network of lines that never made economic sense, given the country's sparse population. At the 1920s peak, it boasted 3,442 miles (5,540 km) of railroads serving a population of 4 million. It was hardly surprising much of this network closed in the 1930s, especially as car use increased.

In a way, it was remarkable that more lines did not close in this period, which is partly explained by the fact that railroad companies had to seek government permission to close lines in many countries, including the US and Britain. Permission was rarely granted, since terminating a service was inevitably unpopular and attracted negative publicity for politicians, meaning that many little-used lines remained open. In Britain, an 1844 Act required railroads to run at least one service a day to serve poorer travelers. This resulted in a phenomenon known as "parliamentary trains," with companies operating the minimum number of trains necessary to circumvent the costs of closure. Some of these "ghost trains" run to this day. Even rather hopeless lines could be kept open to avoid controversy. Renowned chronicler of the Victorian railroads, Jack Simmons, wrote of the Bishop's Castle Railway in mid-Wales,

114,000 miles

(183,465 km)
The length of US rail track closed between 1916 and the present day

Lost lines Many railroad stations, including this one in Canfranc, Spain, were abandoned as a result of the widespread decline and closure of railroad lines around the world. The Canfranc Station was transformed into a luxury hotel, which opened in 2023.

for example, which became insolvent five years after its completion in 1861 yet remained in operation until 1935.

Interwar railroad trends

Relatively few railroads closed around the world in the interwar period. In part, this was because of local opposition to closure, as the railroads were now an established form of public transportation—usually the only one until the advent of buses. Railroad companies were reluctant to sanction closures, too, as it was hard for them to predict the effect of closing branch lines on the network as a whole. Railroad economics are complex, and managers had to determine whether passengers on a branch line would continue to use the system if their local service was no longer provided, before deciding if the revenue they contributed overall made it worth keeping an unprofitable branch line open. This is a continuing conundrum.

In Britain, which boasted over 20,000 miles (32,000 km) of railroads at their peak before World War I, there were few closures in the interwar period, despite growing competition from buses and cars. Just 240 miles (386 km) of track were shut and another 1,000 miles (1,600 km) restricted to freight services. Only the most extreme cases succumbed: the Invergarry and Fort

Augustus branch line in the Scottish Highlands, which was completed in 1903 but never reached Inverness as intended, was closed in 1933 because it was carrying only six people per day. Closures remained the exception, however, until after World War II.

In the US, one type of train suffered major closures in the interwar years. This was the interurban (see pp.56–57), extended tramways that linked neighboring towns on tracks alongside roads. Built cheaply, they sprang up across the nation in the 1910s, usually operating a single carriage, akin to a bus on tracks. At their peak in 1916, these crude railroads covered 15,580 miles (25,073 km), but they were badly hit by competition from cars. Closures started immediately after World War I and accelerated in the Depression after 1929, meaning most interurban lines had a lifespan of barely 20–30 years—very short for the cost of the infrastructure. A remarkable 6,350 miles (10,250 km) were abandoned in the early 1930s, and by the end of World War II, only a few lines survived. All but a handful had shut by 1960. As George Hilton and John Due, authors of *The Electric Interurban Railways in America*, put it: "the interurbans... never enjoyed a prolonged period of prosperity... they played out their life cycle in a shorter period than any other important American industry."

Decline of the streetcar Once part of the most extensive light railway network in the world, the iconic Pacific Electric Red Cars were nearly all scrapped during the interwar period, following pressure from the automobile industry, despite their potential for further service.

"It [Beeching's report] marked the end of our romance with the train... and the rise of the car."

IAN HISLOP, EDITOR OF *PRIVATE EYE* AND RAILROAD ENTHUSIAST

In almost every country with a significant railroad system, there were line closures in the postwar period, and the US was no exception, shutting lines in great numbers. Major railroad companies realized their profits would now come from freight rather than passengers, given the growing competition for suburban journeys from cars and for long-distance travel from planes. Closures required permission from the Interstate Commerce Commission, the federal agency that regulated the railroads.

Railroad service cuts

By the early 1960s, all the main companies were petitioning the commission to close lines, and by the end of the decade, there was a veritable stampede to end passenger services. Many companies used subterfuge to force the commission's hand, using old rolling stock, reducing services, and even demolishing stations to make lines appear uneconomic. Once permission to close was forthcoming, the companies were ruthless about implementing closure. So eager were they to get out of the passenger business, they stopped trains running the minute authorization came through—so commuters of the Chicago, Aurora, and Elgin railroad who had taken the train into town on the day closure was confirmed had to make their own way home. The Louisville and Nashville Railroad dumped its last 14 passengers in Birmingham, Alabama, 400 miles (645 km) short of their destination; only after protests was a bus provided to get them to their final destination.

The pace of US closures became so frantic that the government intervened, creating the state-owned and subsidized rail company Amtrak in 1971 to safeguard the remaining passenger services. It is an irony that the US, which tends to eschew state intervention, still has a nationalized railroad system. Although the nation's network went from a peak of 254,000 miles (408,773 km) in 1916 to 140,000 miles (225,308 km) today, it is still the biggest railroad system in the world, although it is mainly used for freight. Amtrak carries a mere 30 million passengers annually, compared with roughly 1.7 billion in Britain and 1.2 billion in France, both countries with far smaller populations.

In Britain, pressure to close lines came to a head in 1963 with the setting out of a radical plan by the chairman of the British Railways Board, Richard Beeching. He found that the railroad network was very unbalanced, with one-third of the country's 18,000 miles (29,000 km) of track carrying only 1 percent of passengers. His solution was radical. The now infamous Beeching Report, known by its detractors as Beeching's Axe, resulted in the closure of 5,000 miles (8,000 km) of track and a third of the 7,000 stations. While many lines that were clearly not viable were

The Beeching Axe In 1963, Richard Beeching's infamous report, *The Reshaping of British Railways*, drastically reduced Britain's railroad network, cutting vital connections and leaving many towns isolated.

Railroad resurrection Several postwar railroad lines that were once closed have been revived, either as heritage lines such as the Talyllyn in Wales, preserved by enthusiasts, or as fully operational routes on a railroad network.

axed, some major routes were shut down too—subsequently a widespread cause of regret.

In other countries, closures were carried out incrementally, less radically than in the US and more slowly than in Britain. France lost half of its 37,000-mile (59,000 km) network in closures that started in the 1930s until, to protect the remaining lines, the government nationalized the system in 1938. In Eastern Europe, Communist regimes retained their rail systems more-or-less intact as few people could afford cars, but extensive closures took place after the Iron Curtain fell in 1989. However, in recent years, the closure process has been reversed in some countries and railroad mileage has increased, with the reopening of mothballed lines and the construction of new, principally high-speed lines.

Heritage railroads

All these closures had one surprising, beneficial side effect—the creation of a preserved railroads industry largely based on steam trains. Countries where steam trains had until recently remained in service, including Poland, China, and India, attracted enthusiasts, although these have now been replaced by diesel or electricity. However, steam has been preserved in many countries, through the efforts of volunteers repairing and operating sections of old lines as tourist attractions. In Britain, the Santa Specials at Christmas times have proven to be extremely popular.

The first railroad in the world to be preserved as a heritage railroad was the British Talyllyn Railway, a 7-mile (11 km) narrow-gauge railroad opened in 1866 to carry slate down a Welsh valley from quarries to the coast. When its closure was announced in 1951, a group of local people successfully fought to keep the trains running for enthusiasts. The railroad heritage movement has spread around the world since then, and some of these lines even operate regular services that connect with the main line. Old lines continue to be brought back into use for these railroads, including the Welsh Highland Railway, which reopened in 2011 and now, together with the Ffestiniog line, provides a 39-mile (63-km) narrow gauge route across north Wales. In France, too, there are around a hundred such preserved lines, covering 750 miles (1,200 km) of track. These railroads attract 3 million visitors a year, and include a

section of 2 ft (60 cm) narrow-gauge lines used on the Somme front in World War I (see pp.258–265). The US also has a big preservation movement. Its most scenic railroad is the Durango and Silverton Narrow Gauge Railroad, a 45-mile (72-km) line through Colorado. The route was built in 1881–1882 by the Denver and Rio Grande Railway to exploit silver and gold mines in the San Juan Mountains. The remaining section is one of the few in the US that has seen continuous use of steam locomotives since the 19th century.

Some of the most spectacular railroads in the world have been brought back into use after being abandoned. In Ecuador, a 280-mile (451 km) line between the port city of Guayaquil and the highland capital, Quito, has been restored and its steam locomotives are now a major tourist attraction, recreating one of the greatest rail journeys in the world. Thanks to these preserved railroads and the volunteers who work on them, the steam engine will remain a source of admiration for generations to come.

Cinematic railroad The Durango and Silverton Narrow Gauge Railroad owes its preservation in part to its Hollywood success: it has been featured in numerous movies, including *Viva Zapata* (1952) and *Butch Cassidy and the Sundance Kid* (1969).

Underground assembly Before heading under the seabed, the tunnel-boring machines were assembled in a chamber much larger than the main tunnels. Pictured here is one of the vast underground assembly chambers at the British end.

VIVE LE CHANNEL TUNNEL

The opening of an undersea tunnel linking Britain and France in 1994 was the culmination of more than 180 years of debates, discussions, and delays.

The first proposal for a tunnel under the English Channel (although not a rail one) had been made as far back as 1802, by one of Napoleon's engineers. At that time, the journey from London to Paris took about four days (or several weeks if the Channel winds were unfavorable), but the British military, politicians, and even the press were not keen on the idea of a tunnel, fearing that it would leave the island nation vulnerable to attack. Over the next half century, various schemes were mooted, on both sides of the Channel, but they came to nothing. The first serious attempt at digging a rail tunnel was promoted by a Victorian entrepreneur, Sir Edward Watkin, in 1881. Exploratory tunnels were dug at Dover in England and Sangatte in France, but work was abandoned in 1882, largely due to political pressure from the still-unconvinced British.

Misplaced concerns

By the early 20th century, more advanced tunneling machines and the development of electric traction had made the idea of a rail tunnel a more realistic proposition. However, by this time a fit of xenophobic hysteria had seized most of the British military establishment, who were adamant that foreign powers would use the tunnel as a corridor for invasion, a very unlikely prospect since it could easily be blocked off. In fact, Marshal Foch, the Allies' Supreme Commander in the last year of World War I, declared that a tunnel could have shortened the conflict by two years. Nevertheless, these delays in building a tunnel simply meant that the competition kept on speeding up. By 1852, the journey time between London and Paris had been reduced to 12 hours by sea and rail, and 60 years later it took a mere 7 hours. In the 1930s, the glamorous *Flèche d'Or* (Golden Arrow) train-ferry service reduced the journey time to just over six and half hours

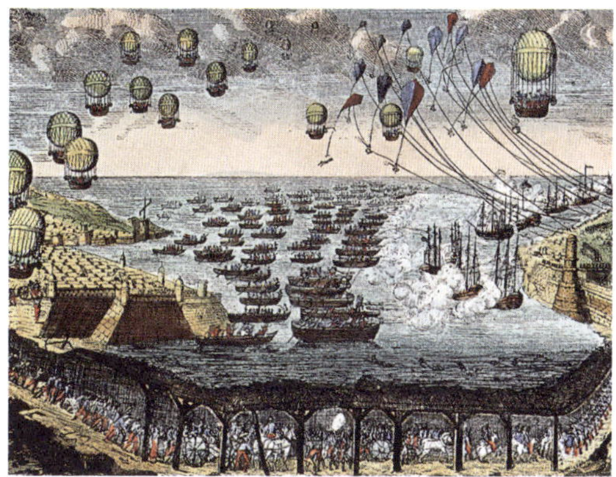

Unfounded fears (right) Concern that a tunnel under the sea could lead to a French invasion of Britain were highlighted in this 1803 engraving, which illustrates French troops walking through the tunnel as ships and balloons attack from sea and air.

and by that time there was also a regular air service between Croydon, just outside London, and Le Bourget, northeast of Paris.

A persisting idea

Although military hysteria dissipated after the end of World War II in 1945, progress on a tunnel remained slow, particularly at the British end, and it was not until 1963 that the British government finally endorsed the idea. By this time, the commercial outlook was promising as the number of travelers from London to Paris was increasing steadily. However, the British were still rather lukewarm about the project and had not yet agreed to a new rail line to link the tunnel to London and beyond. British Rail (BR) suggested a variety of routes, but each one was more expensive than its predecessor. In the end, the cost of the new rail link provided an excellent excuse for the government to cancel the project in early 1975, just as tunneling had begun. This about-turn, which was in fact necessitated by Britain's perilous financial situation, naturally infuriated the French and reinforced their suspicions that Britain was not really serious about a Channel tunnel.

The number of travelers between London and Paris grew from 1 million in 1960 to 2.5 million in 1978

However, the idea for a tunnel refused to go away, and within four years Sir Peter Parker, the chairman of BR, together with his counterparts from the SNCF in France, had resurrected the project by proposing a single-track tunnel—inevitably called the "mousehole"—running "flights" of trains back and forth across the Channel. This somewhat ramshackle idea did not progress, but the principle of building a Channel tunnel received a boost from an unlikely source—Eurosceptic British Prime Minister Margaret

Thatcher. The "Iron Lady" decided that a tunnel could proceed under the Channel, as long as it was privately, not publicly, funded. Along with French President François Mitterand, Thatcher set up a working group and then invited bidders to submit their proposals. Thatcher disliked railroads, so her natural preference was for a road-based, or at least a "drive-through" plan—a bias she shared with Mitterrand—but in the end a plan involving dual rail tunnels won out. A road tunnel was simply too complex given the need for ventilation tunnels in the Channel, which would be a hazard in one of the world's busiest shipping lanes. By the end of 1985, the Channel Tunnel Group/TransManche Link, a consortium of five French and five British contractors plus five banks, had been awarded the contract to build the tunnel.

Rising difficulties

The whole operation was still fiendishly complicated. It took two more years for the Channel Tunnel Act, which officially rubber-stamped the plan, to pass through the British Parliament (although the French procedure took mere days) and the world's investment community was by no means enthusiastic about the tunnel's financial prospects. Financial negotiations were hampered by the geographical spread of the various banks involved, and the sheer number of contractors involved in the plan made the construction process equally complex. However, the balance of power between the interested parties was transformed in early 1987 with the appointment of Alastair Morton as full-time British joint chairman of Eurotunnel, the company that actually held the contract to build the tunnel. During Morton's nine years at Eurotunnel, he saved what was a fundamentally uneconomic venture from disaster by dealing with the British government, the contractors, and the 200 banks eventually involved. He also grappled with BR and SNCF, who would be the main users (to add further complexity, BR was being prepared for privatization at the time). After protracted negotiations about the technology the tunnel would use and the type of links it would enable, a complicated international consortium was formed combining railroad companies from France, Britain, and Belgium.

Spoil containment Five massive lagoons were built to contain the vast amount of excavated spoil from the undersea tunnel, helping manage environmental impact and material disposal.

Crossovers The Channel Tunnel has two undersea crossover points where trains can switch lines, allowing continuous service while sections are closed for maintenance. The UK crossover point, seen here, shows the tunnel-boring machine during construction.

Work begins

Tunneling commenced at long last in December 1987, when the British started digging a service tunnel that would be used for maintenance and emergencies. Starting with the smaller central service tunnel was a good way of testing the tunneling conditions, foreshadowing any geological or practical issues before work on the main rail tunnels began. The French commenced their end of the service tunnel a couple of months after the British and then, in June 1988, the two rail tunnels were started simultaneously from both sides. Thus the Channel Tunnel was, and remains, in fact three tunnels—two rail tunnels separated by a service tunnel. It was the biggest engineering project ever undertaken by France or Britain, requiring 15,000 workers at its peak. However, progress was slower than predicted, causing costs to spiral. In fact, there were no fewer than three major financial crises while the tunnel was under construction and the cost of the project exceeded its budget by more than 80 percent. Nevertheless, on December 4, 1990, the two tunneling teams finally shook hands mid-Channel. Amazingly, the tunnels were only 13 in (330 mm) out of alignment, despite each traveling 15 miles (25 km) from the two starting points.

Completing the tunnels was just the beginning of the process, however. As one observer put it: "turning the tunnels into a piece of complex, safe, and sophisticated transport infrastructure was to prove an altogether different challenge," involving as it did power supply, lighting, ventilation, communication, maintenance provision, and fire detection and suppression equipment. The trains were also incredibly complex, as they had to cope with different power supplies and signaling systems not just in Britain and France but also in Belgium, where some trains would terminate. Safety fears also meant that every piece of equipment had to receive a separate operating certificate for each country, at an estimated cost of over £400 million ($500 million), with a further £200 million ($250 million) lost in the resulting delays. However, the stringent safety requirements have proved their worth: there have been only three serious fires in the Channel Tunnel – all started on shuttles carrying lorries – that closed the Tunnel for short periods, but caused no loss of life.

A major milestone In 1990, French and British workers reached the Channel Tunnel's midpoint with astonishing accuracy, only a couple of inches off, marking a momentous accomplishment in the tunnel's construction.

Official opening

In the end, the tunnel was delayed by a year, far less than occurs on many much smaller projects and actually impressive for such a major one. The contractors handed over the project to Eurotunnel in December 1993, and the "Chunnel"—a nickname that fortunately hasn't stuck—was officially opened by Queen Elizabeth II and President Mitterand in May 1994. Freight trains began traveling through the Tunnel a month later and rail passengers were welcomed in November, on the service now known as Eurostar. On December 22, 1994, the Channel Tunnel inaugurated its pioneering car and truck shuttle service, known as Eurotunnel Le Shuttle, from Folkestone to Calais.

However, in one major respect, the project was incomplete when the Tunnel opened in 1994. Providing a fast line to the tunnel was relatively easy for the French, since all it took was building a branch line to Calais from their new fast line from Paris to Lille and Brussels. By contrast, neither British Rail nor the British government could overcome the difficulties inherent in building an entirely new line from London to Folkestone. BR had never designed a new railroad line, and all the routes it suggested threatened the rich heartland

of Kent, as well as numerous marginal constituencies in South East London. As a result, the Eurostar trains on the British side of the tunnel initially had to travel along tortuous, winding tracks that had been laid a century earlier, taking an hour to travel the 60 miles (96.5 km) from its Waterloo Terminus to the mouth of the Tunnel. The rails were strengthened and the route was provided with new signals and upgraded power supplies, but still, the trains were noticeably much slower in England than in France where they used a *Ligne à Grande Vitesse* (see p.333).

Overcoming the odds

It took until 1996 before work began on a high-speed rail line, now called High Speed 1 (HS1), on the British side. Even when work was finally underway, it was far from simple. The project was beset with financial and construction problems. Excavation of the route revealed many ancient relics, which thrilled archaeologists but caused further delays. Eventually, the first section of the high-speed route through Kent opened in 2003, reducing the journey time between London and Paris by 20 minutes.

The second section of the route, from the North Downs in Kent to a new terminal at St. Pancras in London, was an even bigger engineering problem. It involved tunneling under the Thames River, navigating marshes in east London, building an enormous new station at Stratford, and rebuilding the St. Pancras terminus. The biggest headache, however, was constructing an 11-mile (18 km) tunnel to St. Pancras that would avoid the existing sewers, main railroad lines, and underground system.

Finally, on November 13, 2007, the link was finished, and Eurostar transferred its passenger services from Waterloo to St. Pancras. The switch of terminals marked a historic moment, linking Britain's first high-speed line to its equivalent in Europe and finally completing the project more than 200 years after it had first been proposed. It is the world's longest undersea rail tunnel—23½ miles (37.9 km) of the 31⅜-mile (50.4 km) tunnel runs under the Channel—and has been described by the American Society of Civil Engineers as "One of the Seven Wonders of the Modern World." The Channel Tunnel has proved to be a resounding success, with Eurostar alone carrying more than 11 million people annually through it.

High-speed connectivity The Eurostar, which links London with Paris, Brussels, and Amsterdam, has transformed cross-Channel travel, providing a reliable and efficient route between major European cities.

Number of tons of spoil removed during tunneling under the English Channel

11,023,000

(10,00,000 metric tons)

BUILDING TUNNELS

Tunneling is the most costly and labor-intensive of all engineering enterprises, and, in the early days of the railroads, it was the most dangerous. Working long shifts lit by candlelight in cramped conditions, navvies (see pp.82–87) risked serious injury or loss of life as they burrowed underground using only basic tools. From the mid-19th century, their picks, hand drills, and explosives were gradually replaced by tunnel-boring machines (TBMs), the first of which was used after 1862 to dig the Fréjus Rail Tunnel beneath the Alps (see pp.101–102). Since then, strict safety regulations have reduced risks considerably, and the introduction of computer control has increased the machines' efficiency.

Immersed tunnels

Suitable for routes that cross shallow bodies of water, immersed tunnels on the seabed are a cost-effective alternative to boring beneath it. One of the tunnels built in this way was the Bay Area Rapid Transit (BART) tunnel in San Francisco, in the late 1960s. Sections of the tunnel were floated to the tunnel site; sunk into a precut trench on the seabed; and secured with layers of gravel, concrete, and backfill.

BART tunnel section under construction

Tunneling through In the late 19th century, London Underground tunnels were built using mostly manual labor, with the help of an early TBM called the Greathead shield. Workers dug ahead of the shield, which was then pushed forward by compressed air.

How it works

A tunnel-boring machine (TBM) consists of several connected systems that are operated in different phases of construction to bore and line the tunnel, lay the rails, and convey waste away from the site. The cutting wheel can be as much as 63 ft (19.3 m) in diameter, while the TBM apparatus can be up to 490 ft (150 m) in length.

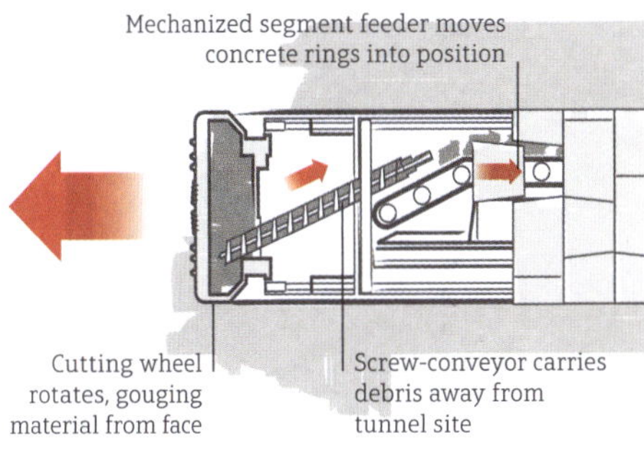

STEP 1: Tunneling phase
During the tunneling phase, the rotating cutting wheel is pressed into the tunnel face at a predetermined rate. Debris is transported away from the cutting face by a screw conveyor (for shale or rock, pictured here) or a series of pressurized pipes (for earth or clay).

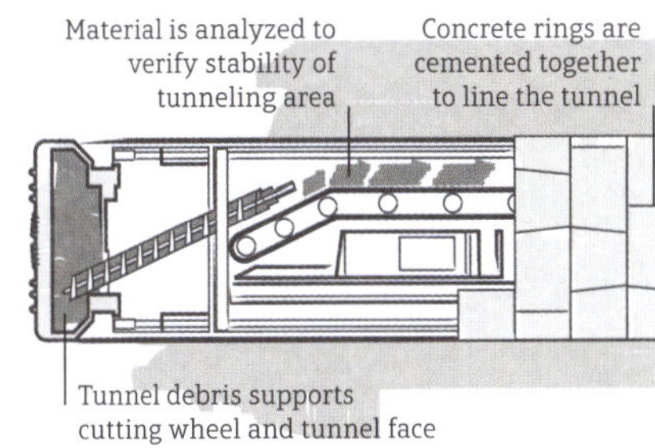

STEP 2: Ring-building phase
The cutting apparatus stops to allow the ring-building phase to commence—the installation of concrete rings to provide a watertight and strengthening lining for the tunnel. The ring segments are cast above ground and moved to the construction site via rail.

The Jungfrau Railway Opened in 1912, this iconic rack railroad ascends through tunnels carved into the Eiger and Mönch mountains, before arriving at the Jungfraujoch—Europe's highest station at 11,332 ft (3,454 m).

SWITZERLAND: THE BEST OF THE BEST

Home to some of the most renowned railroads in the world, Switzerland well and truly embraces trains as an integral element of its national identity.

Switzerland joined the railroad age relatively late, but, as in other countries such as neighboring Germany and Italy, the railroads quickly became a unifying force and a vital component of the nation's prosperity. So much so that today Switzerland can lay claim to having one of the most efficient and well-used railroad networks in the world.

A growing imperative

Surrounded by mountains and beset by cold temperatures and copious snowfall in the winter, Switzerland did not seem like fertile territory for the iron road. Moreover, it did not even become a unified nation until 1848, following a brief civil war between the Protestant and Catholic cantons (states). The new Switzerland adopted a federal state system, similar to that of the US, and the new government prioritized the development and extension of the country's railroad network. So in 1850, two British engineers, Robert Stephenson and Henry Swinburne, were asked to oversee the development of a rail network. The pair suggested a basic, east-to-west line along the valleys between Geneva and Zürich, plus another line from Basel to Lucerne. Rather oddly, though, the capital, Bern, was to be on a branch line. The cantons built these early lines, often with foreign investment and contractors. Stephenson and Swinburne's influence also meant that the Swiss adopted the standard gauge (4 ft 8½ in/1,435 mm) and instituted British-style left-hand running on double-track lines, both of which are still used today.

The iron road's progress remained slow in Switzerland. In the end, unlike most European countries, where the demands of traditional heavy industries such as mining or agriculture fueled railroad expansion, it

In a 2022 test run, Swiss railways set a world record by running a 100-coach, 1.2 miles (1.9 km) train across the Alps

Electric power The transalpine Gotthard line became electrified in 1922. This image from 1930 shows an electric locomotive crossing the Kerstelenbach Viaduct in Amsteg, Switzerland.

was tourism that eventually became the catalyst for further development in Switzerland. From the mid-19th century, increasing numbers of visitors flocked to resorts in the scenic Alps and lakes. However, when pioneering travel agent Thomas Cook took his first tour party to Switzerland in 1863, there was still barely 400 miles (650 km) of railroad in the whole country. It was clear that the country's existing rail network could not cope with the demands of the tourist industry.

Consequently, by the last third of the 19th century, the Swiss federal government was eager to see its railroads develop more rapidly. Furthermore, the country's location in the center of Europe made an efficient railroad network in Switzerland highly desirable for its neighbors, too. They were eager to traverse Swiss territory to create both passenger and freight links across Europe and were happy to invest in Swiss railroads to make that possible. A treaty between Switzerland, Germany, and Italy in 1869 agreed on a strategic link under the Gotthard Pass in the Alps. Completed in 1882, the Gotthard Tunnel (see pp.102–103) linked not just the cantons of Uri and Ticino but also facilitated travel between northern and southern Europe, including Germany and Italy; the Simplon Tunnel (see p.103), opened in 1906, also linked Switzerland with Italy.

Electrifying the tracks

Meanwhile, the railroads continued to spread across the country, including Europe's first rack railroad (see pp.104–105), which opened in 1871. Built to take tourists up the Rigi Mountain above Lake Lucerne, it used a rack-and-pinion system developed by Swiss engineer Niklaus Riggenbach. Three years later, the first 3 ft 3⅜ in (1 m) gauge line opened from Lausanne to Bercher via Echallens, although this was actually built to serve an agricultural area rather than the tourist industry. By adopting a narrower gauge in less accessible or less populous areas, lines could be built much more economically, allowing railroads (and also roadside tramways) to spread into the highest and most remote corners of Switzerland.

After the initial railroad boom of the late 19th century, some speculative railroads went bust and many Swiss people became disenchanted with their railroads being largely owned and operated for the benefit of foreign shareholders. Consequently, in 1898, a referendum on nationalizing the railroads led to the formation of the Swiss Federal Railways in 1902 (officially known as SBB-CFF-FFS to reflect the nation's three principal languages). Over the next few years, the SBB-CFF-FFS acquired approximately 50 percent of the national trackage and embarked on a program to electrify the whole network. Given the country's lack of coal, the Swiss were early adopters of electric traction: the first electrically powered railroad in Switzerland was a 3 ft 3⅜ in (1 m) gauge line between Montreux and Chillon in 1888. The Simplon Tunnel was also electrified from the start, and electric traction was used, too, for the *Jungfraubahn*, completed in 1912.

Further expansion

The two world wars accelerated the electrification process in Switzerland: during World War I, coal shortages caused widespread travel disruption, while World War II affected Switzerland even more, despite its neutrality. The tourist trade that many railroads depended on dried up, and some lines closed after the wars. However, the postwar government soon realized the value of Switzerland's transportation infrastructure and began to invest in the railroads, with the result that by 1960 the entire railroad network in Switzerland was electrified, making it the first country in the world to achieve this milestone.

During the latter half of the 20th century, automobile traffic in Switzerland grew inexorably, as it did elsewhere. With the building of modern highways through and under the Alps, much freight that was once rail-borne transferred to the road. By the 1980s, however, the Swiss public were increasingly concerned about the environmental damage caused by heavy trucks. This eventually led to two major national referenda on the railroads.

The first, in 1987, led to the Bahn 2000 project, which aimed to bring the Swiss rail network into the 21st century. This initiative resulted in the improvement of many lines and the construction of sections of high-speed track that are an integrated part of

The Swiss rail network
Connecting scenic landscapes, Switzerland's fully electric rail network provides efficient travel across the Alps and beyond.

the existing infrastructure rather than, as in many other countries, entirely separate. A second referendum in 1992 approved, by a massive majority, a project called "Alptransit" that regulated the number and capacity of trucks allowed across the Alps. It also prioritized improvements to the rail infrastructure over road building, intending freight to be transferred onto the transalpine railroads.

Transportation of choice

The 1980s also saw the introduction of an impressive integrated national transportation timetable in Switzerland, coordinating rail, bus, and tram services. It means that almost every station in Switzerland has at least an hourly rail service that links to a national timetable plan, giving regular connections with all other routes and modes of transportation. Oddly, although the transportation services are coordinated by the government, its national rail company, SBB-CFF-FFS, owns just under 2,000 miles (3,200 km) of track, with the remaining 1,200 miles (2,000 km) being operated by around 80 different private or semi-nationalized companies, which are tightly regulated. Despite this, the Swiss railroad system is far more streamlined and has far less duplication than many other networks around the world, where competition between different companies resulted in unnecessary or excessive lines being built.

The density of the railroad network in Switzerland is 2.5 times that of the rest of Europe

Signature structure (left) The Bernina Express crosses the imposing Landwasser Viaduct, in Graubunden, Switzerland, along the Albula railroad line. The limestone bridge rises 213 ft (65 m) above the Landwasser River.

Historically, the Swiss electorate, and generally their politicians, have been far more conscious of the implications of their public transportation than most other nations. For example, the standard gauge rail network is the core of a wider transportation system in Switzerland into which local trains (often 3 ft 3⅜ in/1 m gauge), trams, and buses link at all stations. Despite this integrated network, the Swiss still have one of the highest rates of car ownership per capita (about one for every two people), but people use their vehicles far less. In fact, Swiss people make more trips via railroad than any other nation. On average, the Swiss travel 1,312 miles (2,113 km) per person annually by rail. While Japan has consistently led Switzerland in miles traveled per person—the Swiss actually make more individual trips than the Japanese. Given that Japan is a far bigger country with a very dense population, Switzerland's record is all the more remarkable. The key to that success is that the rail network is part of a genuinely integrated public transportation system designed to make nonmotorized travel easier and more efficient. Reliability and punctuality have proved crucial, too, supported by consistent government investment in the railroads (see p.103). Not only is the rail network extensive and well managed, but the cost of rail fares is also highly competitive. In addition to the usual range of discounted season and zonal tickets, it is possible for residents to purchase a national, all-modes (rail, bus, tram, boat) travel card for all their travel needs.

Looking ahead

Today, a growing Swiss population is placing the rail network under increasing strain, and the railroads require considerable investment to keep pace with demand. The Swiss, however, seem up to the task: in Zurich, for example, an expensive series of tunnels has been planned to be open by 2035 to allow trains to pass through the city more quickly and to link expanding suburbs. Railroads, it seems, have become ingrained in the culture and success of Switzerland, and the importance of the iron road shows no signs of waning.

Journey to the summit The Gornergrat Railway, which runs from Zermatt to the summit of the Gornergrat, reaches a height of 10,135 ft (3,089 m) and attracts skiers in winter and hikers in the summer. The famous Matterhorn can be seen from a viewpoint outside the station at Gornergrat.

GOING FASTER: BULLET TRAINS AND HIGH-SPEED LINES

In the 1960s, facing competition from cars, trucks, and airplanes, railroads had to modernize to remain viable. Bullet trains and high-speed lines emerged as the key to revitalizing the railroad industry for the future.

It was the Japanese who led the way with the ground-breaking *Shinkansen* (new mainline), known in the West as the bullet train. It started a trend for high-speed railroads that would spread—albeit rather slowly—around the world.

Japan's geography and pattern of settlement contributed to the genesis of the bullet train, as it had to the development of Japan's railroads in the first place. The country consists of four main islands, but less than a fifth of the land mass is habitable, so most of the population of 124 million is confined to a relatively small part of the country. It was this density of population in lowland regions that created the right conditions for high-speed rail development. In fact, while the high-speed aspect of the *Shinkansen* is emphasized, the new lines evolved mainly because the existing network was running out of capacity.

Railroads in Japan

Japan came late to the railroad age. The island nation had shunned the rest of the world until 1868, when the new Meiji administration sought to modernize the country, opening its doors to the railroads. The first line, which covered the 18 miles (29 km) between Tokyo and Yokohoma, opened in 1872, and the Japanese adopted trains with enthusiasm. The engineers of the line used the narrow gauge of 3 ft 6 in (1,067 mm), the same as in New Zealand as the islands had similar topographies. Later plans to convert to standard gauge to increase traffic on the railroads were opposed by military powers; instead, lines were extended.

Passing Mount Fuji In what has become an iconic image of the meeting of the modern and the ancient world in Japan, the *Shinkansen* bullet trains are pictured here passing in front of snowcapped Mount Fuji.

The pioneer This c.1873 Meiji period illustration depicts a steam locomotive running on Japan's first railroad line at Takanawa in Tokyo.

The railroads boomed in the final few years of the 19th century, and by 1907 there were nearly 4,500 miles (7,250 km) of railroad in operation, all owned by the state-run Japanese Imperial Railways. Development continued steadily between the first and second world wars. By 1945, the total mileage had reached 16,000 miles (26,000 km), nearly a quarter of which was owned privately, with the rest under the control of the renamed Japanese National Railways.

By the 1930s, Japan's first trunk route, the Tokaido line, which linked Tokyo with a series of major cities that included Nagoya, Kyoto, Osaka, and Kobe, was already becoming heavily congested. An entirely new route between Tokyo and Osaka was proposed that would cover the 300-mile (500 km) trip in four hours—an unheard-of speed for a railroad at the time. Work started in 1941 but paused after the Japanese attack on Pearl Harbor triggered the Pacific War.

The Japanese economy took some time to recover from defeat in the war, but by the mid-1950s, the Tokaido line was again running at capacity and the plan for the Tokaido *Shinkansen* was revived. Shinji Sogō, the president of the state-run railroads, persuaded the government that the new railroad line would be viable, as at the time it seemed that cars and planes would make railroads redundant. It was the need for extra train routes that stimulated the *Shinkansen's* development, but to compete with cars it was built on highway principles, with few stops and fast travel times. The high speed was a by-product of the need for capacity rather than an end in itself—a principle that applied to most high-speed

"The bullet train was built to move people at high speeds from one city to another, but it also moved people's hearts and minds in more subtle ways."

JESSAMYN ABEL, *DREAM SUPER-EXPRESS: A CULTURAL HISTORY OF THE WORLD'S FIRST BULLET TRAIN*, 2022 systems around the world. Of course, the high-speed aspect helped attract passengers away from their cars, and also made it possible for rail to compete with aviation over distances of up to 500 miles (800 km), thanks to its city-center-to-city-center routing.

Navigating obstacles

It was decided that Japan's new line would carry only fast electric passenger trains and would use the standard 4 ft 8½ in (1,435 mm) gauge to provide greater capacity and enable use of technology from other railroads. Despite difficult terrain and cost overruns—the eventual cost of 380 billion yen (around or $1.1 billion or £400 million at the time) was twice the original budget—the line was completed five years after work started in 1959. By contemporary high-speed standards, the line was slow, with an average speed of 130 mph (209 km/h), but thanks to its dedicated track and limited stops, the travel time was radically reduced. While the conventional express took 6 hours and 40 minutes between the two main cities, Tokyo and Osaka, the *Shinkansen* made the trip in 4 hours. The *Shinkansen* changed business patterns, too, by making day trips between Tokyo and Osaka possible. Shinji Sogō's faith in the railroad was fully justified. An immediate success, the service carried 100 million passengers in its first three years; by 1976, it had carried one billion. Today, the Tokaido *Shinkansen* alone carries 174 million passengers annually.

It was not an easy ride, however. The service suffered teething troubles, including pain to passengers' ears when trains crossed in the tunnels that accounted for 45 miles (72 km) of the route, and a more embarrassing problem: the air currents generated in the tunnels blew water up from the toilet bowls, much to the users' discomfiture. Eventually, it was decided to pressurize the trains to

Inauguration of the Tokaido *Shinkansen* The Tokaido *Shinkansen* was launched in Tokyo just in time for the 1964 Olympics. The bullet train reduced the travel time between Tokyo and Osaka and became the prototype for high-speed trains worldwide.

solve these problems, which proved expensive but was successful. Interestingly, despite the *Shinkansen*'s popularity, Japanese National Railways faced opposition to building the network it had envisioned. Noise and cost were both concerns, but eventually, in the 1970s, several new lines as well as extensions to the Tokaido line were built. The fastest trains on the Sanyo line travel at 186 mph (300 km/h), a speed that has become the norm across the world for high-speed lines.

Global expansion and influence

Around the world, it was some years before another country followed Japan's lead. Although railroad managers were eager to increase speeds from the 60–70 mph (90–110 km/h) that was standard for express trains by the 1960s, governments remained doubtful as to whether it was worth investing in the "old technology" of train travel. In Germany and France, train speed trials took place, demonstrating that trains could easily reach speeds of 124 mph (200 km/h) for long periods, and attempts were made to speed up services on existing lines. In France, the Paris–Toulouse route was upgraded in 1966 to support 124 mph (200 km/h) running through improvements to tracks and signaling. In Britain, a new diesel service branded InterCity 125 was introduced on routes from London after 1976. However, all used existing lines, which increased journey times as other, slower trains shared the tracks.

To avoid line-sharing, France decided in the 1970s to create a dedicated bullet-style service called the *Train à Grande Vitesse* (TGV); like the *Shinkansen*, the TGV has become a world-renowned brand. At the time, capacity on the key Paris–Lyon route was reaching its limits and it was decided to build a new line, separate from the existing railroad except at the city entrances, where tracks were shared with conventional services. The TGV uses the same gauge as regular trains so it can run on from high-speed sections on to standard tracks for flexibility. The French had created high-speed trains that had beaten the world record several times, reaching an impressive 262 mph (422 km/h) on an experimental track in 1969. Clearly, such speeds would be possible only on a dedicated track, so in 1976, construction of the first *Ligne à Grand Vitesse* started. The Paris–Lyon line was completed in 1981, when the first TGVs started running at a top speed of 168 mph (270 km/h), later increased to 186 mph (300 km/h). The service was an instant success, challenging air travel between the two cities. France embarked on a network of high-speed lines

Comprehensive network
Started in 1964, Japan's high-speed rail network is now more than 1,833 miles (2,950 km) and links the majority of its most populous cities.

356 million

Number of passengers carried on Japanese bullet trains each year

***Train à Grande Vitesse* (TGV)**
The TGV was showcased to the public at the Salon du Train Paris–Montparnasse in June 1979. This event was significant in the lead-up to the 1981 launch of the French high-speed system, which has become an emblem of French modernity and technology.

emanating from Paris. The *Est*, which opened in 2007, operates at the higher speed of 200 mph (320 km/h).

France's high-speed network covered 1,740 miles (2,800 km) by 2021–2022, but it has been surpassed in distance by Spain. In 2005, Spain announced a plan to ensure that 90 percent of the population would live within 30 miles (50 km) of a station served by the Spanish *Alta Velocidad Española* (AVE) network. Spain's first high-speed line, between Madrid and Seville, was completed in time for the Seville Expo '92. It used standard gauge as opposed to the 5 ft 6 in (1,680 mm) Iberian gauge of other Spanish services. This led to a technological development that allows the latest high-speed trains to change gauge without stopping so they can continue journeys off the high-speed network. The expansion was remarkably fast, and Spain now operates half a dozen routes out of Madrid and Barcelona with a total mileage of 2,469 miles (3,973 km).

After France, Germany was the second country in Europe to develop high-speed lines. It opted for a different model by creating high-speed sections rather than whole new routes, so the trains switch frequently between conventional and high-speed lines. Germany launched its *Intercity-Express* (ICE) in 1991, operating at a top speed of 174 mph (280 kph) on the Hannover–Würzburg high-speed railroad.

Ongoing developments

Since the turn of the century, a remarkable number of new high-speed rail services have started running aross the world as the success of the pioneering systems was clear to see. South Korea became the fourth country to adopt high-speed rail technology. Its first train was launched in 2004 after a lengthy and controversial period of development along the Seoul–Busan corridor, linking the country's two biggest cities. Initially, the technology largely duplicated the French TGV system, but as the system has expanded, more homegrown technology has been introduced. In 2024, South Korea signed an international agreement with Uzbekistan for its technology to be used on Uzbekistan's first high-speed line. In 2007, Taiwan inaugurated its high-speed railroad, which runs for 217 miles (350 km) along the west coast of Taiwan, from the national capital Taipei to the southern city of Kaohsiung, using technology based primarily on Japan's *Shinkansen*.

By the mid-2020s, more than 25 countries on all the inhabited continents apart from Australasia were operating high-speed rail services. These include countries—such as Türkiye and Morocco—with high-density populations on key routes, oil-rich states such as Uzbekistan and Saudi Arabia, as well as smaller nations such as Serbia and Portugal. More than 62,137 miles (100,000 km) of dedicated high-speed routes were either in operation or under construction at the start of 2025. Many other countries are considering building their first high-speed line, while several existing users are expanding their routes. Apart from a handful of exceptions in Europe, these lines were used solely for passenger services. By far the world's biggest network is in China (see pp.336–343).

However, it has not been all plain sailing. Major schemes in the UK and the US have both been delayed due to planning and technical difficulties, and this has inevitably resulted in political controversy. In the UK, which has one 68-mile (109 km) line running between London and the Channel Tunnel, a second plan, called HS2, was originally planned to cover much of England with a Y-shaped network running from London to Leeds and Manchester via Birmingham, but it has now been cut back to a 140-mile (225 km) line running between London and Birmingham. In the US, a plan for a 776-mile (1,250-km) route linking San Francisco and San Diego was approved by voters in 2008 but has had financial and planning difficulties, and only a small 119-mile (191-km) section was actively under construction in 2024. Although several plans worldwide have faced delays or widespread opposition, they have almost universally proven successful once opened.

Shinkansen trains feature special automatic air brakes for earthquakes

Disaster at Santiago de Compostella The 2013 accident, Spain's deadliest rail disaster in over 40 years, occurred when a high-speed train traveled too fast on a section where it was supposed to slow down.

Safety on tracks

Safety has been a major factor in the success of high-speed trains. Although there have been three major accidents involving high-speed trains, none occurred at full speed on dedicated lines. In Germany in 1998, a wheel broke at 124 mph (200 km/h) and came off the rails at a bridge—resulting in the derailment and destruction of the full set of 16 cars and the death of 101 people. In China in 2011, due to a signaling error, a train traveling at 62 mph (100 km/h) hit a stationary train on a viaduct, killing 40 people. At Santiago de Compostela in Spain in 2013, a train came off the rails at 120 mph (195 km/h) on a curve with a speed limit of 50 mph (80 km/h), and smashed into a concrete wall, killing 79 people. Oddly, these accidents occurred when the trains were not travelling at high speed. The overall safety record of these new lines has been remarkable due to the vast amounts of effort and money being spent to reduce the potential for accidents.

CHINA, THE NEW PIONEER

China joined the railroad age late in the 19th century, after a false start that led to the destruction of its first line. It has since become a world powerhouse in railroad development.

Despite its false start, China now boasts by far the most extensive system of high-speed dedicated lines anywhere on the globe, a network it is bent on expanding to become the backbone of the nation's transportation infrastructure. China is also home to the world's highest railroad: the Qinghai–Tibet line.

The first railroad line in China was built by Jardine, Matheson & Co., a European-owned trading firm looking to improve access between Shanghai and the nearby port of Woosung. The line was just 10 miles (16 km) long, but its construction in 1876 was mired in controversy: the deeply conservative Chinese officialdom

was reluctant to allow the laying of railroads, fearing it would ruin the livelihood of the vast numbers of those who carried goods for a living. One Chinese official at the time, Yü Lien-yuan, worried that the resulting unemployment would foment unrest:

> “several tens of millions, who earn their living by holding the whip or grasping the tiller, will lose their jobs. If they don't end up starving in the ditches, they will surely gather [as outlaws] in the forests.”

Another official was concerned that coal would run out, arguing that “when one uses coal with such profligacy, coalfields would soon disappear.” In addition to these doom-laden visions, there was much antagonism toward foreigners and foreign-owned concerns at this time. Imperialist shows of might, such as the Opium Wars, lived in very recent memory, and foreign powers had been taking advantage of China's weakness: several European governments, as well as the Japanese, had set up missions along the coast that were effectively a way of obtaining access to China's riches without paying taxes on them. As such, Chinese officials took a dim view of the Shanghai–Woosung railroad, and its European-sponsored construction never received official sanction. Just one year after the railroad opened, Shen Pao-Chen, the governor of the region through which the railroad ran, ordered the line to be

Destroying tracks Printed in the French newspaper *Le Petit Parisien* (1900), this illustration depicts Boxer rebels in China dismantling railroad tracks seen to represent foreign interests.

Running checks Maintenance engineers in Wuhan, China, carry out final checks on two high-speed trains in preparation for the Spring Festival (also known as Chinese New Year) holiday rush in 2018.

First up *Pioneer* was the first locomotive delivered to China, in 1876, for the ill-fated Woosong to Shanghai line.

ripped up and had the equipment shipped to Taiwan, where it was abandoned to the elements.

It was not until 1881 that a permanent railroad line would open in China. Originally intended to be mule-hauled, the line was a 6-mile (10 km) standard-gauge railroad running from a coal mine to a canal at Hsukochuang, about 100 miles (160 km) east of the capital, Beijing. A British engineer, C. W. Kinder, was responsible for the construction, as well as for commissioning China's first locomotive, the *Rocket of China*. These events, however, did not herald a railroad revolution. The government remained reluctant to endorse this ground-breaking method of transportation, despite its success across the world, and very few lines were built in the 1880s. It took the disastrous defeat in the Sino-French War of 1884–1885 to make the Chinese realize that modernization was essential and that railroads could be a catalyst for development. Kinder's line was extended by 20 miles (32 km) in the direction of Beijing. However, a mysterious fire in the Imperial Palace was seen as a sign of celestial displeasure and the line was never completed.

The railroad boom

By 1894, when the Sino-Japanese conflict broke out, little progress had been made and China had a mere 320 miles (500 km) of railroad, compared at the time with 175,000 miles (280,000 km) in the US. However, defeat in the war finally stimulated a railroad boom in China. While Beijing became the center of the network, many other lines were built to serve mines in relatively remote areas. By the time of the Xinhai Revolution of 1911, which created the Republic of China, there were 6,000 miles (9,500 km) of track, a significant increase, but still a relatively small statistic for the most populous country in the world. It was, at the time, half the size of the railroad network in India—a similarly impoverished, but smaller, nation.

Investing in railroads

Growth of the railroads slowed during the period of the Republic as a result of a series of civil wars and the occupation of China by Japan in the late 1930s. Many lines were destroyed in these various conflicts, and by the end of World War II this vast nation still had only 14,000 miles (22,500 km) of workable railroad. After gaining control of the country for the communists in 1949, Mao Zedong invested heavily in the railroad network. Lines were repaired and new ones built, even in difficult mountainous territory. This progress continued after Mao's death in 1976, and by the end of the 20th century, China finally had a network covering most

Built in China In 1881, English engineer Claude Kinder built the *Rocket of China* locomotive in the Tangshan workshops in China. He did so in complete secrecy for fear of being attacked by locals who resented foreign involvement.

of the country. One major gap, however, remained—a line connecting Tibet with the rest of China.

The Tibet connection

Tibet is remote and separated from the rest of the country by the Kunlun Mountains in the north and the Nyenchen Tanglha range in the east. The main Tibetan plateau is a huge, high landmass stretching 1,500 miles (2,400 km) from east to west, and 500 miles (800 km) from north to south. It is home to the largest subarctic permafrost region in the world—which, to put it mildly, is not ideal railroad territory. All land routes to the vast plateau cross mountain passes that climb higher than any peak in the US. As author Abrahm Lustgarten describes in *China's Great Train*, the roads:

> “twist and wind through steep gorges loaded like cannons with unstable rock and snow at their peaks and flushing with torrents of interminable water in their troughs.”

A China–Tibet rail link was seen as a way to cement China's control over this long-disputed area, known by the Chinese as the Tibetan Autonomous Region. Historically part of China, Tibet had declared its independence following the collapse of the Qing dynasty in 1912 but had been reclaimed by the communist-controlled government in 1951 and occupied by soldiers from the People's Liberation Army. Ever since the communist revolution, the government had harbored ambitions to build a railroad line to Lhasa, the capital of Tibet, to help establish control over the territory. However, technical difficulties and lack of money had stood in the way of the project. International experts argued that the railroad simply could not be built, having observed the difficulties of laying railroad tracks on permafrost during the construction of the Baikal–Amur Mainline in eastern Russia (see pp.302–309).

Tibet accounts for an eighth of China's land mass, yet in 2000, it was still the only region in the country without a rail link connecting it to the more developed east. The Chinese government instituted a "Go West" campaign, and the proposed line to Tibet became an important part of that strategy. At the time, Tibet was an undeveloped agrarian region with little connection to the outside world, but there

Propaganda China began to expand and modernize its railroads under the rule of Mao Zedong, who led the revolution of 1949.

was a possibility that mineral resources could be exploited with the help of the proposed railroad.

Building the Qinghai–Tibet line

A precursor to the Tibetan railroad was completed in 1984: an 500-mile (800-km) railroad heading west from Xining (the capital of Qinghai province and the traditional gateway to Tibet) to Golmud, also in Qinghai province.

There are 675 bridges on the Golmud–Lhasa line, which total up to 100 miles (161 km)

The plan to continue the line to Lhasa, however, would not be agreed until over a decade later.

In 1999, President Jiang Zemin launched a campaign to develop western China, which was lagging behind the booming east, and the Tibet railroad became a key part of that strategy. However, there remained some dispute over the best route for the railroad. Golmud, which had been founded in the 1960s as a labor camp for mainly Tibetan prisoners, was now a small city and offered the shortest route to Lhasa. This route involved crossing hundreds of miles of permafrost, however, and there were concerns that the technology to ensure that this could be done was not available. The most obvious alternative route was one from Yunnan province in southern China, but this would be twice the distance of the Golmud route, and so twice as expensive. Eventually, it was decided that it was possible to overcome the permafrost problem, and work started on the 710-mile (1,143 km) line between Golmud and Lhasa in 2001. A railroad constructed in the 21st century benefited from many previously unavailable techniques, but the difficulties of working at such high altitude in a remote region still surpassed that of most previous railroad projects, and the labor force required was enormous—more than 100,000 workers migrated to Tibet to build the railroad at the start of the project. One major challenge was that some sections had to be built on ground that was not quite permafrost—the top layers of soil melted during the summer and so became unstable. To accommodate this, long sections of track were elevated on what

Toil and trouble People building the Qinghai–Tibet Railway worked long, grueling hours in punishing weather conditions, much of it at high altitude where the reduced air pressure and oxygen levels also made the work physically demanding.

were effectively bridges, held up by deep, pile-driven foundations. In addition, passive heat exchangers were installed to cool the track and the surrounding soil.

The human cost of the venture was high, with many workers succumbing to altitude sickness. According to Lustgarten, "Tibetans in nearby villages would see railway officials burying dead workers on the hillsides outside the [Fenghuoshan] tunnel," but the official explanation for the deaths was food poisoning. No casualty statistics have been released by the authorities, who deny that there were any deaths from altitude sickness.

The completed Qinghai–Tibet line

The work began at both ends of the line, and track-laying was completed within four years—the fitting out of signaling and other equipment took another year. Just five years after work started in July 2006, the line opened with much fanfare. The overall cost was around $4 billion—although this may be an underestimate given the difficulties of precisely figuring out the costs of the scheme. On its completion, the Qinghai–Tibet line beat numerous records in railroad construction. It is the highest railroad in the world: the Tanggula Pass, at 16,640 ft (5,072 m), surpasses its spectacular counterpart in the Andes, Peru (see pp.186–191), built almost a century before, by around 820 ft (250 m). Tanggula station is also the world's highest railroad station, and the ¾-mile (1.2 km) long Fenghuoshan tunnel is also the highest railroad tunnel in the world at 16,092 ft (4,905 m) above sea level

The railroad has a capacity of up to eight passenger services per day in each direction. Since the air in Tibet is thin, the carriages on Lhasa trains have special air-conditioning systems to keep oxygen levels healthy, and each seat has its own emergency breathing apparatus. The

"Roof of the world" The line running up from Xining in central China to Lhasa, Tibet, is the highest in the world. It passes through uninhabitable elevations that have a sparse landscape, thin air, and dramatic peaks.

The back of the coin features the Fuxing electric multiple unit

Receiving recognition This coin was released by the People's Bank of China in September 2018 to commemorate the Chinese high-speed rail system, which is seen as emblematic of the nation's modernization program.

China's high-speed rail network reached 29,826 miles (48,000 km) in 2024 and is expected to be 43,496 miles (70,000 km) long by the 2030s

windows are especially large to give travelers the best view, and are protected against the high levels of ultraviolet light on the Tibetan plateau. With all these dangers, passengers are required to obtain a Health Registration Card before traveling from Golmud to Lhasa, and each train has a doctor on board in case of emergencies.

High-speed network

China's belated railroad expansion has continued with the construction of a huge network of high-speed lines. Up until 1993, China's trains were still very slow, averaging just 30 mph (48 km/h), prompting a number of "speed up" campaigns to counter competition from roads and aviation. The result was a series of services that could run at up to 100 mph (161 kph) by the end of the decade. The government, however, had even greater ambitions: the construction of a whole new set of lines in order to radically improve rail services and the nation's infrastructure. A program was thus devised to build the world's biggest network of high-speed lines, defined as more than 124 mph (200 km/h). Some existing lines were upgraded, but for the most part, entirely new lines were constructed—each one faster than the last. The "Mid-to-Long-Term Railway Network Plan" proposed the construction of a national, high-speed rail grid composed of four north–south corridors and four east–west corridors, which, together with upgraded existing lines, would total 7,500 miles (12,000 km).

Speedy growth

The first of these dedicated lines, the Qinhuangdao–Shenyang High-Speed Railway along the Liaoxi Corridor in the northeast, opened in 2003 with a line speed of 124 mph (200 kph), which was upgraded to 155 mph (250 km/h) by 2007. Others soon followed, some opening in time for the 2008 Olympics. One of these was the Beijing–Tianjin Intercity Railway linking northern China's two largest cities and designed for trains running at a speed of 217 mph (350 km/h).

In October 2010, China opened its 15th high-speed rail, the Shanghai–Hangzhou line, and the following year, the key Beijing–Shanghai line, which had a design speed of 236 mph (380 kph), became operational. This gave China more than

5,000 miles (8,000 km) of dedicated high-speed track, more than double that of any other country.

These impressive advances received a setback in July 2011 with a disastrous crash at Wenzhou in which two high-speed trains derailed (see p.335). The crash cast a long shadow, and for a time construction slowed. The program threatened to be delayed, or even shelved, as passenger numbers dwindled in response to the accident, and the top speeds of trains were reduced. However, by 2012, the program had resumed and passenger numbers climbed again. The growth has been even faster than before, with the route length more than doubling in the subsequent decade. This growth has meant that by the end of 2024, there were more than 8,700 daily bullet train services (operated by 2,800 train sets) covering 550 cities in 33 of the country's 34 province-level regions. This amounted to a route mileage of 29,000 miles (46,000 km)—double all the rest of the world's total in operation at the time. About 10 percent of this mileage is on upgraded existing lines but the rest is on newly built track. Parts of the network are operated at 218 mph (350 km/h), the fastest in the world.

Form and function There are different types of high-speed trains, with different models to suit various weather and topographic conditions.

THE RAILROAD RENAISSANCE

The story of the railroad would have been remarkable even if it had simply been consigned to history. However, despite a period of decline, it has outlived pessimistic predictions by enjoying a 21st-century renaissance and a future that looks assured.

This resurgence of the train has not simply been the result of far-reaching technological developments, although improvements have certainly been made. Railroad carriages are rather more comfortable than those of the 19th century, and freight wagons are sturdier and better designed for rapid unloading with the spread of containerization. Signaling is much improved, too, and there have been other sophisticated adaptations to make the railroads faster and more efficient. Despite these advances, train travel in the 21st century would still be immediately recognizable to George Stephenson and other pioneers. Tracks are still usually set 4 ft 8½ in (1,435 mm) apart, and passengers are transported in carriages that stop at stations and are controlled by external signals. However, it is not just improved technology that has resulted in this renaissance but also a widespread recognition of the advantages of rail over other forms of transportation and, crucially, its strong environmental credentials. Railroads remain a particularly relevant mode of transportation in certain markets, both from an economic and efficiency point of view.

Of course, the function of the train today is different. While the railroad was once a monopoly supplier of long-distance transportation, it is now more of a niche industry—but a very important one. Never again will the railroad serve every village and small town. The heyday of the iron road providing the only fast and cheap way of traveling between many places is over; those little village stations and rural halts are lost forever. Nor will railroads dominate the freight market as they once did. Gone, too, are the parcel yards and goods depots once found at every station, wiped out by the truck and the van.

Making a comeback

The railroads had to overcome a very difficult time; there was a point in the postwar period when railroads were regarded as irrelevant (see pp.310–315). The French railroad writer Clive Lamming even gave this phenomenon a name—"*ferropessimisme*," the notion that the decline and marginalization of the railroads was inevitable. But the railroads are still

Railroad resurgence (above) The benefits of rail travel compared to congested roads have fueled a railroad revival, particularly in intercity travel. This 1960 poster was used by British Railways to promote travel by train.

Sparking growth The renewed success of the railroads has led to the construction of many impressive new stations, such as the Liège-Guillemins railroad station in Belgium that opened in 2009.

very much a part of modern life and pessimists have been proved wrong. Many countries are now bemoaning the fact that key lines were closed down and major stations turned into shopping malls or housing developments. Across the world, the railroads are flourishing and will continue to do so for the foreseeable future, because rail is still a very convenient form of travel for passengers and an extremely efficient way of transporting goods.

There are several key markets in which rail travel offers great advantages to passengers. Intercity rail journeys of 300–400 miles (500–650 km)—or further with high-speed lines—may take longer than a flight, but passengers are able to relax or work with the availability of the internet on the train and, unlike far-flung airports, train terminals are located in the heart of the city. Local commutes are also more efficient by rail, whether train or metro, as these trips are usually faster and more reliable than driving, and unaffected by traffic. Trains also offer the best way to enjoy scenic routes, and in some cases, as with the Trans-Siberian (see pp.170–179), are one of the only viable means of transportation across remote areas.

Hauling freight Cargo traffic is highly profitable for numerous railroads, as rail offers a significantly more economical means of moving heavy and large goods compared to road transportation.

Rail is also very well suited to moving large amounts of very heavy, nonurgent freight, such as aggregate and stone, which otherwise damage roads. Trains have a competitive advantage, too, when transporting loads long distances: they are cheaper than convoys of trucks, which require several drivers and may need to stop overnight. Developments in containerization have also made loading and unloading far easier.

Enduring resilience

The railroads have made a remarkable recovery from their postwar nadir, when it seemed their glory days were at an end and that the train would soon go the way of the schooner or the stagecoach. They survived, in most countries at any rate, because of their competitive edge in several markets, and because road transportation has its own limitations. In an age of uncertainty over oil supply, railroads remain a reliable and relatively cheap form of transportation.

The railroads, however, do not stand still. They are continually adapting and evolving—and expanding. In response to competition, services have been sped up and facilities improved; redundant lines and services have been abandoned; and major developments can still be expected. One such example is the wider adoption of in-cab signaling to replace external signals;

Improved signaling Railroad signaling has undergone a significant evolution, with a growing number of trains now managed through in-cab information systems, replacing the traditional reliance on external color-light signals.

this is safer and more efficient, allowing more trains on the track, but will require considerable investment. Moreover, and more significantly, brand-new and reopened lines are springing up in many places.

Continued growth

There is no shortage of exciting forthcoming developments and projects worldwide. Saudi Arabia has several ambitious rail projects, though progress on these has stalled somewhat after their announcement in the 2010s. Russia is boosting capacity on the world's longest railroad, the Trans-Siberian (see pp.170–179), and its sister railroad, the Baikal–Amur Mainline (see pp.302–309). However, fanciful visions of building a line across to Alaska are never going to be realized.

The renaissance of rail is arguably most noticeable in Africa—a continent that has never properly exploited the advantages of rail transportation. There is Chinese investment in several, mainly freight, lines across the continent. The first to be completed was the Mombasa–Nairobi Standard Gauge line, which opened in 2017 and was largely funded by China. Since then, extensions have been completed, and a new line into Uganda has been commissioned. In south west Africa, the Benguela Railway—originally built by the Portuguese colonial authorities in Angola—had fallen into disrepair due to the long-running Angolan Civil War, which began in 1975. With nearly $2.3 billion of investment, the railroad has been rebuilt, and extensions have been added to transport minerals from the Democratic Republic of Congo. Further branches are also being considered for future expansion.

Nigeria also has plans to renew and expand its railroads, and has opened two new commuter lines in the largest city, Lagos, with plans for a third. In South Africa, a 50-mile (80-km) mass rapid transit system, the Gautrain, was fully opened in 2012, linking Johannesburg, Pretoria, Ekurhuleni, and O.R. Tambo International Airport, and plans for a high-speed line between Johannesburg and Cape Town are being examined. Another remarkable project is the Trans-Kalahari Railway on which work started in early 2025, after a long search for funding. The 932-miles (1,500 km) line will run from Botswana, through Namibia's capital of Windhoek to the city of Walvis Bay in the Erongo Region, principally to transport coal and copper ore. There will never be a Cape to Cairo line (see pp.202–211), but Africa will become more rail-oriented than it has ever been.

The growth of the railroads is a worldwide phenomenon. At the start of 2025, the railroad development website, *railway-technology.com*, listed more than 1,000 railroad projects across the world, ranging from small extensions of existing lines to megaprojects involving the construction of a new urban network of light rail and subways. As mentioned previously, there are plans for high-speed lines in numerous countries where previously rail investment had stagnated or declined. High-speed rail is a rising new market as it attracts travelers away from short-haul

Haramain High-Speed Railway Opened in October 2018, the first high-speed line in West Asia connects Medina and the Holy City of Mecca in Saudi Arabia, operating at 186 mph (300 km/h) over its 280-mile (450 km) length.

Metro mania Expansive rail networks, such as the one in Tokyo, Japan, have transformed urban mobility by making efficient travel more accessible than ever.

flights and onto the more environmentally sustainable railroads. It offers not only the prospect of reduced travel times between city centers but also a far more pleasant travel experience.

Meanwhile, the other great boom in railroad development has been the urban metro, and this shows no sign of abating. While in 2013, there were 188 cities with metro systems in 54 countries, by the end of 2024, there were 202 in 62 countries. In the intervening period dozens of extra lines have been added to existing systems. In Shanghai, home to the world's third-busiest metro system, the first line opened in 1993. It took 10 years to add three lines, but the system then expanded rapidly, incorporating 10 more lines over the next decade. By 2035, the city is expected to have 27 metro and commuter lines.

Perhaps one of the most surprising adherents is to be found in car-obsessed Dubai, the largest city in the United Arab Emirates, which first opened a metro line in 2009. The city currently operates two driverless lines, with a third expected to open by 2030.

Trams, or "light rail," are also enjoying a global revival. Old systems are being renovated and many cities, even in the car-dominated US, are opening new lines. In the US, a new type of housing, "transit-oriented development" (high-density development centered around a transit stop), is proving popular as it allows people to commute easily to work, without having to drive. More than 400 cities in the world had light rail systems at the end of 2024, and the route mileage has been growing at about 1 percent annually since 2010.

Stronger than ever

Rail travel has succeeded by seeing off the alternatives. For a time, other technologies were variously put forward as having greater potential to improve transportation, including numerous bizarre monorail plans. The most prominent of these was "maglev"—magnetic levitation (see pp.350–51). Magnetic force is used to elevate the "train" slightly above the special track and then magnets are used to provide forward thrust. The result was a very smooth ride at far higher speeds than conventional trains, along with better acceleration and braking. Despite many decades of research and development, and the introduction of a small number of systems, there are still currently few maglev systems in operation and several have been mothballed as a result of high cost of operation. The Chinese maglev, shuttling passengers between Shanghai and the airport, takes just 7 minutes 20 seconds to cover 18½ miles (30 km) and can potentially reach a speed of 268 mph (431 kph). It has, however, been restricted to 186 mph (300 kph) to reduce power costs. Both China and Japan are building longer lines, but the projects have been beset by financial and technical difficulties. Indeed, the cost of development, the potential risks (there has been one major accident on a German test

The global railroad industry income is projected to grow from $341.8 billion in 2025 to $507.6 billion by 2034

track, resulting in 23 deaths), and the fact that conventional rail is already a tried-and-true technology used across the world, has meant that maglev expansion has been stymied. Airport shuttles at Incheon in Korea and Birmingham in the UK have been scrapped. While there are proposals for lines in several countries, it is clear there is no immediate prospect of this technology replacing rail. A further development of maglev, Hyperloop, which involved very fast pods running in vacuum tunnels was, for a time, widely promoted by tech entrepreneur Elon Musk, but he and other developers have abandoned the technology due to mounting costs and a lack of any economic business case.

In what has proved to be a real surprise to many transportation planners (and past futurologists), the railroads have not only survived to see the 21st century, but are, in fact, booming. As oil becomes scarcer and concerns about environmental impact grow, rail transportation will only appear more attractive. Rail offers convenience, safety, and speed, as well as compatibility with personal technology: travelers can use mobile devices or work on laptops, using time otherwise wasted behind the wheel. The train is becoming more, not less, suited to life in today's world. The 21st century has become the second age of the train.

Urban rail revolution The worldwide surge in metro systems has given rise to architectural gems, such as this metro station in Dubai, showcasing the rapid evolution of rail travel around the world.

MAGLEV TRAINS

Unlike conventional trains with their track-and-wheel interface, maglev (magnetic levitation) trains literally float on air, using powerful magnets to suspend trains at a constant level above a steel rail, or "guideway," and electromagnetic force to propel the trains. Due to a lack of friction, maglev trains are quiet and stable, can accelerate and decelerate fast, and both trains and guideway suffer little wear and tear. However, due to incompatibility with existing railroads, maglev technology has seen limited adoption—the only working commercial systems are in Japan and China. The maglev infrastructure is expensive to build, but operating costs are low and the trains can achieve very high velocity—maglev trains hold the world speed record for rail transportation.

Shanghai shuttle One of the few operating maglev services in the world, the shuttle between Shanghai's airport and the city originally traveled at 268 mph (431 km/h), but its speed has since been reduced to a maximum of 186 mph (300 km/h) to save energy.

How it works

Existing commercial maglev systems use electromagnetic suspension (EMS), in which magnets in the train are activated for both levitation and propulsion by an electric current in the track. This current can be adjusted to determine the train's speed, while electronic sensors monitor the gap between train and guideway.

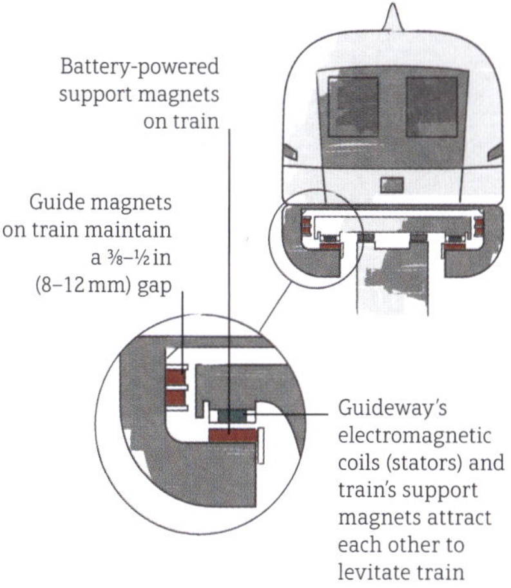

Levitation
Powerful electromagnets on the undercarriage of the train, which wraps around the T-shaped guideway, are attracted by levitation and guidance coils mounted in the rail.

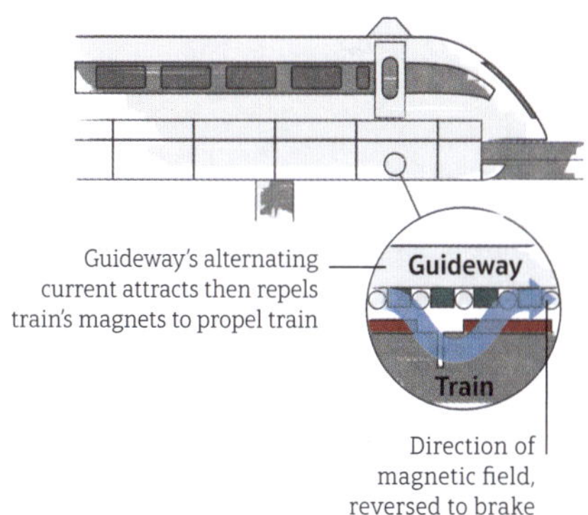

Propulsion
The polarity of propulsion coils in the rail changes constantly, attracting and repelling magnets on the train. The frequency is reversed to stop the train.

Alternative systems

The SCMaglev (Superconducting Maglev, named for the train's powerful magnets) is the latest in a series of high-speed maglev trains developed in Japan. It makes use of electrodynamic suspension (EDS) on U-shaped rails for levitation and propulsion. It has undergone successful trials, though has not yet progressed to commercial use. The completion of the project has been held up by various technical issues, as well as protests from people opposed to the scheme.

A prototype L0 series SCMaglev on a test track

Adapted to succeed A Fuxing high-speed train, specially developed to withstand the cold, icy conditions in northern China, crosses the bridge over the frozen Songhua River in the city of Harbin.

GLOSSARY

Terms in *italic* within an entry are defined under their own headings within the glossary.

Adhesion The frictional grip between the wheel of a train and the rail of a track.

Air cushion A "spring" of air used in modern suspension systems.

Air brake A braking system that uses compressed air as its operating medium.

American A steam locomotive with a *wheel arrangement* of 4-4-0.

Atlantic A steam locomotive with a *wheel arrangement* of 4-4-2.

Baldwin A US *locomotive* manufacturer that was in business from 1825 to 1971.

Ballast The bed of stone, gravel, or cinders on which a rail track is laid.

Bank A steep section of a track that a train requires additional engines to climb.

Berkshire A steam *locomotive* with a *wheel arrangement* of 2-8-4.

Blastpipe The exhaust pipe of a steam *locomotive* that diverts steam from the cylinders into the *smokebox* beneath the *chimney* to increase the draft through the fire.

Bogie See *truck*.

Boiler Cylindrical chamber in which steam is produced to drive a steam *locomotive*.

Boxcar See *van*.

Branch line A secondary railroad line that branches off a *main line*.

Broad gauge Rails spaced more widely than the *standard gauge* of 4 ft 8½ in (1,435 mm).

Buffer A device that cushions the impact of rail vehicles against each other.

Buffer stop / Bumper post The post at the end of a track that halts a train from traveling any farther.

Cab The control room of a *locomotive*, housing the engine crew.

Caboose A railroad car used by railroad workers to monitor track conditions. It is usually attached to the end of a train.

Cant The angle of elevation of a rail, relative to vertical or to its partner rail.

Challenger A steam *locomotive* with a *wheel arrangement* of 4-6-6-4.

Chimney The vertical exhaust funnel of a train. Called a smokestack in the US.

Compound locomotive A steam *locomotive* that uses two sets of cylinders. In such locomotives, the second cylinder is powered by exhaust steam from the first.

Coupler / Coupling The mechanism that connects and holds *rolling stock* together.

Coupling rod A rod that transmits power from a driven axle to the wheels.

Cowcatcher A metal frame projecting from the front of a *locomotive* designed to clear the track of any obstructions.

Cutting A channel dug through the hillside to enable a rail track to maintain a shallow gradient.

Cylinder The core of a steam engine in which a *piston* moves back and forth under the pressure of expanding and condensing steam.

Embankment A raised pathway across a depression in the landscape that enables a rail track to maintain a shallow gradient.

Engine The power source of a locomotive, driven by steam, electricity, or diesel.

Express train A train that passes certain stations on its route without stopping, in order to arrive at its final destination faster.

Firebox The compartment within a steam engine where fuel is burned to provide heat.

Fireman / Stoker / Boiler operator A worker who keeps the *firebox* of an *engine* fed with coal.

Freight / Goods Materials or products transported for commercial gain.

Gandy dancer A track maintenance worker.

Gauge The width between the inner faces of the rails.

Gondola An open-top piece of rolling stock, used to transport loose materials, such as ore and coal.

Handcar A small, open railroad car propelled by its passengers, often by means of a hand pump. Known as a *pump trolley* in Britain.

Hudson A steam locomotive with a *wheel arrangement* of 4-6-4.

Interchange The practice by which railroad companies transport *freight* from other organizations over their tracks.

Interlocking tower See *signal box*

Intermodal Moving either *freight* or passengers by more than one type of vehicle.

Jubilee A steam locomotive with a *wheel arrangement* of 4-4-4.

Junction A place where multiple train lines split or converge.

Lantern A portable lamp with a fuel source. Used by early railroad workers to provide light and to signal to other workers at night.

Level crossing A location where a railroad crosses a road or path at the same elevation.

Level junction A railroad junction where multiple lines intersect, crossing the path of oncoming rail traffic at the same elevation.

Light rail Small, fixed railroads, typically operating within urban environments, e.g, streetcars and trams.

Locomotive An engine-powered vehicle that either pulls or pushes a train along the tracks.

Loop A railroad formation where tracks cross over themselves as they ascend a mountain.

Main line An important line between major towns or cities.

Marshaling yard A railroad yard where freight wagons are loaded and unloaded, arranged, and organized into trains.

Mikado A steam *locomotive* with the *wheel arrangement* 2-8-2.

Monorail A railroad system based on a single rail. Often elevated, and built in urban environments.

Narrow gauge A railroad with a gauge narrower than the standard 4 ft 8½ in (1,435 mm).

Navvies The specialist manual laborers who constructed the majority of the railroads in the 19th century.

Pacific A steam locomotive with a *wheel arrangement* of 4-6-2.

Pantograph A metal arm that connects to an overhead line, providing power to an electric train.

Passenger train A train with carriages intended to transport people. These trains travel between stations at which passengers may embark or disembark.

Passing loop A position on a single-track railroad, where trains traveling in opposite directions can pass each other. Called a passing siding in the US.

Passing siding See *passing loop*

Piston A component of an internal combustion engine that moves up and down against a liquid or gas to provide motion.

Points / Railroad switch A section of railroad that allows a train to move from one track to another.

Prairie A steam locomotive with a *wheel arrangement* of 2-6-2.

Railroad car A covered railroad vehicle used for carrying passengers or cargo.

Rolling stock Used by railroad companies to refer to the entire collection of vehicles that run on their railroad. As a more general, it term refers to any complete locomotive or carriage.

Roundhouse Buildings used to service and store trains. Many used to be arranged around a *turntable*.

Siding A section of track off the main line used for storing rolling stock.

Signal box A control room in which the movement of trains are controlled by means of signals and blocks, ensuring trains travel safely and to schedule. The US term is interlocking tower.

Sleeper A train that can provide beds for all its passengers, particularly for overnight or long-distance journeys.

Slip coach The practice of uncoupling carriages from an *express train*, and braking them to a halt at a station. This allowed passengers to disembark without halting the main train.

Smokebox A component of a steam engine. The smokebox would collect smoke from the *firebox*, after it had heated water to provide steam, and release it though the smokestack or *chimney*.

Smokestack See *chimney*

Standard gauge Rails spaced 4 ft 8½ in (1,435 mm) apart. This is the most widely used gauge.

Station master The individual responsible for the running of a station.

Steam engine An engine that uses steam, produced by heating water with burning fuel, to perform mechanical work.

Subway See *underground*

Switchback See *zigzag*

Tender A carriage containing the fuel and water needed to power a steam train's engine.

Through coach A rail carriage that switches locomotives midjourney, removing the need for passengers to switch trains. Used particularly on long-haul journeys.

Track The permanent fixtures of rails, ballast, fastenings, and underlying substrate that provide a runway for the wheels of a train.

Traction The act of drawing or pulling a load. Can also refer to the adhesive friction of a train to a track.

Truck The undercarriage assembly of a train, incorporating the wheels, suspension, and brakes. Called a bogie in the UK.

Turntable A device for rotating rail vehicles so they can travel back in the direction they came from. Largely obsolete today.

Underground A railroad that operates underground, typically in a major city. Known as a subway in the US.

Unit train A train that carries only one type of goods.

Van A flat-bottomed freight wagon with sliding doors on each side. Known in the US as a boxcar.

Water column See *water crane*

Water crane A track-side device for quickly refilling the water tank of a steam *locomotive*. Known in the US as a water column.

Wheel The wheels of trains are typically cast or forged with an affixed tire of hardened steel.

Wheel arrangement A system for classifying how wheels are placed under a *locomotive*, such as the *Whyte notation*.

Wheel flange A component of a train wheel. The flange extends the wheels to the interior of the train track, preventing the train from running off the rails.

Whyte notation A system classifying *wheel arrangement* by counting first leading wheels, then driving wheels, then trailing wheels (e.g. 0-2-2).

Yard An area with multiple tracks and sidings for the storage, maintenance, and loading and unloading of rolling stock.

Yellowstone A steam *locomotive* with a *wheel arrangement* of 2-8-8-4.

Zigzag A method of track construction on steep inclines. A train ascends the track in a zigzag fashion.

BIBLIOGRAPHY

This is very much a selective bibliography, mainly mentioning books I have used as source material, since there are literally tens of thousands of books on the railroads. Many of these are very detailed and written for a specialist audience, and have consequently not been included in this list. The list is, therefore, aimed at the general reader who wants to know more on the subjects covered in this book, rather than at a specialist audience. I have, of course, made extensive use of my own series of railroad history books, nearly all published by Atlantic. *The Subterranean Railway* (2004, updated 2013) is the story of the London Underground; *Fire and Steam* (2006) covers the story of Britain's railroads; and *Blood, Iron and Gold* (2008) shows how the railroads changed the world. *Engines of War* (2010) demonstrates the importance of railroads in wartime while *The Great Railway Revolution* (2012) is the story of American railroads; *To the Edge of the World* (2013) is the history of the world's longest railroad, the Trans-Siberian. *Cathedrals of Steam* (2021) is the story of the dozen London terminus stations, while *The Story of Crossrail* (2022, published by Head of Zeus) covers the development of the Elizabeth Line.

GENERAL

Erwin Berghaus, *The History of the Railways*, Barrie & Rockliffe, 1964
Gordon Biddle, *Britain's Historic Railway Buildings*, Oxford, 2003
Simon Bradley, *The Railways, Network, Empire, People, Profile*, 2015
Simon Bradley, *Bradley's Railway Guide*, Profile, 2024
David Brandon and Alan Brooke, *The Railway Haters: Opposition to Railways*, Pen and Sword, 2019
Anthony Burton, *Railway Empire*, John Murray, 1994
Anthony Burton, *On the Rails*, Aurum, 2004
Christopher Chant, *The World's Railways*, Grange, 2002
Basil Cooper, *A Century of Train*, Brian Trodd Publishing, 1988
Nicholas Faith, *Locomotion*, BBC Books, 1993
Nicholas Faith, *The World the Railways Made*, Bodley Head, 1990
Tim Fischer, *Trains Unlimited*, ABC Books, 2011
Geoffrey Freeman Allen, *Luxury Trains of the World*, Bison, 1979
Geoffrey Freeman Allen, *Railways Past, Present and Future*, Orbis Publishing, 1982
Geoffrey Freeman Allen, *Railways of the Twentieth Century*, Winchmore, 1983
Jim Harter, *World Railways of the Nineteenth Century: A Pictorial History in Victorian Engravings*, Johns Hopkins University Press, 2005
Murray Hughes, *The Second Age of Rail: A History of High-speed Trains*, The History Press, 2015
Clive Lamming, *Larousse des Trains et des Chemins de Fer*, Larousse, 2005
Andrew Martin, *Night Trains: The Rise and Fall of the Sleeper*, Profile, 2017
Bryan Morgan, ed, *Great Trains*, Crown Publishers, 1973
O.S. Nock, *World Atlas of Railways*, Mitchell Beazley, 1978
O.S. Nock, *Railways Then and Now: A World History*, Paul Elek Ltd, 1975
O.S. Nock, ed, *Encyclopaedia of Railways*, Book Club Associates, 1977
Martin Page, *The Lost Pleasures of the Great Trains*, Weidenfeld and Nicolson, 1975
Steve Parissien, *Station to Station*, Phaidon, 1997
P.J.G. Ransom, *Locomotion: Two Centuries of Train Travel*, Sutton Publishing, 2001
Martyn Pring, *Luxury Railway Travel*, Pen and Sword, 2019
Michael Robbins, *The Railway Age*, Penguin, 1965
Wolfgang Schivelbusch, *Railway Journey: The Industrialization of Time and Space in the Nineteenth Century*, Berg, 1996
Nicholas Wheatley, *Final Journey: The Untold Story of Funeral Trains*, The History Press, 2020
Dixe Wills, *Tiny Stations*, AA publishing 2014
John Westwood, *Railways at War*, Osprey, 1980
John Westwood, *The Pictorial History of Railways*, Bison Books, 2008

EUROPE

H.C. Casserly, *Outline of Irish History*, David & Charles, 1974
Nicholas Faith, *The Right Line: the Politics*, the *Planning and the Against-the-odds Gamble Behind Britain's First High-speed Railway*, Segrave Foulkes, 2007
Peter Fleming, *The Fate of Admiral Kolchak*, Rupert Hart David, 1963 (reprinted 2001 by Birlinn)
Murray Hughes, *Rail 300*, David & Charles, 1988
P.M. Kalla-Bishop, *Mediterranean Island Railways*, David & Charles, 1970
P.M. Kalla Bishop, *Italian Railroads*, Drake, 1972
Allan Mitchell, *The Great Train Race*: Railways and Franco-German Rivalry, Berghahn, 2000
O.S. Nock, *Railways of Western Europe*, A&C Black, 1977
Brian Perren, *TGV Handbook*, Capital Transport, 1998
Albert Schram, *Railways and the Formation of the Italian State in the Nineteenth Century*, Cambridge University Press, 1977
Christine Sutherland, *The Princess of Siberia*, Methuen, 1984
Various authors, *Histoire du Réseau Ferroviaire Français*, Editions de l'Ormet, 1996
Various authors, *ICE: High-Tech on Wheels*, Hestra-Verlag, 1991
Arthur J. Veenendaal, *Railways in the Netherlands*: A Brief History, 1834–1994, Stanford University Press, 2001

THE AMERICAS

Dee Brown, Hear *That Lonesome Whistle Blow: Railroads in the West*, Touchstone, 1977

David Cruise and Alison Griffiths, *Lords of the Line: The Men Who Built the Canadian Pacific Railway*, Viking, 1988

Brian Fawcett, *Railways of the Andes*, Plateway Press, 1997

Sarah H. Gordon. *Passage to Union: How the Railroads Transformed American Life*, 1829–1929, Elephant Paperbacks, 1997

George W. Hilton and John F. Due, *The Electric Interurban Railways in America*, Stanford University Press, 1960

Stewart H. Holbrook, *The Story of American Railroads*, Bonanza Books, 1947

Theodore Kornweibel Jr, *Railroads in the African American Experience*, Johns Hopkins University Press, 2010

Oscar Lewis, *The Big Four*, Alfred A. Knopf, 1938

Albro Martin, *Railroads Triumphant*, Oxford University Press, 1992

Nick and Helma Mika, *The Railways of Canada: A Pictorial History*, McGraw-Hill Ryerson, 1972

O.S. Nock, *Railways of Canada*, A&C Black, 1973

Andrew Roden, *Great Western Railway: A History*, Aurum, 2010

David Rollinson, *Railways of the Caribbean*, Macmillan, 2001

D. Trevor Rowe, *The Railways of South America*, Locomotives International, 2000

John F. Stover, *American Railroads*, University of Chicago Press, 1961

Richard White, *The Transcontinentals and the Making of Modern America*, Norton, 2011

Oscar Zanetti and Alejandra García, *Sugar and Railroads: A Cuban History*, 1837–1959, University of North Carolina Press, 1998

ASIA

Ralph William Huenemann, *The Dragon and the Iron Horse: The Economics of Railroads in China*, 1876–1937, Harvard University Press, 1984

Robert Hardie, *The Burma Siam Railway*, Quadrant Books, 1984

Ian J. Kerr, *Engines of Change: The Railways that Made India*, Praeger, 2007

Ian J. Kerr, *Building the Railways of the Raj*, 1850–1900, Oxford University Press, 1995

Abrahm Lustgarten, *China's Great Train: Beijing's Drive West and the Campaign to Remake Tibet*, Henry Holt, 2008

Deborah Manley, ed, *The Trans-Siberian Railway: A Traveller's Anthology*, Century Hutchinson, 1987

Steven G. Marks, *Road to Power: The Trans-Siberian Railroad and the Colonization of Asian Russia*, 1850–1917, Cornell University Press, 1991

James Nicholson, *The Hejaz Railway*, Stacey International, 2005

O.S. Nock, *Railways of Asia and the Far East*, A&C Black, 1978

Peter Semmens, *High Speed in Japan*, Platform 5, 2000

Roopa Srinivasan, Manish Tiwari, and Sandeep Silas, *Our Indian Railway*, Foundation Books, 2006

Shoji Sumita, *Success Story: The Privatisation of Japanese National Railways*, Profile Books, 2000

John Tickner, Gordon Edgar, and Adrian Freeman, China: *The World's Last Steam Railway*, Artists' and Photographers' Press, 2008

Harmon Tupper, *To the Great Ocean*, Secker & Warburg, 1965

K.R. Vaidyanathan, *150 Glorious Years of Indian Railways*, English Edition Publishers, 2003

Christopher J. Ward, *Brezhnev's Folly: The Building of the BAM and Late Soviet Socialism*, University of Pittsburgh Press, 2009

Various authors, *Guide to the Great Siberian Railway*, 1900, David & Charles reprints, 1971

AFRICA

John Day, *Railways of South Africa*, Arthur Barker, 1963

M.F. Hill, *The Permanent Way: The Story of the Tanganyika Railways*, East African Railways and Harbours, 1958

George Tabor, *Cape to Cairo*, Genta, 2003

AUSTRALASIA

Neill Atkinson, *Trainland*, Random House, 2007

Tim Fischer, *Transcontinental Train Journey*, Allen & Unwin, 2004

C.C. Singleton and David Burke, *Railways of Australia*, Angus & Robertson, 1963

Patsy Adam Smith, *The Desert Railway*, Rigby 1974

Patsy Adam Smith, *Romance of Australian Railways*, Rigby, 1973

INDEX

Page numbers in **bold** refer to main entries.

D

E

F

Q R

S

T

U

V

W

X Y Z

ACKNOWLEDGMENTS

The author would like to thank Nicholas Faith, author of *The World the Railways Made*, for drafting several chapters and advising on various aspects of the book, and Malcolm Bulpitt of the Swiss Railway Society for his draft of the section on Switzerland.

Dorling Kindersley would like to thank the following people for their help in this project: Cyrus McGoldrick for the sensitivity read; Saumya Agarwal, Abhijit Dutta, Janashree Singha, and Hugo Wilkinson for editorial assistance; Katie Cederborg, Michaela Weglinski, and Kathryn Williams for fact checking; Vishal Bhatia, Syed Farhan, Satish Gaur, Ashok Kumar, and Raman Panwar for technical assistance; Aashirwad Jain and Rupa Rao for proofreading; Helen Peters for indexing; Manpreet Kaur, Samrajkumar S, and Vagisha Pushp for Picture Research Administration; and Senior Jacket Designer, Suhita Dharamjit.

The publisher would like to thank the following for their kind permission to reproduce their photographs:
(Key: a-above; b-below/bottom; c-center; f-far; l-left; r-right; t-top)

1 Getty Images: ullstein bild. **2-3 Getty Images:** Science & Society Picture Library. **5 Alamy Stock Photo:** TopFoto / Smith Archive. **6 Getty Images / iStock:** E+ / Oleh_Slobodeniuk. **8 Alamy Stock Photo:** Everett Collection Inc / Ron Harvey (tl). **Getty Images:** Hulton Archive / Price (cr). **Wellcome Collection:** A steam train traveling on a track situated along the sidewalk above the level of the shops in New York; carriages and horse-drawn trolley buses are in the street. Wood engraving by J. R. Brown. (br). **10 Getty Images:** Mondadori Portfolio Premium (bl). **10-11 Alamy Stock Photo:** Heritage Image Partnership Ltd (bc). **11 Dreamstime.com:** Ymgerman (br). **12-13 Getty Images:** Archive Photos / Buyenlarge. **14-15 Getty Images:** SSPL. **16 Alamy Stock Photo:** Washington Imaging (bl). **16-17 Bridgeman Images:** North East Museums. **18-19 Getty Images:** SSPL. **19 Getty Images:** Hulton Archive / Handout (tr). **20 Adobe Stock:** Archivist. **21 Alamy Stock Photo:** The Granger Collection (t). **Bridgeman Images:** Photo © Photo Josse (b). **22 Alamy Stock Photo:** Universal Images Group North America LLC / IMechE (bl). **22-23 Getty Images:** Hulton Archive / Topical Press Agency / Kirby / Stringer. **24 Alamy Stock Photo:** Historic Collection. **25 Bridgeman Images:** © Look and Learn. **26-27 Getty Images:** SSPL. **28 Rainhill Railway and Heritage Society:** (b). **29 Alamy Stock Photo:** World History Archive (b). **Bridgeman Images:** © Look and Learn (t). **30-31 Getty Images:** Greenwell / Daily Mirror / Mirrorpix. **32 Shutterstock.com:** Everett Collection (bl). **32-33 Alamy Stock Photo:** FLHC3 (t). **34 Alamy Stock Photo:** FLHC16 (b). **36-37 Alamy Stock Photo:** Vintage Images (t). **37 Alamy Stock Photo:** Archivah (bc). **38 Alamy Stock Photo:** Pictorial Press Ltd. **39 Alamy Stock Photo:** PhotoStock-Israel / Historic Illustrations. **40 Dorling Kindersley:** Gary Ombler / B&O Railroad Museum, Baltimore, Maryland (cl, bl, cr). **40-41 Dorling Kindersley:** Gary Ombler / Railroad Museum of Pennsylvania (t); Gary Ombler / B&O Railroad Museum, Baltimore, Maryland (b). **41 Dorling Kindersley:** Gary Ombler / B&O Railroad Museum, Baltimore, Maryland (tr); Gary Ombler / Railroad Museum of Pennsylvania (cl, cr, br). **42-43 Alamy Stock Photo:** Lebrecht Music & Arts (b). **43 Alamy Stock Photo:** Colin Waters (tr). **44 Getty Images:** De Agostini / DEA / G. Dagli Orti. **45 Getty Images:** Herbert Hoffmann / ullstein bild. **46-47 Bridgeman Images:** Luisa Ricciarini. **47 Alamy Stock Photo:** Penta Springs Limited / Artokoloro (b). **Bridgeman Images:** © Look and Learn (cra). **48 Alamy Stock Photo:** © Fine Art Images / Heritage Images. **49 Alamy Stock Photo:** Album. **50 Science Photo Library:** CCI ARCHIVES. **51 Alamy Stock Photo:** Classic Image. **52-53 Alamy Stock Photo:** INTERFOTO / History. **54 Alamy Stock Photo:** Chronicle (b); Lebrecht Music & Arts (t). **55 Alamy Stock Photo:** History and Art Collection. **56 Toledo Lucas County Public Library:** Harry H. Hamm Company (b). **57 Alamy Stock Photo:** GRANGER Historical Picture Archive. **58 Dorling Kindersley:** Gary Ombler / Eisenbahnfreunde Traditionsbahnbetriebswerk Stassfurt (bl). **58-59 Getty Images:** Hulton Archive / Fox Photos / Stringer. **60 Getty Images:** ullstein bild (bl). **60-61 Alamy Stock Photo:** Pump Park Vintage Photography. **62-63 Alamy Stock Photo:** North Wind Picture Archives. **63 Alamy Stock Photo:** Glasshouse Images / Circa Images (br). **64 The Metropolitan Museum of Art:** Harris Brisbane Dick Fund, 1933. **65 Alamy Stock Photo:** PD Archive (t); Photo 12 / Buster Keaton Productions (b). **66-67 Getty Images:** SSPL. **66 Rangan Datta:** (bl). **68 Alamy Stock Photo:** Washington Imaging (bl). **68-69 Alamy Stock Photo:** The Print Collector. **70-71 Getty Images:** SSPL. **71 Alamy Stock Photo:** Roland Knauer (t). **72 Getty Images:** ullstein bild Dtl.. **73 Getty Images:** Archive Photos / Stringer (b). **The New York Public Library:** The Miriam and Ira D. Wallach Division of Art, Prints and Photographs: Photography Collection, The New York Public Library. "Elevated railway, Centennial grounds." The New York Public Library Digital Collections. 1876. https://digitalcollections.nypl.org/items/510d47e0-b57c-a3d9-e040-e00a18064a99 (t). **74-75 Alamy Stock Photo:** The Print Collector. **75 Shutterstock.com:** Sudarshan Bhatla (t). **76 Alamy Stock Photo:** AP Photo / Gurinder Osan. **77 Alamy Stock Photo:** Emilio Ereza. **78 Getty Images:** SSPL (bl). **78-79 Getty Images:** Hulton Archive / Stringer. **80 Dreamstime.com:** Sandhya Mandal. **81 Bridgeman Images:** From the British Library archive. **82-83 Getty Images:** SSPL. **84 Getty Images:** SSPL. **85 Adobe Stock:** Archivist (tr). **Leicestershire County Council:** British Railways - S. W. A. Newton Collection (b). **86 Leicestershire County Council:** British Railways - S. W. A. Newton Collection (b). **87 Alamy Stock Photo:** Science History Images / Photo Researchers. **88-89 Alamy Stock Photo:** Imago History Collection. **90-91 Alamy Stock Photo:** EMU history. **91 Fotolia:** (b/right, b/left). **92 Alamy Stock Photo:** The Print Collector / Heritage Images. **94 Alamy Stock Photo:** The Print Collector / Heritage Images. **95 Alamy Stock Photo:** Avalon / Construction Photography (b). **Getty Images:** Hulton Archive / Fox Photos / Stringer (t). **96-97 Library of Congress, Washington, DC:** LC-DIG-pga-03504/The world's railroad scene/Swain & Lewis, des. & lith. 103 State, Chicago. Illinois, ca. 1882. Photograph. https://www.loc.gov/item/2008677250/.. **98-99 Adobe Stock:** Ewald Fröch (b). **99 Alamy Stock Photo:** Logic Images (tr). **100 Alamy Stock Photo:** 19th era (bl). **101 Alamy Stock Photo:** Science History Images. **102 Alamy Stock Photo:** Chronicle. **103 Alamy Stock Photo:** Artmedia (bc). **104-105 Getty Images / iStock:** Milehightraveler (c). **106-107 Alamy Stock Photo:** North Wind Picture Archives. **108-109 Alamy Stock Photo:** The Picture Art Collection. **109 National Portrait Gallery, Smithsonian Institution:** (br). **111 Getty Images / iStock:** DigitalVision Vectors / whitemay. **112 Alamy Stock Photo:** Historic Illustrations (tl). **112-113 Getty Images:** Michael Maslan / Corbis / VCG (b). **114-115 Alamy Stock Photo:** Science History Images. **116 Alamy Stock Photo:** GRANGER Historical Picture Archive. **117 Alamy Stock Photo:** GRANGER Historical Picture Archive (t). **SuperStock:** 3LH-Fine Art (b). **118 Alamy Stock Photo:** History and Art Collection. **119 Getty Images:** Archive Photos / Graphic House / William H. Illingworth / Staff. **120 Alamy Stock Photo:** GRANGER Historical Picture Archive (b); NZ Collection (t). **121 Getty Images:** Hulton Archive / Stringer. **122 Alamy Stock Photo:** The Granger Collection (bl). **124 Alamy Stock Photo:** VintagePostCards (bl). **124-125 Getty Images:** SSPL. **126 Alamy Stock Photo:** The Picture Art Collection. **127 Mary Evans Picture Library:** INS. OF CIVIL ENGINEERS. **128 Alamy Stock Photo:** Shawshots. **129 Alamy Stock Photo:** Shawshots (t). **Dreamstime.com:** Jjfarq (b). **130-131 Alamy Stock Photo:** Pictorial Press. **132 National Museums of Northern Ireland:** (t). **133 Alamy Stock Photo:** Penta Springs Limited / Artokoloro. **134 Getty Images:** Archive Photos / Johns Hopkins University Sheridan Libraries / Levy / Gado. **135 Alamy Stock Photo:** UPI. **136 Getty Images / iStock:** Petia_St (bl). **136-137 Alamy Stock Photo:** Paris Pierce. **138 Dorling Kindersley:** Mike Dunning / National Railway Museum, York (b). **138-139 Alamy Stock Photo:** Album. **140 Alamy Stock Photo:** GRANGER Historical Picture Archive (b). **The Metropolitan Museum of Art:** H. O. Havemeyer Collection, Bequest of Mrs. H. O. Havemeyer, 1929 (t). **141 Getty Images:** Universal History Archive / Universal Images Group. **142 Alamy Stock Photo:** Chronicle (bl). **142-143 Getty Images / iStock:** DigitalVision Vectors / ilbusca. **143 Getty Images / iStock:** DigitalVision Vectors / clu (br). **144 Getty Images:** Corbis Documentary / Patrice Latron (bl). **144-145 Getty Images:** Bettmann. **145 Getty Images:** De Agostini / DEA / Biblioteca Ambrosiana (bc). **146-147 Alamy Stock Photo:** piemags / archive / military. **148 Alamy Stock Photo:** Historic Collection. **149 Getty Images:** Popperfoto. **150 Getty Images:** Hal Morey / Fox Photos / Hulton Archive / Stringer. **151 Alamy Stock Photo:** steeve-x-art. **152 Getty Images:** SSPL (c). **152-153 Getty Images:** Hulton Archive / Fox Photos / Stringer. **153 Alamy Stock Photo:** Historic Images (br). **154 Getty Images:** National Railway Museum / SSPL. **155 Library of Congress, Washington, D.C.:** LC-DIG-ppmsca-28485 / Gillam, Bernhard, 1856-1896, artist. **156 Alamy Stock Photo:** Chronicle. **157 Alamy Stock Photo:** CM Studio (br); World History Archive (tr). **158 Alamy Stock Photo:** Historic Images (tc). **159 Alamy Stock Photo:** Granger - Historical Picture Archive. **160 Alexander Turnbull Library, Wellington, New Zealand:** Railway disaster at Tangiwai. Dominion Post (Newspaper): Photographic negatives and prints of the Evening Post and Dominion newspapers. Ref: EP-Accidents-Rail-Tangiwai rail disaster-01. Alexander Turnbull Library, Wellington, New Zealand. / records / 23201427 (bl). **160-161 Getty Images:** Minnesota Historical Society / Corbis. **162 Courtesy of Hagley Museum and Library:** PRR_11870, Pennsylvania Railroad negative collection (Accession 1993.300), Audiovisual Collections and Digital Initiatives Department, Hagley Museum and Library, Wilmington, DE 19807 / Cumberland Valley Railroad Company car, 1939-10-14 (b). **163 Alamy Stock Photo:** The Granger Collection. **164 Getty Images:** Archive Photos / Chicago History Museum. **165 Courtesy National Gallery of Art, Washington:** Index of American Design. **166 Shutterstock.com:** Everett Collection. **167 Alamy Stock Photo:** The Granger Collection. **168-169 Getty Images:** SSPL / Manchester Daily Express. **170-171 Alamy Stock Photo:** The History Collection (t). **172 Alamy Stock Photo:** Heritage Image Partnership Ltd (b). **173 Alamy Stock Photo:** Album (br); World History Archive (ca). **174 Alamy Stock Photo:** Heritage Image Partnership Ltd (tl). **175 Alamy Stock Photo:** UtCon Collection (b). **176 Alamy Stock Photo:** Heritage Image Partnership Ltd (tl); Photo12 / Ann Ronan Picture Library (br). **177 Adobe Stock:** afrutin (t). **179 Getty Images:** Corbis Historical / Hulton Deutsch (tr). **180-181 Shutterstock.com:** Giuseppe Lami / ANSA via ZUMA Press (c). **181 Getty Images:** Popperfoto (tr). **182 Alamy Stock Photo:** Mirrorpix / Trinity Mirror (tl). **183 Alamy Stock Photo:** The Print Collector / Heritage Images (r). **184 Alamy Stock Photo:** Studiocanal Films Ltd (tl). **184-185 Alamy Stock Photo:** Interfoto / History (b). **186-187 Getty Images:** Manuel Medir. **187 Alamy Stock Photo:** LMA / AW (br). **188 Alamy Stock Photo:** Photo12 / Archives Snark. **189 Alamy Stock Photo:** North Wind Picture Archives. **190 Getty Images / iStock:** tirc83 (b). **Wikipedia:** Ernesto Linares (tr). **191 Bridgeman Images:** Alinari Archives, Florence. **192 Alamy Stock Photo:** robertharding / Michael Runkel (bl). **192-193 Dreamstime.com:** Kalypsoworldphotography. **193 Dreamstime.com:** Michal Stipek (br). **194 Alamy Stock Photo:** Pictures Now (bl). **195 Library of Congress, Washington, D.C.:** Detroit Photographic Co..

197 Alamy Stock Photo: Southern Photo Archives (b). **198 Alamy Stock Photo:** Granger Historical Picture Archive (tl). **199 Alamy Stock Photo:** Heritage Image Partnership Ltd / Curt Teich Postcard Archives (b). **200-201 Alamy Stock Photo:** Gerry White. **Dorling Kindersley:** Gary Ombler / B&O Railroad Museum, Baltimore, Maryland (b). **200 Alamy Stock Photo:** imageBROKER.com / Horst Mahr (cl). **Dorling Kindersley:** Gary Ombler / Virginia Museum of Transportation (cr); Gary Ombler / B&O Railroad Museum, Baltimore, Maryland (bl). **201 Alamy Stock Photo:** David Davies (cr). **Dorling Kindersley:** Gary Ombler / Harzer Schmalspurbahnen (tr); Gary Ombler / Virginia Museum of Transportation (cl). **202 Alamy Stock Photo:** Tibbut Archive (bl). **202-203 Getty Images:** Hulton Archive / Stringer. **204 Mary Evans Picture Library**. **205 Mary Evans Picture Library:** The National Archives, London. England.. **206 Alamy Stock Photo:** Luke Nicolaides. **207 Alamy Stock Photo:** Pictorial Press. **208 Alamy Stock Photo:** Chronicle. **209 Alamy Stock Photo:** World History Archive (t). **Getty Images:** Paul Popper / Popperfoto (b). **210 Adobe Stock:** Archivist (clb). **212-213 Getty Images:** Hulton Archive / brandstaetter images (b). **214 Alamy Stock Photo:** Science History Images / Photo Researchers (b). **215 Alamy Stock Photo:** Chronicle (tr). **216 Bridgeman Images:** © Arkivi UG All Rights Reserved (t). **217 Bridgeman Images:** © Look and Learn (bc). **218 Alamy Stock Photo:** CPC Collection (cl). **Dorling Kindersley:** Gary Ombler / Ribble Steam Railway / Science Museum Group (cr). **218-219 Dorling Kindersley:** Gary Ombler / Railroad Museum of Pennsylvania (b). **219 Dorling Kindersley:** Gary Ombler / Musee de Chemin de Fer, Mulhouse (tl); Gary Ombler / Railroad Museum of Pennsylvania (tr, cl); Gary Ombler / DB Schenker (cr). **Getty Images:** Tomohiro Ohsumi / Bloomberg (br). **220 Dreamstime.com:** Oleksandr Lysenko (br). **221 Getty Images:** Science & Society Picture Library (t). **222 Science Photo Library:** Hagley Museum And Archive (b). **223 Science & Society Picture Library—All rights reserved.:** © National Railway Museum. **224 Getty Images:** Science & Society Picture Library (l). **225 Getty Images:** Bloomberg / Brent Lewin (cra). **226 Alamy Stock Photo:** Smith Archive. **227 Alamy Stock Photo:** Chronicle. **228 Alamy Stock Photo:** Maidun Collection. **229 Alamy Stock Photo:** Eraza Collection. **230 Getty Images / iStock:** DigitalVision Vectors / whitemay. **231 Alamy Stock Photo:** United Artists / Album. **232 Shutterstock.com:** singh_lens (bl). **232-233 Alamy Stock Photo:** Private Collection / AF Eisenbahn Archiv. **234 Dreamstime.com:** Beibaoke1. **235 Dorling Kindersley:** Christopher Pillitz. **236 National Rail Museum, New Delhi:** (b). **237 Alamy Stock Photo:** Dinodia Photos RM. **238 Alamy Stock Photo:** Sam Kovak (t). **Shutterstock.com:** Sudarshan Bhatla (b). **239 Getty Images / iStock:** Shalender Kumar. **240-241 Getty Images:** Popperfoto. **242-243 Alamy Stock Photo:** incamerastock (l). **244 Alamy Stock Photo:** Pump Park Vintage Photography (tl). **245 Bridgeman Images:** Granger (b). **National Postal Museum, Smithsonian Institution:** (tc). **246 Bridgeman Images:** © Look and Learn (bl). **247 Getty Images:** VCG / Corbis Historical / Library of Congress (tr); VCG / Corbis Historical / Scheufler Collection (bl). **248 Mary Evans Picture Library:** Onslow Auctions Limited (ca). **249 Getty Images:** Hulton Archive / Fox Photos (b). **250 Alamy Stock Photo:** Heritage Image Partnership Ltd (b). **251 Alamy Stock Photo:** Prisma by Dukas Presseagentur GmbH / Schultz Reinhard (tr). **252 Alamy Stock Photo:** Trinity Mirror / Mirrorpix (bl). **253 Alamy Stock Photo:** PF-(wararchive) (t). **254 Ron Fisher:** (b). **254-255 Alamy Stock Photo:** piemags / archive / military (tc). **255 Alamy Stock Photo:** Chronicle (br). **256 Dorling Kindersley:** Railroad Museum of Pennsylvania / Gary Ombler (cla, bl). **Dreamstime.com:** Greg Kelton (tr). **256-257 Dorling Kindersley:** Virginia Museum of Transportation / Gary Ombler (clb). **257 Dorling Kindersley:** Gary Ombler / B&O Railroad Museum, Baltimore, Maryland (ca, br); Virginia Museum of Transportation / Gary Ombler (tr). **258-259 Getty Images:** Roger Viollet / Neurdein (b). **260-261 Alamy Stock Photo:** Private Collection / AF Eisenbahn Archiv (tl). **261 Alamy Stock Photo:** Smith Archive (br). **262 Alamy Stock Photo:** Zip Lexing (t). **263 Alamy Stock Photo:** Balfore Archive Images (br). **264-265 Alamy Stock Photo:** The Picture Art Collection (tc). **266 Library of Congress, Washington, DC:** (bl). **267 Alamy Stock Photo:** gotravel. **269 Alamy Stock Photo:** Smith Archive (b). **270 Getty Images:** John Springer Collection / CORBIS (t). **271 Alamy Stock Photo:** sjbooks (tr). **Getty Images:** 500px / damián sa (bl). **272 Dorling Kindersley:** Gary Ombler / Verkehrshaus der Schweiz, Luzern, Switzerland (tr); Railroad Museum of Pennsylvania / Gary Ombler (cra). **273 Dorling Kindersley:** DB Museum, Nurnburg, Germany / Gary Ombler (cr); Railroad Museum of Pennsylvania / Gary Ombler (tl); Virginia Museum of Transportation / Gary Ombler (tr). **Shutterstock.com:** RoongsaK (crb). **274-275 State Library of South Australia:** B 58892 / 373 (t). **274 State Library of South Australia:** B 59187 (bl). **276 State Library of South Australia:** B 39864 (l). **277 Department of Infrastructure, Transport, Regional Development, Communications and the Arts:** Bureau of Infrastructure and Transport Research Economics (BITRE), 2024, Yearbook 2024: Australian Infrastructure and Transport Statistics, Statistical Report, BITRE, Canberra ACT. **State Library of South Australia:** B 14102 / 60 (bl). **278 Getty Images / iStock:** BeyondImages (bl). **279 Kāpiti Coast District Libraries MauMahara collection.:** (t). **Reproduced with the permission of KiwiRail Holdings Limited:** New Zealand Railways. Publicity Branch: Joy of school holidays, tripping by train. Book early at Railway offices, government tourist bureaux, and other travel agencies / Railway Studios. Issued by New Zealand Railways Publicity Branch. By authority, E V Paul, Government Printer, Wellington [ca 1940]. Ref: Eph-E-RAIL-1940s-01. Alexander Turnbull Library, Wellington, New Zealand. / records / 23152676 / Reproduced with the permission of KiwiRail Holdings Limited (br). **280-281 Getty Images:** Corbis Historical / Hulton Deutsch (l). **282 Getty Images:** Science & Society Picture Library (tl). **283 Getty Images:** Mirrorpix / NCJ Archive / Thomson (b).

284 Getty Images: Hulton Archive / Topical Press Agency (bl). **284-285 Getty Images:** Science & Society Picture Library (tr). **286 Getty Images / iStock:** L Feddes (bl). **286-287 Getty Images:** ullstein bild Dtl. / Gircke (tr). **288-289 Getty Images:** Bettmann (bl). **289 COURTESY OF THE B&O RAILROAD MUSEUM:** (tr). **290 Alamy Stock Photo:** Archive PL (tl). **291 Getty Images:** SSPL / National Railway Museum (b). **292 Alamy Stock Photo:** Daniel Dempster Photography (cr); Thomas J. Peterson (bl). **John Gateley:** (cl). **292-293 Dorling Kindersley:** Railroad Museum of Pennsylvania / Gary Ombler (tc); Science Museum Group / Ribble Steam Railway / Gary Ombler (br). **293 Alamy Stock Photo:** Richard Brown (cl); Frank Paul (cr). **Getty Images:** Science & Society Picture Library (tr). **294-295 Alamy Stock Photo:** Vintage_Space (r). **296 Alamy Stock Photo:** Shawshots (t). **297 Dreamstime.com:** Lawrence Peter Mcguire (br). **298 The Australian War Memorial. :** Arthur Francis Seary. **299 Alamy Stock Photo:** Stephen Faulkner (tr); Pictorial Press Ltd (br). **300-301 Alamy Stock Photo:** Imaginechina. **302 Getty Images:** Bettmann (cr). **303 Alamy Stock Photo:** Photo12 / Ann Ronan Picture Library. **304 Alamy Stock Photo:** colaimages (bl). **305 Getty Images:** The Asahi Shimbun (t). **306 Roland Smithies / luped.com:** (bl). **307 Getty Images:** Albert Liberman (r). **308 Getty Images:** Albert Liberman (bl). **309 Adobe Stock:** Andrei Stepanov (t). **310-311 Adobe Stock:** KarSol. **312 UCLA Library Digital Collections:** Los Angeles Times Photographic Collection. **313 Getty Images:** Central Press / Hulton Archive (br). **314 Getty Images:** SSPL (tl). **314-315 Alamy Stock Photo:** Inge Johnsson (b). **316-317 Alamy Stock Photo:** Avalon / Construction Photography. **317 Shutterstock.com:** Kharbine-Tapabor (br). **318-319 Alamy Stock Photo:** qaphotos.com (b). **319 Alamy Stock Photo:** qaphotos.com (tr). **320 Alamy Stock Photo:** qaphotos.com (bl). **321 Alamy Stock Photo:** Paul Quayle (t). **322 Getty Images:** Peter Breining / San Francisco Chronicle (bl). **322-323 Bridgeman Images:** From the British Library archive (c). **324-325 Dreamstime.com:** Janoka82. **326 Alamy Stock Photo:** Carl Simon / United Archives GmbH. **328-329 Dreamstime.com:** Tawatchai Prakobkit (t). **329 Getty Images / iStock:** mbbirdy (br). **330 Alamy Stock Photo:** Album (bl). **330-331 Dreamstime.com:** Nuttawut Uttamaharad (t). **332 Getty Images:** Sankei Archive (b). **334 SNCF - Societe National des Chemins de Fer:** Archives and Documentation Department (Optimservices -SARDO)—(CNAH). **335 Getty Images:** AFP Photo / Aeromedia (bl). **336-337 Getty Images:** VCG (b). **337 Alamy Stock Photo:** Historical Images Archive (tr). **338 Alamy Stock Photo:** Photo Vault (br). **Bridgeman Images:** British Library archive (tl). **339 Alamy Stock Photo:** INTERFOTO / History (r). **340 Getty Images:** China Photos (bl). **341 Alamy Stock Photo:** View Stock (t). **342 Alamy Stock Photo:** Imaginechina Limited (cla). **342-343 Getty Images:** Feature China / Future Publishing (b). **344 Alamy Stock Photo:** Steve Vidler / mauritius images GmbH (cr). **345 Dreamstime.com:** Allard1 (t). **346 Dreamstime.com:** Wellphotos (bc). **Getty Images / iStock:** Bim (t). **347 Dreamstime.com:** Matyas Rehak (br). **348 Alamy Stock Photo:** GUIZIOU Franck / hemis.fr (tl). **349 Getty Images:** owngarden (b). **350-351 Alamy Stock Photo:** View Stock (t). **351 Alamy Stock Photo:** BJ Warnick / Newscom (bc). **352-353 Getty Images:** Yuan Yong / VCG

Cover images: *Front and Back:* **Shutterstock.com:** David Franklin; *Front:* **Alamy Stock Photo:** Tibbut Archive c

Endpaper images: Alamy Stock Photo: lovemydesigns; **Dreamstime.com:** Baloncici, Claudiodivizia, Contact2297, Colleen Farrell, Moose Henderson, Mark Higgins, Himeiji, Lawcain, Manjunatha S, Parkbenchpics, Puripat Penpun, Salonibithale, Szebas, Yinan Zhang; **Getty Images:** Moment Unreleased / Taidgh Barron; **Getty Images / iStock:** Attack-Rabbit, whitemay

COLORIZED IMAGES

Some images in this book have been digitally colorized.

MAPS

Maps are provided throughout the book to illustrate selected railroad lines and other features. Please note that these are for general information only and are not intended to be comprehensive. Place names are given according to the period the map depicts.

CONVERSIONS

Unless specified, figures are approximate and are given to the nearest round number. Where currency conversions are given, the conversion is calculated to the approximate exchange rate of the period, unless specifically stated otherwise.

NUMBERS

"Billion" indicates the short-scale definition, or 1,000 million.

DK DELHI

Senior Editors Anita Kakar, Suefa Lee
Deputy Managing Art Editor Vaibhav Rastogi
Senior Art Editor Anjali Sachar
Project Art Editor Rupanki Kaushik
Art Editor Mitravinda V K
Picture Researcher Geetam Biswas
Team Lead Picture Research Sumedha Chopra
Deputy Manager Picture Research Virien Chopra
Jacket Designer Rhea Menon
Senior Jackets Coordinator Priyanka Sharma Saddi
Pre-production Designer Anurag Trivedi
Pre-production Image Editor Nityanand Kumar
Senior Jacket DTP Designer Harish Aggarwal
Pre-production Coordinator Tarun Sharma
Senior Managing Editor Rohan Sinha
Managing Art Editor Sudakshina Basu
Pre-production Manager Balwant Singh
Pre-production Image Manager Pankaj Sharma
Creative Head Malavika Talukder

DK LONDON

Senior Editor Miezan van Zyl
US Senior Editor Jennette ElNaggar
Senior Art Editor Duncan Turner
Senior Production Editor Andy Hilliard
Senior Production Controller Meskerem Berhane
Managing Editor Angeles Gavira
Managing Art Editor Michael Duffy
Art Director Maxine Pedliham
Publishing Director Georgina Dee
Design Director Phil Ormerod
Managing Director Liz Gough

Established in 1846, the Smithsonian is the world's largest museum and research complex, dedicated to public education, national service, and scholarship in the arts, sciences, and history. It includes 21 museums and galleries and the National Zoological Park. The total number of artifacts, works of art, and specimens in the Smithsonian's collection is estimated at 155.5 million.

Smithsonian National Museum of American History

Amanda Moniz, Curator

Smithsonian Enterprises

Licensing Coordinator Avery Naughton
Editorial Lead Paige Towler
Senior Director, Licensed Publishing Jill Corcoran
Vice President of New Business and Licensing Brigid Ferraro
President Carol LeBlanc

Content previously published in *The Iron Road* in 2014

First American Edition, 2025
Published in the United States by DK Publishing,
a division of Penguin Random House LLC
1745 Broadway, 20th Floor, New York, NY 10019

25 26 27 28 29 10 9 8 7 6 5 4 3 2 1
001–350184–Oct/2025

Published in Great Britain by
Dorling Kindersley Limited

ISBN 979-8-2171-2832-7

DK books are available at special discounts when purchased in bulk for sales promotions, premiums, fund-raising, or educational use. For details, contact: DK Publishing Special Markets, 1745 Broadway, 20th Floor, New York, NY 10019
SpecialSales@dk.com

Printed and bound in India

www.dk.com

This book was made with Forest Stewardship Council™ certified paper—one small step in DK's commitment to a sustainable future.
Learn more at www.dk.com/uk/information/sustainability

ADULT RETURN
NAMBOUR
TO
EXPO
(A)
Oradea Ag. 9
BULETINUL
Nr.
Clasa
0584
ATM MILANO
LINEE ORDINARIE URBANE
735
0.497.701
LIRE
50
002
serie 8316
37399
PICCADILLY CIRCUS
5p
30657
MARKET
1962
1963
TURN BACK
FOLLOWING
CAR OR COACH
LIFT
MINUTES
SYDENEY
METRO
AUTOBUS
2
6602
Cluj Napoca 20
CJ
Bihor
Lei 38
6602
Row
Seat
1963
JAPAN RAIL PASS
(ORDINARY 21 DAYS)
2023.10.10
This pass is non-negotiable.
¥66200(A)
4121
C. Supliment
Tren accelerat
Oradea Ag. 3
CJ
Cl. II Lei 3000
4121
TUMSAR RD
RAIPUR JN
هرات
افغانستان
(مناراهوتل)
Economy Return
CHILD'S TICKET
LEDGER CHARGE
BRISBANE
TO
CAIRNS
0223
NO. OF ORDER ISSUED
I BEG TO APPLY FOR THE FOLLOWING PRIVILEGE TICKET
Economy Return
LEDGER CHARGE
BRISBANE
TO
Maryborough
ROCKHAMPTON
TO
BRISBANE
Not Transferable
Bowen Hills
BRITISH RAILWAYS BOARD
2nd CLASS WEEKLY SEASON TICKET
31
Rate £2.17.6
VALID UNTIL
23 DEC 67
FLEET
WATERLOO
北京
Beijing
Z1次
哈尔滨
Haerbin
2010年11月14日21:14开
¥411.00 元
当日当次车有效
JOURNEY
HAPPY JOURNEY
KENGERI To PANDAVAPURA
Help us to keep the station and train clean
Swachh Bharat
ROMA
metrebus
A Roma paghi la sosta anche con il telefonino!
atac.roma.it/sosta